Media Ethics

Second Edition

To Atisaya–I thank Goodness for you every day.

Media Ethics

Second Edition

Key Principles for Responsible Practice

Patrick Lee Plaisance
Colorado State University

Los Angeles | London | New Delhi
Singapore | Washington DC

Los Angeles | London | New Delhi
Singapore | Washington DC

FOR INFORMATION:

SAGE Publications, Inc.
2455 Teller Road
Thousand Oaks, California 91320
E-mail: order@sagepub.com

SAGE Publications Ltd.
1 Oliver's Yard
55 City Road
London EC1Y 1SP
United Kingdom

SAGE Publications India Pvt. Ltd.
B 1/I 1 Mohan Cooperative Industrial Area
Mathura Road, New Delhi 110 044
India

SAGE Publications Asia-Pacific Pte. Ltd.
3 Church Street
#10-04 Samsung Hub
Singapore 049483

Acquisitions Editor: Matthew Byrnie
Associate Editor: Nancy Loh
Editorial Assistants: Gabrielle Piccininni
                        and Sarita Stark
Permissions Editor: Jennifer Barron
Marketing Manager: Liz Thornton
Project Editor: Veronica Stapleton Hooper
Copy Editor: Codi Bowman
Typesetter: C&M Digitals (P) Ltd.
Proofreader: Scott Oney
Indexer: Molly Hall
Cover Designer: Gail Buschman

Printed in the United States of America

Library of Congress Cataloging-in-Publication Data

Plaisance, Patrick Lee.

Media ethics: key principles for responsible practice / Patrick Lee Plaisance, Colorado State University.

pages cm
Includes bibliographical references and index.

ISBN 978-1-4522-5808-9 (alk. paper)

1. Mass media—Moral and ethical aspects. I. Title.

P94.P55 2013
175—dc23   2013027199

This book is printed on acid-free paper.

SUSTAINABLE FORESTRY INITIATIVE

Certified Chain of Custody
Promoting Sustainable Forestry
www.sfiprogram.org
SFI-01268

SFI label applies to text stock

13 14 15 16 17 10 9 8 7 6 5 4 3 2 1

Brief Contents

Detailed Contents

3   Ethics Theory: Application to Media   37

4   Technology   55

5   Transparency   71

6 Justice 97

7 Harm 123

10　Community　201

11　Conclusion　231

Preface

This second edition extends and refines the primary focus of the first: to provide students with a solid foundation for understanding and applying key ethical principles critical for responsible media practice. Unlike most of the media ethics case study texts, this puts ethics theory front and center in a way that is accessible and designed to raise the level of classroom discussion. By focusing on the philosophical foundations of key principles in an easily understandable yet thought-provoking way, this book attempts both to illustrate the deliberative nature of ethics and to provide knowledge necessary to add substance to students' claims and judgments about media behavior. It offers explanations that link theory with practice through the work of Aristotle, Immanuel Kant, John Rawls, John Stuart Mill, W. D. Ross, Philippa Foot, and others. With this focus, the author hopes students may develop a greater understanding of the work of ethics—both how challenging it is and how engaging it can be in everyday life. Thus, this book is an attempt to reinforce the need to apply philosophy and to counter intellectual and ethical laziness. "The undisciplined mind," Dewey said, "is averse to suspense and intellectual hesitation; it is prone to assertion" (Dewey, 1976, p. 197).

Without this understanding, ethical deliberations are less likely to transcend simplistic gut-level responses, veiled partisan preferences, and gross generalizations about media systems and behavior. By its nature, an ethics discussion is likely to be wide ranging and, to some extent, reductive. And it is unreasonable to expect media ethics students—or even most media ethics instructors, for that matter—to spend large chunks of their time immersed in reading the original works of the theorists covered here and painstakingly bringing them to bear on specific media practices. But students are ill prepared to make solid ethical arguments or to get beyond reflexive restatements of value claims and relativistic thinking if they have a weak grasp of the philosophical basis for guiding principles. This book attempts to provide students with a critically needed yet not overwhelming dose of philosophy to ensure that the *ethics* in media ethics actually means something more than making armchair judgments that this journalist was wrong or that public relations firm was irresponsible.

NEW TO THIS EDITION

The second edition of *Media Ethics* aims to refine and expand the thrust of the first edition in two ways. The first is to clarify its presentation of the theories used in the philosophy of ethics that are relevant to media practice. The second is to emphasize how these theories can help us negotiate challenges presented in our digital media world. The new edition provides four significant features:

- A new chapter, "Key Frameworks," which presents the distinguishing features of virtue ethics, duty ethics, and consequentialist ethics. This chapter provides a condensed account of each approach and discusses the strengths and limitations of each.
- A new chapter, "Technology," which introduces students to the philosophy of technology and explores the ethical implications of the world of social media and emerging media technologies. This chapter is designed to more comprehensively link ethics theory to our digital media world. It also is intended to set the stage for substantive discussion on topics such as what values might be embedded in technologies, and how the architecture of social media influences the ways in which we communicate with each other.
- A dozen new and revised Case in Point examples of media practice. Each of the six "key principles" chapters features a new case illustrating a dilemma in digital media, addressing topics such as greenwashing, geo-fencing, data mining, and PR use of social media.
- Updated discussion of theorists and principles throughout the chapters, more effectively linking the classics with modern-day writers who suggest ways to adapt the claims of Aristotle, Kant, and others for contemporary life. Each chapter also has been updated to include recent examples of applied principles and media practices.

LINKING ETHICS THEORY AND PRACTICE

In this era of interactivity and intense media scrutiny, real-life cases and examples of behavior that raise questions of media ethics are a dime a dozen. There is a healthy variety of case study books from which media ethics instructors can choose. There are useful collections of cases, scandals, and model behavior available on the Web. And most good media ethics instructors are continuously collecting their own examples—from trade journals, mainstream media, and daily Web postings by media ethicists—for use in their classes. This text is intended to do what most of the published case study collections in media ethics do not. Not only do many media ethics case study texts provide only a minimal account of the principles that should inform media behavior; they make little effort to explain the philosophical justifications for asserting the principles in the first place. They provide plenty of material on *media,* yet they are often thin on *ethics*—and their purported ethical discussions too often center on normative standards and best practices rather than on a true application of the philosophy of ethics.

This book also features a large number of case studies that serve to illustrate how key principles are relevant in the real world of media practice. It combines ethics theory with media practice through dozens of cases of media behavior that raise ethical questions. In addition to illustrative examples of media behavior that are discussed throughout the text, each of the book's six principles chapters features four boxed Case in Point studies relevant to the chapter topic—one each from the areas of journalism, public relations, and advertising and another on a relevant aspect of digital media. But this is not a case study textbook. The heavily used media ethics case study textbooks now on the market do an excellent job of providing real-world instances of media practice that raise important ethics questions. Some of the cases in these books present exemplary models of ethical behavior. Other scandalous cases illustrate what happens when media professionals fail to meet their ethical duties. The best cases are genuinely difficult gray areas that lend themselves to legitimate arguments in support of dramatically opposite courses of action or that make us struggle to find new ways to seek common ground and acceptable compromises among conflicting values and stakeholders.

Some may quibble with the perceived lack of comprehensiveness of the list of key principles featured in this book. Other lists may include concepts such as freedom, stewardship, care, and others. But each concept in this book is considered to be, either implicitly or explicitly, central in media ethics research and theory as well as in professional codes of ethics. Several also subsume related concepts—the notion of freedom is an important component of this book's chapter on autonomy, for example.

This book also covers concepts such as transparency and community that are not normally discussed at length in other media ethics case study texts. While these are often mentioned in the media ethics literature, they rarely are the focus of any substantial discussions since they may be perceived as beyond the scope of media studies. However, the ways in which both students and professionals understand how respect is manifested in communication and what "community" encompasses have enormous implications for what counts as "responsible" media behavior. This reflects a subtext throughout all the main chapters, which is an examination of the liberal Enlightenment assumptions on which much of our Western individualistic culture is based. Acknowledging these assumptions and understanding the implications of them is critical not only for media practitioners interested in cultivating a "public sphere," but for students with diverse expectations of media performance. For example, students immersed in our self-centric culture and with only a vague notion of the centrality of "community" to the human experience may be less likely to understand the need for journalistic investigative techniques.

With this book's deliberative focus and its accessible synthesis of key strands of philosophical thought, the author hopes to provide a useful resource for media ethics instructors and for the media professionals of tomorrow.

REFERENCE

Dewey, J. (1976). *The middle works, 1859–1952* (Vol. 9, J. A. Boydston, Ed.). Carbondale: Southern Illinois University Press.

Acknowledgments

This book would not have been possible without the support, mentorship, and inspiration of a wide range of people. Foremost is my wife, Atisaya, whose generous spirit, gracious forbearance, and sharp editing continually provide me with a needed foundation, both of the moral and more earthbound kinds. My son Carter and my daughter Simone are blessings that daily replenish my sense of wonderment. I am indebted to my media ethics students over the years for enabling me to envision this project, for continually challenging me, for cultivating my optimism for the future, and for suffering through early drafts of chapters. The warm and supportive mentorship of Clifford Christians and Jay Black over the years has been humbling and inspiring.

I also owe a debt of thanks to Matthew Brynie at SAGE for his encouragement and support, and I am grateful for the valuable criticism and suggestions of my reviewers: John Ferré of the University of Louisville, Jenn Burleson Mackay of Virginia Tech, Susan C. Worley of Juniata College, Cathy M. Jackson of Norfolk State University, Ryan J. Thomas of Washington State University, Antoinette F. Winstead of Our Lady of the Lake University, and Christopher Meyers of California State University–Bakersfield. Also thanks to Jay Black of the University of South Florida, Jack Breslin of Iona College, Kris Bunton of the University of St. Thomas, Dane S. Claussen of Point Park University, J. William Click of Winthrop University, David Craig of the University of Oklahoma, Bryan Denham of Clemson University, Walter B. Jaehnig of Southern Illinois University, Jeffrey J. Maciejewski of Creighton University, Anthony Moretti of Point Park, Bonita Dostal Neff of Valparaiso University, Maggie Jones Patterson of Duquesne University, William E. Sledzik of Kent State University, Ernest L. Wiggins of the University of South Carolina, and Wendy N. Wyatt of St. Thomas.

Introduction

Any theory of activity in social and moral matters . . . which is not grounded in a comprehensive philosophy seems to me to be only a projection of arbitrary personal preferences.

—John Dewey

The purpose of this book is to improve the effectiveness of ethical thought and decision making among the media professionals of the future. It aims to help students become more savvy and effective readers of the moral compass that we all have within us. Using another navigational analogy, the author hopes this book helps students develop a sophisticated and sensitive "ethics radar" that they can use to spot and intelligently deal with ethical issues. More immediate, this book's goal is to help improve classroom conversations about media ethics.

A solid foundation for ethical thinking in media is needed now more than ever. Media ethics scandals have become a regular feature of news. Media practices have become the object of public scrutiny as never before. Public distrust of the news media is at an all-time high and shows no sign of reversing. The volume of questionable, unethical, and downright shoddy media content in print, in broadcast, and on the Web is dizzying. More often than not, students of the media today are prone to cynicism about ethical claims and are likely to conclude that there is little they can do except to further insulate themselves in a media world tailored to their own narrow personal interests—a technology-driven "balkanization" of communities that commercial media companies are all too happy to encourage in their efforts to "monetize" every opportunity for media content. Journalism is a profession in profound flux, as news organizations struggle to move out of a broken business model and find ways to become economically viable (and still credible) on the Web. News increasingly is a product of collaboration between journalists and ordinary citizens uploading on-the-scene video and dispatches as events happen in real time. The public relations and advertising industries, at the global corporate level, are suffering from a "churning" of accounts in which their most important client often is themselves. And corporate public relations practitioners, like their journalistic counterparts, are adjusting to a brave new world of heightened public scrutiny, demands for transparency, and high-stakes challenges to manage sometimes stark stakeholder conflicts.

A common reflexive response to all the resulting mediocre or unethical (or both) journalistic, promotional, and informational media content is to throw up our hands and conclude that any serious talk of media ethics is superfluous and futile. Indeed, ethicists today understand that theirs is often the voice in the wilderness, that ethical concerns are routinely dismissed as quaint or irrelevant in many discussions of the commercial media juggernaut. For many, the casual setting aside of ethical concerns in the media is symptomatic of a broader societal subordination of moral claims to unreflective desires for expediency and gratification—if technology allows us to do it, it must be good and it must be okay. Clifford Christians, a prominent media ethicist, neatly summarizes this development:

> In our day, morality has appeared to reach the end of the line. The social fashion
> is to be emancipated from moral standards and to disavow moral responsibility.
> We are witnessing the demise of the ethical, living in what Nietzsche called the era
> beyond good and evil. . . . Popular culture gets caught up in the technological
> imperative, producing the visually interesting, creating programs at times of
> artistic wholeness, but driven by the conditions of aesthetic space rather than
> ethics. (2005, p. 4)

The position of this book, however, is that we must resist this form of ethical indifference with every fiber of our moral beings. Understood correctly, our ethical beliefs constitute the essence of our humanness. Our moral life is just as real, immediate, and insistent as our physical and intellectual ones. If we take our existence as moral agents seriously, we must be engaged ethically to ensure, as much as possible, that our values shape our technology and our media, not the other way around. The credibility gap and the ethics scandals that plague our media system now often are the result of precisely that failure of media professionals to fully consider or acknowledge their obligations as moral agents.

Granted, we should be careful about making gross generalizations about media based on the most offensive examples. There is plenty of upstanding and inspiring work in the media—a quick look at the recipients of the Pulitzer, Emmy, and public relations Gold Pick and Silver Anvil awards every year in journalism and public relations can easily counter cynical or disdainful attitudes. But far too many ethical lapses of journalists and public relations practitioners are the result of allowing decidedly amoral factors—deadline pressures, stark economic imperatives, corporate and "branding" interests—to define the quality of their work. Too often, media professionals have not performed the front-end work of ethical deliberation required to embody terms such as *integrity* and *responsibility.* They have not thought through the ethical implications of their behavior—or worse, they have subordinated important ethical considerations in favor of more expedient motives. Too many journalists fail to fully consider the potential harm caused by their work and the opportunities and duties to minimize it. Too many public relations practitioners fail to grasp the critical relationships among the ideas of public service, transparency, conflict of interest, and credibility.

For a credible and effective media system to survive, it is more important than ever for the next generation of media consumers and practitioners to understand and insist on the importance of ethical standards. We need *more* ethical engagement, not less. When we disengage, we compound the problem. The time to think deeply about ethics is now, when students are considering career choices and developing personal and professional values, not in the heat of on-the-job deadlines and pressures that will surely fill the void left by any lack of grounding in ethical values—and just as surely result in regrettable decisions that undermine credibility.

Students interested in careers in journalism, public relations, advertising, or other media-related fields obviously must be well versed in the ethical standards, duties, and obligations that help define them. But this book also is intended to serve a broader cross-section of students, including those from other majors who are taking a media ethics course as an elective with no intention of pursuing media work. As media consumers, we all must be somewhat savvy about how the media system works. Part of our "media literacy" is having a grasp of professional standards and principles. While we all might fancy ourselves media experts in this information age, we cannot intelligently assess media practices or judge media content if we do not have an understanding of the ethical principles that are supposed to drive those practices and that content.

The discussions in each of the key principles chapters are not meant to provide definitive explanations. They are meant to provide a starting place to think about them in a substantive way. Chapters 5 through 10 provide a survey of the roots of the featured principle in classical philosophy, together with discussions of how contemporary thinkers have said we should understand the principle—both of which, it is hoped, set the stage for thoughtful application of these principles to media practice. Much of the book draws from and synthesizes, with an emphasis on accessibility, theorists from a wide range of disciplines, including mass communication research on media sociology and audience effects, as well as philosophy, developmental psychology, political science, and sociology. In addition to the Technology chapter, each principles chapter also features a "cyberspace" section that considers how each principle might be relevant in the online world. This is not meant to imply that new media technology raises fundamentally different or new ethical questions. Quite the opposite—the intent of each cyberspace section is to show that, while we have a tendency to think of the online world as a place where the rules have changed, a solid understanding of key principles suggests that the "new" online questions are rarely new—instead, they are the latest manifestations of long-standing ethics issues regarding our moral obligations in our communication with others.

Several values that many assume to be essential in media ethics are conspicuously absent here. The values of truth, accuracy, and honesty don't receive much attention in this book. That's not because they are unimportant. They absolutely are. They are broad ideals that all of us can relate to. But philosophically speaking, they are manifestations of the principles that this book does feature. For example, truth telling is obviously a key value in media work and in fact is mentioned in several professional codes of ethics. Ethics codes for public relations, marketing, and advertising all include pledges to honor the value of truth, though this value often is understood in an "instrumental" sense—that is, people using media channels to persuade or advocate are expected to avoid outright lies but to use truth selectively in the service of promoting a cause or product or interest. In journalism, truth is considered an "absolute" rather than an instrumental value: It is important not only for what it does, but as an end in itself. Truth seeking is what sets journalism apart from all other forms of communication. Even this lofty notion of truth is complicated and elusive, however. Factual accuracy is a critical dimension of truth seeking. Journalists are expected to be meticulous in verifying facts and using credible sources. But journalists occasionally feel compelled to use deceptive tactics to uncover stories. Also, journalists' scrupulous reporting of false statements can actually hinder our ability to discern the truth of an issue or controversy. And the truth rarely is revealed in a single instance but rather is the result of an incremental compilation of knowledge, a process of uncovering over time. We also know that truth in the postmodern world is anything but monolithic, and abstract proclamations on the value of seeking the truth are rarely fruitful. That is why this book, instead of extolling the obvious importance of truth seeking, strives to lay out the philosophical reasons for *why* we ought to value truthfulness: because it is how we fulfill our obligations that Immanuel Kant and other philosophers say we have to honor everyone's fundamental human dignity and capacity for reason. Similarly, other buzzwords in media ethics such as *integrity* and *accountability* are too often vague platitudes that will not be directly addressed by this book. In fact, these and other widely called-for qualities are the products of conscientious work and solid ethical deliberation. Once we understand what exactly such ethical deliberation requires of us, tossing around moralistic claims about "having integrity" is neither helpful nor necessary. If we, as students of the media and as media professionals, are committed to the philosophically more meaningful principles of justice, transparency, and others discussed in this book, our work consequently will be characterized by honest, accurate, and principled pursuit of the truth.

The aim here is to explain the philosophical basis and rationalizations for these concepts in an accessible way that will encourage more sophisticated thinking about and application of these concepts. While each chapter incorporates contemporary, media-related examples of the concept, these examples are presented to illustrate how the broader philosophical principles underlying the concept can and should be brought to bear in our ethical deliberations.

It is critical that all of us—whether we are or will become practitioners in the media business or continue as media consumers—recognize our obligations as moral agents. Those obligations require us to understand the scope and meaning of key principles. Those principles can and should be used to guide and gauge media behavior regardless of the type of media being discussed—whether it be journalism, public relations, advertising, or marketing with media. But these principles do apply to varying degrees and, in some cases, in different ways according to the type of message or content addressed. Each of the four types of communication just mentioned serve very different functions in society, and so there are different expectations and standards for each. But as moral agents, we must address the same ethical issues regardless of context—including questions of transparency, potential harm, and conflicting values. This book emphasizes that the importance and application of these key principles are not substantially altered by the use of new media technologies. Electronic formats and forms of delivery do not necessarily pose fundamentally new questions of ethics, nor should they be somehow considered exempt from standards of ethical conduct. Online journalists may struggle with the question of how to document corrections and content changes made to stories published on the Web, for example, but such discussions should be considered simply the latest way to frame debates about expectations of accountability and transparency.

This book's approach to media ethics, then, can be described as foundational. That is, the book's focus is not on presenting a series of contemporary examples that serve to start "ethical" discussions; instead, it is designed to get students familiar and comfortable with the epistemic nature of the fundamental elements of ethics. Too often, the author finds that discussions that claim to be ethical in nature are really veiled political discussions intent on justifying the perceived "right" decision. What gets lost is the fact that ethics is concerned not with the final decision but with the posing of the right questions. The book focuses on the importance of this deliberative process in an accessible way that will help students hone their ability to ask the right questions that are informed by key ethical principles. Then, through contemporary examples, it shows students how these principles can effectively guide our deliberations in all sectors of media practice.

REFERENCE

Christians, C. G. (2005). Ethical theory in communications research. *Journalism Studies, 6*(1), 3–14.

CHAPTER 1

Ethics Theory
An Overview

Ethics is a branch of moral philosophy that is rooted in the writings of Aristotle, Epictetus, and other ancient Greeks who were concerned with the nature of goodness. Modern moral philosophers continue their work to understand how we know right and wrong, how "rightness" and "goodness" should be defined, and whether these qualities are intrinsic in acts and objects or whether the concepts are products of our intuitions. Because ethics and moral philosophy are closely related, students often mistakenly assume the two—ethics and morality—are interchangeable or mean the same thing. And because both fields are concerned with such fundamental questions that involve things that make us human, students who are being introduced to the field of ethics often wonder what all the fuss is about. *Isn't it obvious when something is either good or bad?* they ask. Why all this handwringing and hairsplitting over things that should be clear to anyone with half a conscience? In his discussion of Aristotle, Christopher Johnstone offers some words that help clarify why ethics is such an urgent matter of concern today:

> Questions of morality and ethics have become even more troubled, vexed by the acknowledgment that there are multiple sets of culturally grounded values having validity in our society, that moral absolutes are not universally recognized, and that individual autonomy is a value that sometimes outweighs adherence to accepted norms. So now it is more difficult than ever to justify moral claims, to argue for ethical judgments in ways that will be persuasive to society as a whole. (2002, p. 16)

Say you're about to go on a date and your companion shows up in a new outfit. He asks cheerily, "How do you like my new look?" You think it makes him look like some cartoon figure out of the 1970s. Are you going to be brutally honest, or are you going to reply with a little white lie in the interest of having a fun night out? Or imagine yourself as the manager of a fast-food restaurant supervising some coworkers who also are your good friends and who you know are struggling to make ends meet. One day you notice them huddled together at the end of their shift, getting ready to go home. When you walk over, you see they have stuffed their backpacks with food from the restaurant—far more than what they're normally allowed to eat on the job. Are you going to take disciplinary action or are you going to look the other way? Each of these scenarios poses an ethical dilemma. Whether we recognize them as such or not, we all are faced with multiple ethical questions—both large and small, sometimes trivial, sometimes momentous—every day. And depending on a wide range of factors that we discuss in this chapter and the next, we will decide on what course of action to take. The point here is that ethics deals with issues and questions that are not clear-cut. Sometimes, we will have gut-level reactions to dilemmas that will suggest what the right thing to do is. But many dilemmas raise ethical questions precisely because they present a gray, murky case in which there is no immediately apparent answer that is the "right" one—in fact, there may be *no* options that seem fully satisfactory. A student may decide to plagiarize material for a term paper, or a reporter may fabricate a quote to spice up a story. We may want to call these acts "moral failures," but they don't really pose questions of *ethics* because both behaviors constitute clear violations of policies set forth to define what is acceptable and what is not. There is no gray area in which to debate whether student plagiarism or journalistic fabrication is okay in some cases. People will always have many self-serving justifications for such cheating, but philosophically speaking, if we are taking our obligations as moral agents seriously, the question to cheat or not to cheat does not usually offer us *compelling, equally legitimate* reasons for doing it or not. Ethics, then, is not typically concerned with such black-and-white questions. Ethicists have much bigger and more difficult fish to fry.

ETHICS DEFINED

Surveying the work of moral philosophy in general and ethics in particular, we can come up with a working definition of ethics as a form of inquiry concerned with the process of finding rational justifications for our actions when the values that we hold come into conflict. Philosopher Henry Sidgwick wrote that "the aim of Ethics is to systematize and free from error the apparent cognitions that most men have of the rightness or reasonableness of conduct" (1981, p. 77). Another philosopher, R. A. P. Rogers, also offers a variation on this, calling ethics "the science which investigates the general principles for determining the true worth of the ultimate ends of human conduct" (1965, p. 1). The work of ethics, then, has always been epistemic—that is, it's focused on questions of how we actually know what we claim to know. How exactly do we justify an act as being "right?" Moral philosopher Margaret Walker defined ethics as "pursuing an understanding of morality, which provides understandings of ourselves as bearers of responsibilities in the service of values" (2000, p. 89). Johnstone said ethicists strive to "illuminate the processes by which . . . [moral] decisions are made in order to provide insight into the nature and conditions of competent moral judgment" (2002, p. 17). Obviously, ethics and morality are closely related. In our everyday talk, we often treat them as interchangeable and synonymous terms. And ethical decision making can provide a strong basis for making *moral* claims. But the two are not the same, and understanding the difference often can help avoid muddled thinking and gross generalizations. *Morality* generally refers to a set of beliefs that we embrace to help us understand what is good and what is bad in the world. We don't usually question the validity of these beliefs. Truth is preferable to falsehood. Human beings require respect because of their humanness. All the religions of the world provide various systems of belief that place premiums on these and other claims about goodness. For moral philosophers, however, questions about what exactly makes claims of goodness true are of critical interest. What exactly are the properties that make something good, how do we perceive goodness, and how do we know what we know about it? With these kinds of questions, moral philosophers have struggled to get to the bottom of some of the most fundamental issues that make us human.

Ethics, on the other hand, deals with our struggle to justify doing or not doing something when various values of our belief system clash. *Ethics* refers to our efforts to articulate our reasons for putting greater weight on some moral claims than others in certain dilemmas. In contrast to morality's focus on the quality of goodness, ethics focuses on the *rightness* of a given action: How can we say this particular action would be the right thing to do? These moral dilemmas, according to philosopher Philippa Foot, comprise "a special case of the dilemma that exists wherever there is evidence for and evidence against a certain conclusion. What is special is that the conclusion is about what the agent ought to do" (2002, p. 177). Honesty, communal action, and respect for privacy all may be values that we hold dear as part of our belief system. But they can bump against each other—as well as a host of other values—in all kinds of ways. Ethics isn't concerned about making moralistic claims, but about the deliberation we have to go through to properly balance the competing claims. Ethicist Deni Elliott effectively described the distinction between ethics and morality when she said, "Ethics begins when elements of a moral system conflict" (Patterson & Wilkins, 2014, p. 4). Ideally, the real work of ethics is to strive to provide "complete" accounts of both what we should do and why we should do it. Moral philosopher Robert Audi (2004) called these the twin goals of "normative" and "epistemic" completeness. Through solid and careful deliberation, Audi said we should be able to explain the *normative* duties that we have—that is, what we *ought* to do. These kinds of claims are called normative claims, as opposed to descriptive claims about "how things are." Second, Audi said, we ought to be able to explain *why* these claims should motivate us in certain ways—what he refers to as having an *epistemic* understanding of why such claims are valid:

> We want knowledge both of what we should do and of why we should do it.
> Epistemic completeness is needed for a theory to give us the comprehensive
> moral guidance we seek as moral agents; normative completeness is needed to
> enable us to explain—and, correspondingly, justify—the moral judgments we
> arrive at on the basis of the facts that indicate our obligations. (Audi, 2004, p. 86)

These goals are complicated by the fact that our culture and political ideology shape and shade how we think and talk about values and standards. Whether this is a good thing is the subject of vigorous, ongoing debate among ethicists. Several contemporary ethics theorists have suggested that the way we think about ethics in the Western world has an inherent bias in favor of individual freedom and in opposition to claims that emphasize universal truths and community welfare. This bias has fostered a dangerous relativistic mind-set, they argue, that implies that freedom means it's okay to do as one chooses with little need for concern for one's effects on others. "Individual autonomy has been the axis of classical theory," said Clifford Christians (2005, p. 3), a pioneering media ethics theorist. This is a problem because in our era of globalization, we ought to be working to discover basic moral standards that can be accepted universally instead of pushing particular Western ideas of morality onto other cultures. "Universal human solidarity, its radical opposite, ought to be the centerpiece of ethics now" (Christians, 2005, p. 3). This tension is further explored in Chapter 10.

Recall the definition given earlier that describes ethics as a form of inquiry concerned with the process of finding rational justifications for our actions when the values that we hold come into conflict. Let's take a closer look at some key elements of that description; doing so will likely help clarify our thinking about how to apply ethical principles to actual cases later.

It's About the Journey, Not the Destination

Ethics is about our *thinking process*. The experience of learning about ethics can be frustrating for students who expect to walk out of class armed with clear-cut answers for how to deal with different types of problems. But in fact, such direct answers are rare in ethics. Instead, ethics is concerned with asking the right questions. The focus is on the quality of the *deliberative process* and not on the outcome. This can be discomforting because so much of Western culture is goal oriented. We care deeply about good performance, about results, about the bottom line—often with only passing interest in how we achieve those goals or what we do to attain "success." But expecting ethics to provide the necessary "correct" answers usually just leads to *moralizing*—making broad, often unsubstantiated claims about a course of action that some will accept as reflecting their moral beliefs and others won't. As we have discussed, most ethical dilemmas don't present any fully acceptable solutions and instead offer several options that are unsatisfactory in some way. The trick is to figure out which one is most justifiable as you see it and which embodies key values.

> ### Ethics Versus Morals
>
> *Morals* refers to a system of beliefs that we use to make judgments about good and bad. *Ethics* refers to our efforts to reason our way through a dilemma in which two or more central values of our moral system clash. Ethics, according to ethicist Deni Elliott, begins when elements of our moral system conflict.

Trust Your Gut, but Use Your Brain

Ethics is based on *rational justifications*. When faced with a dilemma, many of us may have gut instincts that suggest what the right thing to do is. But in ethics, that's just the beginning. What is it exactly about truth telling, for example, that makes it so important to us when dealing with others? Why exactly do we say we value the idea of not harming others? And when telling the truth will inevitably lead to some type of harm to someone, under what circumstances can we say that we would be willing to tolerate that harm? Conversely, when exactly would it be okay to withhold the truth or deceive someone to prevent certain types of harm? To answer any of these questions, we must have a solid understanding of the philosophical basis for both truth telling and avoiding harm. Otherwise, we risk making decisions based on simplistic moral claims that may not have much credibility for people who don't have the same beliefs. Good ethical decisions can be defended with solid, evidence-based reasoning, not just a series of moral claims. And remember, this does not mean the decision you make will be ironclad. Ethics is not about pleasing everyone, because true dilemmas can plausibly be dealt with in opposite ways. Whichever you choose, people are likely to be upset, and you will be subjected to charges that you are "unethical." Rather, what's important in ethics is the quality of your reasoning for doing or not doing something.

The Art of the Uneasy Compromise

Ethics helps us negotiate among *conflicting values*. The example just mentioned, about two key values of honesty, or truth telling, and avoiding harm to others, is a classic conflict. But there are others. We all value our privacy, but we may also see belonging to and participating in a community as important. We value courage but also camaraderie, loyalty as well as independence. Social psychologists who have studied the nature of human values say cultures and societies generally have a list of widely agreed-upon values, including the ones just mentioned, that are all important to us; differences lie in the relative priority given to single values in certain circumstances (Rokeach, 1973, 1979). It's not that these and other values ever become unimportant; it's just that we choose which ones should be favored to help solve a given problem. It should be clear that having a strong moral belief system doesn't exempt us from having conflicting values. In ethics, it's not enough simply to say we have strong moral feelings about what we should do. We are forced to prioritize our values many times every day, whether we acknowledge doing it or not. Ethical decision making, however, often requires us to think more deeply about these values and why one should drive our deliberations more than another. That often means accepting that some values, as important as they are, must be temporarily subsumed in the service of things that we deem more important, given the circumstance. This process of compromise obviously can be very difficult, but it is greatly helped by a clear understanding of the values that we are talking about.

> ### Ethics: How Is It Defined?
>
> Ethics is the process of finding rational justifications for our actions when simultaneously held values come into conflict.

KEY THINKERS THROUGH THE AGES

Key values and principles used in ethics theory come from a range of thinkers and writers throughout history. Some have changed how we talk about ethical issues; others have added critical new elements or perspectives on claims long accepted as wisdom.

Throughout this book, we discuss the nature of key moral principles and suggest ways to apply them based on the work of many different theorists and theoretical approaches. Following are quick summaries of some central figures in the evolution of ethical thought. The list is by no means exhaustive, and actually, it just scratches the surface of the field. But those thinkers listed here often provide the most useful insights for our efforts to apply moral standards in our assessments of media behavior.

Aristotle

A student of Plato and later tutor to Alexander the Great, Aristotle produced the first known theoretical treatise on ethics. In his *Nicomachean Ethics,* Aristotle argued that human goodness requires using our rationality to live a life of virtue. His idea of the virtues refers to two categories: intellectual (wisdom, understanding, prudence) and moral (including courage, justice, and truthfulness). The moral virtues in particular require us to search for a proper intermediate point between extreme examples of excess or deficiency. To act courageously, for example, is to avoid foolhardiness as well as cowardice. His requirement that we seek this balancing point between two extremes is known as *Aristotle's Doctrine of the Mean.* But Aristotle also recognized that human beings are not strictly rational creatures. He pointed out that a "good" life must incorporate both rationality and passion. He acknowledged that emotion and desire have roles to play in decision making. Aristotle also argued that while a life of contemplation of the virtues represents the highest good, it is insufficient without corresponding social action and engagement. Aristotle, Johnstone (2002) said, "Calls upon us to recognize that we are social, communal beings; that we live in communities; and that performance of our proper excellences must include a practical involvement in the life of these communities" (p. 30). Another key element of Aristotle's virtue ethics is his claim that all of our actions should not only reflect the virtues as discussed; they should also promote and maintain "human flourishing," or the capacity of every human to strive to reach his or her potential. Behavior that undermines or thwarts human flourishing is, by its nature, morally questionable.

Aristotle 384–322 B.C.

SOURCE: Kunsthistorisches Museum, Wien (Vienna).

Immanuel Kant

A major German Enlightenment theorist who argued that we could discern moral laws just as we perceive laws of nature, Kant proposed a complex system that detailed the duties we have as moral agents. At the core of his system is the claim that our human capacity for reason enables us to know these duties and that freedom enables us to act on them. On these two pillars—rationality and liberty—rest his central claim that we are obligated to act morally as the only way to carry out our duties to others. By moral action, Kant meant that we test our decisions by asking whether they can be *universalized*—whether it would be acceptable if everyone applied the decision as a standard of behavior. Such moral requirements, he said, were "categorically imperative"—they were among the core moral obligations that all of us must meet. In this respect, Kant's *deontological,* or duty-based, system contrasts sharply with other systems, such as Mill's utilitarianism, that place the focus of our moral judgments on the consequences of our actions. Since our reasoning capacity is what enables us to act morally, and since liberty enabled us to act on our reasoning, Kant insisted that we had a primary duty to respect this capacity in every human being. People are owed respect not because of what they do or who they are, but because they are human beings with a capacity for reason. This universal moral obligation requires that we treat individuals as ends in them-

Immanuel Kant 1724–1804

SOURCE: Corbis.

selves and never solely as a means to attain other goals or desires we may have. To do otherwise undermines both a person's autonomy and rationality.

John Stuart Mill

A key figure in the development of utilitarianism as a moral system, Mill argued that pleasure alone is desired for its own sake and, thus, constitutes the sole source of moral goodness. All actions, then, must be evaluated on the basis of how much overall pleasure they produce. By *pleasure,* Mill did not mean merely the satisfaction of vulgar impulses and animalistic desires; he argued that "virtue" also is desired as a pleasing pursuit by more refined individuals. He also sought to show how various pleasures should be ranked on more than just a qualitative basis, and he said his theory of utility also would be effective in bringing about justice. In contrast to Kant's duty-based system, Mill's *teleological* approach claims that the moral worth of an act—that is, whether it generates pleasure or happiness for those affected—lies in its consequences, and he,

John Stuart Mill 1806–1873

SOURCE: Hulton Archive/Getty Images.

thus, attempts to subject moral theory to a sort of empirical testing. While the general theory of utility often has been reduced to the rather simplistic claim that we should choose that act which creates the greatest amount of happiness or benefits for the greatest number of people, Mill was concerned about how to determine which actions are likely to produce the "aggregate" good that would benefit a community as a whole. He also insisted that special protection be given to people whose interests might be sacrificed for the good of the community.

W. D. Ross

Ross advocated a moral system that was called "intuitionist" because it claimed that we had an inherent ability to recognize what our moral duties were. In his landmark book *The Right and the Good* (1930), he argued that "rightness" and "goodness" are objective features of the world in just the way that shape, size, and mass are objective features. His theory was similar to the duty-based theories of Kant and others in that he believed we had certain prima facie obligations—standards of behavior that require us to honor several key values in all our interactions with others. They include duties of fidelity (including promise keeping and truth telling), duties of gratitude and justice, and duties of self-improvement and of "not harming others." Ross believed there is structure to the rightness of principles. Certain basic considerations should be weighted more heavily than others. Duties of avoiding harm, of fidelity, and of reparation are weightier than considerations of beneficence, for example. This theory is important because it helps us think more clearly about moral conflicts. Ross allows us to think of moral conflict not as a conflict of *duties,* but as a conflict of moral *reasons* to do or not do something. Ross argued that any thinking individual could see that we all are bound by these duties, but he also said the ways in which we fulfill or honor them will depend greatly on the circumstances in which we find ourselves. We must think deeply about cases in which these duties might conflict, and come up with good reasons for saying, for example, that breaking a promise is acceptable only in certain situations, as when an unexpected situation requires me to act so that someone else is not harmed but also results in my missing an appointment.

W. D. Ross 1877–1940

SOURCE: © National Portrait Gallery, London.

John Rawls

Unsatisfied with the utilitarian moral framework that has dominated political theory since it was first outlined in the 19th century by Jeremy Bentham, Rawls proposed an alternative system that promoted the idea of justice, not utility, as the primary goal of society. In his landmark 1971 book, *A Theory of Justice,* Rawls (1999) argued that the principle of justice is the foundation of social order. The goal of society is not to promote the greatest good for the greatest number of people but to promote justice. This means focusing on how a community ought to distribute scarce "goods"—a term that refers to just about everything that one might want to have, from wealth to opportunity to liberty to self-respect. If we are serious about promoting justice, how would we adopt social policies to do so? Rawls offered a provocative rhetorical device to help us see what kind of decision-making process might best ensure justice in a world of limited goods. Imagine, he said, that you are a member of a community charged with negotiating policies that everyone is to live by. And imagine that each individual is rational and has general knowledge of how the world works—they know about economics, psychology, and so on—and that they know they have individual goals and ambitions. However, each individual has no *particular* knowledge of their place in the world—they are ignorant about their own personal characteristics, skills, talents, status, abilities, and dis-

John Rawls 1921–2002

SOURCE: Jane Reed/Harvard News Office.

abilities. Rawls called this theoretical construct the "veil of ignorance." If all of the conditions were true for a group of people, what kind of decisions would they make about the distribution of goods? Rawls argued that they would first declare that everyone is guaranteed liberty. He said they then would set social policies designed to protect the *least advantaged* in society since any one of the negotiators could conceivably be among them once the veil is lifted. They would, thus, conceptualize justice as *fairness*.

Philippa Foot

For decades, philosophers have been arguing over how exactly we know what makes something "good." Unlike the truth of scientific "facts," our moral judgments cannot rest merely on observations of the state of things, most philosophers have argued. Yet this left many feeling that deciding that something was *good* was simply to have some sort of intuition about its goodness, since it wasn't objective or verifiable. This was conventional wisdom—until an unassuming Oxford theorist named Philippa Foot developed a different approach. Foot, who taught at Oxford and UCLA and who was the granddaughter of President Grover Cleveland, argued that we can indeed point to "objective" reasons for saying one thing is good and another is not, and we can do so by simply pointing to the natural world. Part of what drove Foot was the haunting memory of Nazi atrocities and her desire to find a way to conclude absolutely that the Nazi horrors were morally wrong, and avoid a moral standoff in which they could be justified in any way. "Faced with the Nazis, who felt they had been justified in doing what they did, there could simply be a stand-off," she said during an interview in 2003. "And I thought: 'Morality just cannot be subjective in the way that different attitudes, like some . . . likes and dislikes, are subjective'" (p. 34). Rather than get hung up defining the

Philippa Foot 1920–2010

SOURCE: Getty Images.

good, she said, we are much better off focusing on the value of various traditional virtues Aristotle wrote about—temperance, courage, and so forth—and recognizing how our human needs require us to act accordingly. Published when she was 80 years old, her landmark 2001 book, *Natural Goodness,* argues that vice is a defect in humans just as a poor root system is a defect in an oak tree, or that poor vision is a defect in an owl: both claims simultaneously are normative (e.g., they are claims about the way things *ought* to be) and also factual. Her neo-Aristotelian approach helped revive the popularity of virtue ethics by arguing that the good of human flourishing required certain moral behaviors such as minimizing harm and keeping promises just as certain objective conditions enabled the natural world to flourish. The goodness of virtuous living is the same whether we're talking about the needs of a tree or the needs of a human being, she argued: "The meaning of the words 'good' and 'bad' is not different when used of features of plants on the one hand and humans on the other; but is rather the same as applied, in judgment of natural goodness, and defect, in the case of all living things" (2001, p. 47).

Seyla Benhabib

A political philosopher born and raised in Turkey but who pursued her academic career in the United States, Benhabib's internationalist perspective provides a useful "middle way" approach that seeks to take the best of Kant's call for universal ethical standards as well as feminist criticisms that his "worship" of reason and the premium he placed on impersonal claims of justice too often trump important relationship values such as empathy, care, and cooperation. Too often male Enlightenment thinkers have talked of the moral rights of individuals as if people are theoretical models—they generalize everyone into an ideal rational being, Benhabib argued in her 1992 book *Situating the Self: Gender, Community and Postmodernism in Contemporary Ethics.* This "generalized other" results in priority given to ideals such as duty, respect, worthiness, and dignity in most ethical frameworks. But this is far too "disembodied" to reflect the way we actually live, Benhabib argued. Instead, people ought to be treated as "concrete": each individual is a special case with his or her peculiar history, identity, and emotional responses that should be respected in and of themselves. This, she argued, means we must place priority on a very different set of ideals: responsibility, care, bonding, and sharing. If we govern our actions with these, she said, we confirm not only the "humanity" of those with whom we interact, but also their human "individuality." Thus, Benhabib promoted a moral framework that retains universalism as a good that we ought to aspire to, but also seeks to supplement this "impartialist ethic" based on Kant with an "ethic of care" that feminist theorists say is essential if our moral standards are expected to reflect how we actually live our lives. Her effort to counterbalance male-dominated ethical theory reflects a spectrum of feminist thought that offers a wide range of proposed ethical frameworks. These include Nel Noddings (1984), who argued that society's emphasis on "law and justice" is inherently male, while values such as "receptivity, relatedness and responsiveness" are inherently female. Feminist theory does not seek to idealize women or feminine traits but instead is "marked by its attention to how actors and systems are concretely embedded in and marked by gender, class, race, historical circumstance," as communication theorist Linda Steiner explained (1989, pp. 164–165). She argued that a broad "feminist ethic" is more likely to be focused on how media should maintain and promote social networking and relationships. It should, she said, "address questions about whose interests are regarded as worthy of debate, who gets to talk, and who is regarded as an effective communicator to whom others must listen" (Steiner, 1989, p. 158)—questions that recur in Benhabib's work.

Seyla Benhabib 1950–

SOURCE: Mike Marsland/Yale University.

IDEALISM AND RELATIVISM

Many factors influence and shape how we tackle ethical questions—our values and upbringings, what our peers have to say, our levels of maturity, our personalities. But two major things that profoundly affect our ethical decision making are idealism and relativism. *Idealism* refers to how strongly we feel about the pursuit of humanitarian goals, such as believing that everyone should be concerned with the welfare of other people. The belief that world affairs can and should be ordered to place a priority on maximizing everyone's well-being is central to the moral codes of many people. But others may be less idealistic about the world and may place less emphasis on other people's welfare. These people believe that, while it's important to avoid harming others, potential harm must be considered in the context of the overall good—that harm sometimes may be necessary to produce good.

Relativism refers to the belief that the only way we can decide what's ethical and what's not is to rely on our experiences and internal moral compass. People who reject the idea of universal moral rules that exist outside of individual experience subscribe to a relativistic approach to problems—they don't believe there are any legitimate moral absolutes that are capable of helping us figure out the best course of action in a given dilemma. Relativists rely on a more individualistic perspective.

Your Ethical Ideology

The general way in which you believe the world works—your ideological worldview—shapes how you are likely to approach ethical problems and try to resolve them. Your ethical ideology is largely based on two factors:

Idealism: The extent to which you believe that the best outcomes always result if broad, humanitarian goals drive your actions

Relativism: The extent to which you endorse an individualistic approach—you reject the possibility that there are universal moral standards that can help solve all ethical questions

Together, our degree of idealism and our degree of relativistic thinking make up what's called our *ethical ideology*—our worldview or belief system about the relationship between the individual level and global level that, in turn, shapes how we're most likely to deal with ethical problems. Social psychologists have long been interested in the link between our moral values and our moral behavior, and they have studied how different ethical ideologies influence decision making among a wide range of populations. In 1980, one sociologist came up with an effective way to measure people's idealism and relativism. Donelson Forsyth's Ethics Position Questionnaire (EPQ; presented as Table 1.1) presents 20 statements. Respondents are asked to what extent they agree or disagree with each. There are no right answers. Based on their scores, people who take the EPQ fall into one of four different categories in Forsyth's taxonomy of ethical ideologies (see Table 1.2).

INTENT VERSUS CONSEQUENCE; MEANS VERSUS ENDS

When we make a judgment about an act, what exactly are we judging? Are we assessing what a person's motive is in doing it, or are we passing judgment on the impact or effect the act has on others? Or are we taking both intent and consequences into consideration? How much weight should we assign to a well-intentioned act that turns out to be very harmful? The distinction is crucial to several of the theorists described earlier. Media ethicist Deni Elliott (1991) provided a

Table 1.1   Forsyth's Ethics Position Questionnaire

Below is a series of general statements. Each represents a commonly held opinion, and there are no right or wrong answers. You will probably disagree with some items and agree with others. We are interested in the extent to which you agree or disagree with such matters of opinion.

Please read each statement carefully. Indicate the extent to which you agree or disagree by placing in front of the statement the number corresponding to your feelings, where

1 = Completely disagree

2 = Largely disagree

3 = Moderately disagree

4 = Slightly disagree

5 = Neither agree nor disagree

6 = Slightly agree

7 = Moderately agree

8 = Largely agree

9 = Completely agree

_____ 1. A person should make certain that his or her actions never intentionally harm another even to a small degree.

_____ 2. Risks to another should never be tolerated, irrespective of how small the risks might be.

_____ 3. The existence of potential harm to others is always wrong, irrespective of the benefits to be gained.

_____ 4. One should never psychologically or physically harm another person.

_____ 5. One should not perform an action which might in any way threaten the dignity and welfare of another individual.

_____ 6. If an action could harm an innocent other, then it should not be done.

_____ 7. Deciding whether or not to perform an act by balancing the positive consequences of the act against the negative consequences of the act is immoral.

_____ 8. The dignity and welfare of people should be the most important concern in any society.

_____ 9. It is never necessary to sacrifice the welfare of others.

_____ 10. Moral actions are those which closely match ideals of the most "perfect" action.

Total your scores for items 1–10 and divide by 10. Your resulting 'I' score: _____

_____ 11. There are no ethical principles that are so important that they should be a part of any code of ethics.

_____ 12. What is ethical varies from one situation and society to another.

_____ 13. Moral standards should be seen as being individualistic; what one person considers to be moral may be judged to be immoral by another person.

_____ 14. Different types of moralities cannot be compared as to "rightness."

_____ 15. Questions of what is ethical for everyone can never be resolved since what is moral or immoral is up to the individual.

_____ 16. Moral standards are simply personal rules which indicate how a person should behave, and are not to be applied in making judgments of others.

_____ 17. Ethical considerations in interpersonal relations are so complex that individuals should be allowed to formulate their own individual codes.

_____ 18. Rigidly codifying an ethical position that prevents certain types of actions could stand in the way of better human relations and adjustment.

_____ 19. No rule concerning lying can be formulated; whether a lie is permissible or not permissible totally depends on the situation.

_____ 20. Whether a lie is judged to be moral or immoral depends upon circumstances surrounding the action.

Total your scores for items 11–20 and divide by 10. Your resulting 'R' score:_____

* An 'I' score between 1 and 5 represents a low degree of idealism; score between 6 and 10 is high.

* An 'R' score between 1 and 5 represents a low degree of relativism; score between 6 and 10 is high.

Where do your scores place you on the 'taxonomy of ethical ideologies'?

SOURCE: Forsyth (1980).

valuable example to help us see the difference. Imagine, she said, that you could choose your next-door neighbor. You interview one applicant, Jones, and you ask him how he feels about murder. Jones assures you that he doesn't kill people. When you ask him why he doesn't, he says, "I'm afraid I'll get caught and put in jail." You put the same question to another applicant, Smith, who replies, "I could never kill a person because I believe in the sanctity of human life. I don't think I could kill even in self-defense." As Elliott suggested,

> It takes little reflection for most people to decide that they prefer Smith to Jones as a neighbor. There is always a chance that Jones might come up with a way to murder a noisy neighbor without getting caught. Smith, on the other hand, appears to be motivated by an internal principle rather than fear of external consequences. (p. 18)

Good ethical reasoning also considers the validity and rationales of the methods, or means, used to achieve our goals or ends. Does the end justify the means? If our goals are honorable, does that mean that any strategy used to achieve them is automatically honorable too? Clearly not; we are well aware how a "successful" person with ill-gotten gains can be vulnerable to scorn and punishment. Our capacity for moral agency is part of what makes us human; *how* we accomplish our goals says as much about who we are as what we choose as our goals. Otherwise, the only real values that could be said to motivate us would be self-interest, greed, and expediency. Sure, we often feel compelled to bend the truth or tell a little white lie to keep the peace or prevent hurting someone's feelings unnecessarily, or even to obtain something we feel we deserve but would not otherwise receive. But if we truly hold honesty as a key value, then as moral agents, we should be able to make a rational, defensible case for why deceit or subterfuge are acceptable and are not merely self-serving or expedient. Our methods should embody our values as much as our goals do.

Table 1.2 Forsyth Taxonomy of Ethical Ideologies

Idealism	Relativism	
	High	Low
High	**Situationists** Reject moral rules; ask if the action yielded the best possible outcome in the given situation	**Absolutists** Assume that the best possible outcome can always be achieved by following universal moral rules
Low	**Subjectivists** Reject moral rules; base moral judgments on personal feelings about the action and setting	**Exceptionists** Moral absolutes guide judgments but pragmatically open to exceptions to these standards; utilitarian

SOURCE: Forsyth (1980).

We must understand "ends" not only as what we aim to accomplish and aspire to, but also as a way to perceive others. Kant and other ethicists have argued that we have an absolute moral duty to treat others as ends in themselves and not as means to accomplish our goals. Otherwise, we reduce other human beings to objects or mere tools, which is a failure to properly appreciate the specialness of being human. Furthermore, as we will see, Kant's categorical imperative requires that I treat people as deserving of respect for its own sake because if it were acceptable for everyone *not* to do so, chaos would ensue. Kant says this is critical because our highest value must be placed on our capacity for freedom and moral agency. Failure to treat others as ends in themselves in effect denies our humanness—such behavior implies it is acceptable to treat fellow human beings the same way we might treat the inanimate tools we used to accomplish certain jobs. We must interact with others in ways that maximize their ability to exercise free will or reason. To fail to do so is to fail to recognize our existence as rational beings who, by the presence of our will to reason, are obligated to act morally toward others. These distinctions in how we approach ethical dilemmas are further explored in the next chapter.

For Discussion

1. Think about how you have talked about your sense of "ethics" and your "morals" in conversations with others. Do you typically use them synonymously?

2. What are some values that you have that often clash in daily life?

3. Think of a time in your life when your decision to uphold a principle that you claimed to value resulted in some cost or sacrifice on your part.

4. Take the Forsyth Ethics Position Questionnaire yourself. What is your ethical ideology?

5. How might your degree of relativistic thinking, as reflected in the EPQ, shape the way you deal with ethical problems? How might your level of idealistic thinking do so?

6. Which of the central ethicists and philosophers seems to resonate most with you?

7. Kant and others are concerned that we should avoid treating other people only as means but rather treat them as ends in themselves. Can you think of examples of each?

8. Consider a recent difficult decision you had to make that affected other people. How much weight did you place on the effects or consequence of your decision? How much weight did you place on whether the decision embodied principles that you think are important?

REFERENCES

Audi, R. (2004). *The good in the right: A theory of intuition and intrinsic value.* Princeton, NJ: Princeton University Press.

Benhabib, S. (1992). *Situating the self: Gender, community and postmodernism in contemporary ethics.* London, England: Routledge.

Christians, C. G. (2005). Ethical theory in communications research. *Journalism Studies, 6*(1), 3–14.

Elliott, D. (1991, autumn). Moral development theories and the teaching of ethics. *Journalism Educator,* 18–24.

Foot, P. (2001). *Natural goodness.* Oxford, UK: Oxford University Press.

Foot, P. (2002). *Moral dilemmas and other topics in moral philosophy.* Oxford, UK: Clarendon Press.

Foot, P. (2003). The grammar of goodness: An interview with Philippa Foot. *The Harvard Review of Philosophy, 11,* 32–44.

Forsyth, D. R. (1980). A taxonomy of ethical ideologies. *Journal of Personality and Social Psychology, 39,* 175–184.

Johnstone, C. L. (2002). Aristotle's ethical theory in the contemporary world: Logos, phronêsis and the moral life. In S. L. Bracci & C. G. Christians (Eds.), *Moral engagement in public life: Theorists for contemporary ethics* (pp. 16–34). New York, NY: Peter Lang.

Noddings, N. (1984). *Caring: A feminine approach to ethics and moral education.* Berkeley, CA: University of California Press.

Patterson, P., & Wilkins, L. (2014). *Media ethics: Issues and cases* (8th ed.). Boston, MA: McGraw-Hill.

Rawls, J. (1999). *A theory of justice.* Cambridge, MA: Belknap Press of Harvard University.

Rogers, R. A. P. (1965). *A short history of ethics.* London, England: MacMillan.

Rokeach, M. (1973). *The nature of human values.* New York, NY: Free Press.

Rokeach, M. (1979). *Understanding human values: Individual and societal.* New York, NY: Free Press.

Ross, W. D. (1930). *The right and the good.* Oxford, UK: Clarendon Press.

Sidgwick, H. (1981). *The methods of ethics.* Indianapolis, IN: Hackett.

Steiner, L. (1989). Feminist theorizing and communication ethics. *Communication, 12,* 157–173.

Walker, M. U. (2000). Naturalizing, normativity, and using what we know in ethics. *Canadian Journal of Philosophy, 26*(Suppl.), 75–101.

Key Frameworks

If ethics is concerned with how we argue about weighing values, rather than simply trading moral claims about what is "good" or "right," what exactly does ethics look like? How do we draw on ideas of goodness and rightness to say, for instance, that someone's private information ought to be included in news accounts in some instances but not others? Ethical deliberation focuses largely on our values, so it certainly cannot be completely divorced from the everyday moral standards that we regularly embrace—standards of respect, of truthfulness, of stewardship, of freedom, of connectedness. Moral philosophers are concerned with how exactly we can discern the goodness implied in these and other ideas. In ethics, of course, it is important to be familiar with the moral basis of these principles. But ethicists spend less time asserting their goodness and more time trying to express why one should be given more weight than others in a particular situation. They do so in part by relying on different philosophical theories that frame principles in specific ways. In fact, the philosophy of ethics really comprises multiple philosophies, all of which have their uses and their limitations.

This chapter provides a brief description of three such key philosophies, or frameworks that we commonly draw on in our ethical thinking: **virtue** ethics, **duty** ethics, and **consequentialist** ethics. Each offers us distinct ways to bring key principles, what we think of as ideas reflecting goodness, to bear on ethical dilemmas. They order or frame principles for us and, thus, are valuable in constructing ethics-based cases that argue why one course of action should be considered more defensible than another. As we delve into each, there are a few things to keep in mind. First, while the three philosophies here are arguably the predominant ones referred to in Western ethics, they are certainly not the only ones. Communitarian ethics, for example, offers yet another alternative frame, and it is featured in Chapter 10. Second, these philosophies are not mutually exclusive. There are some overlaps. While the principle of transparency discussed in Chapter 4, for example, can be referred to as a "virtue," it could also be described as a reflection of our moral "duty" to behave in certain ways that connote respect for others. Third, these philosophies are not absolute. Rather than monolithic bodies of thought, each of these frames offers variations on main themes. The theory of justice featured in Chapter 6, for instance, can be considered one of several forms of consequentialist thinking. Fourth, these philosophies are not static. They have evolved over time—and they continue to evolve. Many contemporary thinkers, for instance, have set forth how the work of Aristotle can gain renewed relevance and serve useful purposes when applied to today's world.

VIRTUE ETHICS

Virtue ethics frames moral questions in this way: What would someone with a proper understanding of honorable behavior do in a given situation, and how might one cultivate a character that predisposes one to embrace virtuous behavior as a lifestyle? The cultivation of individual character to become models of virtue, rather than the rightness or wrongness of specific actions, is the focus of virtue ethics. Pursuit of virtue is what constitutes a good human life. The lack of specificity in virtue ethics has long been criticized as a deficiency of the theory: How useful is it when the notion of a good character seems so vague and ill-defined? Yet as suggested in the previous chapter's brief discussion of Aristotle, virtue ethics is not as vague as some suggest. And among virtue theory's many strengths is its flexibility in allowing that being virtuous can depend largely on the personal and professional situations in which we find ourselves. Media ethicist Sandra Borden neatly summarizes this in her book on virtue ethics and journalism:

> An occupation's purpose provides it with moral justification . . . if it can be integrated into a broader conception of what is good for humans. . . . Thus, the theory can explain why members of some groups have rights and responsibilities that do not apply to outsiders (such as cutting someone's chest open with a surgical instrument or going into a war zone to take photographs). It also can explain why it may be morally desirable to prefer one person over another when faced with conflicting interests (the way a professional prioritizes her clients). Virtue theory's emphasis on the habitual disposition to do the right thing . . . takes morality out of the realm of calculations and into the realm of moral responsiveness. (2007, pp. 16–17)

The "habitual disposition to do the right thing" is the *telos,* or end purpose, of virtue ethics. How we actually apply virtues, such as courage, wisdom, or prudence, may well depend on the context of the dilemma we are faced with. But a crucial aspect of virtue theory says that being virtuous is not merely whatever we, as individuals, decide it is. The theory argues that if we think about it, we will realize that we have *objective* reasons for acting virtuously because such behavior is essential for all humans to flourish, to reach their potential. The theory calls on us to build a character that reflects the virtues because doing so serves us well as human beings and as moral agents linked to others in community—just as an oak tree must have a healthy root system to be what it is meant to be.

Virtue ethics was originally articulated in the works of Socrates and Plato, and later was refined by Aristotle. Rather than dwelling on how we know goodness, Aristotle's writings are focused on identifying and articulating the *highest* good, which he says has specific characteristics: It is innately valuable; that is, we desire it for its own sake and not for what it allows us to accomplish, and all other goods are desirable because they help us attain this highest good. Aristotle argues that the highest good is the state of "living well," translated from the Greek word *eudaimonia*. Philosopher Richard Kraut describes Aristotle's general call:

> What we need, in order to live well, is a proper appreciation of the way in which such goods as friendship, pleasure, virtue, honour and wealth fit together as a whole. In order to apply that general understanding to particular cases, we must acquire, through proper upbringing and habits, the ability to see, on each occasion, which course of action is best supported by reasons. Therefore practical wisdom, as he conceives it, cannot be acquired solely by learning general rules. We must also acquire, through practice, those deliberative, emotional, and social skills that enable us to put our general understanding of well-being into practice in ways that are suitable to each occasion. (2010, p. 1)

We do not strive to live well for the sake of some other goal, he argues. Everything we might seek in life—prosperity, health, other resources—we do so because they promote well-being. Virtuous activity enables us to live well by serving as the reason we pursue "lesser" goods. Since our capacity for reason is what distinguishes us from other animals, he argues, using our reason effectively is what happiness, or living well, consists of. Just as in everything else, reasoning well implies a sense of excellence, and so we must pursue virtuous action.

Doctrine of the Mean

Just as a skilled worker knows how to avoid doing too much or too little of something to ensure a job well done, we all must strive to see what behavior might constitute an excess or a deficiency of a given virtue. Since courage is a desirable virtue, we admire courageous people because they understand that some dangers are worth facing, and others are not: They do not flee from every threat, for that would be cowardly; also, they do not mindlessly attack all comers without any sense of fear, for that would represent foolhardiness or recklessness. The same sense of ideal behavior holds for every other virtue Aristotle discusses. Finding the perfect point of moderation between excess and deficiency, or the "sweet spot" of virtuous behavior, is not a matter of mathematical calculation, but of an ability to fully understand the situation one finds oneself in. Aristotle's argument here, that every virtue is a state of behavior that lies between two "vices," one of excess and the other of deficiency, is known as his "doctrine of the mean." Critics have suggested that this doctrine is not very helpful in many types of dilemmas. While his logic makes sense in desirable emotional responses we might have to situations—Aristotle says we may well feel anger, yet we must guard against acting on excessive outrage, for example—it is less useful when faced with choices such as whether to honor a promise to attend a social event or cancel because of an unforeseen obligation. Yet Aristotle is explicit in saying it is not possible to put together an ethical decision manual: Life is too varied and complex for a series of rules to be useful. This does not mean that we are then free to individually decide what is good; just because unique situational circumstances may determine what it means to act virtuously, that is not the same as saying good behavior is *relative* only to our own beliefs and values.

Virtue as Practice

Aristotle was largely preoccupied with setting forth a theory about cultivating the character of the individual. Yet contemporary philosophers have worked to show how his system is useful in arguing what we should do on a social level. These "neo-Aristotelians" say Homeric and Aristotelian accounts of virtue always assume the fact that features of our social and moral lives are widely accepted as important and as necessary conditions for virtuous behavior. In the Homeric tradition, virtues are presented as qualities crucial for effectively performing certain *social roles.* Similarly, for Aristotle, the virtues as he often describes them are not ends in themselves, but are instrumental in the broader aim of achieving "happiness," or *eudaimonia.* Today's virtue ethicists, such as Alisdair MacIntyre, argue that the idea of the value of virtuous behavior applies both to the individual and to society as a whole. "[T]his notion of a particular type of practice as providing the arena in which the virtues are exhibited . . . is crucial to the whole enterprise of identifying a core concept of virtues," MacIntyre argues (2007, p. 187). He makes the distinction between what he calls *external* goods—things or acts that benefit single individuals—and the social benefits resulting in some work as *internal* goods. For example, the medical profession's importance to general public health, as opposed to single patients, is an example of an internal good. The kinds of work that we value primarily for the internal goods they provide, MacIntyre argues, constitute the basis for virtue in professional behavior. We must understand this work as a "practice" that is distinct from other work focused on delivering strictly external goods (e.g., factory work, retail transactions, etc.):

> By "practice" I . . . mean any coherent and complex form of socially established cooperative human activity through which goods internal to that form of activity are realized in the course of trying to achieve those standards of excellence which are appropriate to, and partially definitive of, that form of activity, with the result that human powers to achieve excellence, and human conceptions of the end and good involved, are systematically extended. (MacIntyre, 2007, p. 187)

Practices involve "standards of excellence and obedience to rules" and are aimed at attaining internal goods or things that contribute to the common good regardless of who actually receives them. Media professionals, when deliberately informing their work with the "standards of excellence" that are attached to their "practices," are able to deliver internal goods such as providing information and analysis that enables the public to participate in a vigorous democratic life (journalism) or providing messages and advocacy of perspectives that contribute to a vibrant marketplace of ideas (public relations). "When one chooses a role, one must submit to the expectations that accompany that role," Borden notes. "To enter into a practice, you must submit to the authority of the standards and the internal goods of that practice" (Borden, 2007, p. 22).

Human Flourishing

Rather than getting tangled up in philosophical debates over our motives and duties, virtue ethicists who have followed Aristotle urge us instead to focus on the rules and behaviors that contribute to our "flourishing." They use this term in a broad sense to accommodate the diversity of society and the wide range of interests we all may have. By flourishing, most philosophers mean what we all need to enjoy the fruits of our labor, to reap the benefits of collaboration and community engagement, and to have the means and resources to enable us to strive toward and reach our individual potential. So for us to flourish, we would need, among other things, a social system that is just and that maximizes liberties; encourages engagement, cooperation, and generosity; and frowns on more selfish impulses that can threaten to undermine these. "Men and women need to be industrious and tenacious of purpose not only to be able to house, clothe, and feed themselves," philosopher Philippa Foot (2001) argued, "but also to pursue human needs having to do with love and friendship. They need the ability to form family ties, friendships, and special relations with neighbours. They also need codes of conduct. And how could they have all these things without virtues such as loyalty, fairness, kindness, and in certain circumstances obedience?" (pp. 44–45). Just as modern-day philosophers have said that Aristotle's ideas of cultivating character have a social dimension, they have done the same for his notion of the highest virtue of "living well," or *eudaimonia:* it cannot simply be concerned with the good life of individual people; a life well lived must encompass one's social roles and responsibilities to do more than just make oneself happy. Human flourishing must refer to virtuous behavior that cultivates and protects a vibrant society. MacIntyre (2007) suggested that people's social environment offers everyone a range of goods and expertise that we all draw on to build our lives. Others also have coined the phrase "moral ecology" to refer to a "social vision of the good life with members both cooperating and competing but sharing at least overlapping visions" of what it means to flourish personally and socially (Huff, Barnard, & Frey, 2008, p. 286). Theorist Nick Couldry (2010) describes it this way: "'Virtues' are the means by which stable dispositions to act are well specified, but the reference point by which virtues are specified are not particular 'values,' but precisely those facts about shared human life on which potentially we can come to agree" (p. 66).

For some, all this might sound a bit too vague to serve as a reliable set of guidelines that help us identify what exactly virtuous action would mean in certain situations. But such flexibility is important, virtue theorists say. And they argue that it is really not as difficult to figure out what we mean by flourishing in specific cases as some might suggest. Moral philosopher Philippa Foot has done more than most to help make Aristotle's writings about virtue relevant to our contemporary world. In her 2001 landmark work on virtue ethics, *Natural Goodness,* she argued that acting morally, if we think about it, stems naturally from our ability to apply our reasoning skills to situations. "[T]he fact that a human action or disposition is good of its kind will be taken to be simply a fact about a given nature of a certain kind of living thing," she argued (2001, p. 3). Rather than focusing on abstract concepts such as sacredness of life, goodness, and duty, Foot argued that by concentrating on traditional virtues and vices such as temperance and avarice, we can see the concrete connections between the conditions of human life—the presence and absence of the various necessary goods—and the objective reasons for acting morally. Vice, she argued, is a defect in humans the same way that poor roots are a defect in an oak tree or poor vision a defect in an owl: The two assessments have clear normative implications, yet are also entirely factual:

> [V]irtues play a necessary part in the life of human beings as do stings in the life of bees. . . . In spite of the diversity of human goods—the elements that can make up good human lives—it is therefore possible that the concept of a good human life plays the same part in determining goodness of human characteristics and operations that the concept of flourishing plays in the determination of goodness in plants and animals. (2001, pp. 35, 44)

Foot (2001) refers to the notion of "Aristotelian necessities" such as being able to "bind each other's wills" as being recurrent in the course of our daily lives; we rely on others to perform certain duties and meet certain obligations that benefit us (p. 46). This "require-ment" that we rely on the collaboration of others is essential for human flourishing, and no different from the requirement that a healthy oak tree have sturdy roots:

> Thus the structure of the derivation is the same whether we derive an evaluation of the roots of a particular tree or the action of a particular human being. The meaning of the words "good" and "bad" is not different when used of features of plant on the one hand and humans on the other, but is rather the same as applied, in judgement of natural goodness and defect, in the case of all living things. (Foot, 2001, p. 47)

DUTY ETHICS

While virtue ethics is focused on what kind of person we ought to be and what character traits we should cultivate, duty ethics is concerned with setting out what we ought to do if we take our status of moral agents seriously. Also known as deontology (from the Greek word *deon,* meaning duty), duty ethics argues that there are moral obligations that we are all bound by and that these obligations must motivate our behavior. This framework also is set in contrast with consequentialist ethics, which we'll examine next, in that it force-fully argues that since these moral "duties" define what action is right, our moral judg-ments cannot rest on the outcomes, or consequences, of those acts. Some choices, deontologists argue, simply cannot be justified by their effects: No matter how much they might result in some "benefit," some choices are simply morally wrong because they fail to reflect our duty to behave in a certain way. This is why deontologists often state that the "right" takes priority over the "good." While bringing about some benefit, or good, through one's actions is obviously desirable, our success at doing so cannot be the basis of our moral judgments because that would imply that any sort of underhanded or evil "means" can be justified by a good outcome. Rather, the "right" must come first: Knowing our moral duties to treat others properly, to avoid harm, to respect certain values is the surest guide to making the best decisions. It is our intended ends and our intended means that defines our moral selves. As Thomas Aquinas argued, if we intend something bad as an end, or even as a means to achieve what we perceive as some other good result, we are said to have "set ourselves at evil," and this is something that, as moral agents, we are not allowed to do. Kant's duty-based moral system is the classic example of a deontological approach: An act cannot be judged as right or wrong based on its consequences, but only on whether the person performing the act understood his or her obligations as a moral agent. Performing a certain act may have negative consequences for some people, but such results are not what make that a bad or immoral act; its rightness exists independent of any resulting outcome. A lie is immoral, according to this view, not because of what it may do (that is, result in harming someone), but because of what it is—an act of deception that denies our moral obligation to treat all human beings with the dignity that they deserve. A lie does so because it denies the recipient the right to exercise reasoning capacity. This issue is further explored in Chapter 5.

One's *intent,* then, is the center of moral gravity in duty ethics, rather than one's character (virtue ethics) or the results of one's actions (consequentialist ethics). But even here, we must be specific. Intending to cause harm, for example, can be quite different from "believing" an act will be harmful, "risking" harm by taking an action, inadvertently "causing" harm, or "predicting" an action might be harmful. "For example, we can intend to kill and even try to kill someone without killing him; and we can kill him without intending or trying to kill him, as when we kill accidentally," philosophers Larry Alexander and Michael Moore (2012) write. "Intending thus does not collapse into risking, causing, or predicting . . . [I]t is intending alone that marks the involvement of our agency in a way so as to bring obligations and permissions into play" (p. 6). Since Aquinas, deontologists have argued extensively over how exactly we should define *causing* evil and how that might be different from *allowing* evil.

As much as duty-ethics philosophers emphasize the role of our motivation in making moral judgments, they also are concerned with the *rights* of individuals whose fates are determined by what we do. As moral agents, we all have the right, they say, not to be used only as a means for bringing about good consequences without our consent. People cannot use our bodies, our labor, or our abilities without our say-so. Yet our intents and our rights are not always compatible, and, thus, duty-ethicists continue to debate about the exact nature of our moral duties. Should one person in a lifeboat be killed and eaten so that all the others can survive? Should Siamese twins who are likely to die soon be separated by doctors to harvest the organs of the first to die to give to the second? Should villagers follow the orders of a tyrant to select one among them to be shot to avoid all of them being killed? Your answers to these will differ depending on whether you place a premium on our moral duty to prevent wider harm or whether you emphasize the right of individuals not to be used against their will (Alexander & Moore, 2012). This issue is best illustrated by two commonly used hypothetical scenarios that confront us with situations in which certain people are likely to die and that present us with different options to respond. The first is called the "Trolley Problem," where you witness an out-of-control trolley barreling down the tracks toward a group of five unsuspecting track workers, and you are near a switch that could divert the trolley to a spur. The five workers would be spared, but a sixth worker on the spur would likely die. The second is called the "Transplant Problem," in which a surgeon has five patients in dire need of organ transplants. Are there moral grounds for the surgeon to kill a moderately healthy sixth patient to use his organs to save five lives? For most deontologists, the two scenarios show not only that our motivations matter more than the consequences of our acts, but that our motivations must be guided by an understanding of the fundamental rights of individuals to be treated in a certain way:

> In Trolley, a runaway trolley will kill five workers unless diverted to a siding where it will kill one worker. Most people regard it as permissible and perhaps mandatory to switch the trolley to the siding. By contrast, in Transplant, where a surgeon can kill one healthy patient and transplant his organs to five dying patients, thereby saving their lives, the universal reaction is condemnation. . . . The injunction against using [others against their wishes] arguably accounts for these contrasting reactions. After all, in each example, one life is sacrificed to save five. Yet there appears to be a difference in the means through which the net four lives are saved. In Transplant, the doomed person is used to benefit the others. They could not be saved in the absence of his body. In Trolley, on the other hand, the doomed victim is not used. The workers would be saved whether or not he is present on the second track. (Alexander & Moore, 2012)

Notice the different line of reasoning here that "rights" ethicists use for justifying the switching of the trolley tracks: Strictly speaking, the one worker is not "used" as the means to save the others, even though his death is made inevitable. Other duty-ethics philosophers argue that if we switch the tracks *with the intent* to kill the single worker, that act remains morally impermissible, even if it results in saving the others. Whether such a move is justified is the focus of ongoing debate among various duty-ethicists.

Categorical Imperative

Immanuel Kant is arguably the foremost architect of duty-based ethics. In his extensive writings, he sets forth the nature and role of rationality. With an inexorable logic, Kant argues that what makes us special as beings is our God-given capacity for reason, and with the proper use of that reason, we can fully discern ways in which we are morally obligated to respect and honor that reasoning capacity—in every case, for everyone. Thus, the fundamental principle of our moral duties, he says, is the "categorical imperative": We are to "act only in accordance with that maxim through which you can at the same time will that it become a universal law" (1797/1991, p. 395). It is an *imperative* in that it commands us to do something—Kant does not order that we perform specific actions to be "moral"; instead, he commands us to exercise our *wills* in a particular way. And it is *categorical*—that is, it applies to all of us unconditionally, simply because we possess rational wills, without reference to any of our personal goals or interests. For Kant, this categorical imperative calls on all of us to think more deeply about doing or not doing something. Philosopher Robert Johnson (2012) summarizes how the categorical imperative calls on us to consider the morality of an action:

> First, formulate a maxim that enshrines your reason for acting as you propose. Second, recast that maxim as a universal law of nature governing all rational agents, and so as holding that all must, by natural law, act as you yourself propose

to act in these circumstances. Third, consider whether your maxim is even conceivable in a world governed by this law of nature. If it is, then, fourth, ask yourself whether you would, or could, rationally *will* to act on your maxim in such a world. If you could, then your action is morally permissible. (pp. 10–11)

But saying we all must act only if the action can be defended as a universal standard of action for everyone does not mean duty ethicists think we all must act in lockstep, with no consideration for the unique differences in our lives. Context matters. So in many cases, the moral obligations we have can be "agent-relative"—that is, they may apply just to us because of our relation to the individuals impacted by our actions. One person may feel obligated to act a certain way with family members to avoid moral failure, but that feeling of duty may not apply in the company of strangers.

The idea is that morality is intensely personal, in the sense that we are each enjoined to keep our own moral house in order. . . . Agent-centered theories and agent-relative reasons on which they are based not only enjoin each of us to do or not to do certain things; they also instruct me to treat *my* friends, *my* family, *my* promises in certain ways because they are *mine,* even if by neglecting them I could do more for others' friends, families, and promises. [emphasis added] (Alexander & Moore, 2012, pp. 5–6)

Conflicting Duties

Immanuel Kant boldly claimed that "a conflict of duties is inconceivable" (1780, p. 25). But as we have seen, this claim is optimistic at best. Philosophers have since struggled with how best to reconcile clashing duties in countless actual and hypothetical dilemmas. Philosopher W. D. Ross neatly laid bare the doubtfulness of Kant's claim, saying even our most careful deliberations can involve what he called "moral risk":

We come . . . after consideration to think one duty more pressing than the other, but we do not feel certain that it is so. . . . For, to go no further in the analysis, it is enough to point out that any particular act will in all probability in the course of time contribute to the bringing about of good or evil for many human beings, and thus have a *prima facie* rightness or wrongness of which we know nothing. (1930, pp. 30–31)

But that doesn't negate the reality of our moral obligations, Ross said. By laying out his theory of duty, Ross provides a sort of modified and less rigid deontological approach than Kant's. Ross said we are bound by several of what he called *prima facie* duties— obligations that should be self-evident to any reasoning individual. Like the categorical imperative, his list of duties binds all people in all situations. We have a duty to honor the notion of **honesty**. We must keep the promises we make (**fidelity**). We have a duty to right the wrongs we have committed (**reparation**). We have a duty to express **gratitude** and return favors to those who have helped us. We have a duty to promote general welfare and **justice** for all. We have a duty to avoid harming others (**nonmaleficence**). And finally, we have a duty to constantly strive for **self-improvement**. There should be little argument over whether these duties are real and objectively true; they are "a hard-wired and evolutionarily advantageous set of rules that any morally mature human" should understand, philosopher Christopher Meyers argued (2011, p. 317). But Ross recognizes that there will be plenty of situations in which these conflict, and we are expected to make reasoned arguments for placing greater moral weight on some over others in given situations. For example, in a case that may pose serious harm to someone, our duty to minimize or avoid harm may well take precedence over a promise we made. While such an open-ended theory may be perceived as daunting, its embrace of moral uncertainty in our daily lives should actually be seen as a strength of this approach, Meyers argues. Ross's efforts to set forth universal duties yet acknowledge the contextual basis for how we apply them "is a far more accurate reflection of humans' moral reasoning, both in fact and in capability," Meyers writes (2003, p. 93).

> Persons can, I think, grasp universal moral truth at the abstract level, but our moral decision making in actual cases is fraught with uncertainty and ambiguity. Ross, better than any other theorist, captured this tension. . . . Even the most duty-bound most morally committed person will make mistakes because of inadequate information, but such a person should not be held morally accountable for those mistakes. (2003, pp. 93–94)

CONSEQUENTIALIST ETHICS

Ross's approach arguably serves as a bridge of sorts between a duty-based ethics and a consequentialist approach. We certainly have obligations to act morally and to uphold certain duties, but we also need to think about, and defend, the consequences of actions to the extent possible. As its name suggests, consequentialist ethics argues for shifting the moral weight in decision making from character and intent to how much good our decisions produce. Here, whether an act is morally justified depends only on the results of that act. Just as in the other ethical lines of thought discussed, there are several variants on consequentialist ethics, only a few of which will be discussed here. But the contrast among the three ethical frameworks should be clear. For virtue ethicists, lying, for example, is rejected because it represents a failure to act virtuously and it undermines the basis of trust and collaboration that are essential to human flourishing. For duty ethicists, lying is rejected because it fundamentally disrespects the capacity for independent rationality that all humans have. For consequentialist ethicists, lying is rejected because it is too likely to result in an overall diminishment of positive or good outcomes. And under some forms of consequentialist thinking, a lie that arguably results in more good than harm would be justifiable.

The most common phrase associated with consequentialist ethics is "providing the greatest benefit for the greatest number of people." And the most common form of this framework is *utilitarianism*—an act is judged based on how much "utility," or good outcome, it provides. The early proponents of utilitarianism in the 17th and 18th centuries argued for a *hedonistic* definition of utility: Pleasure is the only intrinsic good, and maximizing it was the sole basis for judging acts. Later, others refined and expanded what constituted the "good" beyond mere pleasure, to include broader, higher-order goods such as freedom, knowledge, skill in the arts, and the like. John Stuart Mill articulated this type of utilitarianism in the 1860s. Yet contemporary philosophers continue to debate just what sorts of consequentialist principles can be useful in ethical dilemmas. Not all pleasures are considered valuable in the same ways for everyone, so which pleasures should carry moral weight? Can we really perceive all possible pleasures and act with sufficient foresight to promote them? How can we rank different kinds of pleasures against each other? Even Mill, one of the foremost architects of utilitarianism, eventually came to the realization that a direct pursuit of happiness as an end in itself can lead only to disappointment. The only truly happy people, he wrote late in life, are those "who have their minds fixed on some other object than their own happiness; on the happiness of others, on the improvement of mankind, even on some art or pursuit, followed not as a means, but itself an ideal end" (Vrooman, 1911, p. 168). The ways in which we perceive pleasures as valuable, and what we count as a maximization of those pleasures worth promoting, could result in quite different variations of utilitarianism. In consequentialist ethics, what appears to be a straight forward idea—maximize benefits, or pleasure, for the greatest number of people—can quickly become very complicated. Still, the general approach of utility has arguably become the foundation of the Western democratic legislative system. Many of our laws and legislative efforts center on maximizing benefits for the greater number of people. It serves as the powerful basis for an enduring political system. But it can be more challenging to see how utilitarianism, given questions such as those above, can serve as an effective moral framework.

One way supporters say it can is to think about promoting things that benefit society, rather than focusing on aggregate goods benefiting individuals. This would help account for cases when "pain" is perceived as somehow valuable. "For example," one contemporary philosopher argued, "even if punishment of a criminal causes pain, a consequentialist can hold that a world with both the crime and the punishment is better than a world with the crime but not the punishment, perhaps because the former contains more justice" (Sinnott-Armstrong, 2011, p. 8). So instead of narrowly having to determine whether a single act would produce a specific benefit or pleasure, this "holistic" utilitarianism compares "the whole world (or total set of consequences) that results from an action with the whole world that results from not doing that action," he argues. "If the former is better, then the action is morally right" (Sinnott-Armstrong, p. 8). This is the difference between using utility as a "standard" with which to judge the rightness of an act, and using it as a "decision procedure." The latter is virtually impossible since we are not omniscient and cannot possibly anticipate every outcome of our actions. So most consequentialists argue for the former, as Sinnott-Armstrong explains: "Just as the laws of physics govern golf ball flight, but golfers need not calculate physical forces while planning shots; so overall utility can determine which decisions are morally right, even if agents need not calculate utilities while making decisions" (2011, p. 10). We cannot be held accountable for simply failing to foresee all the possible consequences of our actions, but utilitarians argue that we are accountable for our *intended* consequences and for failing to observe likely, or *foreseeable,* outcomes.

The kind of consequentialism described previously can be called *act utilitarianism,* since it is concerned with the outcomes of specific actions. But it should be clear that this approach can raise as many questions as it answers, and so other consequentialist thinkers advocate for an alternative known as *rule utilitarianism;* that is, we should judge actions not on specific anticipated outcomes, but on how likely they are to uphold other agreed-on principles or rules. Under this approach, an act is morally wrong if it violates a rule whose acceptance has better consequences than what would likely be the outcome without the rule. John Rawls, a political philosopher who was long dissatisfied with utilitarianism as a moral theory, articulated his theory of justice as an alternative in the 1970s. His theory, which is more fully discussed in Chapter 6, argues that the promotion of social justice should be the primary aim of all public policy, and he sets forth a novel way to think about making decisions that do so. Since under his theory all actions are judged according to a certain standard—in his case, whether they promote justice—it can be considered an example of rule utilitarianism.

Just as the purer forms of virtue ethics and duty ethics can seem overly demanding or rigid, so too can rule utilitarianism—maybe more so, as there are so many forms that the "good" can take, and that can give the most innocuous activity moral weight. Sinnott-Armstrong (2011) neatly summarizes this:

> When I watch television, I always (or most always) could do more good by helping others, but it does not seem morally wrong to watch television. When I choose to teach philosophy rather than working for CARE or the Peace Corps, my choice probably fails to maximize utility overall. If we were required to maximize utility, then we would have to make very different choices in many areas of our lives. The requirement to maximize utility, thus, strikes many people as too demanding because it interferes with the personal decisions that most of us feel should be left up to the individual. Some utilitarians respond by arguing that we really are morally required to change our lives so as to do a lot more to increase overall utility. Such hard-liners claim that most of what most people do is morally wrong, because most people rarely maximize utility. (p. 19)

Criticisms of Utility in Ethics

As mentioned earlier, consequentialism serves as quite an effective political philosophy, and, thus, the basis for much democratic action. Yet its value as a *moral* theory has been undermined by persistent skepticism that it sounds good but remains too vague to be of much use, and that it leaves too much of what we care about out of the moral equation. While utilitarian thinkers offer defenses against each of these attacks, these are some key criticisms that suggest utility is a shaky basis for moral thinking:

❐ If the outcome of our actions is all that matters, then do we have any concrete moral duties? Surely we do, critics argue. "Consequentialism runs up against the belief, held by ordinary persons and by some philosophers, that certain actions are intrinsically wrong, regardless of their good consequences, such as telling a lie so as not to hurt someone's feelings, or helping a terminally ill person to die so as to relieve them of pain," wrote William Stafford (1998, p. 79).

❐ Useful, universalizable definitions remain elusive. As discussed earlier, what forms of "happiness" or "good" should count as those that should be maximized? What should we do in cases when we must choose to promote one good over another? Should we concentrate on short-term benefits? Long-term benefits? What constitutes the greatest number of people in a given situation? And who gets to decide these questions?

☐ Though rule utilitarianism might ease the pressure of considering the merits of every single action we take, our inability to predict future outcomes—positive and negative—still limits our ability to be sure of our choices. Our lack of omniscience still seems to be a moral liability in this framework.

☐ The theory of utility invites us to conflate the one with the many. That is, it tempts us, in considering what would maximize benefits for the greatest number of people, to assume that what is in the interest of an ideal reasonable being is somehow the same as what would be beneficial for everyone.

☐ Thomas Jefferson repeatedly cautioned against the "tyranny of the majority," and while Mill and other utilitarians expressed strong concern for the notion of social justice, their theory leaves open such a threat. History is full of examples of paternalistic, racist, and sexist thinking that presumed all kinds of now-repugnant practices justly benefitted the majority—child labor, slavery, and women treated as property.

CONCLUSION

This chapter began by saying these three frameworks are not mutually exclusive. Indeed, the ways in which the three overlap are as instructive as are their distinct emphases. The duty theory of Ross is a good example. While his articulation of our moral obligations clearly places him in the deontology camp, at least three of his prima facie duties—the duties we have to promote justice, to promote the general welfare of others, and to avoid harming others—are focused on accomplishing specific outcomes, or *consequences*. And yet another of his duties, to pursue self-improvement, clearly is rooted in Aristotle's call to cultivate the *virtues* in our character (Meyers, 2003). Rarely do we find ourselves to be thinking or acting as strict virtue ethicists, deontologists, or utilitarians. We all approach ethical questions from a web of experiences, perceived obligations, and expectations. We care about what others expect of us, what we expect of ourselves, and how we might affect others by what we do. In one case, we may place priority on the obligations, or duties, we feel we have—to avoid harming someone, to honor a promise, regardless of the immediate consequences. In another, we may be more concerned about outcomes and will work to bring about the "good" result that we feel is most necessary. No one way is the right way. And that doesn't mean it ultimately is only up to what you can justify with your own personal beliefs and values, regardless of whether they are shared by others. *Situations* might be unique, but such *relativistic* thinking, as we saw in Chapter 1, fails to acknowledge that ethics is nothing if not *relational*—thinking and acting with knowledge and mindfulness of how our actions impact others. Good ethical deliberation is informed thinking and having awareness that each approach assigns moral weight to quite different things.

For Discussion

1. How might Aristotle's notion of the doctrine of the mean help us in arguing for certain behavior in media?

2. What exactly might Philippa Foot mean when she says that there are "objective" reasons for behaving in certain ways?

3. The human capacity for reason seems to be an important idea in all three frameworks. How so?

4. Are there "duties" that are specific to journalism? To public relations? To media marketing?

5. Consider the notion of privacy. How might journalists weigh it differently under an *act* utilitarian model as opposed to a *rule* utilitarianism?

REFERENCES

Alexander, L., & Moore, M. (2012). Deontological ethics. *The Stanford Encyclopedia of Philosophy.* Retrieved from http://plato.stanford.edu/archives/win2012/entries/ethics-deontological/

Borden, S. L. (2007). *Journalism as practice: MacIntyre, virtue ethics and the press.* Burlington, VT: Ashgate.

Couldry, N. (2010). Media ethics: Towards a framework for media producers and media consumers. In S. J. A. Ward & H. Wasserman (Eds.), *Media ethics beyond borders: A global perspective* (pp. 59–72). New York, NY: Routledge.

Foot, P. (2001). *Natural goodness.* Oxford: Oxford University Press.

Huff, C. W., Barnard, L., & Frey, W. (2008). Good computing: A pedagogically focused model of virtue in the practice of computing (Part 2). *Journal of Information, Communication and Ethics in Society, 6*(4), 284–316.

Johnson, R. (2012). Kant's moral philosophy. *The Stanford Encyclopedia of Philosophy.* Retrieved from http://plato.stanford.edu/archives/sum2012/entries/kant-moral/

Kant, I. (1780). *The metaphysical elements of justice: Part I of the Metaphysics of Morals* (J. Ladd, Trans.). Indianapolis, IN: Hackett.

Kant, I. (1991). *The metaphysics of morals* (M. Gregor, Trans.), Cambridge, UK: Cambridge University Press. (Original work published 1797)

Kraut, R. (2010). Aristotle's Ethics. *The Stanford Encyclopedia of Philosophy.* Retrieved from http://plato.stanford.edu/archives/win2012/entries/aristotle-ethics

MacIntyre, A. (2007). *After virtue: A study in moral theory* (3rd ed.). Notre Dame, IN: University of Notre Dame Press.

Meyers, C. (2003). Appreciating W. D. Ross: On duties and consequences. *Journal of Mass Media Ethics, 18*(2), 81–97.

Meyers, C. (2011). Reappreciating W. D. Ross: Naturalizing prima facie duties and a proposed method. *Journal of Mass Media Ethics, 26*(4), 316–331.

Ross, W. D. (1930). *The right and the good.* Oxford, UK: Clarendon Press.

Sinnott-Armstrong, W. (2011). Consequentialism. *The Stanford Encyclopedia of Philosophy.* Retrieved from http://plato.stanford.edu/archives/win2012/entries/consequentialism

Stafford, W. (1998). *John Stuart Mill.* London, England: MacMillan.

Steiner, L. (1989). Feminist theorizing and communication ethics. *Communication, 12,* 157–173.

Vrooman, F. B. (1911). *The new politics.* New York, NY: Oxford University Press.

CHAPTER 3

Ethics Theory
Application to Media

Ethics often is a frustrating subject. Not because people are resistant to it, though talking about ethics can often be discomforting as people "think out loud" while they grapple with dilemmas. Not because people are intimidated, though they sometimes may feel inadequate to the task of talking about philosophical principles. Not even because ethics, when done right, involves hard intellectual work. People are frustrated because, by its nature, ethics is more about questions than it is about answers. More specifically, ethics is about getting good at asking the right questions, which, in turn, clarify the problem and enable us to explore more effectively possible solutions or acceptable compromises.

People may find ethics frustrating, but they also understand it as important—urgent, even. Every media sector requires a set of skills that communication students must learn: what makes an effective anecdotal lead for a news story, how to propose a communication strategy to a corporate client, or when a well-edited video package requires a wide shot and a voice-over. Ethics addresses individual actions or behaviors, but it also deals with the big picture. It addresses big questions about how we see ourselves as professionals and as moral beings. It requires us to connect the microlevel (what is the best decision in response to a single question) to the macrolevel (how might this decision help promote or reflect a broader mission or obligation of the media). Ethics goes to the very heart of why we have a media system and what we think it ought to do. Not every communication student has an interest in uncovering and writing that award-winning human interest news feature. But we are all media consumers. Every media student has a stake in ethical judgments on media practice.

ETHICS VERSUS WRONGDOING

It's become common in everyday talk to equate being unethical with being "bad" or with failing in some important way. As we have seen, ethics is understood as dealing with finding the best or "most right" solution among many less-than-satisfying options. Ethics refers to the quality of the value judgments we make on matters big and small. So it may be natural to conclude that someone perceived to have chosen the "wrong" course of action has acted badly. But we must remember that the focus of ethics remains on the deliberative process rather than on the final decision. And even though we commonly call "wrong" or inappropriate actions "unethical," doing so can obscure the fact that ethics is about how we grapple with the difficult gray areas. Nearly every day in the media, a host of scandals, wrongdoing, and questionable acts are presented as unethical. Yet many of these, while they obviously involve important questions of values and principles, aren't really ethical issues because they are relatively cut-and-dried. Mary Jones has defrauded people for personal gain. John James has lied to cover up past transgressions. Company X withheld important information on a defective product to protect its profit margin. There is little gray area to debate in these types of cases. If we're serious about our obligations as moral beings, we don't usually argue whether it's ever okay to defraud or maliciously deceive others.

Similarly, some bad behavior on the part of media professionals is clearly just that: deeds or activity over which there is simply no reason for debate. In November 2003, the fast-food restaurant KFC (formerly named Kentucky Fried Chicken) launched a new television advertising campaign for its Original Recipe fried chicken. But it was clear that this was not just another campaign. In addition to seductive photos of piping hot chicken platters and biscuits, the ads featured provocative talk about fried chicken as particularly *healthy.* In one of the two ads, produced by the advertising agency Foote, Cone, and Belding, a woman arrives home and tells her husband, "Remember when we talked about eating better? Well, it starts today." She puts a KFC bucket of fried chicken on the dining table, and a voice states that two Original Recipe chicken breasts have less fat than a Burger King Whopper. In the second ad, a man says to his friend, "Is that you, man? You look fantastic!" Asked about how he got slimmer, the friend says, "Eatin' chicken." Critics were quick to call the ads outright lies. Complaints prompted the Federal Trade Commission (FTC), which polices advertising for deceptive practices, to investigate. Even the magazine *Advertising Age,* the industry's premier trade journal, published a critical editorial calling the ads "laughable and damaging." The FTC concluded that KFC ads were indeed misleading. The commission said that while two KFC fried chicken breasts have slightly less total fat than a Whopper, as the ad said, they also have more calories, more than three times the trans fat and cholesterol, and more than twice the sodium of a Whopper. In a settlement with the FTC, the fast-food company agreed to stop making claims about the health value or weight loss benefits of any of its food without explicit evidence. However, some FTC officials urged tougher action, such as heavy fines. "Companies should not be allowed to benefit monetarily from this kind of deception, especially when the health and safety of consumers are compromised," said FTC Commissioner Pamela Jones Harbour (Mayer, 2004, p. E1).

In April 2003, weeks after American and British troops began fighting in Iraq, *Los Angeles Times* photographer Brian Walski transmitted a photo of Iraqi civilians fleeing the city of Basra as they were being directed by a British soldier. But Walski, in an apparent attempt to increase the dramatic effect of the photo, combined elements of two shots of the same scene into one—resulting in several individuals being duplicated in the same image. His digital manipulation amounted to a kind of deception that violated basic photojournalistic standards of accuracy and truth telling. Walski was fired after a photo editor spotted the discrepancies, but not before his image ran on the front page of the *Times* and other papers. Later, Walski, a 20-year photojournalism veteran, expressed remorse. "There are no gray areas [in the policy]. The line is very clear here and I crossed it," he said. "After a long and difficult day, I put my altered image ahead of the integrity of the newspaper and the integrity of my craft" (Johnston, 2003, p. 10).

Jayson Blair was a young star just out of college when he was hired as a staff writer at the *New York Times* in 2002. He was assigned to help cover some of the most significant national stories at the time: the series of sniper shootings that killed six and terrorized the Washington, D.C., area, and the patriotic homecoming of Army private Jessica Lynch after she was ambushed, injured, captured, and held for nine days before her rescue and subsequent television movie. But Blair's prodigious output was based on a web of half-truths and outright fabrications. The ensuing scandal led to the ouster of both the executive editor and managing editor of the *Times*. In May 2003, the paper ran a 7,000-word front-page story detailing Blair's lies in dozens of stories (Barry, Barstow, Glater, Liptak, & Steinberg, 2003).

That unprecedented *mea culpa* story should be required reading for students taking classes in news reporting, writing, and interviewing because the Blair episode is a defining event for a generation of journalists—much like the fabrications of *Washington Post* writer Janet Cooke, who, in 1981, had to return her Pulitzer Prize for a feature story on an eight-year-old heroin addict who didn't exist, were for an earlier generation. But do the failings of KFC, Walski, or Blair present us with truly *ethical* dilemmas? All certainly illustrate violations of clearly stated professional values and standards. But beyond that judgment, there's little to debate from an ethical perspective. Both offer relatively black-and-white cases of wrongdoing. Calling any one of them a true case of media ethics is like charging a hit-and-run driver with being impolite: It misses the point of the ethics enterprise. Cases such as Jayson Blair's, as astonishing, controversial, and damaging as they may be, are easy. Brazen examples of using media deceptively, such as the KFC ads, offer little room for real ethical debate. Ethics is about the much more difficult cases that present dilemmas with few absolutes. They make us work much harder, they require us to think more deeply about the values we claim to uphold, and they don't often allow us to make satisfying pronouncements such as "They broke the rules" and then move on.

Consider the case of Eason Jordan, Cable News Network (CNN), and Saddam Hussein. During the 1990s, CNN sought to be the "network of record" for international affairs, highly valuing its access to governments around the world. But that access often came with a price, and nowhere was that clearer than in Iraq under Saddam Hussein, whose regime routinely monitored, harassed, and censored foreign journalists. As chief news executive for CNN, Jordan said he made more than a dozen trips to Baghdad to lobby the Hussein government to keep the CNN bureau open. Ensuring that CNN could report from Baghdad meant, Jordan said, that it could not report on the horrible reality of Hussein's regime. When news made the government unhappy, bad things happened. Journalists were ejected from the country if their reports portrayed Hussein in a negative light. CNN regularly faced the threat of harassment. Sometimes those threats were carried out. Jordan said that a CNN cameraman was abducted and tortured. Iraqi citizens who spoke to reporters later disappeared. "Each time I visited, I became more distressed by what I saw and heard—awful things that could not be reported because doing so would have jeopardized the lives of Iraqis, particularly those on our Baghdad staff," Jordan (2003, p. A25) wrote. Only in April 2003, when American forces ousted Hussein and occupied Baghdad, did Jordan feel able to reveal the various ways in which the cable network compromised its news reporting to maintain access. In a newspaper column with the headline "The News We Kept to Ourselves," Jordan wrote, "I felt awful having these stories bottled up inside me. . . . At last, these stories can be told freely" (p. A25).

Jordan clearly believed that the compromises his network made were the right ones. But other journalists around the country were stunned and outraged, and they argued that while Jordan meant well, he violated fundamental ethical standards of public trust and accuracy. In its zeal to protect its access to an evil regime, CNN failed to convey to the world the regime's true nature, sugar-coating the reality in Iraq instead. Critics accused CNN of moral failure. One of them argued that instead of portraying CNN as Hussein's victim, Jordan should have apologized for cooperating with the regime. "Reading Mr. Jordan now, you get the impression that CNN had no ethical option other than to soft-pedal," wrote one such critic. "But there were alternatives. CNN could have abandoned Baghdad. Not only would they have stopped recycling lies, they could have focused more intently on obtaining the truth about Saddam" (Foer, 2003, p. A18). Others suggested that if CNN had demonstrated more moral courage and shown Hussein's brutality more accurately, the world community might have responded more aggressively to isolate the regime in ways that could have averted outright war.

CNN faced a high-stakes dilemma involving journalistic values of minimizing harm, truth telling, access, and independence. Jordan argued that some news out of Baghdad, however much it was controlled by Hussein's propaganda henchmen, was better than no news. Lives were at stake, he said. His compromise was ethically principled and justified, according to his supporters. The news about Iraq that CNN could get out to the world was better than no news at all. But others weren't so sure. Once journalists agree to such controls, the slippery slope to unethical collusion is a short one, critics argued. If the driving value of a news organization is to tell the truth to the world, then a compromise that results in propaganda is unacceptable. CNN essentially bartered its credibility—the soul of any news outlet—for the cheap ticket of a ringside seat to a brutal regime, they argued.

A CHECKLIST FOR ETHICAL REASONING

Once we understand this context of ethical values for media practice, we can more confidently approach ethical dilemmas such as the one posed by CNN and Eason Jordan. But we still need a place to start. As noted earlier, ethics is about asking the right questions. We are more likely to do that with a method or a process that helps us identify and examine the various layers and surfaces of a complicated dilemma.

The MERITS Model

Theorists have offered a variety of ethical checklists and tools to use for ethical reasoning. Drawing from the best of them, the model provided here offers a structured series of questions designed to encourage good ethical decision making. The Multidimensional Ethical Reasoning and Inquiry Task Sheet (MERITS) is intended to direct focus to the values involved in an issue, the philosophical principles that can help guide good decision making, the interests of various stakeholders, and the moral duties and considerations that should be part of any credible ethical deliberation.

The MERITS model obviously is not intended to uncover the definitive "ethical" course of action that should be taken in a given dilemma. Different people may well emerge from the model with very different decisions and equally compelling justifications for them. And without a fuller exploration of key principles provided later in this book, effective use of the model would be difficult. For example, the discussion of Kant's theory of human dignity, as discussed in Chapter 5 (Transparency), will be helpful in working through the Normative Frameworks section of the MERITS model. But ideally, if we can become effective in knowing which questions to ask and keep our focus on the appropriate ethical issue (as opposed to political, personal, or economic ones), more solid ethical reasoning and heightened self-awareness is likely to emerge from the resulting deliberations.

PERCEPTIONS OF BIAS IN THE MEDIA

Many ethical judgments made about the behavior of media workers inevitably devolve into charges of bias. Critics of the news media in particular are quick to suggest that individual journalists or entire news organizations slant the news in favor of a political or ideological perspective or covertly push an agenda. A solid understanding of the nature of bias is helpful, then, in assessing media behavior. The intrepid media critic can find countless examples of subjective wording in the news that appears to support a political view. Media watchdog Web sites of nearly every political stripe serve up a list of such examples on a daily basis, giving both conservatives (see http://www.aim.org; http://www.mediaresearch .org) and liberals (see http://www.fair.org; http://www.bigmedia.org) ample ammunition to argue their case of media bias. In 2003, the *Los Angeles Times* ran a front-page story about a measure requiring Texas doctors to provide materials to women seeking abortions that include information about adoption agencies and color photos of fetuses. The story's use of derisive language, such as referring to the "so-called counseling" requirements of such measures (Gold, 2003), prompted a scathing memo from the *Times* editor to the entire newsroom warning that such "liberal" bias should never appear in the news (Carroll, 2003).

Charges of liberal bias in the news have become increasingly common in the past two decades. This is due in part to research that shows that American journalists are increasingly unlike the average American. They tend to be generally better educated, less religious, and more affluent than the average citizen. The field of journalism tends to attract people with a reformist, if not liberal, streak who question the status quo and who are more likely to challenge power structures. "Journalists are skeptical, confrontational and iconoclastic, which means they challenge the establishment, while conservatives want to conserve it. So the better journalists do their job, the more likely conservatives are to see them as liberal," according to media critic David Shaw (2003, p. E33). In a 2002 survey, 37% of journalists asked said they called themselves Democrats, and 19% called themselves Republicans

Multidimensional Ethical Reasoning and Inquiry Task Sheet (MERITS)	

1. Conflicting Values

Identify and explain the key values in conflict in a dilemma. Examine the importance of each and articulate the conflict.

- Explain how each value might be given priority and thus offer a solution.
- Decide which value should be given priority and justify it.
- Will your decision promote key concepts such as justice, respect, transparency, etc.? How so?
- Are these concepts overridden by some other compelling interest?
- If they are, justify the exception that your decision creates.

2. Normative Framework

Consider which philosophical approach is most applicable and articulate how it should guide ethical thinking in this case.

- Does the dilemma primarily pose a question of unequal power relations or of fairness? Consider how Rawls could be applied.
- Does the dilemma primarily pose a question of possible special treatment, equality, or the relative importance of truthfulness? Consider how Kant could be applied.
- Does the dilemma primarily pose a question of a balancing of rights or of the relative usefulness of moderation? Consider how Aristotle could be applied.

3. Stakeholder Interests

Identify all potential parties that would be affected by your decision or have a legitimate interest in the outcome.

- What exactly is the potential harm faced by various stakeholders, and how might you minimize it?
- Which stakeholder should be given priority? Justify, drawing from the appropriate philosophical framework.
- Which stakeholder appears to have the most to gain from your decision? Which appears to have the most to lose?
- How might you accommodate secondary stakeholders?

4. Duties and Effects

Consider how all your options reflect the moral duties you may have and how they may advance your effectiveness as a moral agent.

- To whom are you directly responsible or accountable?
- What duties do you have in your role as media professional?
- Once you decide on a justifiable course of action, consider whether your decision emphasizes certain duties or values over others. What are they?
- Is your decision duty-based, or is it based on your desire to produce a certain outcome?
- How would you feel about your decision if it were to be widely publicized?

(Weaver, Beam, Brownlee, Voakes, & Wilhoit, 2007). Of 143 journalists who made political contributions from 2004 to the start of the 2008 campaign, 125 of them gave money to Democrats or liberal causes (Dedman, 2007). This pattern of politics among individual journalists has long been used as proof by conservative critics that the news media are biased in favor of the liberal point view. "Everybody in journalism is pro-choice, pro-gun control and for gay marriage," argued former MSNBC primetime pundit Tucker Carlson. "When you only have people [in the media] that all think the same, you do not have good coverage" (Flannery, 2006).

Yet focusing on the apparent personal biases of individual journalists often can be simplistic and misleading, omitting the bigger picture. Many claims of political bias cynically assume that journalists are eager to abandon their professionalism to score political points in their news stories. Yet few things would serve to destroy credibility faster, which as we've seen is something that journalists obsessively strive to protect. Claims that individual journalists promote a political agenda, liberal or otherwise, are like saying the assembly line workers in an automaker plant are responsible for the design of the cars. Professional norms, newsroom socialization, and corporate structures often are far bigger influences on news content. The corporate interests of media companies can be considered pro-business and largely conservative. "Every day I read the Business section of the *New York Times*. Not the Labor section, not the Environment section," said media critic Eric Alterman, referring to two sections of the paper that do not exist. "These are conservative assumptions" (Flannery, 2006). Steven Smith, editor of the *Spokesman-Review* in Spokane, Washington, said generalizations about journalists being this or that are suspicious. "There have been studies that show journalists tend to be more socially liberal than American society as a whole," he wrote. "But generalizations begin to crumble when you start talking about fiscal politics, government activism, etc." (Smith, 2007).

General claims of bias also tend to ignore what volumes of social-psychology research tell us about how we process messages: The judgments we make about media messages often say as much or more about our own ideologies than they do about the messages themselves. Most important is research that helps us understand how we cognitively process messages and work that has documented what researchers call the "hostile media phenomenon."

Information and Cognition

Psychologists have documented that we all use a set of "filters" to guard against being overwhelmed by media messages. These filters are shaped largely by our personal and political values and by our natural impulse to have those values validated. First, we selectively *attend* to certain messages and not to others. We tend to gravitate to messages that affirm our worldviews. It is human nature to pay attention to media outlets and messages that we like and to keep away from those that may challenge our beliefs or opinions, though some recent research has suggested that we will seek out conflicting information in certain conditions (Baran & Davis, 2006, pp. 150–155). Second, in general, we *perceive* messages in ways that reinforce our beliefs. In other words, we will assess and judge quotes, claims, or entire news stories as credible based on how much they reflect our values. Any criticism of our points of view will be scrutinized as questionable or wrong, and we are likely to uncritically accept claims that coincide with our opinions. And third, we selectively *retain* the messages that we've absorbed. We are more likely to recall media content that reflects our beliefs. Recent research suggests this process is more complicated than previously thought; it depends greatly on how important we perceive the message to be and its "symbolic" value to us.

Hostile Media Phenomenon

In 1985, Stanford University researchers asked a group of Arab students to watch a collection of television news reports on the so-called Beirut Massacre crisis of 1982 and provide responses. The researchers then asked pro-Israeli students to view the same news accounts. The result? Both groups were convinced that the news reports were biased against their point of view. Later research confirmed this "hostile media effect," in which groups of partisans, or people with strong feelings on a particular issue, tend to be convinced that news coverage of the issue is biased, or hostile, to their point of view, or at least less agreeable to their point of view than to the opposing viewpoint. Furthermore, the best-informed partisans on an issue are most likely to see bias against their side because they perceive the news as lacking important context. "If I think the world is black, and you think the world is white, and someone comes along and says it's gray, we will both think that person is biased," one researcher noted (Vedantam, 2006). Other researchers found a similar pattern in how people perceive news by looking at their assessments of news reports on the use of monkeys in lab research. When animal rights activists and research supporters were asked about media coverage of the topic, both groups expressed the concern that the coverage was more sympathetic to the opposing view (Gunther & Chia, 2001).

Bias, then, is usually more complex than we think. Sure, we may be able to point to some blatant, black-and-white examples of personal bias in newswriting. But that's the tip of the iceberg. In general, we must understand bias as a *dynamic of interaction* among our opinions, assumptions, and ideologies and what's on the page or on the screen. Often, our claims of bias will reveal more about us than they will about what's in the media. But why is this important in the context of media ethics? It's critical to keep in mind that our personal and political baggage, and not just "objective" facts about media content, will shape and color the judgments we make about media behavior. If we assess media as ethical or unethical based on a rather simplistic understanding of bias, our ethical deliberations are likely to be ill informed and will lack compelling force. Simplistic claims of bias are more likely to lead to moralistic charges and countercharges than to intelligent ethical deliberation.

VALUES IN THE MEDIA

The firestorm that erupted over the disclosure that an independent cable news network sanitized its coverage of Hussein was, at bottom, an argument over which journalistic values should be given greater weight in a particular situation. In such a hostile, even dangerous context, Eason Jordan clearly placed a premium on minimizing the very real threat of harm that could result in CNN's work as a journalistic organization—physical harm not only to his employees, but also to Iraqi citizens, and to his news sources. Fear of such harm led him to accept a compromise in CNN's news reports about Hussein and to pull back on coverage that might offend the dictator. Jordan's critics, on the other hand, placed more importance on the journalistic value of truth telling, arguing that his compromise irreparably harmed the credibility of CNN as a trusted news organization and, consequently, undermined its very basis for existence. Both sides promote compelling, legitimate claims about the obligations of journalists. Which argument you endorse will largely depend on which values you feel should be given greater weight in this case and the quality of your articulation of the reasons why this should be so.

As the CNN–Hussein example shows, the personal and professional values that we hold are not mutually exclusive. That is, our decision to uphold one value doesn't necessarily mean that we must abandon another. It's a matter of prioritizing values that we hold simultaneously. As humans, we are constantly required to assess our value systems as we face questions or issues that must be resolved. We all have various interests and goals, and we all wear many different hats and play multiple roles. But social psychologists have found that we pretty much identify a similar list of key values that are important to us—values such as honesty, friendship, courage, community, health, and love. To say that we believe in something as a "value" is to say that we have an enduring belief that "a particular mode of conduct or that a particular end-state of existence is personally and socially preferable to alternative modes of conduct or end-states of existence," according to Milton Rokeach, a leading theorist of human values (Rokeach, 1968, p. 550). However, we may rank widely accepted values differently. In doing so, we acknowledge that in many cases, we simply cannot fully uphold all of our values. Something has to give. Some values must be given priority, while others get second billing in certain cases. Over the past few decades, research into how we construct our resulting "value systems" suggests that the ways in which we do this "value ordering" help determine how we approach different types of problems. "Values serve as criteria for selection in action" and "become criteria for judgment, preference and choice," according to one theorist (Williams, 1979, p. 283). This is why understanding the nature of our values is so important in the work of ethics. If we are unable to build a compelling, articulate explanation of why we are placing more weight on one value over another in a given case, any ethical position we choose to take is not likely to have much credibility. Neither Eason Jordan nor his critics provide the one and only "true" or best course of action based on the facts; each side must be judged based on the strength of their articulations about why certain prioritized values provide a more ethical justification for one course of action over another.

What are the key values for good media practice? There are many. The codes of ethics for journalists, public relations practitioners, and even marketers and advertisers emphasize honesty, transparency, respect, minimizing harm, and public service, among other values. But at bottom, media practitioners of all stripes, regardless of *why* they are using media channels, aspire to have one thing: credibility.

Credibility

Whether they are seeking to inform the public of newsworthy events or trying to sell a product with a catchy new ad campaign, serious communicators are concerned about being perceived as *credible* sources of information. That ethereal thing called credibility increases or recedes based on how intended audiences perceive the communicator to be upholding or reflecting the other key values just mentioned. If a communicator is believed to be deceptive or dishonest, unconcerned with others' welfare, or oblivious to everyone's obligation to use media in a socially responsible way, that communicator provides potential audiences with little or no compelling reason to pay attention to his message. Journalism students in particular learn early on that credibility is the only real currency they have. If audiences no longer believe that journalists serve as credible sources of information, their very reason for existence evaporates. Public relations professionals also are realizing the importance of credibility in building trust with multiple publics and stakeholders. As a result, media professionals who take their *professionalism* seriously are always talking about how they can protect their credibility. For journalists, that often means an unflinching commitment to the pursuit of the truth, even when that pursuit becomes unpopular, and a scrupulous avoidance of sensationalism and conflicts of interests. Conscientious journalists know that their credibility can depend, paradoxically, on *not* protecting the public from discomforting truths or images. For public relations executives, that means placing client loyalty and advocacy in the context of broader social responsibility to avoid the dismissive labels of "spin doctor" or propagandist. Good public relations consultants know that withholding potentially damaging information during a crisis to stave off short-term client embarrassment often comes at the cost of long-term credibility. In a survey of honor codes and standards in advertising around the world, two researchers said all of the codes and standards reflect five key principles embraced by ad agencies, professional groups, and trade organizations. The idea of credibility is implicit in nearly all of them:

1. A sense of responsibility to consumers, community concerns, and society

2. Decency, honesty, and truth

3. Avoidance of misrepresentation and deception

4. A sense of fair competition

5. The protection and promotion of the reputation of the advertising industry (Spence & Van Heekeren, 2005, p. 26)

Credibility clearly is tied with many other key values that drive good media practice. What also should be clear is that these values transcend media sectors: That is, they are important in defining ethical behavior across the board, regardless of whether the intent of the communicator is to inform, persuade, or sell. Some values have greater relevance to some sectors than others—the idea of loyalty, for example, is of greater concern to public relations practitioners than it is to journalists. And the *weight* normally given to certain values may differ according to the intent of the communicator. Truth is an end in itself for journalists, whereas campaign strategists routinely view truth in a more instrumental way, as a means for success in the marketplace of ideas. Rather than assuming truth is monolithic, we should understand that our use of truth often is selective, and we should be able to reflect on the reasons why this is so. Some advertising ethicists have proposed an "ethical continuum" that illustrates when ethical questions might be raised regarding our selective use of the truth (Figure 3.1). But these broader concerns over the importance of honesty, public service, and socially responsible use of media drive ethical media practice regardless of our motives in our media use. Keeping this in mind, consider some key values embraced by different media sectors.

Figure 3.1   Ethical Continuum for Advertising

Complete truth			Total lie
◄───►
Factual	Persuasive	Embellished	Deceptive
Probably ethical	*Possibly unethical*	*Illegal*	

SOURCE: Murphy, Laczniak, Bowie, & Klein (2005, p. 160)

Values in Journalism

The protection of credibility drives much of journalistic decision making, and this overarching concern is reflected in several key values that are detailed in the code of ethics adopted by the Society of Professional Journalists (SPJ) in 1996. The SPJ code offers four primary directives and provides more detailed points regarding how they should be understood and how they should inform journalists' work. For example, under the first, "Seek truth and report it," the code states that journalists should "tell the story of the diversity and magnitude of the human experience boldly, even when it is unpopular to do so," and they should "support the open exchange of views, even views they find repugnant." Under the "Minimize harm" category, it says that journalists should "recognize that gathering and reporting information may cause harm or discomfort"; that they should "be sensitive when seeking or using interviews or photographs of those affected by tragedy or grief"; and that they should remember that "pursuit of the news is not a license for arrogance." (It is important to note that the code says that journalists must "minimize" harm, not "avoid" all potential harm. This distinction is crucial. As we discuss later, some forms of perceived harm may be inevitable in the course of good journalism and in the free flow of ideas.) Under the "Act independently" category, the code states that journalists should "remain free of associations and activities that may compromise integrity or damage credibility," and they should "deny favored treatment to advertisers and special interests and resist their pressure to influence news coverage." Under the "Be accountable" category, the code states that journalists should "clarify and explain news coverage and invite dialogue with the public over journalistic conduct," and they should "abide by the same high standards to which they hold others."

A Code of Ethics for Journalists From the
Society of Professional Journalists Code of Ethics

Public enlightenment is the forerunner of justice and the foundation of democracy. The duty of the journalist is to further those ends by seeking truth and providing fair and comprehensive accounts of events and issues. Conscientious journalists from all media and specialties strive to serve the public with thoroughness and honesty. Professional integrity is the cornerstone of a journalist's credibility.

Key directives of the SPJ code:

- *Seek truth and report it.* Journalists should be honest, fair, and courageous in gathering, reporting, and interpreting information.
- *Minimize harm.* Ethical journalists treat sources, subjects and colleagues as human beings deserving of respect.
- *Act independently.* Journalists should be free of obligation to any interest other than the public's right to know.
- *Be accountable.* Journalists are accountable to their readers, listeners, viewers and each other.

The complete code can be found at http://www.spj.org/ethicscode.asp.

Values in Public Relations

The code of ethics adopted by the Public Relations Society of America (PRSA), while more elaborate than the SPJ code in many areas, covers similar bases. It can be considered more practical because, in addition to a "statement of professional values," the PRSA code also offers a discussion of some key provisions, such as competition and disclosure of information, and how those provisions should be understood in public relations work. Some are familiar and fairly straightforward, such as expertise, honesty, and fairness. Others are more industry-specific yet still must be understood in a broad context of what it means to be "professional." Independence, or moral autonomy, is one of these. This principle is addressed in Chapter 8 (Autonomy). Regarding the principle of advocacy, PR professionals move beyond working merely as a hired hand when they fully understand their role in the Jeffersonian notion of the "marketplace of ideas." This refers to the claim by Jefferson and other early American leaders that a healthy democracy requires virtuous participation in such a marketplace, from which will arise the best policies. When considered as efforts to promote perspectives, interests, and causes in ways that maintain the integrity of the marketplace, the work of public relations gains moral legitimacy. That legitimacy is lost when advocacy work is done in a way that undermines or corrupts that marketplace, through misinformation, deception, and failure to provide important information. Similarly, when the PRSA value of loyalty is properly understood in the context of professional practice, PR workers understand that they are more than mere mouthpieces paid to do a client's bidding and that being professional means you are conscious of your moral obligation to serve a broader notion of the public good as well. Daryl Koehn, a theorist who has written extensively on the nature of professionalism, addresses the question of client loyalty:

[A full understanding of the nature of professionalism] enables the professional to avoid many problems which necessarily arise if and when professionals falsely assume that they must act as the unconditionally loyal servant of the individual client at hand. . . . A professional is an agent who freely makes a public promise to serve persons (e.g., the sick) who are distinguished by a specific desire for a particular good (e.g., health) and who have come into the presence of the professional with or on the expectation that the professional will promote that particular good. . . . The Greek *prophiano* became the Latin *professio*, a term applied to the public statement made by persons who sought to occupy a position of public trust. *And it is trust, not the perceived power of the professional to manipulate things or people, that bestows moral legitimacy* [emphasis added]. (1994, pp. 58, 59, 172–173)

A Code of Ethics for Public Relations Professionals From the Public Relations Society of America Member Code of Ethics

The level of public trust PRSA members seek, as we serve the public good, means we have taken on a special obligation to operate ethically. . . . These values are the fundamental beliefs that guide our behaviors and decision-making process. We believe our professional values are vital to the integrity of the profession as a whole.

Key professional values:

- Advocacy
  - o We serve the public interest by acting as responsible advocates for those we represent.
  - o We provide a voice in the marketplace of ideas, facts, and viewpoints and aid informed public debate.

- Honesty
  - o We adhere to the highest standards of accuracy and truth in advancing the interests of those we represent and in communicating with the public.

- Expertise
  - o We acquire and responsibly use specialized knowledge and experience.
  - o We advance the profession through continued professional development, research, and education.
  - o We build mutual understanding, credibility, and relationships among a wide array of institutions and audiences.

- Independence
  - o We provide objective counsel to those we represent.
  - o We are accountable for our actions.

(Continued)

(Continued)

- Loyalty
  - We are faithful to those we represent, while honoring our obligation to serve the public interest.
- Fairness
  - We deal fairly with clients, employers, competitors, peers, vendors, the media, and the general public.
  - We respect all opinions and support the right of free expression.

The complete code can be found at http://prsa.org/aboutUs/ethics/preamble_en.html.

Values in Marketing and Advertising

Professional associations that represent media advertisers have recognized the fact that they, too, are obligated to uphold these more general values if they take their duties as moral agents seriously. Both the American Advertising Federation and the American Marketing Association as well as more specialized niche industry groups have adopted codes of ethics that echo the standards and themes found in the codes for journalism and public relations. This may come as a shock to media students. Ethical advertising and marketing—is there such a thing? But these groups realize the importance of at least publicly stating the ethical dimensions of using media channels to sell stuff—and of proclaiming that the duties involved in being a moral agent don't go away just because the motive is profit. We all might be able to point to examples of advertising and marketing that suggest ethical standards are thrown out the window when they are no longer convenient. More interesting, perhaps, is how little this might bother us as media consumers. Marketing and advertising ethicists argue that industry professionals are obligated, just as is everyone else in media, to uphold ethical principles. To those who believe imposing ethical standards on advertising is futile, ethicists argue such standards are needed more than ever and should span a wide variety of practices, if advertising as an industry is to remain viable and credible:

> Ethical concerns range from the spokesperson used (e.g., well-known actors plug seemingly low-cost life insurance aimed at the elderly), to the message itself (e.g., the use of large print price appeal headlines with small print disclaimers by car rental companies and airlines), the media utilized (e.g., visual pollution caused by billboards), and the suitability of a particular ad for its intended audience (e.g., when children are audience members). (Murphy, Laczniak, Bowie, & Klein, 2005, p. 153)

One advertising researcher, examining the attitudes of college students toward sex appeals in advertising, found that more relativistic students were less bothered by the use of sexual suggestiveness in an ad. Female students, regardless of their levels of relativism, said the use of sex in advertising was unethical. This should give advertisers pause—particularly those interested in tapping the affluent, media-savvy "Gen Yers" now in college. "Advertisers should consider the moral implications of advertising content in the planning process, not after a campaign has been launched," the researcher concluded (Maciejewski, 2004, p. 103). Other advertising scholars have urged firms to appoint an ethics committee to anticipate possible problems and avoid creative work that may cross a line. Such a committee would make sure that creative directors are mindful of ethical concerns from the start.

A Code of Ethics for Marketers From the American Marketing Association's "Ethical Norms and Values for Marketers"

Marketing practitioners must recognize that they not only serve their enterprises but also act as stewards of society in creating, facilitating, and executing the efficient and effective transactions that are part of the greater economy.

Key professional values:

- *Honesty*—to be truthful and forthright in our dealings with customers and stakeholders
  - We will tell the truth in all situations and at all times.
  - We will honor our explicit and implicit commitments and promises.
- *Responsibility*—to accept the consequences of our marketing decisions and strategies
  - We will make strenuous efforts to serve the needs of our customers.
  - We will avoid using coercion with all stakeholders.
  - We will acknowledge the social obligations to stakeholders that come with increased marketing and economic power.
  - We will recognize our special commitments to economically vulnerable segments of the market such as children, the elderly, and others who may be substantially disadvantaged.
- *Fairness*—to try to balance justly the needs of the buyer with the interests of the seller
  - We will represent our products in a clear way in selling, advertising, and other forms of communication; this includes avoidance of false, misleading, and deceptive promotion.
  - We will reject manipulations and sales tactics that harm customer trust.
  - We will not knowingly participate in material conflicts of interest.
- *Respect*—to acknowledge the basic human dignity of all stakeholders
  - We will value individual differences even as we avoid stereotyping customers or depicting demographic groups (e.g., gender, race, or sexual orientation) in a negative or dehumanizing way in our promotions.
  - We will make a special effort to understand suppliers, intermediaries, and distributors from other cultures.
  - We will appropriately acknowledge the contributions of others, such as consultants, employees, and coworkers, to our marketing endeavors.

(Continued)

(Continued)

- *Openness*—to create transparency in our marketing operations
  - o We will strive to communicate clearly with all our constituencies.
  - o We will explain significant product or service risks, component substitutions, or other foreseeable eventualities that could affect customers or their perception of the purchase decision.
  - o We will fully disclose list prices and terms of financing as well as available price deals and adjustments.
- *Citizenship*—to fulfill the economic, legal, philanthropic and societal responsibilities that serve stakeholders in a strategic manner
  - o We will strive to protect the natural environment in the execution of marketing campaigns.
  - o We will give back to the community through volunteerism and charitable donations.
  - o We will work to contribute to the overall betterment of marketing and its reputation.

The complete code can be found at http://www.marketingpower.com.

A Code of Ethics for Advertisers From the American Association of Advertising Agencies Standards of Practice

Advertisers "must recognize an obligation, not only to their clients, but to the public, the media they employ, and to each other. . . . Unethical competitive practices in the advertising agency business lead to financial waste, dilution of service, diversion of manpower, loss of prestige, and tend to weaken public confidence both in advertisements and in the institution of advertising."

Creative Code

We, the members of the American Association of Advertising Agencies, in addition to supporting and obeying the laws and legal regulations pertaining to advertising, undertake to extend and broaden the application of high ethical standards. Specifically, we will not knowingly create advertising that contains:

- False or misleading statements or exaggerations, visual or verbal
- Testimonials that do not reflect the real opinion of the individual(s) involved
- Price claims that are misleading
- Claims insufficiently supported or that distort the true meaning or practicable application of statements made by professional or scientific authority
- Statements, suggestions or pictures offensive to public decency or minority segments of the population.

We recognize that there are areas that are subject to honestly different interpretations and judgment. Nevertheless, we agree not to recommend to an advertiser, and to discourage the use of, advertising that is in poor or questionable taste or that is deliberately irritating through aural or visual content or presentation.

The complete statement can be found at http://www.aaaa.org/EWEB/upload/inside/standards.pdf.

From the Better Business Bureau's Code of Advertising

- The primary responsibility for truthful and non-deceptive advertising rests with the advertiser. Advertisers should be prepared to substantiate any claims or offers made before publication or broadcast and, upon request, present such substantiation promptly to the advertising medium or the Better Business Bureau [BBB].
- Advertisements which are untrue, misleading, deceptive, fraudulent, falsely disparaging of competitors, or insincere offers to sell, shall not be used.
- An advertisement as a whole may be misleading although every sentence separately considered is literally true. Misrepresentation may result not only from direct statements but by omitting or obscuring a material fact.

The complete BBB advertising code can be found at http://us.bbb.org.

Clearly, the profession of marketing claims to adhere to standards similar to those of other media sectors. Indeed, the code for marketers is, in many ways, more comprehensive and philosophically grounded than the advertising codes featured in this chapter. And yet it is worth considering how a commercial culture can appear to exempt marketers in the media from these same expectations.

For Discussion

1. Consider the value of honesty as discussed in the various codes of ethics for journalists, public relations executives, and advertisers. Even though all media sectors claim it as a key value, we clearly have different expectations about the "truthfulness" of content in TV news programming versus TV advertising, for example. Does this mean we give advertisers a pass when it comes to ethical media use? If so, why do you think this is the case?

2. Think of a recent media-related scandal that you've heard of. Does it present a genuine ethical dilemma? How so?

3. Are you sympathetic to the argument made by CNN news executive Eason Jordan regarding his decision to pull back on aggressive news coverage of Hussein's regime? Or would you side with Franklin Foer and his critics? Why?

4. Consider which media outlets you tend to use and trust. What might this suggest about your tendencies, beliefs, and opinions?

5. Is there a social issue you are passionate about or on which you hold strong positions? Has the media coverage of that issue disappointed you in some way? Are you more critical of news accounts on the topic?

REFERENCES

Baran, S. J., & Davis, D. K. (2006). *Mass communication theory: Foundations, ferment and future.* Belmont, CA: Thomson Wadsworth.

Barry, D., Barstow, D., Glater, J. D., Liptak, A., & Steinberg, J. (2003, May 11). Correcting the record: *Times* reporter who resigned leaves long trail of deception. *New York Times,* p. A1.

Carroll, J. (2003, May 22). Memo on abortion and liberal bias (unpublished).

Dedman, B. (2007, June 14). Journalists dole out cash to politicians (quietly). *MSNBC.com.* Retrieved from http://www.msnbc.msn.com/ id/19113485/

Flannery, D. C. (2006, January 17). Pundits debate biases in American press. *Daily Nexus.* Retrieved January 18, 2006, from http://www.dailynexus .com/news/2006/10631.html

Foer, F. (2003, April 14). CNN's access of evil. *Wall Street Journal,* p. A18.

Gold, S. (2003, May 22). Texas OKs disputed abortion legislation. *Los Angeles Times,* p. A1.

Gunther, A. C., & Chia, S. C. (2001). Predicting pluralistic ignorance: The hostile media perception and its consequences. *Journalism & Mass Communication Quarterly, 78*(4), 688–701.

Johnston, C. (2003, May). Digital deception. *American Journalism Review, 25*(4), 10–11.

Jordan, E. (2003, April 11). The news we kept to ourselves. *New York Times,* p. A25.

Koehn, D. (1994). *The ground of professional ethics.* New York, NY: Routledge.

Maciejewski, J. J. (2004). Is the use of sexual and fear appeals ethical? A moral evaluation by Generation Y college students. *Journal of Current Issues and Research in Advertising, 26*(2), 97–105.

Mayer, C. E. (2004, June 4). KFC misled consumers on health benefits. *Washington Post,* p. E1.

Murphy, P. E., Laczniak, G. R., Bowie, N. E., & Klein, T. A. (2005). *Ethical marketing.* Upper Saddle River, NJ: Pearson Prentice Hall.

Rokeach, M. (1968). The role of values in public opinion research. *Public Opinion Quarterly, 32*(4), 547–559.

Shaw, D. (2003, March 23). "Bias" that bends over backward to right itself. *Los Angeles Times,* p. E33.

Smith, S. (2007, June 21). News is a conversation. *Spokesman Review.* Retrieved from http://www .spokesmanreview.com/blogs/conversation/archive.asp?postID = 15653

Spence, E., & Van Heekeren, B. (2005). *Advertising ethics.* Upper Saddle River, NJ: Pearson Prentice Hall.

Vedantam, S. (2006, July 24). Two views of the same news find opposite biases. *Washington Post,* p. A2.

Weaver, D. H., Beam, R. A., Brownlee, B. J., Voakes, P. S., & Wilhoit, G. C. (2007). *The American journalist in the 21st century: U.S. news people at the dawn of a new millennium.* Mahwah, NJ: Lawrence Erlbaum.

Williams, R. M. (1979). The concept of values. In D. L. Sills (Ed.), *International encyclopedia of the social sciences* (Vol. 16, pp. 283–287). New York, NY: Macmillan and Free Press.

CHAPTER 4

Technology

We live in a thoroughly digital world, from our reliance on unseen cloud computing to the ubiquity of USB outlets. Media technology, more specifically, has reshaped the way we live in countless ways. It has changed how we consume media. It has guided our transition from passive audience members to armies of active content producers. It has liberated us and empowered us in unprecedented ways. Depending on who's talking, it is making us significantly smarter than previous generations, or it is turning us into stupid, gadget-fixated zombies. In fact, we arguably have moved into an era in which all of our references to "media" assume that *digital* media is what we mean—the online versions of traditional print sources, social networking sites that have become relied-on media sources in their own right, the streaming video that we now expect to accompany every piece of information, the cellular-based information economy that is transforming media content of every kind. When we refer to "talking" with others on our phones, we are less likely to refer to an actual voice conversation, but instead to an exchange of text messages: In 2009, the amount of data sent as text, e-mail, and streaming video on mobile networks surpassed the amount represented by phone conversations for the first time. While every chapter in this book addresses issues raised by media technology, it is worthwhile to consider the meanings and ramifications of the digital form itself. It has reshaped our daily habits. It has influenced how we interact with one another. It has transformed how we see the world around us. Some of these effects may seem obvious; others are more subtle but just as important—and perhaps even disturbing when we really consider them. Rather than documenting the present state of (and the ethical questions raised by) an ever-changing digital media landscape, this chapter focuses on the broader contours, and general features, of our digital media in an attempt to have us think more deeply about the implications of our digital—and digitized—lives. It explores what we do with media technology and also examines what media technology does to us. And of course, such exploration ultimately enables us to consider, as savvy consumers and producers, the ethical questions posed by media technology. Too often, the wonders of media technology seduce us into focusing only on what they enable us to do. Evgeny Morozov (2011) refers to this tendency as our casual "cyber-centrism" that "prioritizes the tool over the environment" (p. xvi). What he means is that we can become so wrapped up in the wonders of digital possibilities that we allow our technology to supersede moral concerns. This chapter seeks to balance that seduction with the concerns of ethicists who urge us to think deeper, to consider *what technology does to us* as well. As long ago as 1984, Albert Borgmann argued that we have a moral obligation to resist mindlessly placing a premium on the convenience that devices offer us. Similarly, David Noble famously wrote, "Technology leads a double life, one which conforms to the intentions of designers and interests of power and another which contradicts them—proceeding behind the backs of their architects to yield unintended consequences and unintended possibilities" (2011, p. 325). With our media technologies today, the warnings of both theorists have only gained in resonance, as Evgeny Morozov argues:

> The fact that a given technology has multiple affordances and is open to multiple uses . . . does not obviate the need to closely examine its ethical constitution, compare the effects of its socially beneficial uses with those of its socially harmful uses, estimate which uses are most likely to prevail, and, finally, decide whether any mitigating laws and policies should be established to amplify or dampen some ensuing effects. . . . The way forward is to clearly scrutinize both the logic of technology and the logic of society that adopts it; under no circumstances should we be giving technologies—whether it's the Internet or mobile phones—a free pass on ethics. All too often the design of technologies simply conceals the ideologies and political agendas of their creators. (2011, pp. 296, 298)

HOW WE THINK ABOUT TECHNOLOGY

Do media technologies—the way we use them, the way they influence our behavior—pose fundamentally new ethical questions? Are there ethical issues that are encountered only online? Or are the ethical issues posed by the digital world—issues of harm, of justice, of autonomous agency, of privacy—simply the latest manifestations of long-standing concerns? Most ethicists agree that the digital world rarely poses fundamentally new ethical questions. Instead, it simply presents the latest repackaging of privacy, of deception, of harm. "Deceptive behaviour in cyberspace is . . . not a new moral issue though it raises the problem of 'moral distance' with extra urgency," argues Cees Hamelink in his book, *The Ethics of Cyberspace* (2000, pp. 34–35). "The speed of digital communication does not create new forms of immorality, but makes it possible to commit immoral acts so fast one hardly notices." Professional media organizations such as the Society of Professional Journalists and the Public Relations Society of America have not felt compelled to draft separate codes of digital ethics to promote responsible online behavior. However, the digital media landscape has challenged producers and consumers alike to consider ways to translate expectations of good behavior as well as "netiquette" standards that govern civility and rudeness.

Technological Determinism

There are deeper concerns as well. No doubt technology has improved human existence in countless ways. Yet our assumption that we can best address our social problems with more technological innovation is not without a dark side. In our reliance on technology, it is easy to assume that every advance is a positive one. From that assumption, it is not a big step to see the development of technology as an inexorable march of progress—a march that not only is unquestioned, but that we as individuals are powerless to stop or control. Technology, then, is *determining* the makeup of our social lives. Rather than being harnessed to help promote values we embrace, technology comes to determine those very values, and even promote other values as normal that we may have not seen as such before. For the technological determinist, technology controls history and becomes the basis for virtually all human activity. Rather than serving our social and cultural priorities, the march of technology becomes an end in itself. As theorist Neil Postman (1992) famously said, "The uses made of any technology are largely determined by the structure of the technology itself—that is, that its functions follow from its form" (p. 7). Of course, such determinism raises a multitude of ethical questions. Maybe the march of technological innovation is unquestioningly good. But if it isn't, then are we at the mercy of the values it promotes? If we are powerless to influence or control it, what does that say about the free will that we trumpet, in a culture that cherishes liberty so much? In much of our technological development, the two highest values are efficiency and convenience. In our often unquestioning embrace of this march of progress, we, too, are invited to place a priority on these values in our lives—sometimes at the expense of other social values, such as trust, human contact, and safety. Once again, Morozov (2011) usefully uncovers the important ethical issue here:

> If technology's march is unstoppable and unidirectional, as a hoard of technology gurus keep convincing the public from the pages of technology magazines, it then seems pointless to stand in its way. If radio, television, or the Internet are poised to usher in a new age of democracy and universal human rights, there is little role for us humans to play. However, to argue that a once-widespread practice like lobotomy was simply a result of inevitable technological forces it to let its advocates off the hook. Technological determinism thus obscures the roles and responsibilities of human decision makers, either absolving them of well-deserved blame or minimizing the role of their significant interventions. . . . By adopting a deterministic stance, we are less likely to subject technology—and those who make a living from it—to the full bouquet of ethical questions normal for democracy. (pp. 290–291)

An example of this is seen in how we have come to use mobile-phone technology in our daily lives—and how we have allowed this technology to reorder social values. Most of us can't be separated from our cell phones for more than a moment. The connectivity and immediacy of information access they afford us are wonderful things. This dependency has moved into the driver's seat of millions of automobiles. Auto makers have even encouraged it, turning out new models with built-in features such as colorful touch screens, voice-activated systems, and Bluetooth connectivity. Yet mobile technology's convenience has clashed with public safety values, with disastrous results. While most responsible drivers understand it is foolish to text and drive (and doing so is illegal in most states), compelling research has documented just how *any* cell phone use siphons off cognitive attention required to drive safely. The cognitive energy to navigate a smart phone and carry on a phone conversation far outstrips all other potentially distracting activities such as talking with a passenger or fiddling with a radio tuner. And researchers have found that using a hands-free system makes little difference. A driver distracted by cell phone use is four times more likely to cause an accident. And driver reaction times are reduced to the same as a driver with a blood-alcohol level beyond the legal limit in most states (Richtel, 2009). In fact, about 5,000 people are killed by distracted drivers every year, thousands more are injured, and millions of dollars in damage occur as a result of our newfound habit behind the wheel. Such numbers should make anyone who claims to be a responsible motorist pause before reaching for the phone while driving. That we see so many cell phone–using motorists is arguably a classic example of a deterministic adoption of technology, in which its uses follow its form, as Postman (1992) said, in a way that is largely unquestioned and that invites us to displace our values of safety and consideration of others with values of convenience and efficiency. As Arthur Welzer, a political scientist at Michigan State University, argued, "To the extent that we view ourselves as helpless pawns of an overarching and immovable force, we may renounce the moral and political responsibility that, in fact, is crucial for the good exercise of what power over technology we do possess" (Welzer quoted in Morozov, 2011, p. 290).

The Human as a Technological Being

Other philosophers have urged us to look even deeper, to consider how human nature and technology might even be intertwined. Twentieth-century German philosopher Martin Heidegger famously said, "The essence of technology is by no means anything technological" (1954/1977, p. 4). What he meant by that is "the technological" is not a thing or even a process, but a state of mind. Our fascination with and constant turning toward technology reflects a more fundamental notion of human nature: Over the centuries since the ancient Greeks, we have lost an ability to see the world as they did, not only as a collection of resources to be exploited, but as a reality to be appreciated as an end in itself. The Greeks, of course, made use of the world as well, but their two ways of understanding nature—not just *techné* but also *poiésis*—led to a more holistic and healthy existence, Heidegger suggested. Our approach to the world, in contrast, is almost exclusively technical. We see the river not for how it exists in the present—an expression of geological time, a thing of grace, power, and majesty—but as a resource, something to be made into an instrument that is useful: a source of nourishment, a mode of transportation, and a site from which to draw hydroelectric power. This impulse comes from a specific use of our powers of reason, which informs our desire to impose "order" in our environment. "Modern science's way of representing [the natural world] pursues and entraps nature as a calculable coherence of forces," he wrote (Heidegger, 1954/1977, p. 21). This "ordering" and what he called our "challenging" of the natural world to make it into usable things, our *instrumentalizing* of nature, obviously has its value and its place in our lives. But it has overwhelmed all other ways of "seeing" and, thus, has stunted our sense of reality, our sense of the world. So paradoxically, our focus on things when we talk about technology actually blinds us to the true, deeper nature of what is the technological. We have become "constrained to obey" the imperative of seeing the world only through a technological lens, and we will never be truly free until we recognize it as a sort of self-imposed handicap because this lens, he said, prevents us from fully understanding ourselves, as the ancient Greeks did. We start seeing nature only as a reflection of our powers to control it, to manage it—in other words, we only see a superficial reflection of ourselves, oblivious to our deeper human essence that resides "within" the world, not merely controlling it from "without." "So long as we represent technology as an instrument, we remain held fast in the will to master it," he wrote. "We press on past the essence of technology" (p. 32). Ultimately, man himself may be seen only as a tool, a resource, undermining the moral demand that each individual is accorded dignity, is respected because he *is*. The way out of this trap, Heidegger suggested, is to constantly question our motives and fully consider our actions— to second-guess, whenever possible, our tendency to see everything as a potential resource with negotiable value.

The Commercial Soul of the Digital World

Most of us understand that the World Wide Web is heavily commercial in nature. While theorists and commentators have long applauded its liberating, empowering, and community-building possibilities, the fact is that much of the platform has been harnessed in ways to generate revenue. As a result, all kinds of distinctions and boundaries— the personal and the professional, the communal and the commercial—are constantly being tested and sometimes blurred altogether. It may seem a bit spooky when banner ads for bridal services start popping up on Web sites you visit soon after you mention wedding plans in e-mails to friends sent from your Google account. But Google is providing that free e-mail account precisely in exchange for the right to troll your incoming and outgoing mail for key words and then selling that information to advertisers. We are invited to use Google products because the ensuing extraction of personal data is how the company makes money. "If you've mentioned anxiety in an e-mail, done a Google search for 'stress' or started using an online medical diary that lets you monitor your mood, expect ads for medications and services to treat your anxiety," wrote law professor Lori Andrews (2012, p. SR7). Similarly, Facebook is "free" only because it's an effective way for Mark Zuckerberg to gather personal data coveted by advertisers, who then use this access to "micro-target" advertisements to us based on our interests and web-surfing histories. "It's a digital data vacuum cleaner on steroids, that's what the online ad industry has created," said Jeff Chester, executive director of the Center for Digital Democracy. "They're tracking where your mouse is on the page, what you put in your shopping cart, what you don't buy. A very sophisticated commercial surveillance system has been put in place" (Chester quoted in Story, 2007, para. 8). Many ad executives argue that such practices benefit consumers, who see more relevant ads. And they argue that giving up some "harmless" personal data is a small trade-off for the free content of the Web. "Ultimately, if you want the content to remain free on the Web, you need to at least give us the information to monetize it," said David J. Moore, an advertising executive (Moore quoted in Story, 2007, para 11).

Nonetheless, for most of us, these practices regularly raise questions of privacy: As we are increasingly in the role of customer on the Web, how much control of personal information do we have? How much should we expect to keep? How much commercialization of personal networking sites are we willing to embrace in exchange for the privilege of constant connection with friends? In recent years, government agencies have responded to these concerns; in early 2013, the Federal Trade Commission called for the mobile-phone industry to develop a "do not track" feature that allows people to opt out of routine data collection from their phones, similar to the federal "do not call" registry that people can join to prevent telemarketer phone calls. Flexing its muscle on the issue, the FTC also has been penalizing companies with hefty fines for misleading customers by gathering personal data without their consent by trolling their cell phone contacts lists. One social networking app, called Path, was hit with an $800,000 fine for doing so. "Over the years the FTC has been vigilant in responding to a long list of threats to consumer privacy, whether it's . . . kids information culled by music fan Web sites, or unencrypted credit card information left vulnerable to hackers," said FTC chairman Jon Leibowitz. "The settlement with Path shows that no matter what new technologies emerge, the agency will continue to safeguard the privacy of Americans" (Federal Trade Commission, 2013).

But while much of our concern focuses on such privacy claims, some argue we should be worried about the opposite problem: alienation through the exploitation of information for purposes that are not intended (Bakardjieva & Feenberg, 2000). Data mining and third-party use of personal data shared on social networking sites can threaten to undermine the sites' civic value, they warn. Others have suggested that there is a disconnect between how all of us are reduced to data points, relentlessly profiled by digital marketers into forensically reidentifiable "objects of (algorithmic) computation" (Manders-Huits, 2010, p. 52), and how the same commercially driven sites offer us attractive spaces to build and present our personal identities. Stereotyping, law professor Lori Andrews says, is alive and well in these kinds of data-aggregation practices:

> Your application for credit could be declined not on the basis of your own finances or credit history, but on the basis of aggregate data—what other people whose likes and dislikes are similar to yours have done. If guitar players or divorcing couples are more likely to renege on their credit-card bills, then the fact that you've looked at guitar ads or sent an e-mail to a divorce lawyer might cause a data aggregator to classify you as less credit-worthy. When an Atlanta man returned from his honeymoon, he found that his credit limit had been lowered to $3,800 from $10,800. The switch was not based on anything he had done but on aggregate data. A letter from the company told him, "Other customers who have used their card at establishments where you recently shopped have a poor repayment history with American Express." (Andrews, 2012, p. SR7)

Manders-Huits (2010) argues that developers of social networking sites must not be driven by exclusively commercial interests, but that they also have a duty to respect our abilities to exercise our freedom to construct "moral" identities online that have more significant meaning than merely existing as an opportunity for microtargeted ads.

Ten Commandments of Computer Ethics

1. Thou shalt not use a computer to harm other people.

2. Thou shalt not interfere with other people's computer work.

3. Thou shalt not snoop around in other people's computer files.

4. Thou shalt not use a computer to steal.

5. Thou shalt not use a computer to bear false witness.

6. Thou shalt not copy or use proprietary software for which you have not paid.

7. Thou shalt not use other people's computer resources without authorization or proper compensation.

8. Thou shalt not appropriate other people's intellectual output.

9. Thou shalt think about the social consequences of the program you are writing or the system you are designing.

10. Thou shalt always use a computer in ways that ensure consideration and respect for your fellow humans.

SOURCE: Computer Ethics Institute (http://www.brook.edu/ITS/CEI/CEI_HP.HTM).

WHAT WE DO WITH MEDIA TECHNOLOGY

Our mobile phones, our customized news feeds, our blogs, and our social media pages all have provided countless benefits. Yet media ethics calls on us to consider the possible downsides of the digital revolution and be mindful of the potential harm we can cause by its use as well. While we do not necessarily need to sympathize or align ourselves with the naysayers and doomsday prophets, it is instructive to examine some key claims from those studying how we use media technology. The convenience of digital media can be overwhelming in a literal sense: It can tend to dominate and neutralize just about every other principle we might value in communication such as the value of context, dialogic engagement, and openness to new ideas. "At a Thanksgiving dinner, I watched a friend's teen text her way through the meal, rarely looking up to relate to the family and friends gathered from faraway places just to be together in her home," wrote Ron Sachs (2013, p. 22), a journalism and PR veteran in Florida. "The disconnection powered by our tech connections makes all of us producers and publishers—but the quality of our interaction often sinks to an all-time low. . . . The frantic daily sprint to constantly stay in touch has helped too many of our children, friends, neighbors, colleagues—and ourselves—to lose touch with the most important principles of human connectedness" (Sachs, 2013, p. 22). And while we have the world at our fingertips, most of us do not regularly take advantage of such wealth; instead, we customize our news and RSS feeds so that we're assured of getting only content that reflects our interests and beliefs. We use the Web to increase our insularity, and, thus, our polarization and preconceived assumptions about people and things outside our digital bubble. We join up in "narrowcast" social networking communities that are composed of people just like us (Parsell, 2008). Since it becomes so easy to shield ourselves from anything we disagree with, our use of media technology can arguably promote extremism and reinforcement of ill-founded opinions impervious to different facts; this, in turn, can erode our ability to relate to one another and recognize shared democratic interests (Sunstein, 2008). The architecture of sites such as Facebook, while wildly popular, also are limiting in significant ways, some argue. Such social networking sites tend "to treat human relations as if they are all of a kind, ignoring the profound differences among types of social relations (familial, professional, collegial, commercial, civic, etc.). As a consequence, the privacy controls of such architectures often fail to account for the variability of privacy norms within different but overlapping social spheres" (Vallor, 2012, p. 8).

Privacy and the Value of Forgetting

Privacy is a perennial issue as boundaries constantly shift. Many of us are still coming to grips with the costs of the convenience of using social networks. We continue to look for ways to reconcile the conflict between our personal motivations for using social media and the profit-driven motivations of the companies to which we hand our personal data. According to theorist Jared Lanier (2010), "The only hope for social networking sites from a business point of view is for a magic formula to appear in which some method of violating privacy and dignity becomes acceptable" (p. 55). Nearly three-quarters of American job recruiters report that they have rejected candidates because of information found online, such as photos and social-networking sites—material many of us might assume is private. Stories of how our uses of the Web undermine privacy are rife in the news media. One example is that of Stacy Snyder, a young teacher in training at a Pennsylvania high school who posted a photo on her MySpace page in 2006 that showed her at a party wearing a pirate hat and drinking from a plastic cup. The photo caption read "Drunken Pirate." Discovering the photo, her supervisor at the high school told her it was unprofessional, and days before her college graduation, university officials denied her a teaching degree. Snyder sued, arguing that the university had violated her First Amendment rights by penalizing her for behavior that was unrelated to any professional obligations. But in 2008, a federal judge rejected her claim, saying that because Snyder was a public employee whose photo didn't relate to matters of public concern, her MySpace post was not protected speech (Mayer-Schönberger, 2009, pp. 1–3).

Some argue that Snyder's predicament suggests how our conception of digital privacy must include a "right to forget" provision. The invasive nature of relentless, permanent archiving of every digital moment, footprint, and posting is warping our collective ability to define ourselves. A society defined by the permanent—and public—recording of everything we do "will forever tether us to our pasts, making it impossible, in practice, to escape them," writes theorist Victor Mayer-Schönberger, who argues for the importance of "societal forgetting" (2009, p. 13). Belying the persistent American myth of the powers of self-reinvention, digital archiving of our personal content is increasingly limiting our abilities of self-definition. "[F]ar from giving us a new sense of control over the face we present to the world, the Internet is shackling us to everything that we have ever said, or that anyone has said about us, making the possibility of self-reinvention seem like an ideal from a distant era," writes legal scholar Jeffrey Rosen (2011, pp. 3–4). Up until now, the limits of human memory largely ensured that people's sins were forgotten, and this also has served to underscore the reality that human beings evolve over time and that we have the capacity to learn from past experiences. Technology is undermining this, with serious ethical implications, as Mayer-Schönberger warns: "Without some form of forgetting, forgiving becomes a difficult undertaking. Or, as T. S. Eliot wrote, '[I]f all time is eternally present, [a]ll time is unredeemable'" (2009, p. 125). As a result, he and other theorists and policymakers are endorsing a "constitutional right to oblivion" and other steps to impose "expiration dates" on certain types of archived data, including our Facebook postings. Many of us willingly allow ourselves to be tracked and followed. How? By routine use of our smart phones, which are packed with sensors and always connected to the Internet:

> If someone knows exactly where you are, they probably know what you are doing. Cellular systems constantly check and record the location of all phones on their networks—and this data is particularly treasured by police departments and online advertisers. Cell companies typically retain your geographic information for a year or longer, according to data gathered by the Justice Department. What's the harm? The United States Court of Appeals for the District of Columbia Circuit, ruling about the use of tracking devices by the police, noted that GPS data can reveal whether a person "is a weekly church goer, a heavy drinker, a regular at the gym, an unfaithful husband, an outpatient receiving medical treatment, an associate of particular individuals or political groups—and not just one such fact about a person, but all such facts." Even the most gregarious of sharers might not reveal all that on Facebook. (Maass & Rajagopalan, 2012, p. SR5)

Online Comments: Too Much of a Good Thing?

Ethicists who study our online behavior ask big questions about whether media technology helps us pursue virtue and build our understanding of what it means to live well, or whether it is undermining us by easing us into echo chambers of our choosing and allowing convenience to trump almost every other value we say is important. The impersonal nature also invites users to do and say things they might not otherwise, posing a recurring dilemma for editors and organizations trying to encourage dialogue and engagement. Consider the "reader comment" feature on most news sites that allows nearly anyone to post a reaction below a story. News organizations promote the feature as a way to encourage engagement with stories, yet the comments often devolve into personal attacks and rants from conspiracy theorists and political fringe dwellers. This poses a dilemma: what to do when the comments become uncivil? In specific instances, many editors have simply shut it down when things get too nasty. "On the rare occasions when the comments get truly out of hand, shutting them off is our prerogative," wrote Felice Belman, editor of the

Concord Monitor newspaper in New Hampshire after reader comments featured personal attacks and details identifying the victim of an assault that the news story intentionally left out. "This story is certainly fodder for public discussion. Unfortunately, it got hijacked . . . by inappropriate comments" (Belman, 2013).

News and Social Media: Valuable Crowdsourcing or Unruly Mob?

Today, when any national event occurs such as a school shooting or a natural disaster, the news in the mainstream media is only half the story. The other half is compiled by thousands of regular folks who become mostly anonymous contributors on social media sites such as Buzzfeed, Reddit, and 4chan. In some cases, the uploaded cellphone images, Tweets, and other posts provide a startlingly instantaneous news narrative that runs parallel with—and often informs—traditional news reporting. At its best, such crowdsourced news results in quick information dissemination by people who are at the scene long before any journalists. At worst, however, it becomes an unruly and often dangerous mob that recklessly spins unfounded accusations and conspiracy theories into the wider world and tramples on journalistic standards of fairness, impartiality, and concern for minimizing harm. The role played by social media during the fast-paced, developing story of the manhunt for the two brothers suspected of setting off the bombs at the 2013 Boston Marathon was both. Seeking to enlist the public, FBI officials released photos of the two brothers, and within hours, tips and responses had them in hot pursuit. However, part of the motive for releasing the photos was to "limit the damage being done to people who were wrongly being targeted as suspects"— damage largely fuelled by the continuous, urgent, and often reckless stream of posts on social media sites. The Boston Police Department, whose active Twitter account had more than 200,000 followers, ultimately pleaded with people to stop posting updates with information they were overhearing on police scanners (Montgomery, Horwitz, & Fisher, 2013). "The Reddit and 4chan army, unguided and without professional restraint, often contributed to the spread of rumors and misinformation," wrote one law-enforcement analyst. "A single botched tweet and a misquote of a police scanner prompted swarms of Redditors to present [an innocent bystander's] head on a platter. While the community can and should partake in the effort to thwart criminals, an unguided mob will make unfortunate mistakes, which social media then amplifies" (Bar-tur, 2013, para. 3). Erik Martin, Reddit's general manager, said his staff "deeply regretted" some missteps. "Activity on Reddit fueled online witch hunts and dangerous speculation which spiralled into negative consequences for innocent parties," he posted on the site. However, in an interview, Martin stopped short of calling for new rules of online behavior. "Reddit is a sort of attention aggregator. It can tell you what to pay attention to, but it is certainly not a replacement for news reporting" (Kaufman, 2013, B1).

WHAT MEDIA TECHNOLOGY DOES TO US

If we think about it, technology does lots of things to us. But for some theorists, the most troubling thing it does is that it invites us to think *less.* Technology can save us time, money, and cognitive effort. One particular way it helps us conserve brain space is that technology is often designed in such a way that discourages us from considering the ethical implications and consequences of our uses of it. Morozov (2013) refers to the example of the electrical appliances in our kitchens. We typically use them and have no way of knowing how much power they consume. "This ignorance is neither natural nor inevitable; it stems from a conscious decision by the designer of that kitchen appliance to free up your 'cognitive resources'" (p. 12), he argues. The same design process is at work with digital communication technology. It often obscures relevant ethical questions. "Take privacy," Morozov continues:

> Opening browser tabs is easy, as is using our Facebook account to navigate from site to site. In fact, we do so unthinkingly. Given that our online tools and platforms are built in a way to make our browsing experience as frictionless as possible, is it any surprise that so much of our personal information is disclosed without our ever realizing it? This, too, is not inevitable: designed differently, our digital infrastructure could provide many more opportunities for reflection. (2013, p. 12)

Morozov's is just one in a flood of recent books sounding that alarm that we're letting media technology run rampant over basic human values. Another, *Virtually You: The Dangerous Powers of the E-Personality,* argues that the Web has largely become a sordid breeding ground that caters to our most infantile impulses, resulting in our "e-personalities"— grotesque versions of ourselves driven by narcissism, grandiosity, and an obsession for instant gratification of every whim (Aboujaoude, 2012). The more optimistic among us continue to debate the ways in which the benefits of our Web use outweigh the downsides. But there is little question that social media are influencing how we communicate and relate to one another. Several theorists go so far as to argue that the ways in which our media technology encourages some types of talk—asynchronous, everything-I-do-is-noteworthy—and discourages others—non-text-based responses and gestures that indicate character—actually hamper our ability to cultivate authentic identities online (Cocking, 2008). This is quite different than fostering dialogue. Two-way communication certainly happens all the time on Facebook, yet pages are arguably dominated by "Look at me!" and "This is what I like!" posts. As a result, such online communication involves considerably more "self-presentation" than does face-to-face interaction. "Past research into everyday conversation showed that a third of it is devoted to oneself, but today that topic has become an obsession thanks to social media," writes science journalist John Tierney (2013, p. D3). "Rutgers researchers classify 80 percent of Twitter users as 'meformers' who tweet mainly about themselves" (Tierney, 2013, p. D3). Some theorists suggest this structural privileging of self-involvement is partly responsible for the surge in narcissistic tendencies among the college generation born in the 1970s, 1980s, and 1990s—the group now known as "Generation Me." Think about how we present ourselves to others in face-to-face communication. Facebook's overwhelming popularity is largely the result of how easy it makes it to communicate instantly with selected groups of people. Yet we seldom think about how Facebook has subtly influenced what exactly our conversations now look like. Media critic Rob Walker explores how social media can reshape how we communicate, and even how we might perceive ourselves:

We're encouraged to record and express everything, all the time. In real time, we can record and distribute the most important moments of our existence, and some of the least. For the generations growing up in the Web era, this mode of being is more or less taken for granted. But the tools we use privilege the moment, not the long term; they also tend to make everything feel roughly equal in importance and offer us little incentive to comb back through our digital scribblings and sort out what might have lasting meaning from what probably doesn't. The results are pretty much the opposite of a scrapbook carefully edited to serve as a memory object but could end up serving that function by default. (Walker, 2011, p. 44)

The architecture of Facebook creates the expectation that we "talk" a very specific way: It invites personal pronouncements and places a premium on individual expression. Such architecture matters. Users of the Web site Tumblr, for example, are well aware of how the site's deliberate structure differs from other social media sites such as Facebook, and many recognize that these distinctions prompt people to behave differently on each. David Karp, the developer of Tumblr, said he always felt the "reader comments" sections of news sites were a mistake because too often commenters must say provocative or outrageous things if they are to be noticed. The feature itself can bring out the worst in people, so Tumblr does not offer a comments feature or a reply-post feature like Facebook. So how do you encourage engagement, like Facebook does, yet still avoid the screamers and hecklers? Karp explained his approach in a magazine profile:

First, Karp notes, you *can* comment on someone else's post, by reblogging it and adding your reaction. But that reaction appears on your Tumblr, not the one you're commenting on. "So if you're going to be a jerk, you're looking like a jerk in your own space, and my space is still pristine," Karp explains. This makes for a thoughtful network and encourages expression and, ultimately, creativity. "That's how you can design to make a community more positive." (Walker, 2012, p. 24)

All this is not to suggest that our use of social media has hopelessly diluted what it means to be a "friend," or that the downsides of our use of media technologies outweigh the positives. No doubt, we have greatly benefitted from the incredible connectivity and information access it has provided us. Theorists, however, suggest that in our romance with technology, we have not thought enough about the downsides—how it has made us less considerate of others in the ways we act in the real world:

Yet lingering ethical concerns remain about the way in which [social networking sites] can distract users from the needs of those in their immediate physical surroundings (consider the widely lamented trend of users obsessively checking their Facebook NewsFeed during family dinners, romantic dates and symphony performances). Such phenomena, which scholars like Sherry Turkle (2011) worry are indicative of a growing tolerance for being "alone together," bring a new complexity to earlier philosophical concerns about the emergence of a zero-sum game between offline relationships and their virtual [social networking site] competitors. They have also prompted a shift of ethical focus away from the question of whether online relationships are "real" friendships, to how well the real friendships we bring to [social networking sites] are being served there. (Vallor, 2012, pp. 13–14)

Moreover, heavy social media users may even be making themselves unhappier than the rest of us by observing the goings-on of apparently "happier" friends and, thus, falling into what researchers have called "the self-promotion-envy spiral." In one study, the longer people spent on Facebook, the more they reported thinking that life is unfair and that they're less happy than their Facebook friends. "The spread and ubiquitous presence of envy on social networking sites is shown to undermine users' life satisfaction," researchers concluded (Tierney, 2013).

Morozov (2011) expresses concern that our unquestioning cheerleader attitude toward the wonders of technology in our lives ignores grim realities of how oppressive regimes around the world use that same technology for more sinister purposes. "The truth is that many of the opportunities created by the free-for-all anonymous Internet culture have been creatively exploited by people and networks that undermine democracy," he argues, citing examples of savvy Web use by criminal gangs and racist groups in Europe, Asia, and Latin America (pp. 256–257). He recounts how ethnic groups have routinely used text messaging in recent years to mobilize attacks on perceived enemies in Australia, the Czech Republic, Kenya, Nigeria, and elsewhere, to devastating and lethal effect. In early 2010, clashes between Muslim and Christian communities in Nigeria killed more than 300 people and were fuelled largely by texts such as one saying, "kill before they kill you. Dump them in a pit before they dump you" (2011, p. 258). In 2005, many Australians received text messages urging attacks on their fellow citizens of Lebanese descent, resulting in scores of injuries. One text said, "This Sunday every f*** Aussie in the shire, get down to North Cronulla to help support Leb and wog bashing day. . . . Bring your mates down and let's show them this is our beach and they're never welcome back" (p. 260). It would be silly to blame such racism on mobile phones, Morozov writes. "But the ease, scale and speed of communications afforded by text messaging makes the brief and previously locally contained outbursts of neo-Nazi anger resonate in ways that they could never have resonated in an era marked by less connectedness" (p. 260). At the very least, he argues, this dark side of texting should make us pause before we impulsively say universal adoption of such technology is unquestionably a good thing. "Perhaps, the freedom to connect, at least in its current abstract interpretation, would be a great policy priority in a democratic paradise, where citizens have long forgotten about hate, culture wars, and ethnic prejudice. But such an oasis of tolerance simply does not exist" (p. 260).

VIRTUES AND VALUES IN MEDIA TECHNOLOGY

Is technology value-neutral? Is there truly a "good" or "bad" technology, or is its value only present when it is put to good or bad uses? We've often heard mantras such as "Guns don't kill people, people do," which implies that the tool is morally inert; its user, not the tool itself, signifies its value. Is media technology analogous? Certainly things that were never designed with malicious intent can be used for harmful ends. And it is true that blaming objects for their harmful effects too often lets people who should be held accountable for their uses off the hook. Yet many technology theorists urge us to reconsider our assumption that technology itself should be considered value-neutral. In fact, technology design and production are bound up with values about what resources they use, how they reflect or perpetuate social and cultural power, and whether they embody notions of stewardship and sustainability. "Technology," wrote Darin Barney, "is intimately bound up in the establishment and enforcement of prohibitions and permissions, the distribution of power and resources, and the structure of human practices and relationships. In technology, justice is at stake" (Barney, 2005, p. 656). More than two decades ago, theorist Clifford Christians (1989) first argued that technology is actually value-laden, not value-neutral. "Technological products are legitimate if and only if they maintain cultural continuity," he wrote (p. 129). What he meant was that we, as designers and users of media technology, have a moral duty to ensure that our gadgets promote ethical living. Does our use of media technology promote a sense of respect for human dignity? Of the notion of stewardship of natural resources? Of justice and healthy communities? Of free expression, reciprocity, and engagement?

Whether we are optimists or pessimists when it comes to the effects of social media on our lives, the claims and examples in this chapter underscore the need for all of us, as moral agents, to be mindful designers and users, and to be conscious of technology's powers of seduction, to be able to place its claims of convenience and efficiency in the context of ethical principles of stewardship, responsibility, and engagement. Aristotle, as Chapter 2 discussed, set forth a framework calling on us to cultivate virtuous lives that reflected and promoted the idea of human flourishing—conducting ourselves and adopting policies with the aim of helping everyone realize his or her fullest potential. "Men and women need to be industrious and tenacious of purpose not only so as to be able to house, clothe, and feed themselves," wrote philosopher Philippa Foot (2001), who sought to adapt Aristotle's work for our contemporary world, "but also to pursue human needs having to do with love and friendship. They need the ability to form family ties, friendships, and special relations with neighbours. They also need codes of conduct. And how could they have all these things without virtues such as loyalty, fairness, kindness, and in certain circumstances obedience?" (pp. 44–45). Foot's work provides a solid foundation on which to begin building a true *ethic* for behavior online. The normative operating principles of justice, transparency, and stewardship that Barney, Christians, and others embrace constitute important guides for articulating standards of virtuous behavior for all aspects of our digital existence: the work of online news writers and aggregators, the duties and responses of audience segments, the obligations of marketers and communicators doing promotional work. At the same time, an ethic of digital flourishing must address the often perilous seductions of digital technology.

For Discussion

1. Respond to the concern that many of us are "cyber-centric," and not always in a good way. In what ways might digital media invite you to "prioritize the tool over the environment," as Morozov argues?

2. The example of the casual practice of distracted driving is offered as one example of technological determinism—the notion that our adoption of technology proceeds regardless of moral considerations. What might be another negative example of such determinism regarding media technologies?

3. Heidegger and other theorists have long argued that technology is more a "state of mind" than having anything to do with machines or gadgets. What is your response to this counter-intuitive argument?

4. Have you been surprised to find yourself the object of online "microtargeting" by advertisers? Were you disturbed by implications it raised regarding your privacy? Were you grateful to be spared ads about things you probably don't care about?

5. Consider the "communities" you have joined based on your interests. Consider how you might be tailoring your RSS and digital news feeds to make sure you don't miss news about the topics that concern you most. Does such activity widen your horizons or limit your exposure to the world?

6. How would you respond to claims that we should all have a "right to oblivion" in the digital world?

7. Consider the claims that the very "architecture" of social networking sites reshapes the way we communicate—and often not in a good way. Given your use of Facebook, Foursquare, and other such sites, how might this be happening?

REFERENCES

Aboujaoude, E. (2012). *Virtually you: The dangerous powers of the e-personality.* New York, NY: W. W. Noton & Company.

Andrews, L. (2012, February 5). Facebook is using you. *New York Times,* p. SR7.

Bakardjieva, M., & Feenberg, A. (2000). Involving the Virtual Subject. *Ethics and Information Technology, 2*(4), 233–240.

Barney, D. (2005). Commentary: Be careful what you wish for: Dilemmas of democracy and technology. *Canadian Journal of Communication, 30,* 655–664.

Bar-tur, Y. (2013, April 22). Boston police schooled us all on social media. Retrieved from http://mashable.com/2013/04/22/boston-police-social-media/

Belman, F. (2013, April 2). Report to readers: No comments, please. Retrieved from http://www.concordmonitor.com/opinion/5436954-95/report-to-readers-no-comments-please

Christians, C. G. (1989). A theory of normative technology. In E. F. Byrne & J. C. Pitt (Eds.), *Technical transformation: Contextual and conceptual implications* (pp. 123–139). Dordrecht, The Netherlands: Kluwer Academic.

Cocking, D. (2008). Plural selves and relational identity. In J. van den Hoven & J. Weckert (Eds.), *Information Technology and Moral Philosophy* (pp. 123–141). Cambridge UK: Cambridge University Press.

Federal Trade Commission. (2013, February 1). Path social networking app settles FTC charges it deceived customers and improperly collected personal information from users' mobile address books. Retrieved from http://www.ftc.gov/opa/2013/02/path.shtm

Foot, P. (2001). *Natural goodness.* Oxford: Oxford University Press.

Hamelink, C. J. (2000). *The ethics of cyberspace.* London, England: SAGE.

Heidegger, M. (1977). *The question concerning technology and other essays* (W. Lovitt, Trans.). New York, NY: Harper & Row. (Original work published 1954)

Kaufman, L. (2013, April 29). Boston attacks trip up Reddit in its turn in spotlight. *New York Times,* p. B1.

Lanier, J. (2010). *You are not a gadget: A manifesto.* New York, NY: Knopf.

Maass, P., & Rajagopalan, M. (2012, July 13). That's no phone. That's my tracker. *New York Times,* p. SR5.

Manders-Huits, N. (2010). Practical versus moral identities in identity management. *Ethics and Information Technology, 12*(1), 43–55.

Mayer-Schönberger, V. (2009). *Delete: The virtue of forgetting in the digital age.* Princeton, NJ: Princeton University Press.

Montgomery, D., Horwitz, S., & Fisher, M. (2013, April 20). Police, citizens and technology factor into Boston bombing probe. *Washington Post.* Retrieved April 22 from http://www.washingtonpost.com/world/national-security/inside-the-investigation-of-the-boston-marathon-bombing/2013/04/20/19d8c322-a8ff-11e2-b029-8fb7e977ef71_story.html

Morozov, E. (2011). *The Net delusion: The dark side of Internet freedom.* New York, NY: Public Affairs.

Morozov, E. (2013, March 31). Machines of laughter and forgetting. *New York Times,* Sunday Review, p. 12.

Noble, D. F. (2011). *Forces of production: A social history of industrial automation.* New York, NY: Oxford University Press.

Parsell, M. (2008). Pernicious virtual communities: Identity, polarisation and the Web 2.0. *Ethics and Information Technology, 10*(1), 41–56.

Postman, N. (1992). *Technopoly: The surrender of culture to technology.* New York, NY: Alfred A. Knopf.

Richtel, M. (2009, July 19). Dismissing the risks of a deadly habit. *New York Times.* Retrieved from http://www.nytimes.com/2009/07/19/technology/19distracted.html?pagewanted = all&_r = 0

Rosen, J. (2011, July 21). The web means the end of forgetting. *New York Times Sunday Magazine,* pp. 1–14.

Sachs, R. (2013, March). New tech realities result in culture of disconnection. *O'Dwyer's, 27*(3), 22.

Story, L. (2007, November 1). FTC to review online ads and privacy. *New York Times.* Retrieved from http://www.nytimes.com/2007/11/01/technology/01Privacy.html?pagewanted = print&_r = 0

Sunstein, C. (2008). Democracy and the Internet. In J. van den Hoven & J. Weckert (Eds.), *Information Technology and Moral Philosophy* (pp. 93–110). Cambridge, UK: Cambridge University Press.

Tierney, J. (2013, March 19). Good news beats bad on social networks. *New York Times,* p. D3.

Vallor, S. (2012). Social networking and ethics. *The Stanford Encyclopedia of Philosophy.* Retrieved from http://plato.stanford.edu/archives/win2012/entries/ethics-social-networking/

Walker, R. (2011, January 9). Things to do in cyberspace when you're dead. *New York Times Magazine, 44*(46), 30–37, 44.

Walker, R. (2012, July 15). Peace, love and Tumblr. *New York Times Magazine, 22,* 24–25, 51.

CHAPTER 5

Transparency

This chapter is based on Plaisance (2007), Copyright www.informaworld.com.

If ethics is all about struggling to find rational ways to balance competing interests and values, the concept of *transparency* assures us that all the players, or stakeholders, are speaking the same language. We humans are, by nature, creatures of community. Our social roles make up a large part of who we are. As social animals, we are specially wired to depend on interaction with others. That is why communication is such a central feature of humanity. There are obvious reasons why we are so dependent on communication: to get information we need to live our daily lives, to participate in our culture, and, indeed, to understand our place in society and develop meaningful relationships with others. But there is another critical but often implicit ingredient of human communication: trust. Imagine a world in which you could freely communicate with anyone you chose, but you could never be sure that what others told you was truthful or accurate, or even whether anyone ever actually cared about such things. If it served someone's whim or interest to lie to you or to give you deliberately false or misleading information, they did so at every opportunity. If that were the norm, our very society would collapse. Notwithstanding the proliferation of political "spin doctors" and one-sided commercial advertising, our communication is based on the notion of *honest* exchange. We refer to this norm of forthrightness, or being aboveboard, as being *transparent*. And society as we know it would not be possible if we did not place a premium on the spirit of openness or transparent behavior.

The concept of transparency is critical to anyone concerned with ethics in communication because it doesn't simply address the *content* of our messages to other people, but requires us to think about the form and nature of our interaction with others. Transparency is not only an issue regarding *what* we say, but also *why* we say it, and even *how* we talk. What are my motives in making the claims I'm making or in writing a story a certain way? Am I being upfront about those motives or is there something I'm not disclosing? Why am I reluctant to disclose it? What does it mean to show respect to someone when communicating with them? These are some key questions that focusing on the concept of transparency force us to consider.

The Latin preposition *trans* means "movement," and *parent* means "visible." According to the *Oxford English Dictionary,* transparency is the quality of "having the property of transmitting light, so as to render bodies lying beyond completely visible." Rather than connote the passive, conventional image of transparency as "allowing everything to be visible," business ethicist Richard Oliver (2004) argued that today's "new" transparency implies the increasing expectation by various stakeholders of "active disclosure." "In other words, the idea of motion or action in transparency has returned to a much earlier understanding of the term, with motive shifting to the left of the equation—putting new *responsibilities* [author's emphasis] on the observed" (Oliver, 2004, pp. 3, 4).

We all understand that we must try to articulate our reasoning as clearly as possible in the interest of providing full disclosure and a basis for accountability. But it's important to understand exactly *why* transparency is so central to the field of ethics and what kind of weight we ought to place on it as a central value.

TRUST AND SECRECY

Some would argue that, as a society, we have achieved more openness, or transparency, than ever—so much so that its virtue is widely taken for granted and universally shared. "There has never been more abundant information about individuals and institutions whose claims we have to judge," Cambridge philosopher Onora O'Neill (2002) wrote. "Openness and transparency are now possible on a scale of which past ages could barely dream" (p. 66). This "high road" toward increasing, pervasive social and commercial transparency is built on new technologies that she says are ideal for achieving openness. These technologies have reaffirmed our claims that openness is the best way to build public trust and accountability. The increased activity and prominence of Web-based media "watchdog" groups and independent bloggers have contributed to the intense public scrutiny of media behavior. The subjects of news accounts now can disseminate their own versions of events, including transcripts that show audiences what journalists chose not to use.

Yet O'Neill (2002) argued that we have not seen a corresponding increase in trust. "On the contrary, trust seemingly has receded as transparency has advanced. . . . Transparency certainly destroys secrecy: but it may not limit the deception and deliberate misinformation that undermine relations of trust" (pp. 68, 70). She concluded,

> Unless there has been prior deception, transparency does nothing to reduce deception; and even if there has been deception, openness is not a sure-fire remedy. Increasing transparency can produce a flood of unsorted information and misinformation that provides little but confusion unless it can be sorted and assessed. . . . Demands for transparency are likely to encourage the evasions, hypocrisies and half-truths that we usually refer to as "political correctness," but which might more forthrightly be called either "self-censorship" or "deception." (pp. 72–73)

Furthermore, other theorists have cautioned that while people are increasingly relying on computer-mediated communication, certain of its characteristics, including its "sensory displacement" and its tendency to "dematerialize" communicators, make it more difficult to foster trust and ensure that a premium is placed on truth (Tompkins, 2003).

Journalists themselves often are ambivalent about their commitment to the ideal of transparent behavior. They have long been reluctant to expose newsroom deliberations to public scrutiny for various reasons, including a fear of undermining another central journalistic tenet: autonomy from outside influences. When asked to rank a set of given values, the journalistic value of being "aboveboard" failed to make the top tier of the six most highly ranked of 24 values (Plaisance & Skewes, 2003).

Similarly, the ideal of transparency also poses challenges in the area of advertising. The line between legitimate persuasive efforts and underhanded manipulation or outright deception can seem elusive, and economic imperatives often tempt advertisers to disregard the distinction. Because of its essential role in our society, commercial speech is legally protected in society—as long as it is not untruthful or misleading. "This recognizes that while advertising serves an economic purpose, it does not have free rein to communicate in order to achieve its goals," Sheehan wrote (2004, p. 4). In other words, advertising content, like any other media content, carries an ethical obligation to be responsible.

Transparency: It's in the Code of Ethics

Many codes do not explicitly list transparency as a key value; instead, the concept is implied in statements throughout the codes that outline what constitutes ethical behavior. The ethics code of the American Marketing Association, however, explicitly calls on marketers to "create transparency" in their operations and "to be truthful and forthright" in dealings with customers and stakeholders. Some other examples include the following:

From the American Advertising Federation

Advertising shall

- Tell the truth, and shall reveal significant facts, the omission of which would mislead the public.
- [Use testimonials that are] limited to those of competent witnesses who are reflecting a real and honest opinion or experience.

The complete statement can be found at http://www.aaaa.org/EWEB/upload/inside/ standards.pdf.

From the Society of Professional Journalists Code of Ethics

Journalists should

- Distinguish news from advertising and shun hybrids that blur the lines between the two.
- Disclose unavoidable conflicts.
- Clarify and explain news coverage and invite dialogue with the public over journalistic conduct.

(Continued)

(Continued)

- Admit mistakes and correct them promptly.
- Avoid undercover or other surreptitious methods of gathering information except when traditional open methods will not yield information vital to the public. Use of such methods should be explained as part of the story.

The complete code can be found at http://www.spj.org/ethicscode.asp.

From the Public Relations Society of America Member Code of Ethics

A member shall

- Preserve the integrity of the process of communication.
- Be honest and accurate in all communications.
- Reveal the sponsors for causes and interests represented.
- Avoid deceptive practices.

The complete code can be found at http://www.prsa.org/aboutUs/ethics/preamble_en.html.

The duty of transparency requires us to acknowledge the moral dimension of all communicative acts, yet it does not require the sacrifice of autonomous agency when opacity or evasion serve legitimate privacy interests. Autonomy requires privacy, as several theorists have pointed out (Bok, 1982; Goffman, 1963; Rosen, 2000). In her essay on the science of deception detection, journalist Robin Henig (2006) noted that learning to lie is an important step in human maturation:

> What makes a child able to start telling lies, usually at about age 3 or 4, is that he has begun developing a theory of mind, the idea that what goes on in his head is different from what goes on in other people's heads. . . . After a while, the ability to lie becomes just another part of his emotional landscape. (p. 76)

Philosopher Thomas Nagel (1998) eloquently stated how neither individuals nor society can survive and flourish without secrecy:

> Each of our inner lives is such a jungle of thoughts, feelings, fantasies and impulses, that civilization would be impossible if we expressed them all, or if we could all read each other's minds, just as social life would be impossible if we expressed all our lustful, aggressive, greedy, anxious or self-possessed feelings, and private behavior could be safely exposed to public view. (p. 15)

Our existence as moral agents requires the exercise of secrecy and, thus, some right to exercise deception in the service of protecting our private selves. Failure to acknowledge the need for secrecy as a key component of autonomous agency leaves us "unable to exercise choice in our lives," as philosopher Sissela Bok said (1982, p. 20). As a mechanism for public policy, disclosure "can increase as well as decrease risks," according to Mary Graham (2002) in her book *Democracy by Disclosure.* "If revelations are distorted, incomplete, or misunderstood, they can misinform, mislead, or cause unwarranted panic" (p. 5).

TRANSPARENCY AS RESPECT

Clearly, achieving transparency as a widely accepted policy of ethical behavior may not necessarily guarantee moral "progress" or alleviate moral confusion. And several theorists have made it clear that we are under no obligation to tell the truth in extreme circumstances, when being truthful threatens one's survival, such as during wartime or if faced with torture. Indeed, this exemption is implied in UNESCO's Universal Declaration of Human Duties and Responsibilities. But if we have a proper understanding of the concept of transparency, in fact, it ought to "limit" deception and misinformation. As we will see, the concept is tightly bound up with the Kantian duty of acting in ways that respect the humanity—or, more precisely, the rational capacity and the free will to exercise that capacity—of others. Even if transparency is not always a sufficient condition for more ethical behavior, its absence is a prerequisite for deception, which, as we know, presents serious challenges for anyone who values ethical behavior.

> **Transparency: How Is It Defined?**
>
> Transparent behavior can be defined as conduct that presumes *openness* in communication and serves a reasonable expectation of forthright exchange when parties have a *legitimate stake* in the possible outcomes of effects of the sending or receiving of the message. It is an attitude of *proactive moral engagement* that manifests an express concern for the *persons-as-ends principle* when a degree of deception or omission can reasonably be said to risk thwarting the receiver's due *dignity* or the ability to exercise reason.

We all have aspirations, agendas, and motivations. But as we struggle with different ethical problems, our responses to the pull of various claims and arguments must be aboveboard. Ethical behavior, by definition, strives to respect the claims of every stakeholder. Ethics is fundamentally concerned with our search for quality in our justifications of what we deem "right." It addresses the nature of our deliberation and the strength of the rationales that we arrive at for a given question. If we cloak our rationales, our real motives, we undermine the ethical enterprise. If we fail in our obligation of full disclosure, we rightfully become open to charges of deception and disrespect, no matter how honorable or accepted our final decision seems to be.

Transparent interaction is what allows us as rational, autonomous beings to assess each other's behavior. Our motivations, aspirations, and intents are fully set forth for examination. "Moral communication," Robert McShea (1990) wrote, "is possible among us to the extent to which we share . . . a common view of the facts" (p. 221). Sissela Bok (1999) argued that when we use deception or stop short of full disclosure, we fail to treat others with the requisite dignity and respect. We fail as moral beings, in effect.

Case in Point: Plugola for a Pundit

In June 2004, the U.S. Department of Education awarded a $950,000 contract to Ketchum, a major international public relations firm, to develop communication campaigns to publicize and promote various federal policies and programs. Part of that deal involved paying $240,000 to Armstrong Williams, a frequent conservative African American commentator on television, to tout the U.S. Department of Education's No Child Left Behind policy. He did so repeatedly, without disclosing the fact that his opinions were being paid for. Soon after news reports revealed the arrangement, Williams apologized for his "ethical lapse." But while Williams said he regretted accepting the payment, he refused to return it. That, he said, "would be ludicrous because they bought advertising, and they got it." Critics also accused Ketchum of undermining the credibility of public relations in general with such underhanded deals that fail to fully disclose relationships with audiences. "At the end of the day, PR is about trying to communicate a message on someone's behalf," said Harris Diamond, chief executive of Weber Shandwick, one of the largest public relations firms in the country. "It is very important that we have transparency in our practices. We have to give very clear guidance on where information is coming from (O'Brien, 2005)."

KANT: THE PRINCIPLE OF HUMANITY

While we strive to articulate the key values and guiding principles for media behavior, it is also valuable to remind ourselves of the philosophical underpinnings of full disclosure. Upholding transparency as a goal in our deliberations is not simply a way to argue the rightness of our decisions. It is how we demonstrate that we are ethical beings from the start. Philosophically, the notion of transparency is rooted primarily in the work of Immanuel Kant. He established what many scholars refer to as his "principle of humanity" in the *Groundwork for the Metaphysics of Morals,* originally published in 1785: "Act so that you use humanity, as much in your own person as in the person of every other, always at the same time as an end and never merely as means" (1785/2002, p. 429). Several contemporary theorists have raised questions about Kant's principle of humanity, wondering whether it truly sets forth a helpful moral criterion (M. Singer, 1961) and whether it successfully helps us understand which actual ends or purposes are morally acceptable (Jones, 1971). Other theorists have defended Kant, arguing that his principle simply provides a criterion for evaluating the pursuit of whatever ends a person may have (Atwell, 1986; Paton, 1971).

This humanity principle is closely related to what is known as Kant's "supreme principle of the doctrine of virtue," which is stated later in his *Metaphysics of Morals* (1797/1991):

> Act in accordance with a maxim of *ends* that it can be a universal law for everyone to have. In accordance with this principle, man is an end for himself as well as for others, and it is not enough that he is not authorized to use either himself or others merely as means (since he could then still be indifferent to them); it is in itself his duty to make man in general his end. (Kant, 1797/1991, p. 198)

This is tied to Kant's "categorical imperative," which defines an act as "moral" if it may be endorsed as acceptable behavior for everyone. So as a moral being, I must strive to ensure that I treat others with respect, not because I may fear them or because I might benefit from doing so, but because if I deal with others in ways that are designed to further my interests, I am effectively reducing people to means to my ends instead of treating them as ends in themselves. This, Kant argues, reduces humans to objects or mere tools, which is a failure to properly appreciate the specialness of being human. Furthermore, as we will see, Kant's categorical imperative requires that I treat people as deserving of respect for their own sakes because if it were acceptable for everyone *not* to do so, chaos would ensue. This is the universalist approach that most commonly defines Kant's deontology, or duty-based moral system, as opposed to other approaches, such as the utilitarianism of John Stuart Mill, which places emphasis on the goodness of consequences of an act. The categorical imperative obviously is a key idea in Kant's moral system. But we do not focus

Kant's Principle of Humanity

All human beings are "ends" in themselves, and, thus, of infinite moral value—not because they may be of use to me, but because they are human beings with free wills and a capacity to exercise reason. Since everyone is an "end" with absolute moral worth, I may not reduce anyone to a mere "means" to accomplish a goal or task, for doing so denies their ability to live as rational beings. In Kant's words, "Act so that you use humanity, as much in your own person as in the person of every other, always at the same time as an end and never merely as a means" (1785/2002, p. 429).

on it here. Rather, his related humanity principle is the cornerstone for the concept of transparency as a key guide for ethical behavior. Once we understand this principle, we will see how it provides the basis for his universalist maxim.

Mill on Transparency

In most of his writings, John Stuart Mill is largely concerned with promoting and refining his political theory based on the idea of utility—that society should embrace as its purpose the creation of opportunities for individuals to pursue their own versions of happiness. He also was concerned with morality and the cultivation of "character" and argued that we had an obligation to act morally toward others. His argument that we have a duty to cultivate "virtue" in our lives echoed Aristotle. While Mill does not specifically address the question of ethical transparency as Kant did, some of his writings on morality make the implicit claim that, as social creatures, we are morally bound to be concerned with the welfare of others and their ability to freely pursue their interests. Mill is explicit in saying that since society provides many services and opportunities that provide happiness, we fail morally if we do not somehow recognize our moral obligation to others. Here is one of Mill's most direct passages on the issue of moral treatment of others:

> There is a standard of altruism to which all should be required to come up, and a degree beyond it which is not obligatory, but meritorious. It is incumbent on every one to restrain the pursuit of his personal objects within the limits consistent with the essential interests of others. What those limits are, it is the province of ethical science to determine; and to keep

(Continued)

(Continued)

all individuals and aggregations of individuals within them is the proper office of punishment and blame. In addition to fulfilling this obligation, persons make the good of others a direct object of disinterested exertions, postponing or sacrificing to it even innocent personal indulgences, they deserve gratitude and honour, and are fit objects of moral praise. . . . The proper office of those sanctions is to enforce upon every one, the conduct necessary to give all other persons their fair chance: conduct which consists chiefly of not doing them harm, and not impeding them in anything which without harming others does good to themselves. To this must of course be added that when we either expressly or tacitly undertake to do more, we are bound to keep our promise. And inasmuch as everyone, who avails himself of the advantages of society, leads others to expect from him all such positive good offices and disinterested services as the moral improvement attained by mankind has rendered customary, he deserves moral blame if, without just cause, he disappoints that expectation. (1961, pp. 143–144)

Kant's principle of humanity argues that we have a moral duty to respect others as ends in themselves simply because they are human beings and, therefore, are capable of *reason,* which becomes the basis for his entire ethical system. "Kant means that when I regard myself as an end in myself, I am regarding myself as a moral agent subject to moral law and so of infinite value," according to a prominent authority on Kantian philosophy, H. J. Paton (1971, p. 176). "I must do this in virtue of my nature as a rational agent, and so must every other man. . . . In virtue of my rational nature as such I must regard—and treat—all persons (including myself) as moral agents" (p. 177). As philosopher John Atwell (1986) noted, this notion of people as rational ends is a central feature in ethics codes across professions:

[This principle] occurs again and again in current discussions of business and professional ethics, where it is said, for example, that workers are not to be treated in the manner of the tools they themselves employ, that medical patients are to be "respected" by their physicians, that human subjects may not be "used" by medical and social science researchers unless "informed consent" has been obtained, and so on in other "practical" areas. Nearly every (if not every) professional code of ethics operative at the present time makes a favorable reference to Kant's principle of humanity, the notion of respect for persons, or the like. (p. 105)

The linkage between the concept of transparency and the Kantian principle of humanity can be seen in the ethics codes for both journalists and public relations professionals, which in their promotion of accountability and disclosure demonstrate a fundamental respect for the rationality and judgment of media consumers. "Be accountable" is one of the four directives of the code of ethics adopted in 1996 and promoted by the Society of Professional Journalists. According to the code, "Journalists are accountable to their readers, listeners, viewers and each other." As a result, journalists should "clarify and explain news coverage and invite dialogue with the public" and "abide by the same high standards to which they hold others" (Society of Professional Journalists, 2006). The code of ethics adopted by the Public Relations Society of America lists "disclosure of information" as a key provision. According to this provision, public relations practitioners can build public trust "by revealing all information needed for responsible decision-making," and the code urges them to "avoid deceptive practices" and "reveal the sponsors for causes and interests represented" (Public Relations Society of America, 2006). Transparency is even an implicit value stated in the American Marketing Association's ethics code, which urges members to avoid false or misleading advertising and "sales promotions that use deception or manipulation" (American Marketing Association, 2006).

Case in Point: Food Lion and ABC's *PrimeTime Live*

In November 1992, ABC's *PrimeTime Live* newsmagazine show aired a segment that charged Food Lion, a Southeast supermarket chain, with selling out-of-date meat and deli products and forcing employees to work "off the clock." To get the story, ABC producers applied for Food Lion jobs and were hired. They went to work with tiny cameras and microphones in their clothes and hair and documented work habits in the meat and deli departments. Food Lion's sales declined by $4.6 billion after the undercover news segment, and the company closed more than 80 stores. The grocery chain later took ABC to court—not on libel or defamation charges or to argue that the segment was false, but to claim that ABC was guilty of fraud and trespass because the producers misrepresented themselves to gain access to the stores. In December 1996, a federal grand jury found ABC and all four producers guilty of fraud, awarding Food Lion a whopping $5.5 million in punitive damages. That was later reduced by a judge to $315,000, then still later to a token $2. The case sparked intense debate over the appropriate use of hidden cameras and other deceptive practices by journalists, and whether the goals of truth telling and serving the public justify such questionable tactics, or means.

Nowhere is Kant referred to in these or most other codes of ethics. Yet they all use his humanity principle as the basis for why behavior ought to be proscribed when it comes to acts of deception of any kind. On the surface, it may be obvious to us why deception, or lies, or false claims in advertising are wrong. They just are, we say. They violate our sense of honesty. These forms of deception are hypocritical if we talk about the importance of "truth" as a value. Philosophically, the roots go much deeper. All of this rests on Kant's fundamental claim that "a good will has a unique and absolute value" (Paton, 1971, p. 171). If this is accepted, then we are prohibited, as moral agents, from subordinating another human being to any lesser ends, including the pursuit of our own interests and desires. But Kant's "positive" moralism charges us to go even further in respecting the human will: "It must indeed be a duty, not merely to refrain from thwarting its manifestation in action, but also to further these manifestations so far as it is in our power to do so" (Paton, p. 171).

Kant outlines that all beings or objects in the world fall into one of three categories: (1) *Wesen*—projected ends, desires, or objects of one's will, which are known as *subjective* ends; (2) *Gegenstände*—natural, nonrational objects that are not dependent on one's will, such as trees, stones, gold, or animals; and (3) *Objekte*—rational beings, which are considered ends in themselves. Again, Atwell's (1986) explanation of how Kant says we should correctly perceive the moral worth, or value, of each, is useful:

> Objects in (1) have no value except that of being willed or desired by someone; things in (2) have only a relative value, specifically, a value of means alone; and rational beings, in (3), have an absolute value, indeed, a dignity, hence they are properly "objects" of respect, or at least their humanity or personality is. To say, then that man "exists" as an end in itself is to say that the "nature" of man designates him as an end in itself: "rational beings are called *persons* because their nature designates them from the start as ends in themselves, i.e., as that which may not be treated merely as means." (p. 108)

Kant's Categorical Imperative

I commit an immoral act when my treatment of another person involves acting on a claim that I would not want to be adopted as a universal standard of behavior for everyone or as a universal law of nature.

We must understand Kant's conceptualization of "ends." Philosopher Onora Nell (1975) suggested that Kant places paramount value on our "will" and on our "rational nature" as ends in themselves because rational nature "is the only possessor of a will which can be good" (p. 106). "If good willing is an end in itself or objective end, then so are rational beings" (p. 108). "There is no conceivable object of the will, i.e., no subjective end, to which persons may be treated merely as means thereto," said Atwell (1986, p. 108) of Kant's claims. "Things may be *used,* in principle, for any end one may have, but persons may never be *used* for any end whatever" (p. 108). We cannot honor the will to reason by treating others merely as means to satisfy our inclinations, for to do so suggests that we would treat fellow human beings the same way we might treat the inanimate tools we use to accomplish certain jobs. If we are serious about the value of freedom and about our duty to honor human reason, Kant said, then we will strive to treat others *as ends in themselves* and not solely as means for the attainment of our personal goals or desires. We must interact with others in ways that maximize their ability to exercise free will or reason. To fail to do so is to fail to recognize our existence as rational beings who, by the presence of our will to reason, are obligated to act morally toward others.

Paton (1971) neatly tied this principle to Kant's widely understood categorical imperative or universalist ethic:

> I will try to put this less technically. Formula I bids me act only on maxims which can be universal laws for all men. Since these laws are laws of freedom, this means that in determining my actions I have to take into account the rational wills of other men: I ought to act only in such a way that as rational beings they can act on the same law as I. Hence their rational wills limit my actions and must not be arbitrarily overridden by me. That is to say, I ought not to use them merely as means to the satisfaction of my own desires. Similarly, I ought not to use my own rational will merely as a means to the satisfaction of my desires. (p. 178)

And yet the implications of Kant's idea here are even more radical. Taken together, our duty to respect the freedom accorded to all rational beings and our duty to avoid treating others as merely ends creates an additional obligation: to accept *the happiness of others* as our own objective end. This is a radical notion, to say the least, and may well sound jarring to our modern sensibilities. Yet it is not entirely unfamiliar; several religions take this "Love thy neighbor as thyself" approach, even if they stop short of providing any rational justifications beyond an article of faith. Nell explained Kant's basis for claiming that we are obligated, as moral beings, to make the happiness of others our concern and to use this concern to guide our actions toward others. We can't necessarily predict what kind of help or cooperation we may need from others, so we cannot be sure how we might be required to act out Kant's categorical imperative. As a result, if we are serious about respecting the freedom of others based on a respect for them as rational beings, their happiness (or objective ends) becomes our concern too because our awareness of them is required for us to respect the will of all rational beings (Nell, 1975, pp. 109–110).

At this point, many students may conclude that Kant's framework is unreasonably rigid and impractical. No doubt, Kant expects a lot of us as moral agents, but how can much of what he says be applicable to our daily lives? One thing to keep in mind is that Kant is talking largely about our idealized selves. Recall that ethics is all about the *normative* world, about how we ought to act, with a full understanding of our duties. Even so, a long line of philosophers has grappled with the implications of his duty-based system. Surely, many have said, there are other ways to recognize that despite our intentions, we must make compromises—including a white lie now and then—in much of our daily lives. Philosopher W. D. Ross (1930), mentioned in the first two chapters, provides a way to soften Kant's rigidity and yet still acknowledge our moral duties. Unlike Kant, Ross emphasizes that our duties stem from relationships, and the proper maintenance of them can require a delicate balancing act. He also recognizes that moral decision making is full of complexity and uncertainty:

> Where a possible act is seen to have two characteristics, in virtue of one of which it is a prima facie right, and in virtue of the other prima facie wrong, we . . . are well aware that we are not certain whether we ought or ought not to do it; that whether we do it or not we are taking a moral risk. We come in the long run, after consideration, to think one duty more pressing than the other, but we do not feel certain that it is so." (1930, pp. 30–31)

Ethicist Christopher Meyers usefully lays out Ross's (1930) categories of perfect, or prima facie, duties (things that should always inform our behavior, regardless of the situation) and imperfect, or actual duties (things we should do when the case allows) (Meyers, 2011, pp. 326–328). Meyers also explains that we often perceive Kant's system as overly rigid because it doesn't seem to leave room for this sort of balancing of duties as Ross does, and that Kant seems to presume that we can be "morally omniscient"—that is, we have all the morally relevant information before us to make a decision. Ross recognizes this is not so; we often resort to guesswork, or speculation, in our efforts to do the right thing. And we also end up making mistakes. Still, Kant usefully points us to broad standards that should inform our behavior. His framework lays out what our better selves might look like. And deception, or lack of transparency, is a fundamental concern when it comes to interacting with others: I treat another person wrongly (that is, use deceptive means to induce someone to act according to my desires) when my treatment of that person involves acting on a maxim that I would not want to be adopted as a universal law of nature. This does not imply that our strictly utilitarian dealings with other people are immoral. As Paton (1971) said, I may go to the post office and give the postal clerk a package to mail, thus treating the clerk as a means to satisfy my desire that it be delivered as I want. Kant's point is that while we might treat people as means in the course of our daily lives, we cannot treat them as *only* means, and we must respect them as ends in themselves as well.

But this theory of universalism strikes many feminist critics as suspicious and even disingenuous. Kant's rigid system, they argue, presents a masculine perspective as the only "rational" one. Seyla Benhabib (1992), a political philosopher, claimed the universalism promoted by Kant, John Rawls, and others is not really universal at all, since it is inherently male focused and systematically devalues or dismisses feminist claims and concerns. Their universalism, she argued, "is defined surreptitiously by identifying the experiences of a specific group or subject as the paradigmatic case of the human as such. These subjects are invariably white, male adults who are propertied or at least professional" (Benhabib, 1992, pp. 152–153). Benhabib seeks to find a middle ground between a strict Kantian emphasis on rationality and the claims of feminists that relationship values too often are trumped by society's worship of reason and claims of justice. Her "conversational" model does not insist that we ought to accept ethical conclusions and standards that apply to everyone, but instead, she suggests that the concerns of "respect" for others and "reciprocity," or a willingness to critique our moral claims from the perspectives of others, are keys to ethical behavior.

Many ethical debates over media behavior center on clashes involving the fundamental values of exercising the First Amendment free speech rights and respecting the dignity and sensitivity of certain groups that may be affected or offended by that exercise. In early 2006, this conflict arose when newspaper editors in Europe and the United States struggled with the question of whether to publish editorial cartoons that negatively depicted the Muslim prophet Mohammed. Although most American papers declined to run the cartoons, which were first published by a Danish newspaper in late 2005, several others did, including the *Philadelphia Inquirer* and the *American-Statesman* of Austin, Texas, claiming it to be a necessary demonstration of their free speech rights. Editors at the two papers also argued that readers should be able to see the cartoons to better understand the controversy surrounding them. Many Muslims, however, believe that Islam forbids *any* depiction, critical or otherwise, of the prophet, and the cartoons struck many Muslims as deeply offensive. The decision to publish the material, for many Muslims, demonstrated a callous disregard for, and even a repudiation of, their religious beliefs by Westerners. It may seem odd to invoke Kant's claim that it is our *rational capacities* that provide the basis for our freedom in a dispute involving religious belief, but the argument that publishing the cartoons was a free speech question would likely strike Kant as hollow and even backward. Freedom celebrated for its own sake has no sound philosophical basis and has no moral force, he might say. Publishing the cartoons without a sufficient understanding of the depth of offense given to Muslims could be considered a failure to adequately engage followers of Islam as ends in themselves; instead, they become merely *means* in an exercise of free speech.

KANT: THE THEORY OF HUMAN DIGNITY

Kant spent much effort in showing why all humans must be treated in a way that respects their autonomy and dignity—he discussed these in the same way that Thomas Jefferson and others have said that we are all born with "certain inalienable rights." Kant elaborated on these claims and became more explicit regarding the value of transparency in his *Metaphysics of Morals,* originally published in 1797. In that work, Kant set forth what could be referred to as a theory of human dignity, arguing that human beings require a certain degree of respectful treatment, not because of any requirements of social norms, but because they are human beings. It is precisely because others exist as rational agents, Kant said, and, thus, are vulnerable to being thwarted or undermined unfairly in various ways that we must accept categorical imperatives that serve to help us universalize our behavior.

Kant's fundamental contention regarding this, according to Paton (1971), is that "an absolutely good will, and even the human being capable of manifesting such a will, cannot be subordinated as a means to any object of merely relative worth without contradiction—that is, without a breach of rational and coherent willing" (p. 177).

> **Kant's Theory of Human Dignity**
>
> Human beings require a certain degree of respectful treatment, not because of social norms, but because of their existence as rational beings. If this is true, we also must accept that the *promotion* of the freedom of others is a moral obligation, since it is only through one's freedom that one can exercise one's capacity for reason.

Indeed, Kant said that as true moral beings, we must go further: We must always seek to *advance* the interests of others and work on behalf of their happiness. Kant's principle of humanity, we have seen, establishes the philosophical link between the basis for our duty to respect the free will of others and duties that may result. His theory of human dignity argues that we are obligated to make this link into something that manifests itself in our daily lives. For unlike rules of law, which generally set forth boundaries of our behavior and guide us on what we *cannot* or *should not* do, the focus of ethics, as we've noted, is more active, or positive: It deals with what we *ought* to do as moral agents with personal and social obligations. As we have seen, for Kant, these moral obligations arise from the absolute value we place on the human free will and reasoning capacity. Paton (1971) said this is what it means to take Kant's abstract categorical imperative and apply it "positively" in everyday life: "[The principle] bids us to act on the maxim of furthering the ends of rational agents. . . . This positive interpretation is for Kant the basis of positive and ethical, as opposed to legal, obligations" (p. 172).

As Paton (1971) said, "We shall never understand Kant aright unless we see him as the apostle of human freedom and the champion of the common man" (p. 171). If we are truly serious about valuing the idea of human freedom, we must accept Kant's claim that the value of human freedom rests not on our mere existence as living and breathing organisms upon the Earth, but on our power of reason. It is the existence of our free will (or *Willkür*), our existence as rational beings, that requires freedom to be given paramount value. Our rationality and free will are what set us apart from the animal kingdom. And only freedom can enable the exercise of both. So, Kant said, in our acceptance of the value of freedom, we are not only acting in our personal interest in ensuring our ability to think and move about without undue restrictions; we are doing so because of our innate and absolute value as rational beings who possess the faculty of reason. We do not have a duty to respect the reasoning capacity of others because it is the fair or polite thing to do; we have a duty to respect the reasoning capacity of others because we have a duty to honor the value of humanity's capacity for reason.

Once we understand how Kant links our freedom and our duty to honor everyone's "will" to reason, the importance of the concept of transparency in all of our communication with others becomes clearer. "The dishonor that accompanies a lie also accompanies a liar like his shadow," Kant wrote in his *Metaphysics of Morals* (1797/1991, p. 225). Contrary to our conventional cultural claims about lying, which generally say a lie is wrong because of the harm it does to the receiver (or based on its consequences), Kant is largely unconcerned with any *effect* of a lie. Any harm to others caused by a lie may be worth avoiding, but Kant says this harm "is not what distinguishes this vice" (p. 225). Remember that the focus of Kant's moral system remains steadily on our *duties;* he has little concern for making moral judgments on the *consequences* of our acts. Consequences have no power to determine whether an act is moral or immoral, Kant said; that is decided by how well we understand our duties and to what extent we carry them out. So it is not the mere consequences of a deception that justify our rejection of it; rather, a lie or act of deception is morally objectionable because, *by its very nature,* it assaults our capacity for rational thought and thwarts the exercise of our free will. Kant's principle of human dignity culminates, as it were, in the special "moral contempt" he reserves for untruthfulness:

> By a lie a man throws away and, as it were, annihilates his dignity as a man. A man who does not himself believe what he tells another (even if the other is a merely ideal person) has even less worth than if he were a mere thing; for a thing, because it is something real and given, has the property of being serviceable so that another can put it to some use. But communication of one's thought to someone through words that yet (intentionally) contain the contrary of what the speaker thinks on the subject is an end that is directly opposed to the natural purposiveness of the speaker's capacity to communicate his thoughts, and is thus a renunciation by the speaker of his personality, and such a speaker is a mere deceptive appearance of a man, not a man himself. (Kant, 1797/1991, pp. 225–226)

The Immorality of Lies

According to Kant, any possible harm that stems from a lie is not what makes it immoral. It is immoral because *by its very nature* it assaults our capacity for rational thought and thwarts the exercise of our free will.

Kant leads us, with an inexorable logic, down a path that establishes the concept of human dignity as an essence that demands something of us in everything we do. Lying and acts of deception become concrete assaults on the innate dignity that we all require as humans. Transparency, or truthful forthrightness, is not just another vogue word, Kant said (1785/2002); it defines much of what it means to live an ethical life. His articulation of the concept of transparency, through his theory of human dignity, challenges us with a question: Do we have the moral courage to do more than "talk the talk" about how we value truth and integrity, all the while exploiting people and situations when it's convenient or serves our interests? Are we up to "walking the walk" and living our lives with a concern for the dignity and well-being of others in everything we do?

Case in Point: Is Dove's "Campaign for Real Beauty" for Real?

Unilever, the multinational parent company of Dove, created a media sensation with its "Campaign for Real Beauty" featuring thought-provoking ads that raised questions about media portrayals of models and their negative impact on the self-esteem of "real" women. Begun in 2004, the campaign included the "Evolution" viral video that won top prizes at the International Advertising Festival in 2007. Also that year, Dove launched a series of ads featuring "lumpier-than-usual 'real women' in their undergarments." However, both Dove and its advertising agency, Ogilvy & Mather, became the target of sharp criticism when it was revealed that even the shots of the "natural" women were Photoshopped by Pascal Dangin, a renowned master of fashion-photo retouching. "Do you know how much retouching was on that?" Dangin was quoted as saying about the Dove photos. "But it was great to do, a challenge, to keep everyone's skin and faces showing the mileage but not looking unattractive" (Neff, 2008).

Similarly, Kant's moral system lends a force and a substance to the notion of human free will that reveal the emptiness of our tendency to mouth platitudes about our right to "liberty" for its own sake. Freedom is *not* just another word, Kant argued; it *defines* us as moral agents and thereby comes with a serious duty or obligation. If you think about it, the challenge Kant poses here is radical indeed—particularly for such an individualistic, objectifying, commerce-driven culture such as ours. What he is asking us is this: Are we up to the task of taking seriously what normally receives only lip service? Rather than reveling righteously in our liberty to do almost whatever we want, do we value freedom enough to let it define how we treat others? Are we ready to respect limits on our own freedom if that's what it means to meet our duty to allow our fellow human beings to exercise their free will? Are we ready to take on the happiness of others as our own *end?*

In essence, Kant's notion of "duty" to others is really a core principle in the mission claimed by journalists, public relations professionals, and other media workers to "serve the public." This notion of "duty" also is reflected in increasing efforts by journalists and news organizations to respond to calls for greater accountability in what they do. Heightened interest in and acceptance of standards of transparency are changing the way people in the media business do their jobs. In the world of journalism, news organizations such as the *Dallas Morning News* now use blogs to explain newsroom decisions (Willey, 2003), if only in an effort to head off criticism. Individual reporters are using their blogs to provide links to sources and other materials to help readers assess their work (J. Singer, 2005, p. 189).

Editors at the *Spokesman-Review* in Spokane, Washington, have begun "Webcasting" their morning and afternoon news meetings, inviting observers to participate in real time (Rosen, 2005). This heightened interest in and acceptance of standards of transparency is found in the realm of public relations as well, echoing as it does the pledge among public relations practitioners to make sure their service to clients also conforms with the broader "public good."

"By a lie a man throws away and, as it were, annihilates his dignity as a man."

—Immanuel Kant, *Metaphysics of Morals*

It should be apparent that the concept of transparency is more than a platitude. Ironically, a rash of business and marketing books have recently been published that trumpet the usefulness of transparency as a smart business strategy (see Ind, 2005; Oliver, 2004; Pagano, 2004). Business leaders are recognizing that the concept is an effective "means" toward success! A central feature of Kant's argument for why we should all avoid treating people as means has itself become a hot commodity by which companies strive to attain stronger commercial profits.

But as Kant showed us, the concept speaks to the core of what constitutes human dignity and what actions respect or dishonor that dignity. The concept, in other words, should be understood as essential to ethical behavior. And since transparency by definition rests in the nature of our interaction—our communication—with others, it must inform every decision made by those in the media industries.

TRANSPARENCY IN THE MEDIA

For journalists, confronted by an often hostile public, transparency is more than academic; it is an essential element of credibility. Journalistic decisions lack transparency when they serve primarily to protect selfish interests or political power or are justifications rooted in defensiveness. In their book *The Elements of Journalism: What Newspeople Should Know and the Public Should Expect,* Bill Kovach and Tom Rosenstiel (2001) offered what they call the "Rule of Transparency," which roughly is an attempt to apply scientific method standards to daily journalism. The rule calls for journalists to regularly disclose the limitations and methods of their news gathering so that the reliability of their work can be assessed by others.

"Transparency means embedding in the news reports a sense of how the story came to be and why it was presented the way it was," Kovach and Rosenstiel (2001, p. 83) wrote. Insisting on transparency "will help over the long run to develop a more discerning public. This is a public that can readily see the difference between journalism of principle and careless or self-interested imitation" (p. 83). The concept of accountability also has changed for public relations practitioners. The industry has been repeatedly stung by revelations of deceptive tactics in the service of private clients, and these examples often have undermined the insistence by public relations officials that their professionalism requires them to serve the public good, just as journalists claim to do. Increasingly, public relations practitioners are realizing, just as journalists have, that cultivating and protecting one's credibility as a source of information is paramount and ought to drive most decisions. But in public relations, that mandate can be even more complicated, given the obligations to client interests that are often in tension with the call for public service.

Case in Point: Product Placement Makes Shows Real, but Is It Ethical?

Authenticity, of course, is a key element of good storytelling. Filmmakers and television producers understand that watching a character grab a Heineken, and not a bottle with a generic "beer" label, helps maintain our suspension of disbelief. Brands create authentic environments and, thus, lend believability for us as audience members. The ethics question surrounding the widespread use of product placement, however, focuses on expectations of *disclosure*. When is the presence of a brand simply an artistic decision, and when is it a financial arrangement? And is it a problem when we can't tell which? Product placement is so common now that we all know it occurs routinely. Sometimes the insertion of brands into the story is ingenious. Sometimes it is ham-handed. But what are the ethical obligations of producers in their treatment of us as audience members? For some, it may not matter that GMC paid a hefty price to have its models exclusively showcased in the *Transformer* blockbusters. But when we are unable to make our own independent assessment, placement raises questions of respect and transparency for many ethicists. Brand placement disclosure has become routine for some programming—Tina Fey's popular *30 Rock* show disclosed in the final credits which brands "sponsored" each episode. For most of us, product placement is of little concern, but critics argue that behind-the-scenes deals impose artistic constraints to ensure that the film or TV show provides a "friendly" environment for the brand. Over time, this can have a serious effect on the kind of programming we see—programming that emphasizes commerce rather than emotionally moving projects. An example of this tension occurred with the production of *Flight*, starring Denzel Washington as a pilot with an alcohol problem and whose preferred beverage was Budweiser. Fearful of the negative association, Anheuser-Busch insisted that Paramount Pictures alter a scene involving a fraught landing so that the Budweiser label was obscured (Holpuch, 2012). This concern over artistic integrity is why Steven Levitan, a producer for the popular TV show *Modern Family*, said he resisted most pitches by companies to get their brands in the script. "We turn down, I would say, about 90 percent" of advertiser requests, he said. "We get offers constantly. We do very few" (Steinberg, 2012). Media critics and ethicists said this is precisely the problem: The imperative of corporate branding threatens to dominate even our artistic endeavors—especially when audiences can't tell the difference between art and ads. "If movies were completely hospitable to placements, they'd be over as an art form," said Mark Crispin Miller. "In the long run, the practice will only work against the interests of marketers as it worsens cinema" (Galician, 2004a, p. 220).

The question of transparency also confronts advertisers and entertainment executives as the phenomenon of "product placement"—the practice of "embedding" a product, brand, or service into a film or storyline in lieu of airing more traditional commercials—becomes increasingly common. Producers usually charge anywhere from $10,000 to more than $1 million to feature a product in a film or TV show, depending on how the product is shown. In many cases, corporations routinely send agents to huddle with screenwriters and Hollywood producers to find ways to feature products or, in some cases, weave entire storylines around a product. Absolut Vodka did precisely this when it invented a drink called the "Absolut Hunk" and persuaded the producers of *Sex and the City* to build an episode around the product. But critics have called such practices unethical, since audiences are rarely informed that they're really watching paid advertising when they presume they're watching creative programming. "Product placement does pose some ethical concerns and I don't think the people involved with placement like to acknowledge that," said media ethicist Edward Wasserman. "You're playing on people's susceptibility" (Odell, 2007, para. 71, 77).

Journalism and Accountability

Journalists who explicitly value transparency demonstrate that they are continually engaged in examining whether their coverage has fully taken into account the interests of all involved in or affected by their coverage. "Transparency—telling the public how the media gets it stories—has become one of the biggest issues facing newspapers," wrote media writer Eric Deggans (2006) of the *St. Petersburg Times*. "Even as readers accept the hundreds of little facts newspapers print daily, they are increasingly seeking the story behind the big stories, leaving editors to struggle with how much they can comfortably reveal" (p. A1). Veteran media critic William Powers (2006) of the *National Journal* agreed. "Something is happening to journalism that happened to government long ago—it's becoming more transparent. The media's sausage factory now has windows, and everybody's looking in and seeing how news is put together" (p. 53). Steven A. Smith, editor of the *Spokesman-Review* in Spokane, Washington, acknowledged that this may strike many in the media business as counterintuitive, or even counterproductive. But for journalistic credibility, it's critical.

> Transparency—which includes being open about mistakes—can kill rumors and conspiracy theories that breed distrust. It can soften criticism, or at least direct it to the appropriate targets. . . . It can enhance credibility, but only if consistently followed. . . . Raising the window, fessing up, speaking directly to readers with a genuine openness actually enhances credibility. (Rosen, 2005, p. 1)

In May 2005, Smith, the editor of the *Spokesman-Review,* sought to do just that by publishing an extensive "Note to Our Readers" that accompanied an explosive set of stories detailing how the city's mayor, an outspoken and powerful conservative politician in the state, had been trolling Internet sites to seek sex with young men and offering favors to them. The mayor, Jim West, admitted to the Internet activity but denied any criminal wrongdoing, and he was ousted in a recall election seven months later. In his editor's note to readers, Smith wrote, "Today's stories speak for themselves. But I know many readers will have questions. Those questions deserve answers" (Smith, 2005, p. A1). He went on to address several anticipated questions: Is the mayor's sexual orientation or sex life a story? Who are the sources for these stories? Why publish the stories now and not when West was running for mayor in 2003 or years before when he was in the state legislature? Smith ended with providing both his e-mail address and his office phone number.

Journalists are continually making judgment calls and deciding what they think the public ought to know. What they sometimes fail to do, however, is to proactively provide full disclosure about the *methods* of their work as a way to increase accountability, as Smith did in Spokane. "We have, without any fanfare or much conversation, moved into an era in which news organizations are expected to explain themselves," said Alex Jones, a former *New York Times* reporter and director of the Joan Shorenstein Center on the Press, Politics and Public Policy at Harvard University. "Twenty years ago, it would not be expected that the *New York Times* would explain itself. The concept of what accountability is has changed" (Deggans, 2006, para. 9).

Being Aboveboard in Public Relations

Recognizing the value of transparent behavior also requires an understanding that a company's relationship with its public and its customers is more than just a financial transaction. It is a relationship that is built on trust. In 1994, several specialists flagged computation flaws in Intel's new Pentium chip. Company officials didn't respond—until complaints started drawing media attention and company credibility began eroding. Public relations officials are increasingly recognizing that stronger proactive work—demonstrating more transparency in how problems are dealt with—is critical in maintaining consumer trust. "Only through transparent dealings with its public will a tech company be able to build and retain the consumer trust upon which it depends," wrote Eric Armstrong, a public relations professional working in the technology industry (Armstrong, 2005). In particular, times of crisis pose urgent, fundamental challenges, forcing public relations professionals to perform tightrope-like roles as both organizational representatives and public counselors. Avoiding potentially discomforting public disclosure can become a powerful temptation. Yet in such crisis communications, "No comment" is not an option for anyone concerned about credibility, public relations ethicist Kathy Fitzpatrick wrote. "Ethical public relations professionals are forthright and honest and counsel clients and employers to adopt responsible communication policies built on principles of openness and transparency" (Fitzpatrick & Bronstein, 2006, p. 13).

Each year in their introductory classes, countless public relations students read about the tactics of a well-known international public relations firm, Hill and Knowlton (H&K), to generate public support for U.S. military action against Iraq in 1990. H&K, working for the Kuwaiti government through a "front" group called Citizens for a Free Kuwait, was accused of misleading the American public about atrocities committed by Iraqi soldiers in its efforts to "sell" the war (MacArthur, 1992; Wilcox, Ault, Agee, & Cameron, 1999). In their widely used public relations textbook, Wilcox and his colleagues asked, "Should H&K have disclosed publicly the sources of funds supporting Citizens for a Free Kuwait? Is the use of a 'front' organization such as Citizens for a Free Kuwait deceptive and a breach of the [public relations industry] code of ethics?" (1999, p. 78). These are most certainly rhetorical questions. Many public relations practitioners and instructors have been diligent in preaching the gospel of transparency ever since.

But that gospel isn't followed by everyone in the industry. Too often, publicists can spend considerable energy cultivating an appearance of credibility by downplaying or masking sources of information or their roles as advocates. If they can get their message out and maybe even win points in the court of public opinion, they say, the means justify the ends. Who cares if it's not clear who's behind the message? Who is harmed if a message campaign *seems* to be coming from journalistic sources? The fact is that anyone who takes seriously the idea that we all have certain ethical obligations should care about such examples of failures to act transparently. Such deception results in multiple types of harm—to the credibility of the client, to the message, and to the professional image of public relations itself. Because of shady PR practices, the Federal Trade Commission adopted rules in 2009 that require anyone using the web for commercial purposes to identify themselves as advertisers. For public relations, this adds an increased burden of disclosure: No longer can PR firms claim that they are not in control of bloggers who are paid for their promotional posts. For example, a campaign featuring a celebrity touting a hotel chain must disclose whether he or she materially benefited from the promotion, such as receiving a free stay (O'Dwyer, 2010).

Advertising: Authenticity or Deception?

Product placement in television shows, Hollywood films, and other entertainment content has exploded from a $1.5 billion industry in 2004 into a $10 billion industry by 2010, according to some estimates. Marketers realized the potential of using movies as vehicles for products when, in 1982, a cute little alien gobbled up Reese's Pieces in Steven Speilberg's film *E.T.* Sales of the candy leapt 65% in three months. Quickly, Hollywood began courting placement deals with corporate agents. Now, hundreds of companies regularly make product placement agreements with film, television, and video game producers. In an analysis of the biggest movies of 1977, 1987, and 1997, researchers found that "an astounding one-quarter of the running time in top-grossing Hollywood movies contained some kind of brand message" (Galician & Bourdeau, 2004, p. 32). In 2007, the European Commission helped TV networks generate more money by allowing more product placement in programming. In Great Britain, producers are required to carry a "PP" icon to indicate to viewers that what they're watching includes product placements. The United States, however, remains the largest market for product placement, according to a report by PQ Media. Manufacturers and corporations are flocking to product placement as new technology such as TiVo allows broadcast audiences to bypass traditional commercials, and they also claim that such arrangements boost the "authenticity" of entertainment programming.

> In real life, no one says, "Gimme a *beer!*" said independent filmmaker Samuel Turcotte. It's ridiculous not to use a brand in such a case in a movie. Moviemakers used to think that using brand names undermined the artistry of the cinema, but today we know that it undermines reality *not* to use them when they would be in real life. There's a difference between reality and whoring to commercialism. (Galician, 2004b, p. 224)

But critics and ethicists, however, insist there is a fundamental element of deception at work in product placement, making it ethically questionable. There is no question that the use of real brands in storytelling is important for producers to cultivate authenticity. For ethicists, that's not the issue. The issue is empowering audiences with information through disclosure so that we can make our own judgments about whether the "creative" work we are seeing is reduced to a vehicle for products to an unreasonable degree. By making deals with companies and shaping a show to accommodate a particular product, producers are not being fully honest about the nature of the content they're presenting to audiences, opponents say. Assessing the practice, they say, has to take into account the expectations of audiences. If people watching a TV sitcom or a movie presume that the events, characters, and props are the result of a creative or artistic effort when in fact they're watching the result of a deal with an advertiser, they are entitled to feel duped. Media critic and ethics professor Edward Wasserman explained:

> The types of products written into a show really ought to be up to the writer. It's part of their creative vocabulary. What product placement does is auction off elements of that vocabulary in ways that I think are not ethically permissible. It turns what is meant to be a creative artist into a huckster. It's not only the choice of products that's at issue, it's what you do with them. What we see is a widening circle of corruption. A company pays to get Cap'N Crunch on Tony Soprano's kitchen table, but part of the deal is that Tony can't pick it up and throw it in Carmela's face. Products not only have to be present and visible, but they have to be treated in a certain way. You're not going to have producers turning up their noses at a company that is paying for their product to be there. (Odell, 2007, para. 75)

Moreover, companies may well be missing out on an opportunity to engage with audiences in new ways through placement strategies. Morgan Spurlock, famous for his *Supersize Me* documentary on eating at McDonald's for a month, playfully explored the world of product placement in his 2011 film, *Pom Wonderful Presents The Greatest Movie Ever Sold,* in which he suggests that companies suffer from an irrational fear of transparency, or full disclosure, in product placement. More seriously, media critic Mark Crispin Miller added that product placement threatens to endanger high-quality entertainment by turning it into a vehicle for selling:

> You think back to those dramas, those comedies that have stayed with you—that have moved you, tremendously, that you want to see again, that you think about for days. Well, those kinds of works are increasingly unlikely, when the stuff that's on TV basically functions to sell Pepsis, to sell Nikes, to sell selling—to sell consumption. (Goodman & Dretzin, 2003)

Ethicists and media critics are not the only ones who have voiced concern. In 2005, members of the Writers Guild of America, which represents thousands of Hollywood scriptwriters, complained that too often they were pushed to reduce their storyline writing to basically ad copy, saying that "the result is that tens of millions of viewers are sometimes being sold products without their knowledge, sold in opaque, subliminal ways and sold in violation of government regulations" (McNary, 2005, para. 5).

TRANSPARENCY IN CYBERSPACE

The Web opens up virtually limitless opportunities to tap new audiences, connect with them in new ways, network with clients and stakeholders as never before, and open new channels for information and greater levels of interaction. But the Web also means unprecedented scrutiny by audiences and stakeholders, less control of what's out there, and possibly greater and more frequent temptations to communicate in ways that are less than upright or above-board. The key strengths of Web technology—its immediacy, its vast reach—create the perfect climate for "sock puppets": techie parlance for fake Internet identities that are intended to deceive users. The accessibility and apparent universality of the Web also may invite communicators to dismiss or gloss over the ethical requirement of transparency, or assume that such old ethical standards don't really apply to the new technology. They would do so at their peril. Newer, cooler, faster channels of communication are not exempt from basic ethical standards. If anything, transparent behavior is gaining even greater currency on the Web, which presents users with overwhelming information options. Who can people trust? Which sources are reliable? How will you know whether you're just getting a sales pitch?

Generating Buzz in the Blogosphere

Transparency has emerged as a serious issue for bloggers and the marketing firms that would like to cash in on potentially vast online audiences. PayPerPost and other similar marketing organizations regularly pay a fee to bloggers who write favorably about certain products and services. One PayPerPost investor said such relationships are harmless, likening them to product placement in movies. "You put an ad inside the text and it's more of a subtle way of advertising," he said. "It doesn't take away from the blogger" (Friedman, 2007, p. C1). But critics warn that such relationships raise questions about what is paid advertising and what is independent commentary and that deliberately concealing the fact that someone is paying for a post is a failure to meet the moral obligations of transparent behavior. In fact, the Federal Trade Commission (FTC) announced in December 2006 that "word-of-mouth" or "buzz" marketing in which bloggers are paid to publicize or plug something is considered advertising and must be labeled as such. To prevent consumers from being misled into believing they're getting unbiased information, bloggers must fully disclose that they're being paid for certain content, the FTC ruled. "We wanted to make clear . . . if you're being paid, you should disclose that," said Mary K. Engle, the FTC's associate director for advertising practices (Shin, 2006, p. D1).

With the "New" News Media, a New Interactivity

Journalists who began their careers before the advent of the World Wide Web often wonder how they ever managed to do their jobs without it. A savvy surfer can identify key information sources in seconds that, before the Web, could have taken a couple of days to nail down. But the new era of Internet interactivity also has broken down the formerly insulated newsroom in ways both exhilarating and frightening. "Journalists who have fought their way up amid the clutter of traditional media are used to having their opinions questioned, but not with the directness and ferocity that the Web encourages," noted one writer (Carr, 2006). For the most part, immediacy created by the new technology has been transformative in a good way for journalists. Even the fact that stories of newsroom scandals now dominate the news more frequently can be considered a good thing: Such news doesn't necessarily mean there are more ethical lapses, but only that there's greater public scrutiny over the news media. And many news organizations have transformed that new immediacy into more loyal and attentive audiences. In 2003, the editorial board of the *Dallas Morning News* launched a blog that offers readers an unprecedented glimpse into the board members' debates and decisions about editorial positions to take. The number of people dropping in on the blog doubled from 2004 to 2005, with a significant increase in reader e-mails to the board (Hull, 2006).

Such proactive examples of harnessing Web transparency to bolster credibility and expand audiences are getting more numerous. But journalists also have learned the importance of transparency on the Web the hard way. Lee Siegel, a culture writer for the *New Republic,* launched a blog and soon was set upon by venomous critics, particularly those who didn't appreciate Siegel's negative comments about TV talk show host Jon Stewart. In response, Siegel began using the pseudonym "sprezzatura" to lash out. At one point, "sprezzatura" wrote, "Siegel is brave, brilliant and wittier than Stewart will ever be. Take that, you bunch of immature, abusive sheep." One reader responded that "sprezzatura" sounded suspiciously like Seigel, to which "sprezzatura" replied, "I'm not Lee Siegel, you imbecile" (Young, 2006). When magazine editors learned of his deception, they terminated Siegel's blog, and he later apologized for his "prank."

For Discussion

1. Even though Kant's moral system doesn't concern itself with the consequences of an act, how might you make a philosophical argument that would justify weighing the effects of an act when assessing whether it should be considered moral?

2. Kant challenges us to take seriously the notion of full disclosure in all of our decision making, but how practical is this for professional communicators? A key part of the job of journalists, for example, is to serve as an information gatekeeper—to continually make judgments about what information or story is worth their time and what can be omitted. How might we reconcile Kant's charge with these kinds of news decisions that need to be made every day?

3. Are there cases in which some deception or obfuscation ought to be justified, either personally or professionally? How would you articulate a definition for such a category of exceptions?

4. Regarding the controversy over the publication of cartoons considered offensive to many Muslims, how might you argue that censoring such cartoons may indeed pose a greater offense to human dignity, as Kant describes it, than printing them might?

5. Go online and conduct a brief search on the Web for the use of the term *transparency*. How is it most often used and understood, and do such uses correspond with Kant's claims of the term as described in this chapter?

6. In what ways are Kant's uses of the term *free will* similar to or different from the uses of the term *freedom* in much of contemporary political debate?

REFERENCES

American Marketing Association. (2006). *Code of ethics: Ethical norms and values for marketers.* Retrieved from http://www.marketingpower.com/content435.php

Armstrong, E. (2005, June 20). Transparency keeps tech-product flaws from being fatal. *PR Week,* p. 6.

Atwell, J. E. (1986). *Ends and principles in Kant's moral thought.* Dordrecht, The Netherlands: Martinus Nijhoff.

Benhabib, S. (1992). *Situating the self: Gender, community and postmodernism in contemporary ethics.* London: Routledge.

Bok, S. (1982). *Secrets: On the ethics of concealment and revelation.* New York, NY: Pantheon.

Bok, S. (1999). *Lying: Moral choice in public and private life.* New York, NY: Vintage.

Carr, D. (2006, September 11). A comeback overshadowed by a blog. *New York Times,* p. C1.

Deggans, E. (2006, January 16). Media struggle with demands for transparency: News consumers now seek enough information to judge newspapers' reporting for themselves. *St. Petersburg Times,* p. A1.

Fitzpatrick, K., & Bronstein, C. (Eds.). (2006). *Ethics in public relations: Responsible advocacy.* Thousand Oaks, CA: Sage.

Friedman, J. (2007, March 7). Blogging for dollars raises questions of online ethics. *Los Angeles Times,* p. C1.

Galician, M. L. (2004a). A leading cultural critic argues against product placement: An interview with Mark Crispin Miller. In M. L. Galician (Ed.), *The handbook of product placement in the mass media: New strategies in marketing theory, practice, trends and ethics* (pp. 219–222). New York, NY: Haworth Press.

Galician, M. L. (2004b). A rising independent filmmaker argues for product placement: An interview with Samuel A. Turcotte. In M. L. Galician (Ed.), *The handbook of product placement in the mass media: New strategies in marketing theory, practice, trends and ethics* (pp. 224–226). New York, NY: Haworth Press.

Galician, M. L., & Bourdeau, P. G. (2004). The evolution of product placements in Hollywood cinema: Embedding high-involvement "heroic" brand images. In M. L. Galician (Ed.), *The handbook of product placement in the mass media: New strategies in marketing theory, practice, trends and ethics* (pp. 15–36). New York, NY: Haworth Press.

Goffman, E. (1963). *Behavior in public places: Notes on the social organization of gatherings.* New York, NY: Free Press.

Goodman, B., & Dretzin, R. (2003, November 9). The persuaders [Television series episode]. R. Dretzin, B. Goodman, & M. Soenens (Producers). *Frontline.* Boston, MA: WGBH.

Graham, M. (2002). *Democracy by disclosure: The rise of technopopulism.* Washington, DC: Brookings Institution Press.

Henig, R. M. (2006, February 5). Looking for the lie. *New York Times Magazine, 76*(83), 46–53, 76.

Holpuch, A. (2012, November). Budweiser wants off this flight: When product placement goes bad. *The Guardian.* Retrieved from http://www.guardian.co.uk/media/filmblog/2012/nov/06/product-placement-film-cases

Hull, D. (2006, December 5). Blogging between the lines. *American Journalism Review* (December 2006/January 2007), pp. 63–76.

Ind, N. (Ed.). (2005). *Beyond branding: How the new values of transparency and integrity are changing the world of brands.* London, England: Kogan Page.

Jones, H. E. (1971). *Kant's principle of personality.* Madison: University of Wisconsin Press.

Kant, I. (1991). *The metaphysics of morals* (M. Gregor, Trans.). Cambridge, UK: Cambridge University Press. (Original work published 1797)

Kant, I. (2002). *Groundwork for the metaphysics of morals* (A. W. Wood, Ed. & Trans.). New Haven, CT: Yale University Press. (Original work published 1785)

Kovach, B., & Rosenstiel, T. (2001). *The elements of journalism: What newspeople should know and the public should expect.* New York, NY: Crown.

MacArthur, J. R. (1992). *Second front: Censorship and propaganda in the Gulf War.* New York, NY: Hill & Wang.

McNary, D. (2005, November 13). Scribes chase blurb bonanza: Product placement perturbs WGA. *Variety.* Retrieved from http://variety.com/2005/more/news/scribes-chase-blurb-bonanza-1117932866/

McShea, R. J. (1990). *Morality and human nature: A new route to ethical theory.* Philadelphia, PA: Temple University Press.

Meyers, C. (2011). Reappreciating W. D. Ross: Naturalizing prima facie duties and a proposed method. *Journal of Mass Media Ethics, 26,* 316–331.

Mill, J. S. (1961). *Auguste Comte and positivism.* Ann Arbor, MI: University of Michigan Press.

Nagel, T. (1998, August 14). The shredding of privacy. *Times Literary Supplement,* p. 15.

Neff, J. (2008). Retouching ruckus leaves Dove flailing. *Advertising Age 79, 1*(19), 53.

Nell, O. (1975). *Acting on principle: An essay on Kantian ethics.* New York, NY: Columbia University Press.

O'Brien, T. L. (2005, February 13). Spinning frenzy: P.R.'s bad press. *New York Times.* Retrieved from http://www.nytimes.com/2005/02/13/business/yourmoney/13flak.html?pagewanted = print& position = &_r = 0

Odell, P. (2007, April 1). Give me a break: Professor Edward Wasserman weighs in on the ethics of product placement. *PROMO.* Retrieved from http://promomagazine.com/entertainmentmarketing/marketing_ star_struck/

O'Dwyer, J. (2010, February). Be wary about "advertising" in social media. *O'Dwyer's, 24*(2).

Oliver, R. W. (2004). *What is transparency?* New York, NY: McGraw-Hill.

O'Neill, O. (2002). *A question of trust.* Cambridge, UK: Cambridge University Press.

Pagano, B. (2004). *The transparency edge: How credibility can make or break you in business.* New York, NY: McGraw-Hill.

Paton, H. J. (1971). *The categorical imperative: A study in Kant's moral philosophy.* Philadelphia: University of Pennsylvania Press.

Plaisance, P. L. (2007). Transparency: An assessment of the Kantian roots of a key element in media ethics practice. *Journal of Mass Media Ethics, 22*(2–3), 187–207.

Plaisance, P. L., & Skewes, E. A. (2003). Personal and professional dimensions of news work: Exploring the link between journalists' values and roles. *Journalism & Mass Communication Quarterly, 80*(4), 833–848.

Powers, W. (2006, January 6). Win, lose, draw. *National Journal,* p. 53.

Public Relations Society of America. (2006). *PRSA member code of ethics.* Retrieved from http://www.prsa.org/aboutUs/ethics/ index.html

Rosen, J. (2000). *The unwanted gaze: The destruction of privacy in America.* New York, NY: Random House.

Rosen, J. (2005). Guest writer Steve Smith: Fortress journalism failed. The transparent newsroom works. *PressThink.* Retrieved from http://journalism.nyu.edu/pubzone/weblogs/pressthink/2005/11/

Ross, W. D. (1930). *The right and the good.* Oxford, UK: Clarendon Press.

Sheehan, K. (2004). *Controversies in contemporary advertising.* Thousand Oaks, CA: Sage.

Shin, A. (2006, December 12). FTC moves to unmask word-of-mouth marketing; endorser must disclose link to seller. *Washington Post,* p. D1.

Singer, J. B. (2005). The political j-blogger: "Normalizing" a new media form to fit old norms and practices. *Journalism: Theory, Practice & Criticism, 6*(2), 173–198.

Singer, M. G. (1961). *Generalization in ethics: An essay in the logic of ethics, with the rudiments of a system of moral philosophy.* New York, NY: Knopf.

Smith, S. A. (2005, May 5). Stories result of 3-year investigation: Note to our readers. *Spokesman-Review,* p. A1.

Society of Professional Journalists. (2006). *Code of ethics.* Retrieved from http://www.spj.org/ethics_code.asp

Steinberg, B. (2012). Why so many brands want to be in *Modern Family*—and why so few will. *Advertising Age, 83*(4), 2, 36.

Tompkins, P. S. (2003). Truth, trust and telepresence. *Journal of Mass Media Ethics, 18*(3–4), 192–212.

Wilcox, D. L., Ault, P. H., Agee, W. K., & Cameron, G. T. (1999). *Public relations: Strategies and tactics.* New York, NY: Longman.

Willey, K. A. (2003). Readers glimpse an editorial board's thinking. *Neiman Reports, 57*(3), 88–90.

Young, C. (2006, September 18). Journalistic ethics gone astray. *Boston Globe,* p. A13.

CHAPTER 6

Justice

At first glance, it may seem odd for a media ethics text to dwell on the idea of justice. What does justice have to do with the media? If we think of justice in broader terms than merely a concern of courts and lawyers, plenty. As we will see, justice is bound with our general ideas of fairness, which is a key value for much of what we perceive as valid communication. Fairness certainly is a central value in the news media. There are all kinds of ways in which decisions about content on media channels, as well as the behavior of media professionals, can affirm or violate our expectations about fairness. But the concept of justice has a much deeper relevance to media use and behavior than standards of fairness and balance. Justice is a foundation for our idea of what constitutes a successful, working society. Sure, it is the role of the court system to carry out "procedural" or formal justice, but our expectation of a "just" society implies the responsible participation of groups and institutions, including the media. It implies that everyone acknowledge the existence of social values that can, and often should, balance and sometimes constrain our selfish impulses. "One may think of a public conception of justice as constituting the fundamental charter of a well-ordered human association," said Harvard University social philosopher and political theorist John Rawls (1971/1999, p. 5).

This chapter discusses some of the key building blocks of the concept of justice as defined by a range of thinkers and reviews some of their ongoing debates over how society should pursue justice. The discussion then turns to one particular theory of justice that provides a provocative and useful model to help us tackle practical questions. This theory, put forth by Rawls, offers a way to bring the abstract principle of justice to bear on nuts-and-bolts questions about clashing social and economic interests and about unequal distribution of power and goods. His model serves as an ingenious invitation to take the vague, lofty claim of social justice seriously and think in practical terms about how a truly just society would deal with common problems. After explaining Rawls's justice theory, the chapter discusses how this theory can be helpful in grappling with specific kinds of media ethics dilemmas.

Justice is such a fundamental requirement of a functioning society that, when we feel its existence, we rarely give it much serious thought. Theorists since Plato have been preoccupied with what exactly justice should value and how it should function—arguably, it poses a greater concern in any social theory than most other virtues. We have bumper stickers that read, "No Justice, No Peace; Know Justice, Know Peace." There are none that make similar statements about other social values such as loyalty, humility, or prosperity. Justice is one of the four cardinal virtues Plato spoke of in his *Republic* (the other three being wisdom, courage, and temperance). But Plato's writings, similar to Aristotle's *Nicomachean Ethics,* asserted that justice is the most important, the one that integrates all the others. Plato actually described an idea of justice "in the soul" and used the term in a much broader sense as behaving rightly, in addition to the idea of justice as a social value.

Benhabib on Justice

As a prominent political philosopher, Seyla Benhabib focuses much of her attention on the idea of justice. She engages extensively with Rawls's theory of justice. But a problem with his theory, she argues, is that it assumes we all are "idealized"—that is, Rawls talks about "people" as if everyone were model characters with identical concerns and circumstances. In reality, this "generalized other" is a projection of the theorist doing the theorizing and, thus, cannot be applied to the real world. A more useful approach, Benhabib argued, is to try to base our claims of justice on what she calls "the concrete other"—that any legitimate theory must accept "every moral person as a unique individual, with a certain life history, disposition and endowment, as well as needs and limitations" (1992, p. 10). So while she agrees that we should aspire to a "universal" notion of justice, it must be supplemented by an emphasis on caring for others by acknowledging the realities of individual lives. Through her feminist critique, Benhabib argued that male philosophers through the ages systematically excluded women from the "public" sphere, in which justice is central, and relegated them to the "domestic" sphere, as a way to enforce sexist social structures.

> The sphere of justice from Hobbes through Locke and Kant is regarded as the domain where independent, male heads of household transact with one another, while the domestic-intimate sphere is put beyond the pale of justice and restricted to the reproductive and affective needs of the bourgeois paterfamilias. . . . An entire domain of human activity, namely, nurture, reproduction, love and care, which becomes the woman's lot in the course of modern, bourgeois society, is excluded from moral and political considerations, and relegated to the realm of "nature." (p. 155)

Through history, the Western concept of justice has largely focused on the avoidance of harmful action. In his play *Oresteia,* Aeschylus expressed its original meaning with the repeated phrase, "What you do shall be done to you." More detailed prohibitions in the same vein of thought are offered in the Ten Commandments. Leibniz and other philosophers claimed that the Golden Rule, "Do as you would be done by," is the basis for justice. The idea was generally that we should refrain from harming others to avoid harm ourselves. So the avoidance of harmful action was largely the subject of justice. But this is only the most rudimentary understanding of justice as we talk about it now. Philosopher W. D. Ross argued that the pursuit of justice, or "the bringing about of a distribution of happiness between other people in proportion to merit" (1930/2002, p. 26), is one of seven duties that everyone is morally obligated to carry out and is one of several ways that people can and should "produce as much good as possible" (p. 27). One of the most prominent theories about how people develop as moral beings, formulated by developmental psychologist Lawrence Kohlberg (1981), is based on the presumption that we develop an ever-increasing moral sense as our notion of what constitutes justice evolves and expands. What we refer to as *justice* now embraces a range of ideas and theories, including the claims that we have certain rights, that these legal rights are based on moral theory and obligations, and that justice also is linked somehow to ideas of fairness, of equality, of impartiality, and to a notion of social good. But these links are not at all simple.

What role should the goal of social justice play in the decisions that media practitioners make? Is a call to be "just" beyond the practical scope of what journalists and public relations professionals should be doing? Our perception of the role that we feel the media should play in society obviously will greatly influence our answers to these kinds of questions. For example, if we believe that public relations professionals essentially serve a corporate function as image builders and liaisons, we might say expecting them to also be advocates of social justice is too much of a stretch. Similarly, if we perceive the role of journalists to be strictly one of dissemination of information, we might argue that they ought to keep any ideas they might have about what is "just" and what is not to themselves and out of their stories. For the journalist or the public relations professional to claim that justice is beyond the scope of the job is to take an overly narrow view—a view that fails to take into account the numerous different roles that media play in our society. The media system is a significant source of political, cultural, and economic power and, as with all sources of power, is subject to calls for accountability—particularly in a democratic society. In advertising, the increasing trend of "socially responsible" campaigns that link brands with social values or causes implicitly recognizes this reality. Advertisers also have bowed to public pressure to scale back their pitches to children, considered a particularly vulnerable group. The cereal giant Kellogg, for example, agreed in 2007 to stop advertising its most sugar-laden products to children through TV because the practice was perceived as unjustly exploiting children (CBS News, 2007). The ways in which the media behave and the roles they perform (or fail to perform) can greatly influence what society conceives as fair or just. So even if media professionals decline to overtly promote a sense of a "just" society, their decisions will have an impact on people's perceptions of justice.

Case in Point: Froot Loops, Cocoa Puffs, and Ads for Kids

Justice, according to John Rawls (1971/1999), requires special consideration for society's most disadvantaged or most vulnerable. Consumer groups have long attacked cereal makers for unethically exploiting, through multimillion-dollar TV ad campaigns, society's most vulnerable population: children. Bowing to pressure, Kraft Foods, the maker of Post cereals, Oreos, and Kool-Aid, stopped advertising its sweetest products to kids in 2004. Two other cereal giants, General Mills and Kellogg, also curtailed their advertising that targeted kids. Kellogg, for example, stopped advertising its most sugary products, including Froot Loops and Pop-Tarts, to audiences where at least half the viewers are

(Continued)

(Continued)

under age 12. The action came after advocacy groups, including the Center for Science in the Public Interest (CSPI), worried about child obesity threatened to sue the company. David MacKay, Kellogg's CEO, said the company was making the move because of increasing concerns about marketing to children. One CSPI study found 54 commercials for Kellogg products in 27 hours of Saturday morning TV; 98% of them promoted foods that the center said had low nutritional value. But since 2008, children are seeing far fewer ads touting sugary cereals, both on television and on Internet Web sites that previously incorporated brands such as Trix and Lucky Charms in interactive games. Companies such as Kellogg, Burger King, and Kraft Foods have even banded together and agreed not to pay television producers to feature their products in programming targeting children. In 2012, the Walt Disney Company extended this trend, adopting policies of accepting only advertising for nutritional foods on its TV channels, radio stations, and Web sites. The policies meant that some popular products, such as Capri Sun drinks and Kraft Lunchables meals, didn't make the cut and were dropped from Disney venues (Barnes, 2012).

Consider the recent controversy in which the *New York Times* and the *Los Angeles Times* published articles exposing an American antiterrorist initiative that involved monitoring international banking transactions without getting the usual court warrants. The Bush administration argued that the program, run by the Central Intelligence Agency (CIA), was a critical tool in the fight against terrorist organizations and that publishing the articles would jeopardize a legitimate program. Editors held the story for more than a year while considering the administration's case for secrecy and bolstering the story with more reporting. The decision to publish was made because editors felt the government did not make a compelling case for its secrecy because the program raised fundamental concerns about civil liberties, and also because, as the editors of the two papers wrote, "Our job, especially in times like these, is to bring our readers information that will enable them to judge how well their elected leaders are fighting on their behalf, and at what price" (Baquet & Keller, 2006). How might the decision to publish the articles despite personal appeals by the president of the United States have reflected, or failed to reflect, our notion of justice?

CONCEPTS OF JUSTICE

"Justice is the first virtue of social institutions, as truth is of systems of thought."

—John Rawls

The way we have understood justice has changed over time. The Aristotelian view of justice was based on individual morality; now, we understand that seeing justice simply as an issue between wrongdoer and victim is simplistic and inadequate. "Whereas the classical conception of justice focused on the just man, the person who is to act justly, the modern view focuses on more general demands of just treatment and the concept of a citizen to whom just treatment is due," according to political philosopher Sirkku Hellsten (2001, p. 95). Not only has it changed over time, but theorists have also come to split justice into two dimensions—one called "conservative" justice and the other called "reformative" justice. The first is concerned with maintaining order and ensuring that social institutions are able to juggle competing interests. When that is done, everyone benefits and is able to partake of the advantages of the social system. "Conservative justice assumes that everyone benefits from a stable social order, however imperfect, and so it aims to preserve stability," according to philosopher David Raphael (2001, p. 4). Reformative justice, in contrast, is what we talk about when we focus on righting perceived social wrongs or expanding the social system to include or benefit groups that have been historically denied or marginalized. This sense of justice "supplements" conservative justice, Raphael said, by "trying to remove the imperfections, redistributing rights so as to make the social order more fair" (p. 4). The tension between these two regularly triggers social and political debates and culture war skirmishes—many of which involve media behavior. In public relations, corporate representatives who may feel obligated to acknowledge the complaints of a group of boycotting consumers also may have to deal with pressure from executives and stockholders worried that the complaints are unfair and threaten company stability. Similar conflicts arise over decisions in the news media. In August 2002, the *New York Times* began including notices of same-sex unions and ceremonies in its listing of marriages. Editors, in an example of exercising "reformative" justice, noted they could no longer justify exclusion of gay couples and that doing so would amount to politically motivated discrimination. Other newspapers followed suit. But opponents of gay marriage strongly criticized the move as eroding traditional values.

Justice as Desert

We also speak of someone getting their "just deserts," or getting what they deserve. We want justice to be based on merit. Impartiality is a key historical idea here. To avoid showing favor is not to blindly insist on complete equality (because that is impossible), but to ignore inequalities that are "irrelevant" to what someone deserves, Raphael said. "One must not favor the rich and the great out of esteem for their wealth and power, and one must not favor the poor and the weak out of pity for their need and vulnerability," he said. "Impartiality, then, discounts inequalities (apart from desert) and so gives equal treatment to equals and unequals alike" (2001, p. 234). The 18th-century economist Adam Smith offered a useful way to think of fairness and impartiality in practical terms. Smith said fairness is often defined by interested, but still "impartial" spectators, such as a crowd watching a race in which a runner seeks to gain advantage by jostling or tripping his rival instead of relying on his strengths:

This man is to [the crowd], in every respect, as good as he: they do not enter into that self-love by which he prefers himself so much to this other, and cannot go along with the motive from which he hurt him. They readily, therefore, sympathize with the natural resentment of the injured, and the offender becomes the object of their hatred and indignation. (1759/1976, p. 83)

While the idea of justice based on *desert* is clearly a part of our culture, others have argued we also think about basing justice on *need*. Aquinas, Augustine, and others have said a just society is one that acknowledges and works to meet a moral obligation to provide for its less fortunate members. Helping the needy, then, was a requirement of justice as well, they said. Any system that fosters further inequality by rewarding those already blessed with gifts widens the already morally offensive gap between rich and poor. This need-based approach says justice "is to aim at equality and to favor the needy in order to reduce inequality" (Raphael, 2001, p. 5). But this notion of justice is one that continues to fuel political debates. The biblical prophets generally did not speak of justice when they addressed the obligation to help the needy. Need as a basis for a system of justice is not universally accepted. "Everyone of course agrees, and always has agreed, that the relief of need is a strong moral obligation; the difference of opinion concerns only the classifying of this obligation under the rubric of justice" (Raphael, 2001, p. 235).

Justice: It's in the Code of Ethics

In some codes, such as that of the Society of Professional Journalists, justice is a key concern that is explicitly addressed. In others, such as those of the American Marketing Association and the Public Relations Society of America, the concept is implied in statements throughout the codes that outline what constitutes ethical behavior.

From the Society of Professional Journalists Code of Ethics

Public enlightenment is the forerunner of justice and the foundation of democracy.

Journalists should do the following:

- Show compassion for those who may be affected adversely by news coverage. Use special sensitivity when dealing with children and inexperienced sources or subjects.
- Give voice to the voiceless; official and unofficial sources of information can be equally valid.
- Recognize that private people have a greater right to control information about themselves than do public officials and others who seek power, influence or attention. Only an overriding public need can justify intrusion into anyone's privacy.
- Balance a criminal suspect's fair trial rights with the public's right to be informed.
- Deny favored treatment to advertisers and special interests and resist their pressure to influence news coverage.
- Encourage the public to voice grievances against the news media.

The complete code can be found at http://www.spj.org/ethicscode.asp.

From the American Marketing Association

Marketers must do the following:

- Foster trust in the marketing system. . . . It requires that marketing communications about goods and services are not intentionally deceptive or misleading. . . . It implies striving for good faith and fair dealing so as to contribute toward the efficacy of the exchange process.
- Recognize our special commitments to economically vulnerable segments of the market such as children, the elderly and others who may be substantially disadvantaged.

The complete code can be found at http://www.marketingpower.com.

From the Public Relations Society of America Member Code of Ethics

A member shall do the following:

- Preserve the free flow of unprejudiced information when giving or receiving gifts by ensuring that gifts are nominal, legal and infrequent.
- Follow ethical hiring practices designed to respect free and open competition without deliberately undermining a competitor.
- Reveal the sponsors for causes and interests represented.
- Avoid deceptive practices.
- Decline representation of clients or organizations that urge or require actions contrary to this Code.

The complete code can be found at http://www.prsa.org/aboutUs/ethics/preamble_en.html.

Justice as Equality

As the previous references to impartiality and equality suggest, our ideal of egalitarianism also is bound into our expectations of what constitutes justice. For Aristotle, unlike many other theorists, the link between justice and equality is strong and prominent in his writings. Indeed, the Greek word for "equal" is also used to express the idea of "fair." Aristotle said, "There is most room for friendship and justice in democracies, where the citizens, being equal, have many things in common" (cited in Raphael, 2001, p. 235). Arbitrary social divisions based on class, race, and other factors easily offend our sense that "all men are created equal." While theorists continue to argue over what exactly a just society would look like, nearly all agree that a central feature of such a society would be a high degree of egalitarianism—the notion that all people are to be treated equally and not on the basis of social status or other factors that are beyond their control. History is filled with competing efforts to realize this kind of equality, and most developed countries have adopted this ideal. Peter Kropotkin, a 17th-century Russian exile who wrote extensively on moral issues and state control, suggested why equality is implicit in the Golden Rule:

The question is an important one, because only those who regard others as their equals can obey the rule: "Do not do to others what you do not wish them to do to you." A serf-owner and a slave merchant can evidently not recognize the "universal law" or the "categorical imperative" as regards serfs and negroes, because they do not look upon them as equals. And if our remark be correct, let us see whether it is possible to inculcate morality while inculcating ideas of inequality. (Kropotkin, 1887/1970, p. 176)

But actual, total equality has not been achieved and may well be impossible—and may not even be desirable. Equality defined as equal access to opportunity is a laudable goal, but its full implementation would likely require extensive state intervention and intrusion into private lives to an unacceptable degree. And the dangers of a fully realized system of equal distribution of goods are even bigger.

The only way to maintain anything like an equal distribution of wealth and material resources would be by the forceful intervention of coercive authority. . . . Such a situation of total equality could only be attained by the extensive loss of liberty and . . . it would be economically inefficient because it would provide no material incentives that reward effort. (Hellsten, 2001, p. 97)

Justice as Fairness

The idea of fairness, however, comes much closer to what we usually mean when we talk about justice in society. And it is even likely to encompass many of the concepts just mentioned, such as impartiality, the meting out of "just deserts," both good and bad, and equal treatment except when there are relevant reasons for discrimination. It might also include a call to help the needy. But its actual definition is much more elusive. Fairness seems to have a stronger quality of comparison than justice; fairness might be contained in our idea of justice, but it also is apart from it. Raphael (2001) attempted to tease out the distinction:

Fairness is a matter of making or allowing the same provision for each or all of the persons concerned. That does not always apply to a situation described as just: a just punishment is one that fits the crime. You could say that it is compared with the crime and contrasted with heavier or lighter punishments for other crimes; but it is not necessarily compared with other instances of punishment for the same crime. If such a comparison is made and a difference of treatment is found, we say the difference is "unfair"—and we could reasonably add or substitute "unjust." But such comparison is not needed in order to describe the punishment as just in the first place. (p. 237)

So fairness might be described as equality in context—as in the expressions "fair play" or "a fair fight." Fairness also is a trait that depends on agreement. When we say we have won a contest "fair and square," it implies that certain rules of the game were agreed to beforehand that allow everyone to respect the outcome. This is why "justice as fairness" is the foundation for a model of a just society put forth by John Rawls in the 1970s. "In justice as fairness," he said, persons . . . implicitly agree . . . to conform their conceptions of their good to what the principles of justice require, or at least not to press claims which directly violate them. An individual who finds that he enjoys seeing others in positions of lesser liberty understands that he has no claim whatever to this enjoyment. The pleasure he takes in others' deprivations is wrong in itself: it is a satisfaction which requires the violation [of our sense of fairness]. (1971/1999, p. 27)

We now focus on his model and discuss how his approach can help us put all this theory to practical use. Rawls's "theory of justice" not only revolutionized our understanding of the concept but also challenged conventional thinking about the very purpose of society. His work has been called one of the most revolutionary works of political theory in the past century (Fishkin & Laslett, 1979). It provides a useful tool for any serious ethical delibera-tions involving dilemmas that raise questions of fairness and of power relationships.

Case in Point: Google Flu Trends: Mistaking Data for Knowledge

Several years ago, Google offered a service to help people figure out "hot spots" around the country with high occurrence of flu. By analyzing flu-related search questions of Google and the location of those search users, together with doing some other statistical calculations, it produced an estimate of how many Americans had the flu. For the peak of the 2012–2013 flu season, Google Flu Trends said nearly 11% of the population was sneezing and coughing. Yet that turned out to be double the estimate of the Centers for Disease Control and Prevention. What went wrong? Scientists suggested that the heavy media coverage of flu, compounded by the swiftness of flu news going "viral" on social networking sites, led Google's algorithms to present a distorted picture of reality. Google, in other words, focused only on the numbers and ignored the context. "Data inherently has all the foibles of being human," said media researcher Mark Hansen. "Data is not a magic force in society; it's an exten-sion of us" (Bilton, 2013, p. B6).

RAWLS AND UTILITARIANISM

Before Rawls published his landmark work, *A Theory of Justice,* in 1971, the philosophy of utilitarianism dominated most discussions of what constitutes a "moral" society. The principle of utility, articulated most forcefully by John Stuart Mill (1859/1991, 1863/1998) and summarized in the work of philosopher Henry Sidgwick (1907), is this: The general principle that should guide social policy is determined by that which maximizes benefit for the majority of people. The "consequentialist" approach was discussed in more detail in Chapter 2. Having as our object the achievement of the greatest amount of happiness for the largest number of people is clearly a noble thing, and utilitarianism has provided the dominant sociopolitical framework for Western societies since Mill's time. Its effect has been profound, and it has served as the basis for much democratic legislation in general. It also has served as a basis for the judicial system, as it has helped theorists and policymakers balance the rights of many with the potential for some to cause harm to others through their actions. As straightforward as the *political* theory of utility sounds, it has drawn extensive criticism as a moral theory. But critics, unable to come up with an acceptable alternative, had been forced to work within a utilitarian framework—until Rawls. He not only abandoned such a framework, but for the first time, he was also able to offer an alternative argument about what society should strive for that he said is morally superior. Happiness, while a laudable goal, should *not* be the standard by which society is built, he said. Basing a society on the maximization of happiness for the greatest number of people also forces us to think of individuals as one monolithic entity. This is a fundamental fallacy that undermines any claim we might make about what decision will produce the greatest benefit for the greatest number, he said. "Utilitarianism does not take seriously the distinction between persons" (Rawls, 1971/1999, p. 24). He elaborated:

> There is no reason to suppose that the principles which should regulate an
> association of men is simply an extension of the principle of choice for one man.
> On the contrary: If we assume that the correct regulative principle for anything
> depends on the nature of that thing, and that the plurality of distinct persons with
> separate systems of ends is an essential feature of human societies, we should not
> expect the principles of social choice to be utilitarian. (p. 25)

Instead of assuming what would most benefit some "model" person and using such assumptions as the basis for policy, Rawls said we must find a way to discern what basic rules would be widely agreed to. Once we do that, we will have a more rational basis for making policy decisions about rights and responsibilities. Rawls suggested that this more rational basis would be a consensus about justice. Justice, he argued, must be the primary value, the foundation for everything else. He said utilitarianism is morally unacceptable because it goes against the demand for justice in our nature as rational beings. "It is an infeasable moral conception because it misrepresents our nature, viewing us as creatures concerned primarily with desire-satisfaction, and failing to see how important freedom and equality are" (1971/1999, p. 58).

Rawls later emphasized that his system of justice should be understood as a *political* doctrine that uses a moral, or more specifically a Kantian approach, and not as a strictly *moral* doctrine. But this is precisely what makes Rawls's theory so innovative and so useful in ethical deliberation, in contrast to utilitarianism. He requires us to take the idea of social justice seriously and try to envision what it would look like "on the ground" and not just as an abstract concept. Trying to build a comprehensive "philosophy" of justice is not likely to succeed, he said, and would probably not be workable. Instead, he said his "justice as fairness" theory is the most practical: "It presents itself not as a conception of justice that is true, but one that can serve as a basis of informed and willing political agreement between citizens viewed as free and equal persons (Rawls, 1985, p. 230). In these and other revisions and clarifications Rawls made later, he appeared, in some ways, to abandon a Kantian approach that he relied on to make his case for his theory of justice. But while his work has drawn criticism for this, the complaints do not lessen the value of his overall framework for practical ethical decision making.

RAWLS AND A THEORY OF JUSTICE

Rawls's landmark book, while more accessible than many such theoretical works, is still dense, complex, and wide ranging. We focus here on his "justice as fairness" model, which he suggests is an approach morally superior to utilitarianism. While outlining his model, this chapter also explains the overall theory of justice on which the model is based. It is important to remember that Rawls's theory challenges both the idea of traditional liberal democracy, which tends to rest on a utilitarian approach, and the idea of a more conservative free enterprise capitalism, which tends toward perfectionism and, thus, encourages a possibly exploitative economic aristocracy or even social Darwinism.

Rawls acknowledged that some members of society gain special privilege because of natural factors such as talent and circumstances of birth. These inequalities will never be eliminated, nor does Rawls wish they could be. But Rawls said a just society will seek to compensate for these "natural" inequalities by investing its resources with the aim of benefiting those who find themselves at the bottom of society's hierarchy. In this respect, Rawls requires us to think about the very purpose of a society in a way that challenges conventional—and comparatively simplistic—notions of "getting ahead" or unfettered pursuit of happiness. With equal liberty for all as the most fundamental principle, Rawls argued that society's most important aim is achieving social justice. And that means placing the "highest social value" on the needs of the neediest. As he acknowledged, what he is doing is nothing less than challenging some fundamental assumptions of the major political systems of the world, including American democratic life: "Such a view is plainly at odds with the rugged individualism of the unconstrained free enterprise economy, and it is equally at odds with the highly controlled communist or socialist state that submerges the individual's autonomy in the quest for greater social welfare" (Gorovitz, 1975, p. 286).

The Veil of Ignorance

So if we are serious about the idea of justice, how exactly would we go about cultivating a truly just society? Rawls began by offering a way to understand human character and invited us to accept it as reasonable. It is rather easy to do so because Rawls asked us to agree on only a few basic assumptions:

- People have some goals that, given the right to live a life of their own design, they are entitled to pursue.
- Whatever those goals may be, their pursuit is dependent on individuals having what Rawls referred to as "primary goods"—things such as liberty and opportunity, health, income and wealth, and self-respect.
- The satisfaction of human wants depends in part on the possibility of engaging in social interaction with others.

Next, Rawls asked us to envision a group of people who come together and are charged to negotiate fundamental principles for their society. Each individual understands that, while they are free agents in the negotiation and are not being coerced, they will be bound to live by the principles that emerge from the talks. It is important to remember that this is a hypothetical situation; it doesn't have to occur in the real world.

So far, so good. Rawls's criteria are simple enough. Then, he set down some more stipulations for the negotiators:

- Each negotiator is a "rational agent" with general knowledge about how the world works. They are all well informed about psychology, physics, economics, sociology, and other areas of "general" knowledge.
- Each of them has a rational "life plan"—a set of goals about what kinds of things would advance personal interests—but has no knowledge of what that plan might be.
- Each is concerned only with advancing his or own interests and is entirely uninterested in the welfare of fellow negotiators. Each knows neither sympathy nor envy at this point.

Up to this point, Rawls was largely echoing the work of John Locke, Thomas Hobbes, and other social theorists throughout Western history who espoused what has been called the "social contract" theory of political legitimacy. But then Rawls imposes a new dimension. He challenges us to imagine a scenario in which, while the negotiators have "general" knowledge about the world, they are utterly ignorant of particular facts about themselves and others. They know nothing about their backgrounds or their personal characteristics—in short, they know nothing about things that would otherwise distinguish them from one another, including age, race, sex, or ability. And even though, as we noted earlier, they know they have life goals they wish to advance, they have no idea what their specific goals are. Rawls called this new constraint "the veil of ignorance." The purpose of this mental exercise, Rawls said, was to eliminate any opportunity for the negotiators to try to angle for agreement on policies that they know would benefit them at the expense of others. As philosopher Samuel Gorovitz (1975) noted, "No biases can occur among rational deliberators beset by the veil of ignorance, since no such negotiator has any idea whether a biased position will help or hinder him once the veil is lifted and he discovers his position in the real world" (p. 279). Rawls called the odd situation that the negotiators find themselves in, with "general" wisdom about the world and "particular" ignorance about themselves, the "original position":

> The aim is to rule out those principles that it would be rational to propose for
> acceptance, however little the chance of success, only if one knew certain things
> that are irrelevant from the standpoint of justice. For example, if a man knew that
> he was wealthy, he might find it rational to advance the principle that various
> taxes for welfare measures be counted unjust; if he knew that he was poor, he
> would most likely propose the contrary principle. To represent the desired
> restriction one imagines a situation in which everyone is deprived of this sort of
> information. One excludes the knowledge of those contingencies which sets men
> at odds and allows them to be guided by their prejudices. In this manner the veil
> of ignorance is arrived at in a natural way. (Rawls, 1971/1999, p. 17)

On its surface, the "original position" poses quite a dilemma: What in the world would such a group be able to accomplish? But for Rawls, the dilemma is precisely what's needed to set the stage for building a just society.

The First Principle: Maximum Liberty for Everyone

Rawls said the negotiators, stuck in this odd predicament, unsure of how they may fare in life after they agree on principles and have the veil lifted, will consider a variety of possible frameworks. They may consider, as Thrasymachus does in Plato's *Republic,* to agree that society's strongest members will benefit the most. They may adopt a Nietzschean approach that says justice is that which advances the ennoblement of humanity and supports the most advanced members of society. Rawls said the negotiators also will consider adopting a utilitarian approach, deciding that what is just is what provides the greatest benefit or happiness for the largest number of people.

But they will reject all of these, Rawls argued, because they will quickly realize that under each system, there will be some segment of the population that will be systematically underprivileged—and since no one knows where they will end up in society, no rational person would risk being among them. Since all of them know they have life goals even though they are in the dark about what they are, Rawls said the negotiators will realize that any framework of justice will have to provide for basic freedoms first. Any kind of arbitrary deprivation of their freedom would be fundamentally unfair, and they would ultimately agree on an initial conception of justice that Rawls called "justice as fairness." They would adopt their first principle ensuring maximum liberty for everyone. In his later work, Rawls revised this first principle: Everyone is entitled to maximum individual liberty insofar as one person's freedom does not unreasonably interfere with the freedom enjoyed by others.

> ### Rawls: The Veil of Ignorance
>
> A hypothetical condition imposed on people brought together to come up with basic principles for their society that everyone will have to live by once the veil is lifted:
>
> - The negotiators have "general knowledge" about how the world works—they are informed about psychology, physics, economics, and so on.
> - They have no "particular" knowledge about their backgrounds or personal details (including race, sex, ability, or social status) that would set them apart from others. They also are ignorant of their personal life goals.
>
> Rawls called this state that the negotiators find themselves in behind the veil the "original position."

The Second Principle: Distribution Favoring the Disadvantaged

Having agreed that basic justice requires equal liberty for everyone, Rawls said, the negotiators must then consider what to do about scarcity in the world. Granting equal liberty is one thing, but a system of justice must provide a way to distribute the limited goods of the world. Rawls called anything that a rational being could want "primary" goods. If there were unlimited resources for everyone, each person would simply take what he wanted.

But the world is not like that, and the negotiators know that scarcity—of material goods and social advantages—prevails. In a context of scarcity, some principles governing distribution are an essential part of a conception of justice as a virtue of social institutions. (Gorovitz, 1975, pp. 280–281)

So again, Rawls said the negotiators will consider a variety of options. Since they could end up among society's least advantaged when the veil is lifted, they will reject systems that would discriminate against certain groups. This includes the utilitarian approach since any one of them could end up in a minority that would suffer for the majority to benefit. "Now obviously no one can obtain everything he wants; the mere existence of other persons prevents this," Rawls said. "The absolutely best for any man is that everyone else should join with him in furthering his conception of the good whatever it turns out to be" (1971/1999, p. 103).

Rawls said they will then realize that unequal distribution of goods could be acceptable—if the distribution of a good somehow benefits the people who don't get any of it. For example, they may agree that giving the physicians among them more transportation resources—a Jeep or an airplane, say—would actually provide a benefit to those who are in greatest need of medical services. The negotiators would agree, in other words, that any unequal distribution of goods should be based on what would benefit *the least advantaged* in society. They would agree to this, Rawls said, because all would recognize that they could end up in that group. Such goods, he said, "are to be distributed equally unless an unequal distribution of any, or all . . . is to everyone's advantage. Injustice, then, is simply inequalities that are not to the benefit of all" (1971/1999, p. 54).

Not everyone can be president or a neurosurgeon or chief executive officer of a major company. But if everyone has an equal chance to such advantaged positions in society, and if the resulting inequalities are arranged in such a way to ensure that society's worst off will benefit in some way, then these inequalities will be acceptable to the negotiators, Rawls said. And so they will arrive at their second principle: Social and economic inequalities are to be arranged such that

- Any unequal distribution of goods results in the greatest possible benefit to society's least advantaged.
- These inequalities are based in public positions that everyone in society has equal opportunity in attaining.

The negotiators will realize the two principles could conflict with each other: restricting the liberty of some individuals

Rawls: Justice as Fairness

The negotiators behind the veil of ignorance, Rawls said, will come to realize that, at bottom, their plan for society must be fair. This idea of justice as fairness will rest on two key principles:

- Everyone is entitled to maximum individual liberty as long as it does not interfere with the freedom of others.
- Social and economic inequalities will be arranged such that (a) society's least advantaged will benefit, and (b) the inequalities are based in positions that everyone has equal opportunity of attaining.

The negotiators also would agree, Rawls said, that the first principle would always have priority over the second.

(violating the first principle, in other words) may help arrange an inequality that satisfies the second principle. Rawls said the negotiators then would specify that the first principle of liberty had absolute priority over the second and would agree that the principles must always be applied serially—in other words, the first principle must be met before the second one is applied. "This ordering means that infringements of the basic equal liberties protected by the first principle cannot be justified, or compensated for, by greater social and economic advantages," Rawls said (1971/1999, pp. 53–54).

THE POWER OF RAWLSIAN JUSTICE

Rawls put forth his theory not to claim that it is "truer" than utilitarianism but simply as a way to build society with conditions that we all can rationally accept—or at least could be led to accept upon reflection. And his theory is not intended to dictate the details of a society when all the agents leave the veil of ignorance and start tackling practical issues of governance. His principles will not, as Gorovitz noted,

> discriminate between social orders within which the means of production or transportation are privately owned and those in which there is public ownership. But they will discriminate between those that are repressive, subservient to vested interest, or discriminatory, and those that function in the interest of providing every citizen with the best possible prospects of pursuing his life plan. . . . Laws favoring the privileged are excluded as unjust, unless they result in benefits which accrue maximally to the least advantaged. (1975, pp. 284–285)

But at the same time, Rawls did not assume that his model would result in a perfectly just society. This is impossible, he said, and all social systems can only strive to come as close to upholding an ideal sense of justice as possible. Indeed, he said, the eventual political system that is built after the veil is lifted may well suffer from problems of injustice, since "there is no feasible political process which guarantees that the laws enacted in accordance with it will be just" (1971/1999, p. 311).

Rawls also was clear that the work of the negotiators does not end with these two principles. Rawls spelled out that they would have to decide on the government structure and legislative procedures that would be needed to apply the principles of liberty and justice to actual social problems. In his later work, Rawls also said that his model is only applicable to more modern, developed societies, such as the United States.

THE VALUE OF RAWLS FOR ETHICS

One of Rawls's key accomplishments is that he avoids putting forth a utopian model of how society should work. Granted, his "veil of ignorance" is a rhetorical device that may strike some as unrealistic, but Rawls made no claims that such a thing needs to exist—only that we can imagine ourselves capable of "considered judgments" that aren't limited by our selfish interests. He argued extensively that even though the veil may not actually occur, it is *feasible* and, thus, provides a way for us to think about a sense of justice worth respecting. Rawls was very clear in saying people are not inclined to act fairly out of the goodness of their hearts; they have to feel invested in a system that they understand requires them to show a certain behavior toward others because their own welfare depends on that behavior. His "veil of ignorance" model helps accomplish this: Everyone agrees from the start what it means to act under principles of fairness because all understand they may end up among society's least advantaged after the rules are set. This, he says, provides "stability" and the basis for moral action:

> Acting fairly is not in general each man's best reply to the just conduct of his associates. To insure stability men must have a sense of justice or a concern for those who would be disadvantaged by their defection [from the rules], preferably both. When these sentiments are sufficiently strong to overrule the temptations to violate the rules, just schemes are stable. Meeting one's duties and obligations is now regarded by each person as the correct answer to the actions of others. His rational plan of life regulated by his sense of justice leads to this conclusion. (Rawls, 1971/1999, p. 435)

Rawls argued that it is indeed in a person's "selfish" interests to accept his model of justice and act according to its constraints, even when that means accepting limits on personal desires. His argument offered three claims:

1. His principles of justice would bond people together in a positive way, reaffirming our understanding of social connectedness and demonstrating that not only does abandoning a sense of justice harm a community; doing so also can harm friends and associates that we care about.

2. Since we intuitively understand how we all benefit by a well-functioning society, his principles of justice help us maintain its effectiveness and, thus, allow us to continue reaping personal benefits.

3. Rawls, drawing from Kant, claimed that since we are rational beings, we cannot but help to place a premium on justice since that is what is required for us to "express our nature as free moral persons" (Rawls, 1971/1999, p. 501). In other words, not only is following principles of justice for our own good, but it is also part of our nature and is required to regulate our other desires.

Feminist Objections to Rawls's Claims

This emphasis on justice has been strongly attacked by feminist critics as inherently male centered and fatally flawed; they argue that a concern for fairness simply doesn't guide how people relate to each other and make decisions, as Rawls assumes it does. Some have questioned whether the "individual" that Rawls talks about can possibly be human. Political theorist Seyla Benhabib (1992) and others have challenged his claims about justice "on grounds that this emphasis excludes the traditionally female sphere of domestic relations and children" (p. 132). She and other feminist thinkers argued that this separation systematically privileges a male-dominated "public" world and devalues the domestic sphere, resulting in an unequal distribution of power. They also argued that our ethical makeup is more accurately defined by how we think about the idea of caring for others, not pursuing justice. Sociologist Carol Gilligan, in her landmark 1982 book *In a Different Voice,* suggested that long-held assumptions about how people's moral development reflected the evolution in their understanding of justice did not necessarily apply to the experiences of women. She found that many women expressed a moral framework that was contextual and tied to relationships with others rather than lofty principles of justice or fairness. Instead, for many women, ethics meant the ability to put oneself in another's shoes and act on feelings of empathy. Benhabib described this difference as "distinguishing between the ethical orientation of justice and rights and the ethical orientation of care and responsibility" (p. 149). One feminist theorist, Nel Noddings (1984), even went so far as to label "law and justice" as inherently male notions and "receptivity, relatedness and responsiveness" as female ideas.

Gilligan (1987) suggested the two approaches are interdependent rather than mutually exclusive: "The moral injunctions, not to act unfairly toward others, and not to turn away from someone in need, captures these different concerns," she wrote (p. 20). And whether Gilligan's "ethic of care" is a viable alternative to Rawls's justice framework is a subject of continuing debate. "Care issues are genuinely moral," Benhabib wrote, "yet the care perspective does not amount to a moral theory with a distinct account of a moral point of view" (1992, p. 187). This is because "care" is an inadequate basis for moral theory since it cannot be universalized. The objects of our care and compassion can never encompass all of mankind but must always remain specific and personal, according to Lawrence Blum (1988). Benhabib uses the example of Mafia family members, whose family code requires mutual "care" and support but also is based on contempt for the lives and property of nongroup members. A morality of care, she argued, can wrongly defend this exclusivist, tribalist culture: "A morality of care can revert simply to the position that what is morally good is what is best for those who are like me. Such a claim is no different than arguing that what is best morally is what pleases me most," which of course amounts to amorality (p. 187).

JUSTICE AS FAIRNESS IN THE MEDIA

But Rawls was clear that his "justice as fairness" approach means everyone—and every social institution—has an important stake in the topic. Rawls also indirectly addressed the question of *fair access* to media, and his comments are worth noting for both journalists and public relations practitioners. "If the public forum is to be free and open to all . . . everyone should be able to make use of it," Rawls said. "The liberties protected by the principle of participation lose much of their value whenever those who have greater private means are permitted to use their advantages to control the course of public debate" (1971/1999, pp. 197–198). For journalists, this suggests a need to be on guard against the temptation to fawn over the famous and the powerful. For public relations, media professor David Martinson (1999) said it means public relations officials have "an ethical obligation to strive to open the channels of communication to the traditionally underrepresented" (p. 23). For advertisers, it has meant embracing "socially responsible" campaigns in which companies identify products and services with "just causes." It also has meant that advertisers are increasingly embracing the idea of "stakeholder" in its broadest sense, where a company's stakeholders are not just investors, customers, or markets, but the environment, the disadvantaged, and even the well-being of all living things.

Case in Point: Media Slap Down
O. J. Simpson's Pseudo-confession

Twelve years after O. J. Simpson's ex-wife and a friend were found murdered in Los Angeles, the former football star attempted a public resurrection of sorts by writing a book that described hypothetically how he would have killed them. The book, titled *If I Did It*, was published by ReganBooks, owned by the Fox TV network parent company, News Corp., and was shipped to bookstores in 2006, before public outcry forced News Corp. CEO Rupert Murdoch to cancel the project and call it "ill considered." A two-hour interview with Simpson, scheduled to air on Fox stations during November 2006 "sweeps" week, also was canceled after advertisers withdrew and many Fox affiliates refused to broadcast the segment. Simpson was paid $3.5 million for the book deal and TV appearance. Clearly, the Simpson deal was killed only after it became apparent to Fox executives that it was no longer going to be profitable. But the sense of injustice, among both media workers and the public, in allowing Simpson to benefit from the killings was palpable. While Simpson was acquitted for the murders in what many called "the trial of the century," he was later found liable for the deaths in a civil suit and was ordered to pay $33.5 million to the victims' families. Nearly 50,000 people signed a petition on the Web site Dontpayoj.com, demanding that the media projects be scrubbed. "I think that over the long run, people can see the difference between truth and falsity, and that they are repulsed by garbage and material that takes advantage of a horrible situation for material gain," said Fordham University media professor Paul Levinson (Zurawik & Madigan, 2006, p. C1).

Confusion Over What's Fair in Journalism

Journalists traditionally have taken pride in their perceived mission to give voice to the voiceless. Such priority given to the most disadvantaged in society is inherently Rawlsian—in pointing out the plight of society's most vulnerable, journalists hope to provide an overall social good. But many different kinds of dilemmas do not present a clear answer about what constitutes a "just" decision by those in the news media. Recent research has confirmed patterns of reliance on negative stereotypes regarding race and other factors (Poindexter, Smith, & Heider, 2003). And journalists are often accused of unethical behavior when turning their scrutiny to private individuals unwillingly caught up in a public controversy. Rawls's justice theory invites news professionals to think hard about what would be fair news coverage in the "original position," when they must think about the possibility that they could end up on the other side of the camera or microphone. This should not be used as an excuse to shrink from aggressive coverage or to automatically allow complaints of individuals to trump stories of vital public interest. Veteran journalist and former *Washington Post* ombudsman Joann Byrd (1992) explained why there is such a disconnect between the public's understanding of fairness—in terms of people getting the coverage that they deserve based on merit—and journalists' definition of fairness as having nothing to do with what is "owed" to individuals and everything to do with serving a broader public interest. Parents who think their child should be featured in the paper because she won a science fair assume that coverage should be a reward for effort, for example. But journalists see fairness very differently. Byrd explained:

> Organizations with publicity chairs who believe their cause is getting short shrift fall under the same basic criteria for fairness as groups with tickets to sell and people who say their third-party candidate is invisible, the same basic goals as desperate parents whose adorable 3-year-old will die without a liver transplant. Fairness, to these people, is a function of need. . . . Journalistic fairness is more like the fairness of a jury trial or the craps table: It is what you get from a fair, detached procedure. . . . Journalists may not agree on an all-purpose definition of what news is, but we are sure what it's not: It is *not* what serves people who think that fair news coverage is a bigger slice of the pie for their event or their position. News judgment does *not* serve subjects, sources or groups, but the broader public. (p. 106)

Still, when covering emergencies or disasters, journalists often are driven by the desire to capture the greatest amount of drama possible; often too little thought is given to the need for sensitivity. Journalists might take a few moments to envision how, behind the "veil of ignorance," all the parties involved may insist on coverage that (1) gives victims and families more control of news coverage (following the first principle of maximum liberty) and (2) pays the greatest respect to the most vulnerable people in such situations.

Recall the controversy over the articles published about Central Intelligence Agency monitoring of international banking transactions—a decision made after extensive lobbying by Bush administration officials not to run the stories and after the *New York Times* held the story for more than a year while pondering the issue. How might Rawls be applied to this case? Rawls's first principle would require us to insist on making freedom of speech a priority. Failure to do so is a ticket to the tyranny of government propaganda and censorship. Insisting on free speech, even speech perceived as threatening to those in power, requires us to acknowledge that the news media often will publish or broadcast material that will be antagonistic. Second, using the veil of ignorance model, we would need to consider policies that we would want the news media to abide by to ensure that the most vulnerable population in a given situation would be protected. An argument in defense of the Bush administration's insistence on secrecy regarding the bank-monitoring program might suggest that the most vulnerable population in this case might be potential victims of a terrorist attack that might have been thwarted if the program had not been exposed. Therefore, such an argument might make a case that the media had a moral duty *not* to publish the stories. Conversely, an argument in support of publishing them might use the veil of ignorance differently and point to the much larger population of unwitting, presumably innocent, and *actual* victims of the unwarranted monitoring. The news media's first commitment is to the public, this argument might say—particularly when questions regarding basic civil liberties are raised in the course of antiterrorism efforts waged in their name.

Dialogue and Dissemination

Questions of justice often arise for public relations professionals in both their consultations with clients and their dealings with the public and the press. In their book *Managing Public Relations,* James Grunig and Todd Hunt (1984) said that public relations officials tend to be "careerist"—they place greater value on salary, management approval, and job security than on other values associated with professionalism: integrity, accountability, responsibility. In a survey of members of the International Association of Business Communicators, 55% considered it "somewhat ethical" to present oneself misleadingly if it is the only apparent way to reach a goal. Service as an aggressive advocate for a paying client is admirable. But as professionals, public relations practitioners strive to be more than mere publicists; if they take the question of social responsibility seriously, then they also are sensitive to questions of justice. This connection between PR claims that it is a "profession" and the notion of public service central to professionalism was discussed in Chapter 3. A full understanding of the nature of professionalism "enables the professional to avoid many problems which necessarily arise if and when professionals falsely assume that they must act as the unconditionally loyal servant of the individual client at hand," writes Daryl Koehn, who adds that it is this element of broader service to the public, not exclusively to a single client, that "bestows moral legitimacy" (1994, pp. 58, 173). The "veil of ignorance" model offered by Rawls is a useful reminder for everyone in public relations that they are significant players in a social system and that such status requires community-building efforts that take into account the plight of the most vulnerable when formulating communication strategies.

Public relations theorists have touted "two-way symmetrical" models of work as the fairest and most ethical (Grunig, 1989; Grunig & Hunt, 1984; Pearson, 1989). Others, however, question whether such "reciprocal dialogue" is realistic or even desirable. In public relations, such emphasis on reciprocity, in some cases, "saddles public relations with ethically questionable quid pro quo relationships" and results in pandering and doublespeak (Stoker & Tusinski, 2006, p. 158). Dialogue, paradoxically, "can be tyrannical and dissemination can be just" (Peters, 1999, p. 34). Focus on straightforward public distribution or dissemination of information, they say, requires public relations practitioners to keep their eye on the ethics of communication—on trust, source credibility, and responsible action. Media professors Kevin Stoker and Kati Tusinski suggested that the popular "systems theory" of public relations that emphasizes "stakeholders" is morally questionable:

> Only those stakeholders considered valuable to the organization's success or possessing the most valid claims might be considered worthy of dialogue. . . . The irony of ethical communication based on systems theory and dialogue is that its

very emphasis on equality, consensus and agreement could promote inequity in the selection of publics (even those considered most vulnerable), a false consensus . . . and disparate treatment of publics based on [their usefulness] to the organization. (2006, pp. 164–165)

Case in Point: Shades of Green in Marketing PR

Few companies want to be left behind by the environmental sensitivity bandwagon, and as a result, we are bombarded with advertising and campaigns to persuade us that brands really are taking steps to improve or limit harm to the environment. But several companies have opted to spend advertising dollars to project an image of ecofriendliness while making no actual effort to clean up their act. This practice, known as "greenwashing," has been used to describe companies such as Dow Chemical, General Motors, BP, DuPont, and the agribusiness giant Archer Daniels Midland (Allen, 2009). Greenwashing also has attracted the attention of state prosecutors as well as the Federal Trade Commission (Kewalramani & Sobelsohn, 2012). However, debate continues over when companies cross the line from honest image cultivation to disingenuous greenwashing.

Branding and Justice in Ads

More than ever, corporations are scrutinized and monitored by consumers who expect corporate responsibility and responsiveness to social issues. Customers want to know how company profits are used. They want to assess a company's environmental impacts. And increasingly, economic power is translated into political power as consumers seek companies that reflect their social interests and shun those that don't. Call it pocketbook justice. Consequently, the way companies promote their brands is changing. "Branding is no longer only a relationship between the brand and the consumer; instead, the branding process can involve information related to both the integrity and the ethical behavior of the corporation producing the brand," Sheehan wrote (2004, p. 251). So we see advertising by BP that never mentions British Petroleum but touts an enterprise that is "Beyond Petroleum" and is defined by a profound environmental sensitivity. One recent ad featured a construction worker who is quoted, "I figure that the oil companies pay the motor companies not to put out a vehicle that's cleaner, healthier for our environment," and then provides information that suggests BP is a different kind of oil company.

Advertisers are increasingly driven to show consumers that they're committed to supporting "just causes" and not simply increasing profit margins. Kenneth Cole ads, for example, feature messages on AIDS awareness and gun control. Retail giant Target advertises that it donates 1% of sales to local schools. After the September 11, 2001, attacks, Revlon and other companies pledged a portion of their profits to victims. Conversely, companies are sometimes forced to counter negative images with new marketing in the face of consumer retribution for perceived examples of misbehavior. Nike suffered when consumer groups publicized claims that the footwear manufacturer relied on Asian sweatshops, which offended many people's sense of justice and corporate responsibility. In 2010, advertising watchdog units forced Tyson, the chicken products giant, to remove television commercials for chicken nuggets that showed children pushing away nutritious meals, only becoming happy when presented with chicken nuggets. The Children's Advertising Review Unit, a policing agency of the ad industry, said the ads were clearly targeted toward children under 12 and discouraged them from pursuing well-balanced diets.

JUSTICE IN CYBERSPACE

The idea of justice often is understood as a feature of our political system, but how is our use of technology related to justice? Contrary to conventional wisdom, technology is neither value-free or politically neutral (Barney, 2005; Christians, 1989). Technology should be understood broadly, technology expert Darin Barney said, as a "political outcome" that springs from the interests of scientists, innovators, investors, and other players in a web of "relationships and institutions in and through which power is differentially . . . distributed" (2005, p. 656). Cell phone technology, for instance, did not "arise as if by magic from the disinterested progress of science," but from a complex political, social, and economic context. Media ethicist Clifford Christians (1989) elaborated on this point:

> [Technological tools] combine specific resources—know-how, materials, and energy—into unique entities, with unique sets of properties and capabilities. Any technological object, therefore, embodies decisions to develop one kind of knowledge and not some others, to use certain resources and not others, to use energy in a certain form and quantity and not some other. There is no purely neutral or technical justification for all these decisions. Instead, they arise from conceptions of the world, themselves related to such issues as permissible uses, good stewardship, and justice. (p. 125)

The way we use new media technologies, then, such as blogs, online interactive news sites, and customized search engines that track buying patterns or political interests, *do* in fact have a potential to either promote or threaten our idea of social justice.

News and the Web

What does it mean for journalists to "serve their communities" when the Internet is radically changing our very definition of community? The ability to customize news has accelerated the trend of audience fragmentation, with everyone increasingly "balkanizing" themselves by limiting their exposure to news based on their narrow interests. At the same time, the Web's rapid diffusion of information through these groups may exaggerate the effect of news. Because of active online, issue-oriented communities, coverage of something at one place has more impact in other regions. As a result, Web-based communication "may ultimately contribute to an intensification of conflict," according to R. Kelly Garrett (2006, para. 19), an information technology researcher.

The Web has flattened geography, enabling online communities to spring up based on a wild range of affiliations including interests, hobbies, and politics. This has presented new opportunities to serve—print and broadcast organizations have scrambled to stake a presence in the blogosphere with their staff bloggers on topics ranging from politics to pets. But it poses new problems, too. How can the freewheeling, opinionated culture of blogging mesh with traditional journalism standards? The exciting interactivity of the Web is challenging journalists of all stripes to reconsider their commitment to "giving voice to the voiceless." In the rush to use the online world, journalists also must be careful about making dangerous assumptions about who exactly they are serving. While Internet access is rapidly expanding and is taken for granted by many, it is not ubiquitous. Globally, policymakers continue to be worried by a widening "digital divide" that separates information technology–savvy societies from others. In many African and southeast Asian countries, fewer than 1% of the population enjoy Internet access. And even if these populations could log on, they're not equipped to understand most of the content they would find. This global inequality in access and content raises major questions of social justice. "The Internet dramatically lowers barriers to entry into the marketplace of ideas," wrote Andrew Chadwick (2006), a political theorist. "Yet there are vast regions around the world and large swaths of the populations of wealthy countries whose cultures are not adequately reflected in the online environment. . . . The content divide reinforces the physical access divide, creating a vicious circle of exclusion" (p. 53).

"Stealth" Media Campaigns

Public relations professionals, like journalists, also must be mindful of what constitutes a just use of the media system. The codes of both groups cite the need to maintain and contribute to a robust "marketplace of ideas." However, "stealth" communication campaigns or manipulative strategies can raise questions about equal treatment and fairness, particularly in the freewheeling blogosphere. While such tactics may advance client interests, they also can do so at the expense of other people and their ability to use media content effectively. Public relations workers at Walmart, seeking to counter recent negative news coverage about the chain's low wages and health benefits, began "feeding" bloggers tips and suggested topics that reflected positively on the company. The material, however, was not attributed to Walmart sources. Glenn Reynolds, the founder of Instapundit.com, said that strategy appeared to violate a basic blogosphere rule: "If I reprint something, I say where it came from," he said. "A blog is about your voice, it seems to me, not somebody else's" (Barbaro, 2006, p. C1). Such stealth advocacy campaigns, posing as sponsor-free content, have the potential to corrupt the marketplace and threaten the idea of "just" use of media, putting audiences at a disadvantage in making independent judgments about which claims are credible or unbiased and which are not.

While advertisers understand the importance of cultivating brand loyalty among young consumers, the debate over what strategies targeting youth are appropriate continues. A recent Federal Trade Commission report criticized developers of popular educational and gaming apps for failing to give parents basic explanations about the personal information they collect. Among 200 children's apps available on Google and Apple platforms, only 20% reported their data collection practices; such practices could be used to find or contact children or track their activities across different apps without their parents' knowledge or consent, regulators warned (Singer, 2012).

For Discussion

1. Describe the differences among systems of justice based on desert, on need, and on equality.

2. Explain how Rawls's concept of "justice as fairness" is different from utilitarianism.

3. In his "veil of ignorance" model, Rawls said negotiators have "general" knowledge about how the world works and yet are ignorant about their personal characteristics that would set them apart from one another. How might this scenario be used by public relations officials to draw a crisis communication plan for a multinational corporation?

4. How might the "veil of ignorance" scenario be used by a news organization to help write guidelines for covering a major disaster, such as a terrorism incident or an earthquake that strikes a metropolitan area?

5. Do you think Rawls's principle of social justice suggests that the news media are morally obligated to be more aggressive in spotlighting examples of injustice and in advocating for social change? Why or why not?

6. Think about how you use Web-based technologies to get news and information. Can you think of examples of how these new technologies raise possibilities for media use that could be considered unjust according to the principles discussed in this chapter?

In contrast, public relations theorist Robert Heath (2001) argued that public relations practitioners with a proper understanding of the responsible use of rhetoric embody the notion of justice in their advocacy work. Rhetoric, he said, helps groups create and identify shared meanings through dialogue and "empowers participants." "It explains how public relations helps to establish marketplace and public policy zones of meaning" and requires public relations practitioners to consider *how* they can responsibly create meanings that "justify norms and build relationships vital to society" (p. 33).

REFERENCES

Allen, A. (2009, April 2). The "green" hypocrisy: How Americas corporate environment champions pollute the world. *24/7 Wall St.* Retrieved from http://247wallst.com/2009/04/02/the-%E2%80%9Cgreen%E2%80%9D-hypocrisy-america%E2%80%99s-corporate-environment-champions-pollute-the-world/

Baquet, D., & Keller, B. (2006, July 1). When do we publish a secret? *New York Times,* p. A15.

Barbaro, M. (2006, March 7). Wal-Mart enlists bloggers in its public relations campaign. *New York Times,* p. C1.

Barnes, B. (2012, June 5). Promoting nutrition, Disney to restrict junk-food ads. *New York Times,* p. B1.

Barney, D. (2005). Commentary: Be careful what you wish for: Dilemmas of democracy and technology. *Canadian Journal of Communication, 30,* 655–664.

Benhabib, S. (1992). *Situating the self: Gender, community and postmodernism in contemporary ethics.* London, England: Routledge.

Bilton, N. (2013, February 25). Data without context tells a misleading story. *New York Times,* p. B6.

Blum, L. A. (1988, April). Gilligan and Kohlberg: Implications for moral theory. *Ethics, 98,* 472–491.

Byrd, J. (1992). Fair's fair—unless it isn't. *Media Studies Journal, 6*(4), 103–112.

CBS News. (2007, June 14). *Kellogg won't market sugary cereals to kids.* Retrieved from http://cbsnews.com/stories/2007/ 06/14/health/printable2926923.shtml

Chadwick, A. (2006). *Internet politics: States, citizens and new communication technologies.* New York, NY: Oxford University Press.

Christians, C. G. (1989). A theory of normative technology. In E. F. Byrne & J. C. Pitt (Eds.), *Technical transformation: Contextual and conceptual implications* (pp. 123–139). Dordrecht, The Netherlands: Kluwer Academic.

Fishkin, J., & Laslett, P. (1979). *Philosophy, politics and society* (5th ed.). Oxford, UK: Basil Blackwell.

Garrett, R. K. (2006). Protest in an information society: A review of literature on social movements and new ICTs. *Information, Communication & Society, 9*(2), 202–224.

Gilligan, C. (1982). *In a different voice: Psychological theory and women's development.* Cambridge, MA: Harvard University Press.

Gilligan, C. (1987). Moral orientation and moral development. In E. F. Kittay & D. T. Meyers (Eds.), *Women and moral theory* (pp. 19–33). Totowa, NJ: Rowman & Littlefield.

Gorovitz, S. (1975). John Rawls: A theory of justice. In A. de Crespigny & K. Minogue (Eds.), *Contemporary political philosophers* (pp. 272–289). New York, NY: Dodd, Mead.

Grunig, J. E. (1989). Symmetrical presuppositions as a framework for public relations theory. In C. Botan & V. Hazelton (Eds.), *Public relations theory* (pp. 17–34). Hillsdale, NJ: Lawrence Erlbaum.

Grunig, J. E., & Hunt, T. (1984). *Managing public relations.* New York, NY: Holt, Rinehart & Winston.

Heath, R. L. (2001). A rhetorical enactment rationale for public relations: The good organization communicating well. In R. L. Heath (Ed.), *Handbook of public relations* (pp. 31–50). Thousand Oaks, CA: Sage.

Hellsten, S. (2001). Theories of distributive justice. In R. Chadwick (Ed.), *The concise encyclopedia of ethics in politics and the media* (pp. 94–105). San Diego, CA: Academic Press.

Kewalramani, D., & Sobelsohn, R. J. (2012, March 20). Greenwashing: Deception claims of "eco-friendliness." *Forbes.* Retrieved from http://www.forbes.com/sites/realspin/2012/03/20/greenwashing-deceptive-business-claims-of-eco-friendliness/

Koehn, D. (1994). *The ground of professional ethics.* New York, NY: Routledge.

Kohlberg, L. (1981). *The philosophy of moral development: Moral stages and the idea of justice.* Cambridge, MA: Harper & Row.

Kropotkin, P. (1970). Anarchist communism: Its basis and principles. In R. N. Baldwin (Ed.), *Kropotkin's revolutionary pamphlets.* New York, NY: Dover. (Original work published 1887)

Martinson, D. L. (1999, Winter). Is it ethical for practitioners to represent "bad" clients? *Public Relations Quarterly,* 22–25.

Mill, J. S. (1991). On liberty. In J. Gray (Ed.), *"On liberty" and other essays* (pp. 23–128). New York, NY: Oxford University Press. (Original work published 1859)

Mill, J. S. (1998). Utilitarianism. In R. Crisp (Ed.), *Utilitarianism* (pp. 47–107). Oxford, UK: Oxford University Press. (Original work published 1863)

Noddings, N. (1984). *Caring: A feminine approach to ethics and moral education.* Berkeley: University of California Press.

Pearson, R. (1989). Business ethics as communication ethics: Public relations practice and the idea of dialogue. In C. Botan & V. Hazelton (Eds.), *Public relations theory* (pp. 111–131). Hillsdale, NJ: Lawrence Erlbaum.

Peters, J. D. (1999). *Speaking into the air: A history of the idea of communication.* Chicago, IL: University of Chicago Press.

Poindexter, P. M., Smith, L., & Heider, D. (2003). Race and ethnicity in local television news: Framing, story assignments and source selections. *Journal of Broadcasting & Electronic Media, 47*(4), 524–536.

Raphael, D. D. (2001). *Concepts of justice.* Oxford, UK: Clarendon Press.

Rawls, J. (1985). Justice as fairness: Political not metaphysical. *Philosophy and Public Affairs, 14,* 223–251.

Rawls, J. (1999). *A theory of justice.* Cambridge, MA: Belknap Press of Harvard University. (Original work published 1971)

Ross, W. D. (2002). *The right and the good* (P. Stratton-Lake, Ed.). Oxford, UK: Clarendon Press. (Original work published 1930)

Sheehan, K. (2004). *Controversies in contemporary advertising.* Thousand Oaks, CA: Sage.

Sidgwick, H. (1907). *The methods of ethics.* London, England: Macmillan.

Singer, N. (2012, December 11). Children's apps fall short on parental disclosure, U.S. says. *New York Times,* p. B1.

Smith, A. (1976). *The theory of moral sentiments* (D. D. Raphael & A. L. Macfie, Eds.). Oxford, UK: Clarendon Press. (Original work published 1759)

Stoker, K. L., & Tusinski, K. A. (2006). Reconsidering public relations' infatuation with dialogue: Why engagement and reconciliation can be more ethical than symmetry and reciprocity. *Journal of Mass Media Ethics, 21*(2–3), 156–176.

Zurawik, D., & Madigan, N. (2006, November 21). Simpson book, TV special canceled: News Corp. drops plans amid public, station outrage. *Baltimore Sun,* p. C1.

CHAPTER 7

Harm

$\mathbf{A}$s difficult as it may be to believe—given widespread examples of news stories, graphic photos, and advertising that are arguably harmful or insensitive—most media practitioners are continually mindful of the need to minimize potential harm, avoid outright harm to people, or at least seriously weigh claims of harm. Most advertisers don't set out to drive away potential customers by being harmful or insensitive; they just want to be provocative, but they may fail to fully appreciate the impact of their work. Journalists who cover law enforcement regularly agree not to include in their stories details that could jeopardize an ongoing investigation when police make a compelling argument that doing so would undermine their case. Respected public relations officials push their clients to make public safety a top priority, even when doing so may run counter to their client's immediate interests. These examples of using communication channels in responsible ways should not be surprising. They are rooted in broad, long-standing moral principles about our obligations to others. Many philosophers and social theorists have offered different arguments for why a concern for potential harm should be an intrinsic part of all our social interactions. A few notable ones include the following:

- Immanuel Kant (1785/2002) argued that, as moral agents, we are duty-bound to give all the respect to others that the idea of human dignity demands for everyone. This means treating others as "ends" in themselves and never merely as a "means" to further our goals. For Kant, any action that undermined people's capacity for reason and their ability to exercise free will violated this requirement and, thus, was immoral. He went further, saying that, when possible, we also have a duty to *advance* the interests of other people, since by doing so we can help maximize their capacity to exercise free will. So minimizing harm, for Kant, is only the starting point for determining what it means to be a moral person.
- John Stuart Mill (1859/1991) included in his theory of utility the so-called harm principle, which states that the only purpose for which power can be rightfully exercised over community members against their will is to prevent harm to others. While Mill was concerned mostly with building a framework that allows government to limit someone's freedom only for the protection of others, many theorists since have explored what exactly should fall under Mill's category of

preventing harm. Several thinkers, as we shall see, caution against using the term *harm* too loosely because doing so invites paternalistic thinking and unreasonable restrictions on liberty.

- William D. Ross (1930/2002) outlined a moral system to help us understand what constitutes goodness by defining seven essential duties we have as moral agents, such as promise keeping, reparation, and gratitude. Another of his duties is a duty of "not injuring others." Ross called these obligations "*prima facie* duties" because while all of them are relevant in determining what is "right," they can indeed conflict. Ross and others have argued that we must reason our way to why one duty should "override" others in a particular case.

W. D. Ross on Harm

In a more perfect world, each one of us would, when confronted with a dilemma, have all the facts, options, and possible outcomes and consequences laid out in front of us. But we are not omniscient. Even the most morally upright people will make mistakes because of lack of information, miscommunication, misperception, and so on. This is one reason why the philosopher W. D. Ross listed "nonmaleficence," or avoiding harm to others, as one of the central duties we are obligated to honor. Other duties include promise keeping, justice, gratitude, and self-improvement. All of them, Ross said, are prima facie duties: They are self-evident to any individuals who are serious about their existence as moral agents. The duty of nonmaleficence is a bit different from most of the other duties, however. While the others (except for the duty of beneficence, or charitable conduct) get their "moral weight" from previous acts, avoiding harm is, as Meyers (2003) described, "forward-looking"—it gets its moral weight from anticipated outcomes of a decision. Ross also said that avoiding harm should be a stronger guide for our behavior than beneficence. One of the reasons Ross argued that avoiding harm must have major moral weight is that it helps explain why even the best of intentions can result in harm or evil, and so any moral theory that only considers *consequences* to have moral value is inadequate. "Any particular act will in all probability in the course of time contribute to the bringing about of good or evil for many human beings, and thus has a *prima facie* rightness or wrongness of which we know nothing," Ross (1930/2002, p. 31) wrote. Meyers (2003) added, "Even the most duty-bound, more morally committed person will make mistakes . . . but such a person should not be held morally accountable for those mistakes" (p. 94).

But of course simply mouthing a commitment not to harm others doesn't help us much. Disagreements and competing claims about what exactly constitutes "harm" often form a central issue in ethical dilemmas. How we see harm is closely tied to what moral philosopher Marion Smiley (1992) calls our "valuation of personal integrity"—how we define goodness in ourselves and others through the relative weight we place on values such as autonomy and self-sacrifice. In the clash of values that defines all ethical problems, it is the idea of potential or actual harm and our desire to avoid or minimize it that conflict with other competing values such as truth telling, public service, and accountability. "While the prevention of harm is clearly of value to most people, so too is the ability of individuals to guide their own lives according to the projects that they have established for themselves," Smiley said. "The problem is that these projects do not always coincide with the prevention of harm. Hence, we are forced to balance the two in ways that are never totally satisfactory" (p. 114). Countless media ethics dilemmas show us a difficult, murky gray area in which this commitment is not easy to translate into practice. Who exactly might be harmed by a particular decision? On what are they basing this claim of possible harm? Will a relatively minor harm suffered by one individual or group spare a larger population much more serious harm? What exactly constitutes this broad notion of harm, and who gets to decide? And how can journalists and public relations officials make these decisions without being paternalistic and condescending—without assuming they know best what their audiences need even if people object?

Harm: How Is It Defined?

According to many theorists, it *should* include

- Acts that explicitly "set back" someone's interest.
- Acts that undermine someone's human dignity.
- Wrongful acts that may not explicitly cause harm, such as trespassing.

It *should not* include

- Unhappy or unwanted physical or mental states.
- Acts that offend, annoy, or hurt one's feelings.
- Acts that shock, anger, or embarrass someone.

When trying to determine whether doing something may pose harm and how it might be avoided or minimized, it is critical to have a solid understanding of what harm *is*—what kinds of behaviors or actions the concept of harm should be understood to include and what it does not cover. The concept of harm has multiple dimensions and multiple possible meanings. Public relations practitioners must be mindful of information and claims that can pose a very real threat of harm to a client's business viability or public image, threats of harm to their long-term professional credibility, and threats to the broader public interest. Journalists must weigh claims of harm from sources and news subjects as well as from audience members. To be sure, it is the duty of all professionals who use the media to act responsibly in minimizing harm and avoiding unnecessary harm. But our ability to do so depends on the clarity of our understanding of exactly what harm is. As media consumers, we are often quick to pass judgment on practices we deem "harmful" without fully grasping the nature of those practices. This routinely happens with journalists documenting events that make us uncomfortable. During a civil rights march in Selma, Alabama, a photographer for *Life* magazine witnessed sheriff's deputies shoving children to the ground. Instead of documenting the actions of the deputies, the photographer stopped taking photos and assisted the children. Martin Luther King Jr. heard about the incident and spoke with the photographer: "The world doesn't know this happened, because you didn't photograph it. I'm not being cold-blooded about it, but it is so much more important for you to take a picture of us getting beaten up than for you to be another person joining in the fray" (Smith, 2008, p. 438).

Often, tossing around broad, general claims of possible harm without fully understanding what is meant serves only to muddy our ability to reason through the rhetoric. In the context of media, the specific harm of a decision can be particularly slippery to grasp, since it often involves assumptions about possible effects of media content—whether it be a graphic photo, a racy ad, or coverage of a hot-button issue—on unseen audience members. In public relations, it is commonly argued that decisions to disclose (or not to disclose) information can potentially "harm" a client, or the public interest, or someone's reputation, or a firm's credibility. In journalism, arguments often flare over whether a controversial or insensitive article or photo "harms" a news subject by invading privacy, or whether controversial content "harms" readers by offending them.

WHAT CONSTITUTES HARM?

Should all of these possibilities be put under the umbrella of possible harm? In general, no. The idea of consent is a key notion in all of the cases just mentioned; *Volenti non fit injuria* ("To one who has consented no wrong is done"), Aristotle stated in his *Nicomachean Ethics*. This approach has been a cornerstone of law ever since. Socrates and the Stoics argued that the only harm that should concern us is the "moral harm" we commit when we "degrade" or "corrupt" a person—even if by doing so that person somehow benefits or profits. Epictetus even argued that it was so harmful simply to have a "poor character" that he thought any legal punishment for resulting acts was redundant. Such a person is punished enough, he argued, just by being the sort of person he was. Since then, several theorists have been concerned about building a universal framework for moral responsibility for the assessment of harm and, when harm could have been prevented, establishing standards to make judgments about the "blameworthiness" of anyone who chooses not to prevent harm. Philosopher John Harris (1973) claimed that to discover that a person is morally responsible for external harm is to discover that she is both causally responsible for it and morally to blame. Several theorists have cautioned that, for good public policy, we must use a definition of *harm* that is more specific than the way many armchair media critics may understand it.

In media, harm can take several forms. Consider *To Catch a Predator,* the controversial series on NBC's *Dateline* magazine program. The show quickly became a ratings booster when it began in 2004. NBC hired a pedophile watchdog group, Perverted Justice, to pose as girls and boys in chat rooms, engage in sexual conversations, and lure pedophiles to a sting house equipped with hidden microphones and cameras. The show's host, Chris Hansen, then would confront them. In 2006, the show began working closely with local police, whose officers would swoop in and arrest the sex offender suspects.

By August 2007, more than 250 men had been arrested in the sting operations. Slightly fewer than half had been convicted of a crime. But problems began in November 2006, during sting operations with police in Murphy, Texas. The four-day sting led to 25 arrests.

Perverted Justice decoys realized that one man engaging in sexual online chat with them was a local prosecutor, Louis Conradt. Conradt did not take the bait and go to the sting house. Instead, local police SWAT team members—followed by an NBC camera crew—surrounded his house and broke down the door. Conradt shot himself in the head. Rival ABC news-magazine show *20/20* aired an investigative story that suggested NBC producers had crossed the line in their collusion with local police to get a good show. NBC faced two lawsuits regarding the show. And all of the charges against the two dozen men arrested in the Murphy sting have been dropped because of questions surrounding the legitimacy of evidence gathered through the show.

By late 2007, NBC appeared to be scaling back its commitment to the show, dramatically decreasing the number of operations aired compared with previous years. And critics as well as others involved in the show have pointed to evidence suggesting that the show resulted in several types of harm:

- *Harm to NBC's journalistic reputation.* Most journalists are extremely wary of being perceived as working as an arm of the law, believing that such a perception seriously undermines their credibility. The *To Catch a Predator* segments fitted cameras and microphones onto police officers, and two Murphy police detectives involved in the show said local police officials allowed NBC producers to call the shots on the sting operations to ensure dramatic footage. In May 2007, a former *Dateline* producer filed a lawsuit against NBC, claiming that she was fired because she opposed what she called the program's "unethical practices."
- *Harm to subjects of news coverage.* While no one is eager to defend suspected pedophiles, the show encouraged audiences to "convict" them without due process. Their reputations—including those who were never charged or convicted—were irrevocably damaged. Conradt obviously suffered the ultimate form of physical harm. Referring to the damage done by the show, one judge concluded that there were sufficient facts to suggest Conradt's suicide was foreseeable and that "the police officers and NBC acted with deliberate indifference and in a manner that would shock one's conscience" (B. Ross & Walter, 2008).
- *Harm to the public's trust in law enforcement.* After Conradt's suicide, his sister, Patricia, sued NBC News in an effort to hold the network liable for her brother's death. She argued that NBC was irresponsible and contributed to the alleged violation of her brother's civil rights. In February 2008, a federal judge refused to dismiss the $105 million suit, ruling that "a reasonable jury could find that NBC crossed the line from responsible journalism to irresponsible and reckless intrusion into law enforcement" (B. Ross & Walter, 2008). Conradt agreed to drop her case when NBC settled the lawsuit for an undisclosed amount in June 2008. Ethics consultant Jack Marshall (2007) argued that NBC's tactics create a slippery slope. While no one wants to defend suspected pedophiles, "if we so uncritically accept unethical conduct from television producers . . .—turning private humiliation into public sport—the temptation will only become stronger to give police a pass on the abusive bending of ethical standards in the pursuit of public safety" (p. A56).

- *Harm to NBC's economic interests.* Clearly, NBC faces potentially costly damages should they lose in court. But advertisers also appeared to become wary of being associated with the show's content. "We're all concerned with what content we're associating ourselves with," said a director for a national advertising agency in charge of broadcast spots (Stelter, 2007, p. C1). Later *Predator* episodes appeared to include significantly fewer national spot ads than earlier shows, observers noted. The series also is expensive to produce. NBC paid Perverted Justice, the pedophile watchdog group, a consulting fee of about $70,000 for each episode (Stelter, 2007).

The substance of these harms is apparent. Whether any or all of these types of harm are outweighed by other compelling benefits or ethical values is the subject of continuing debate.

"Setting Back" Interests and "Wronging" Others

In his landmark work, *Harm to Others* (1984), social philosopher Joel Feinberg built a largely legalistic framework for properly understanding the notion of harm and how it should be handled by the law and the courts. He discussed various dimensions of "injuring" or "wronging" others and how different kinds of harm should be punished. According to Feinberg, a harm is an act or state that "sets back" the interest of someone else, such as reasonable interest in career, health, reputation, or privacy. This "setting back" of some-one's interest has to be concrete—it has to be something that explicitly makes the person's state of affairs, or the person's ability to attain reasonable goals, worse off than if the act had not been done. And it must be something that "sets back" important desires, like rais-ing a family or accomplishing a long-term project, and not more trivial interests such as seeing a movie or walking a dog. "Not everything that we dislike or resent, and wish to avoid, is harmful to us," Feinberg wrote (1984, p. 45). "[It is critical that we distinguish] between the harmful conditions and *all* the various unhappy and unwanted physical and mental states that are not states of harm in themselves" (p. 47). He continued,

> [Unpleasant or objectionable] experiences can distress, offend, or irritate us, without harming any of our interests. They come to us, are suffered for a time, and then go, leaving us as whole and undamaged as we were before. The unhappy mental states they produce are motley and diverse. They include . . . transitory disappointments and disillusionments, wounded pride, hurt feelings, aroused anger, shocked sensibility, alarm, disgust, frustration, impatient restlessness, acute boredom, irritation, embarrassment, feeling of guilt and shame, . . . bodily discomfort, and many more. . . . Like various pleasures of the moment, these passing unpleasantnesses are neither in nor against one's interests. For that reason, they are not to be classified as harms. (pp. 45–46)

Feinberg's work is critical to our understanding of what is meant by harm from a *legal* standpoint. He proposed his conceptualization of harm primarily to help lawmakers properly weigh when government should intervene in public affairs and impose restric-tions on individual freedoms. But his definition also is helpful from a moral standpoint because it requires us to think about the nature of our effects on others and our obliga-tions to them. Kant said we must act in ways that always respect the human dignity of others, but that does not mean we must always be fearful of offending people's tender sensibilities. Insisting that such relatively minor offenses be considered "harms" risks turning us into a sinister society of paternalistic, censorious vigilantes. Likewise, ensuring a healthy, vigorous public sphere, or marketplace of ideas, means our sensibilities and our ideals about decency are going to get bumped and jostled. As creatures of community, we should expect to be upset or occasionally offended as a natural part of living in a social system and interacting with others who have different or competing interests, perspectives, and motivations. On the other hand, Feinberg (1984) also said we must include acts that "wrong" others among legitimate "harms" even when specific interests may not have been set back:

> One person *wrongs* [author's emphasis] another when his indefensible (unjustifiable and inexcusable) conduct violates the other's right, and in all but certain very special cases such conduct will also invade the other's interest and thus be harmful in the [second] sense. . . . For example, so-called harmless trespass on another's land violates the landowner's property rights and thereby "wrongs" him even though it does not harm the land. (pp. 34–35)

HARM AS A CULTURALLY BOUND CONCEPT

Obviously, in many cases we do equate being offended with being harmed in some way, and our laws reflect this. Public nudity is prohibited. Store clerks are barred from selling cigarettes to minors. These and similar measures enforce norms or standards that we as a society have embraced, even though the harm prevented may not be readily apparent. Of course, our approach to understanding what constitutes harm is based on very Western Enlightenment concepts of the autonomy of the individual and on a scientific method that emphasizes empirical discovery and testability. Other cultures place a much greater premium on the notions of social order, public reputation, and "saving face." Accordingly, behaviors that may threaten these are more likely to be considered as genuine "harms" even if they may not explicitly "set back" clearly defined interests of individuals or groups.

Minimizing Harm: It's in the Code of Ethics

In some codes, such as that of the Society of Professional Journalists, harm is a key concern that is explicitly addressed. In others, such as that of the Public Relations Society of America and the American Advertising Federation, the concept is implied in statements throughout the codes that outline what constitutes ethical behavior.

From the Society of Professional Journalists Code of Ethics

Journalists should:

(Continued)

(Continued)

- Show compassion for those who may be affected adversely by news coverage. Use special sensitivity when dealing with children and inexperienced sources or subjects.
- Be sensitive when seeking or using interviews or photographs of those affected by tragedy or grief.
- Recognize that gathering and reporting information may cause harm or discomfort. Pursuit of the news is not a licence for arrogance.
- Recognize that . . . only an overriding public need can justify intrusion into anyone's privacy.
- Balance a criminal suspect's fair trial rights with the public's right to be informed.

The complete code can be found at http://www.spj.org/ethicscode.asp.

From the Public Relations Society of America Member Code of Ethics

A member shall:

- Preserve the integrity of the process of communication.
- Protect privileged, confidential or insider information gained from a client or organization.
- Act promptly to correct erroneous communications for which the practitioner is responsible.
- Avoid deceptive practices.
- Encourage clients and customers to determine if a conflict exists after notifying all affected parties.

The complete code can be found at http://www.prsa.org/aboutUs/ethics/preamble_en .html.

From the American Advertising Federation

Advertising shall:

- Refrain from making false, misleading, or unsubstantiated statements or claims about a competitor or his/her products or services.
- Be free of statements, illustrations or implications which are offensive to good taste or public decency.

The complete statement can be found at http://www.aaaa.org/EWEB/upload/inside/standards.pdf.

From the American Marketing Association

Marketers must:

- Do no harm.
- Value individual differences even as we avoid stereotyping customers or depicting demographic groups (e.g., gender, race, sexual orientation) in a negative or dehumanizing way in our promotions.

The complete code can be found at http://www.marketingpower.com.

Smiley (1992) argued that we tend to think about claims of harm in a relatively straight-forward, objective way—X can be considered a harmful act and Jones can be held responsible for it. But in fact, our understanding of harm and our assignment of responsibility for it is based on a variety of political and social norms that are culture bound. Preventing harm, he said, turns out to be a highly complicated "socially and politically charged enterprise" that often requires us to weigh our own social and political values (p. 115). Smiley took the widely used example of the debate over how to ease Third-World hunger and starvation. He noted the considerable disagreement not only over who is in the best position to prevent it, but also over how we might best prevent it in the future.

> While some of us argue that a large-scale redistribution of wealth to the third world is necessary, others contend that it is more important that we reinvest in our own economic system or even let famine take its own course. . . . While some of us might be willing to hold ourselves causally responsible for such famine . . . others would presumably not be willing to do so. (p. 113)

People who would hold themselves somehow responsible in this debate may well criticize those who don't. And that, Smiley said, illustrates how even our perceptions of what constitutes harm (and thus our assignment of blame or responsibility) is inevitably bound by social and political norms:

> [To criticize those who refuse to take responsibility] would not be fair to at least some of them. For surely there are those who look at the huge amount of suffering in the world and conclude that we can alleviate it better through the sustenance of our own capitalist system than through a wholesale distribution of wealth. Moreover, even if we could label these individuals "selfish," it is not obvious that selfishness is so bad in this context. Indeed, what we call selfishness might be defined by others as a way of placing very high value on their own privacy or personal objects. (1992, p. 114)

This debate shows, Smiley said, that our understanding of harm and our assignment of responsibility for it is based on a variety of political and social norms that are culture bound. Even if we were determined to place a premium on the value of avoiding harm in whatever moral theory we choose to adopt, Smiley argued, "we would have to explore the social and political considerations that ground our judgments of causal responsibility in practice" (1992, p. 115).

Case in Point: Using Sex to Sell Stuff

Sex in advertising is nothing new. "We want to be sexy, we want to be provocative," said a creative director responsible for the racy 2007 ad campaign for Belvedere Vodka that featured women in fishnet stockings getting spanked in public. Consider this description of a recent Dolce & Gabbana ad

(Continued)

(Continued)

that ran in *Esquire:* A woman, fully clothed in a tight dress and spike heels, lies on her back, hips raised as a bare-chested man holds her down and four other men look on. The menace in the situation is underscored by the fact that the woman is blankly unsmiling and some of the men appear to have slight sneers on their faces. The National Organization for Women attacked the ad for depicting what they called a "stylized gang rape." Even advertising executives have become uneasy about such examples of over-the-top sexualized imagery in ads. In 1991, an *Advertising Age* editorial blasted beer ads that featured sexualized women and urged brewers to realize that objectifying women in advertising contributes to sexist cultural attitudes. Noting that women make up about half of the luxury vodka market, Wally Snyder, CEO of the American Advertising Federation, asked, "How can we conclude that a potential customer angered by advertising will purchase the brand? I believe that women searching for an upscale vodka would be more attracted to a brand connecting to them through ethical advertising." Of the Dolce & Gabbana ad, Snyder said, "It is difficult for me to see how this ad advanced Dolce & Gabbana, which markets upscale Italian fashions to women. Moreover, it certainly did not advance the image of the advertising industry" (Snyder, 2007, 2008).

UNDERSTANDING HARM IN THE MEDIA

Two cases illustrate the very real harm that can be involved in media work:

- When a bomb exploded aboard Pan Am flight 103 as it flew high above Scotland in December 1988, the world was stunned by what later was proved to be a major act of international terrorism. It also seemed to have paralyzed a woefully understaffed public relations section at the airline. Although news of the holiday crash, which killed all 259 aboard and 11 people on the ground, traveled quickly, the airline failed in several ways to adequately handle pressure from the public and the media and failed to provide adequate counseling and facilities for bereaved family members. In some cases, relatives of victims were informed of their losses over the phone—by sales representatives never trained in grief counseling. The airline had an inadequate emergency plan for such a crisis. The resulting damage to the company's image and marketability proved fatal. Less than two years after the crash, Pan Am filed for bankruptcy.

- In October 2006, a milkman named Charles Carl Roberts IV planned and executed the murders of five Amish girls, ages 7 to 13, after taking them hostage in a rural Pennsylvania schoolhouse and binding their hands with duct tape. He carried a suicide note explaining how he had been tormented by desires to molest young girls since the death of his premature daughter nine years earlier. When he began shooting the girls execution-style, police stormed the school, and he turned the gun on himself. The resulting culture clash between the swarm of media crews and the reclusive Amish community, which renounces the use of automobiles and modern appliances, was striking. Local families rolled past satellite trucks in their horse-drawn carts. Local media outlets attacked national journalists for "invading" the community and acting in disrespectful ways. The Amish community, media critics said, was treated as a spectacle for national consumption through what some called oversaturated and excessive news coverage of the event's most lurid details, particularly by the *Philadelphia Inquirer*. In describing the intrusion of the media on the traumatized Amish community, one writer commented:

At one place, where cables from a television truck crossed the road, a horse pulling a wagon froze in fear, rearing back, whinnying, spooked by the foreign objects. The animal could have been a metaphor for the Amish themselves. As they passed nervously, staring straight ahead, it was as if any contact with the outsiders, the modern people, could end only one way—badly. (Grogan, 2006, p. A15)

These are clearly two cases in which either the actions of media professionals failed to prevent harm or the specific steps taken to prevent harm compromised other professional values. But not all such examples of harm in the media are so explicit. Often, claims of possible harm from media behavior trigger widespread disagreement over whether such claims are valid, or when media professionals should take such claims into account in the course of their work. Just because a news story may appear overly intrusive does not automatically mean that the coverage is harmful. The definitions of harm offered by Feinberg (1984) and other theorists are quite different from the ways many media professionals often talk about possible harm. In public relations and in journalism, harm often is thought of much more abstractly, and communicators often place greater weight on the *potential* for harm that could result. This is understandable since media professionals undertake special relationships with different audiences. Those relationships are defined by expectations of honest discourse, a sense of responsibility, and a degree of trust.

Even when actual harm results from something the media does, the assignment of responsibility or blame is not always immediately clear. Consider the case of Rigoberto Ruelas, a south Los Angeles elementary school teacher. As part of the trend of using metrics to assess teacher effectiveness that has swept across the country, Los Angeles used data analysis, based on seven years of student scores on state tests, to rate their teachers in 2009 and 2010. Supporters of the assessments say they are an important way to hold teachers accountable to parents and communities. Teachers unions and other opponents say they are unfair and misleading, as they do little to measure intangible values teachers bring into the classroom and rely almost exclusively on student test scores. After the teacher ratings were completed in Los Angeles—the country's second largest school district—the *Los Angeles Times* published the ratings of every teacher in LA. Ruelas, who taught fifth grade, was rated "less effective than average" by the district. About a month later, his body was found in a ravine in Angeles National Forest. His death was ruled a suicide. Hundreds of protesters marched on the *Los Angeles Times* building. In a statement, *Times* editors defended the publication of the teacher rating database, stating that "it bears directly on the performance of public employees who provide an important service," and that "parents and the public have a right to judge the data for themselves" (Lovett, 2010). A suicide prompted by a media story certainly falls under the category of harm in one sense, but should the *Times* be held somehow responsible?

Yet considered on a broader scale, the subject of suicide can pose such a significant potential harm that psychologists have long pressed journalists to think carefully about how they cover stories of people killing themselves. For decades, communication researchers and crisis counselors have been concerned about the likelihood that news coverage of suicides, especially teen suicides, could prompt other troubled individuals to take their lives as well. Psychologists refer to this phenomenon as media or suicide "contagion." Research has strongly suggested that media depictions can "model" behavior that encourages vulnerable people with preexisting suicidal dispositions to imitate the act—particularly when a suicide gets front page coverage and when stories focus on the death of a celebrity figure who is seen as an attractive model. Some researchers (Romer, Jamieson, & Jamieson, 2006) have found that news reports on suicide in six U.S. cities were associated with an overall increase in local suicide deaths. Newspaper coverage was associated with deaths for people younger than 25 and for people older than 44, while TV coverage was associated with deaths only in the younger group. So how can the news media responsibly cover the issue of suicide without either marginalizing it as a pressing social problem or encouraging imitative acts? Government agencies and private suicide prevention groups have encouraged news media to follow guidelines designed to discourage imitation:

- Downplay romantic or sensational aspects of suicide.
- Downplay suggestions that suicide resolves problems for victims.
- Use the word *death* in headlines instead of *suicide*.
- Avoid extensive detail about the suicide.
- Provide information on how to identify symptoms of depression that can lead to suicide.
- Provide contact information for local counseling and crisis services.

Most communicators, particularly in a commercial media system such as ours, are loath to offend their audiences and so are inclined to talk about potentially offensive materials as potentially *harmful* because such materials can be considered breaches in that trust. Advertisers may want to push the envelope and use dramatic imagery or techniques to elevate their product or service above the "clutter," but if target audiences are offended, advertisers may feel that they have crossed the line: They can be said to have caused "harm" because their offensive message has turned off potential customers. This is a valid business concern and would be more acceptable if our social life could be described only in economic, "transactional" terms. But it cannot, as much as we may be encouraged to do so by our commercial-saturated media system. Many moral philosophers have suggested that applying the notion of harm in this way is problematic as an ethics argument because it defines *harm* in terms that are too broad to allow for important distinctions in how we interact with people.

Case in Point: Odwalla, Crisis Communication, and *E. coli* Poisoning

In October 1996, more than 60 people fell seriously ill and a 16-month-old Colorado girl died in a case of *E. coli* poisoning that health officials soon traced to contaminated apple juice made by Odwalla, Inc. The company hired Edelman Public Relations to formulate and manage its response to the potential public relations disaster. Among Odwalla's first actions was to recall all of its apple juice products within 24 hours of being notified by health officials of the epidemiological link. Federal health officials later cleared Odwalla's California processing plant as the source for the contamination, focusing instead on practices of the company's apple suppliers. But the company did suffer financially: Sales revenue for 1996 dropped about $5 million, the company settled more than a dozen civil suits filed by victims of poisoning, and in 1998, Odwalla pleaded guilty to 16 misdemeanor charges of selling adulterated food products and agreed to pay a $1.5 million fine—the largest criminal fine in a food injury case in Food and Drug Administration history (Thomsen & Rawson, 1998, p. 45). Regardless, Edelman's response is considered by many an example of effective crisis communication that limited harm to the public and to the company's viability. "By being open and empathetic with the public, consumers and the media, Odwalla was able to seize the initiative and take control of the crisis before it destroyed the company," one observer said. "By knowing its audiences, Odwalla was able to effectively communicate its key messages by using the media to its advantage" (Evan, 1999, p. 17). Here are some features of the public relations response:

- Odwalla executives were made available for every possible media request.
- The company held media updates twice daily during the crisis.
- The company set up an 800 number staffed 20 hours a day, and company executives made personal calls to all their distribution accounts within 48 hours.
- Edelman helped Odwalla establish an advisory board to help develop and implement state-of-the-art juice pasteurizing techniques.
- The company invited federal Food and Drug Administration inspectors to its facilities and provided footage of plant operations for media use.

However, many advertising experts do recognize the potential for ads to create a form of "indirect" harm. This may include what Sheehan (2004) refers to as "psychological" harm stemming from the "creation of unhealthy desires and the development of attitudes toward issues such as materialism, waste, environmental destruction and social injustice" (p. 11). This form of harm is difficult to precisely measure, often prompts unsubstantiated (and often uninformed) claims about media effects, and evokes frustration among advertisers—all of which can contribute to the problem, according to Sheehan: "Although such harm should not be downplayed, it may be a better use of time and energy to accept some responsibility for the harm, recognize the role that mass media as a whole play in the harm, and move on to other issues" (p. 11). When it comes to children, however, research on gender stereotypes in advertising does suggest a very real potential for harm by imposing rigid norms for how girls and boys should "be." There is more advertising targeted to boys than girls, and each gender is defined in very conservative terms. Sheehan summarizes some key findings:

> Boys are seen driving vehicles and using building equipment and are seen building and taking things apart. Boys also are featured in advertisements for science and math toys. When boys play with other boys, they play with male toys such as trucks and computers. Girls are seen playing with dolls, housekeeping equipment and products relating to vanity. When girls play with other girls, they play with girl toys such as dolls. . . . Girls tend to be inactive, playing quietly in the house, whereas boys are active and are often seen playing outside. (p. 170)

As advertisers constantly rely on such rigid gender characterizations, critics argue that children internalize these roles and are not encouraged to explore roles—or even emotions—that are associated with the opposite gender. This, they say, can be harmful psychologically.

Moreover, consumer groups have long been concerned that unbridled advertising threatens to create and affirm social norms that benefit the corporate bottom line but are ultimately harmful to society. This is why advertising targeted to children, either directly or indirectly, has become a central battleground:

> Advertisers are attuned to kids' developmental stages—to their need for peer approval, status, independence. The overwhelming message is that things make the person; that what's important is what you have, not what you are. These pressures influence children's development as citizens, as well as consumers. The barrage of advertising encourages continuous consumption and acquisition at the expense of reasoned decision-making, thrift and environmental sensitivity. At a time when kids need to learn how to consume thoughtfully, numerous promotional messages are teaching the opposite. (Consumers Union, 1998, para. 37)

Public relations professionals, often charged with the responsibility of helping manage and cultivate client image and building relationships based on trust, naturally tend to see threats to their public image or reputation as genuinely harmful. And in many instances, such threats should be considered legitimate "harm" that could "set back" a client's interest. Of course, depending on the issue, that interest may or may not be considered an overriding interest that ought to outweigh other obligations, such as to the professional notion of public service, to our obligations to protect the integrity of the profession, and even to a broader Kantian notion of truth telling or transparency. And there should be no presumption that client interests are beyond question and automatically outweigh these other obligations, media ethicist Tom Bivins noted. "Despite the commonly voiced belief that the primary loyalty of public relations practitioners is to the client, we know that significant moral concerns can arise from ignoring third parties," he cautioned (2006, p. 25). Journalists, speaking broadly, often face the opposite challenge. Whereas public relations practitioners may be inclined to talk about harm too loosely, journalists tend to claim an overly narrow definition of what exactly constitutes harmful content or behavior—or at least are more interested in justifying potentially harmful content or behavior by falling back on a vague defense of "serving the public interest." Some theorists (Coleman &

May, 2004) have urged journalists to think in a more sophisticated way about potential harm to third parties in their work and to respect the concerns of a broader circle of story subjects, sources, and audiences. If journalism is indeed to become a fully developed profession, they say, journalists should demonstrate a heightened sensitivity to ideas of informed consent, confidentiality, and full disclosure like that found among medical doctors, anthropologists, and professionals of other fields.

Advertising to Children: Ensuring Ethical Practices

The Children's Advertising Review Unit, a self-policing agency of the advertising industry, promotes eight "core principles" intended to protect children from harmful advertising practices:

1. Advertisers have special responsibilities when advertising to children or collecting data from children online. They should take into account the limited knowledge, experience, sophistication, and maturity of the audience to which the message is directed. They should recognize that younger children have a limited capacity to evaluate the credibility of information, may not understand the persuasive intent of advertising, and may not even understand that they are being subject to advertising.

2. Advertising should be neither deceptive nor unfair, as these terms are applied under the Federal Trade Commission Act, to the children to whom it is directed.

3. Advertisers should have adequate substantiation for objective advertising claims, as those claims are reasonably interpreted by the children to whom they are directed.

4. Advertising should not stimulate children's unreasonable expectations about product quality or performance.

5. Products and content inappropriate for children should not be advertised directly to them.

6. Advertisers should avoid social stereotyping and appeals to prejudice, and are encouraged to incorporate minority and other groups in advertisements and to present positive role models whenever possible.

7. Advertisers are encouraged to capitalize on the potential of advertising to serve an educational role and influence positive personal qualities and behaviors in children (e.g., being honest and respectful of others, taking safety precautions, and engaging in physical activity).

8. Although many influences affect a child's personal and social development, it remains the prime responsibility of the parents to provide guidance for children. Advertisers should contribute to this parent–child relationship in a constructive manner.

HARM MORE PRECISELY DEFINED

In addition to Feinberg, other philosophers have weighed in on this issue and expressed similar cautions about using the term *harm* too loosely or narrowly. According to Joseph

Raz (1986), one harms a person when one diminishes the person's prospects or decreases his range of possibilities. In his critique of Mill's harm principle, philosopher Nils Holtug (2002) argued for a "moralized" concept of harm that is not based solely on the possible "negative effects" an act may have on others' welfare. Some people may be offended by homosexual acts, or by Salman Rushdie's *The Satanic Verses,* or by scientific intrusions into the process of life such as in-vitro fertilization, Holtug said. If these examples were said to be harmful to those whose sensibilities were offended by them, then we are using the term *harm* too loosely and are inviting excessive state intervention into our social lives (p. 364). Similarly, broad claims that certain media content, such as a controversial advertisement or a news story that exposes misconduct, causes harm to individuals who may find it offensive or embarrassing often overreach. True, there has been extensive media effects researched that strongly suggests that, in certain circumstances, certain types of media content have an (often negative) effect on certain audience segments.

Case in Point: Crowdsourced
News Tests Limits in Boston Bombings

For a fast-moving story such as the manhunt for the two suspects in the deadly 2013 Boston Marathon bombings, social media appears to be perfectly suited: Sites can harness the eyes and ears of thousands of regular folk who are often on the scene long before any journalists. The resulting real-time stream of cell-phone images, Twitter updates, and other posts created fascinating digital narratives on Buzzfeed and other sites, complementing and often informing mainstream news accounts. This instantaneous, hybrid news is the new journalism. It can be wonderfully empowering as consumers transform into contributors and creators. It can also be a nightmare. Citizens tweeted mistaken information from police scanners, unleashed baseless rumors, and even enabled people to point fingers at innocent bystanders as suspected accomplices. In one forum on the popular Reddit site, users uploaded thousands of photos and spearheaded a massive search for anyone with "suspicious" backpacks like the ones used by the bombers. "Find people carrying black bags," wrote an anonymous Reddit moderator. "If they look suspicious, then post them." Such reckless vigilantism created a dangerous atmosphere, police officials said. "In addition to being almost universally wrong, the theories developed via social media complicated the official investigation," police said (Montgomery, Horwitz, & Fisher, 2013).

Relationships among lower levels of scholastic achievement and more frequent instances of aggressive behavior among adolescent boys who are heavy viewers of television programming have been compellingly documented (Comstock & Scharrer, 1999). Research also has suggested that men who watch pornographic material are likely to express "desensitized" attitudes toward women (Harris, 1994; Traudt, 2005). Theorists also have long argued that advertising that sexualizes, marginalizes, and generally devalues women as objects is harmful because it undermines girls' self-esteem by promoting impossible and restrictive norms of beauty and femininity (Myers & Biocca, 1992; Silverstein, Perdue, Peterson, & Kelly, 1986). In these and other cases, the claims of harm are much more concrete and significant than mere claims of being offended by violent or sexual content. It can be argued that, in these areas, research strongly suggests that actual harm has indeed occurred or people's interests have been "set back" by media content. Indeed, a 1991 editorial in *Advertising Age,* the premier trade magazine for the advertising industry, acknowledged the harmful effects of advertising—specifically, beer ads—that objectify women. "Clearly, it's time to wipe out sexism in beer ads; for the brewers and their agencies to wake up and join the rest of America in realizing that sexism, sexual harassment and the cultural portrayal of women in advertising are inextricably linked" ("Brewers," 1991, p. 28). Debates continue over quantifying the claims of harm, over the culpability of certain content providers, what would be acceptable free-speech restrictions to curb or minimize harm, and whether content providers have a social obligation to take measures to prevent such claims of harm.

MILL'S HARM PRINCIPLE

What many contemporary theorists and critics refer to as Mill's "principle of harm" is actually presented by Mill as his "liberty principle" in his landmark 1859 essay, *On Liberty.* Both references are accurate since the principle Mill put forth is deeply concerned with building a framework intended to balance the two fundamental yet often conflicting interests: ensuring maximum individual freedom and also acknowledging that freedom can and should be restricted when it can reasonably prevent actual or threatened harm to others. His principle, stated in Chapter 1 of *On Liberty,* reads thus:

> That the sole end for which mankind are warranted, individually or collectively, in interfering with the liberty of action of any of their number is self-protection. That the only purpose for which power can be rightfully exercised over any member of a civilized community, against his will, is to prevent harm to others. (1859/1991, p. 30)

Mill was concerned here about *actual* harms suffered by individuals without state intervention, but he also said such intervention is permissible to prevent *potential* harms. Later, in Chapter 4 of *On Liberty,* this was made explicit: "Whenever . . . there is a definite damage, or a definite risk of damage, either to an individual or to the public, the case is taken out of the province of liberty, and placed in that of morality or law"(p. 96). And it is important to understand that Mill was not saying that causing harm to others is *sufficient* to justify restrictions on liberty, only that it is a *necessary* condition. Mill gave the example of someone succeeding in a competitive examination, in which those who performed less well could say

> ### Mill's Harm Principle
>
> "The sole end for which mankind are warranted, individually or collectively, in interfering with the liberty of action of any of their number is self-protection.
> [And] . . . the only purpose for which power can be rightfully exercised over any member of a civilized community, against his will, is to prevent harm to others" (Mill, 1859, para. 9)

that their interests were set back or harmed. Mill was clear: There will always be winners and losers in a democratic society. But society "feels called on to interfere, only when means of success have been employed which it is contrary to the general interest to permit—namely, fraud or treachery, and force" (p. 109).

Philosophers still debate over the precise implications of Mill's words on liberty and harm; some (Lyons, 1997) have argued that Mill, in addition to allowing restrictions on one's liberty when someone was causing harm to others, also allowed that people can be compelled to "cooperate in joint undertakings and to act as a good Samaritan" (p. 117), stemming from the benefits he receives as a community member. Others (Brown, 1972) have argued that such claims overstate Mill's principle and that he does not allow restrictions on conduct unless that conduct that is interfered with can itself be considered harmful or dangerous to others. Lyons argued that Mill made clear that freedom may be limited only for the purpose of preventing harm to other persons, but the conduct that is interfered with need not itself be considered harmful or dangerous to others. Indeed, Lyons posited that "cooperation requirements" that interfere with individual freedom to serve a greater good and not just to prevent an immediate or threatened harm are encouraged by Mill. "For they may well provide the *only* means of preventing or eliminating some significant harms, such as malnutrition and starvation, emotional disturbances, illness and disease, vulnerability to attack, homelessness, and so on," he argued. "A principle that excluded other ways of preventing or eliminating harm would restrict such efforts very seriously" (Lyons, 1997, p. 122). Philosopher Richard Vernon (1998) suggested that it is a mistake even to read the so-called harm principle as providing any standard at all for deciding what kind of speech or acts to restrict. Mill's argument, he noted, has been used to simultaneously argue why violent pornography should be restricted (because it poses a definite "public harm" that the state has a valid interest in preventing) and why it should be allowed (because Mill construed "harm" more narrowly, some said, as a definable injury to a particular individual, and porn cannot be shown to do this). "No known definition of 'harm' captures and excludes the cases that Mill apparently wants to capture and exclude," Vernon wrote. "It is difficult to see that the idea of harm is doing any independent work as a criterion of legislative or policy choice" (p. 121).

Mill was clear that liberty may be restricted and that people may be compelled to do something (that is, serve on a jury, give court testimony, defend one's country, and so on). But he was adamant that liberty should not be restricted for "paternalistic" reasons—for reasons that assume the government knows what's best for people and should regulate behavior when people don't act in their own best interest. Yet even the strongest supporters of Mill's utilitarian argument in general have criticized his claims that *any* paternalistic act poses a serious and unacceptable violation of individual liberty. They say that Mill wrongly assumed that everyone is wholly and wisely informed about what's in their best interests while everyday life regularly demonstrates that this is not the case. Philosopher H. L. A. Hart, who is largely sympathetic to Mill's utilitarian framework, said Mill's arguments against any sort of paternalism seem "fantastic":

> No doubt if we no longer sympathize with this criticism this is due, in part, to a general decline in the belief that individuals know their own best interest. Mill endows the average individual with "too much of the psychology of a middle-aged

man whose desires are relatively fixed, not liable to be artificially stimulated by external influences; who knows what he wants and what gives him satisfaction or happiness." (Hart quoted in Dworkin, 1997, p. 70)

Others have argued that the limitations of Mill's harm principle also point to a general failure of utilitarianism to account for fundamental injustices or to address how unequal distribution of goods and wealth raise questions about moral agency. Utilitarianism goes wrong, Arneson (1997) argued,

> In regarding only aggregate totals or averages of welfare while ignoring altogether the value of equal distribution of welfare among persons. . . . It is polemically slanted insofar as it highlights harmonious, rosy possibilities and ignores equally likely but more troublesome cases which pose acute conflicts of distribution. (pp. 87, 92)

This objection also reflects a more general problem with Mill's overall argument for his theory of utility in guiding decision making. Having as our object the achievement of the greatest benefit for the largest number of people is clearly a noble thing. And Mill, in his efforts to build a usable framework to help ensure a harmonious social life, never lets us understate or dismiss the centrality of individual freedom as a driving value. But the devil, for most utilitarian theorists, has always been in the details—in the practical application of Mill's abstract claims. Who determines the nature of the potential harm involved? How are we defining "benefit," and is our focus on the short term or on the long term? The theory spelled out in Mill's famous *On Liberty* is understandably a landmark in social and political theory and undergirds much of our majoritarian democratic ideals, and rightly so. But Mill's framework is much less useful in the realm of ethics because it invites blanket assumptions and gross generalizations on the kinds of key questions just mentioned. By maintaining such a high level of abstraction, Mill also discouraged serious explorations into the various types and dimensions of harm. Indeed, his abstraction can result in some significant contradictions, particularly when we try to apply his utilitarian framework to media behavior. How can media practitioners *not* act somewhat paternalistically when they are trying to serve the public interest in part by serving as "gatekeepers" and continually making decisions about what the public should know? Mill's emphasis on freedom also can be undermined by the tendency of his harm principle to lead us to judgments about the potential "harm" that certain kinds of content may pose to audiences—a very paternalistic way of "protecting" audiences that Mill would find objectionable. Lapsing into what could be called our default utilitarian thinking, it is easy to claim that controversial content—narrowly sexualized images of women in advertising, say—can cause serious harm to young women (and there is research to suggest a link between exposure to such content and young females' self-esteem), and, thus, should be controlled in some way. This sort of harm may indeed be the type of content that we may want to restrict. Our debate would likely focus on how exactly the nature of the harm might outweigh First Amendment values. Yet Mill's harm/liberty principle, with its narrow focus on *state* action and its absence of a more substantial explication of the various dimensions of harm as discussed here, is of little help in such a debate.

Case in Point: Data Mining Shopper Behavior: Invaluable or Invasive?

Data analytics has become an essential tool of retail marketing: mining the buying habits of regular shoppers to anticipate their needs and interests and targeting ads and discounts accordingly to cultivate brand loyalty. Grocery and retail chains have regular access to purchasing data through popular "frequent shopper" memberships. Such customer "profiling" through data mining, however, can raise ethical questions. Target stores, among the most aggressive in such data mining practices, recently came up with a reliable method to identify which young families shopping at Target were expecting to have a baby—specifically, when women were in their second trimester, long before they started buying baby products. The ability to make such predictions is invaluable to retailers trying to build loyalty and target ads. Analysts saw 25 products that constituted a "pregnancy prediction" score and that women bought more of during their second trimester, including unscented lotions, bags of cotton balls, and calcium, magnesium, and zinc supplements. Product fliers highlighting coupons for these and other products were then sent to their addresses. In one instance, an angry Target customer in Minneapolis complained to store managers when his high school daughter started receiving pregnancy-related coupons. A few days later, he called to apologize: It turned out she *was* pregnant (Duhigg, 2012).

HARM IN CYBERSPACE

How are our values influenced or, as philosopher Jacques Ellul (1965) argued, warped by technology? Do new electronic forms of communication pose fundamentally new ethical questions? Several theorists have cautioned that the developing legal standards for the online world need to reflect our obligations as moral agents as well. As the discussion in Chapter 4 noted, online media can pose very real harms—undermining privacy, inviting vigilantism, and distorting our understanding of the wider world. Media ethicist Paula Tompkins (2003) and others also have argued that online technology forces us to consider the very cornerstone of human communication: the idea of trust. "The questions themselves are not new—whether we have been deceived, whether the reality we believe to be true is indeed true, or whether we can trust what we perceive" (pp. 194–195). Issues of full disclosure, social responsibility, and respect for human dignity apply as with any other communications venue—even though the anything-goes, democratic, and often anarchist nature of the Internet may invite some users to believe they may somehow be exempt from such moral considerations. Bloggers have proposed several "blogger codes of ethics," a few of which have been widely embraced (Beeson, 2005; Kuhn, 2005). The immediacy and control that computer-mediated communication (CMC) appears to give users is a paradoxical power because the same attractive traits of the technology also can invite deception and miscommunication—some forms of actual harm, in effect. CMC increasingly allows us to feel like we're there when communicating, and it allows us to communicate asymmetrically with people, controlling when we attend to messages and when to continue or cut off exchanges. Tompkins says this actually can threaten feelings of trust because such features allow us to "limit social negotiation of meaning" and undermine our "social" understanding of communication by placing priority on individual senders and receivers (p. 197). In other words, we gain control and immediacy at the expense of true social experience. In certain contexts, this could be considered a degree of harm because of claims of deception and misrepresentation.

Developing case law on claims of harm and defamation stemming from online content is inconsistent. Legal and moral responsibility is often difficult to assess because of the open, democratic, and often anonymous nature of online postings, bulletin boards, and other types of cyberspace forums. Here again, theorists are struggling to identify standards for what constitutes harm. What are the legal and moral responsibilities of an Internet service provider, or ISP, to control content and prevent harmful or hateful content? Should our values and expectations change to accommodate new technology? The question of liability has become an urgent one for ISPs, which are struggling to balance the role of mere *distributor* of content and their interests in controlling the content being distributed through their networks.

> If the online service provider has the ability to control the acts of the bulletin board operator, then the bulletin board operator is deemed the agent of the online service provider and the online service provider shares in the legal responsibility for the acts of the bulletin board operator. (Lipinski, Buchanan, & Britz, 2002, p. 145)

Some theorists have called for a "moral" reassessment of Internet responsible-use standards to address what they see as a philosophical deficiency in the way case law is handling questions of liability in cyberspace. Lipinski and colleagues (2002) argued that

> the failure to require ISPs to be legally accountable for defamation could lead to a situation where the common good or "civil discourse" will not be served or privileged, and where individuals, who are affected by defamation and hate speech, will have no form of moral or legal protection in cyberspace. . . . ISPs are not value free forums operating on moral neutral grounds. As Internet communications become more and more prevalent and readily available, we must acknowledge the power they indeed have over society and how it is shaped in technological *and* philosophical terms. Just as television has been critiqued and, yes, blamed, for its influence over society, the Internet too faces such critiques. (p. 155)

WHEN CONCERN FOR HARM AND OTHER DUTIES CONFLICT

There is a reason why most codes of ethics that address the concept of harm frame our ethical obligations to *minimize* harm or avoid *unnecessary* harm instead of intoning that we must avoid or prevent harm altogether. In the realm of media interaction, as in many other areas of life, some degree of harm is inevitable. There are cases in which professionals regularly decide that upholding one value or another—whether it be carrying out a broader public service or keeping a promise—should outweigh claims of possible harm. While we all acknowledge that we have a fundamental duty not to harm others, if we're serious about our obligations as moral agents, "the fact that an act will cause harm is invariably a moral reason not to do it, though not necessarily an overriding one," theorists point out (McNaughton & Rawling, 2006, p. 432). As we've emphasized earlier, it is not enough to simply say something is bad and leave that as our justification for doing or not doing something. The quality of our ethical deliberation rests in the strength of the *reasons* we give. This is one reason why moral philosopher W. D. Ross and his discussion of our often-conflicting prima facie duties can be helpful. While Mill never let us underestimate the respect and weight owed to our idea of liberty, and Kant required us to fully consider what it means to be morally obligated to treat others in certain ways, Ross illuminated how we may weigh competing obligations. "He allows us to think of moral conflict not as conflicts of *duties* but as a conflict of moral *reasons*," moral philosopher Philip Stratton-Lake said (W. D. Ross, 1930/2002, p. xxxviii). Ross was clear about the duties that we have, including avoidance of harm, but his system is largely dependent on context. Any broad generalizations about duty that do not sufficiently consider the facts of a specific case carry little weight in Ross's system. He cautioned that it is a mistake to presume in any ethical deliberation that "every act that is our duty is so for one and the same reason. . . . No act is ever, in virtue of falling under some general description, necessarily actually right; its rightness depends on its whole nature and not on any element of it" (pp. 24, 33). Moral philosopher Robert Audi (2004) described Ross's approach to resolving conflicts as similar to Aristotle's insofar as the two seek to apply practical wisdom to moral problems. "For Ross as for Aristotle, a rule may emerge *on the basis of the resolution* one reaches. But there is not necessarily any rule that the agent or anyone else need ever have been aware of, *antecedently* governing each particular case one may encounter" (p. 27).

Audi, in suggesting an approach that blends the contextual strength of Ross with the power of Kant's more absolutist system, offered an example to illustrate how we might reason our way through conflicting obligations. Recall our earlier discussion about Kant and his categorical imperative: I may justify an act if it can be universalized as a standard of behavior for all. Audi suggested applying the categorical imperative to proposed compromises, or to proposed "violations" of prima facie duties. He posed the example in which he realizes that his sick daughter could have a serious setback and that only he can keep watch over her, which would entail breaking a promise to meet a friend for lunch, forcing him to make a needless trip to the restaurant. Kant's imperative, Audi suggested,

> requires asking whether we can (rationally) universalize our maxim, which in my example may be plausibly taken to be "If the only way to keep my sick child safe is to break a promise to a friend at the cost of inconvenience, but in a way that friend would not (at least on careful reflection about the facts of the case) resent, then I will break it." (2004, p. 90)

We can use Kant's "intrinsic end formulation" (always treat humanity never simply as a means, but always at the same time as an end), Audi said, in a way that "rationally" justifies violating what Kant called a "perfect" or absolute duty, such as promise keeping. He then proposed to justify breaking his lunch date due to his daughter's illness:

Suppose I risked my daughter's health to keep a promise of the kind in question, I would apparently fail to treat her as an end in the relevant sense. I would be putting her in serious danger for a less than weighty reason; treating her as an end, in the sense I take to be most pertinent, requires caring about her good both to a significant degree and for its own sake. The point is not that if I kept the promise, I could not still care about the child at all; it is that the treatment is not appropriate to the level of care that goes with treating persons as ends or with my relationship to her. . . . Moreover, in breaking the promise I would not be treating or using my friend merely as a means. I would not *use* my friend at all, as I would be lying to get the friend's car for a trip to the liquor store. (2004, pp. 91–92)

Media professionals must cultivate a similar ability to build compelling, rational arguments when their decisions are likely to cause harm. In late 2004, journalists around the country had to grapple with claims of the potential harm they would cause if they chose to identify the woman who had accused Los Angeles Lakers star Kobe Bryant of rape. Virtually all mainstream media outlets withheld her name during coverage of the investigation and run-up to the criminal trial (her name and other details were made widely available on the Web, primarily by sites maintained by Bryant's fan base). But when prosecutors dropped the case against Bryant when the woman backed out as a witness, only to file a civil suit against Bryant for monetary damages, journalists faced a conundrum. The two metropolitan papers in Denver took opposite courses: The *Rocky Mountain News* named the woman in its coverage of her civil suit; the *Denver Post* did not. Much of the arguments made by editors at each focused on how to define fairness and how to minimize harm to all the stakeholders in the story. And the competing arguments were equally compelling. At *Rocky Mountain News,* publisher John Temple essentially argued that allowing her anonymity while every other plaintiff in civil court was not threatened to undermine the integrity of the system. The harm she may suffer by being identified, Temple argued, was outweighed by his broader concern for fairness. Not so, the editors of the *Denver Post* argued. The woman already had received threats on her life and clearly suffered from the social stigma of rape even when her identity was not publicized. The harm posed by naming her outweighed any disadvantage her anonymity may pose to Bryant, they argued. The point here is not to conclude the *Rocky Mountain News* acted unethically and the *Post* did not, or vice versa. Both news organizations took the concern of harm in its various dimensions seriously, and both spent considerable effort justifying their decisions in a rational way. The argument was not of which paper carried out its duty to minimize harm and which did not; the argument was one over competing reasons to do or not to do something.

The challenge, then, for all media professionals concerned about ethics is to constantly assess the value and integrity of the content we want to distribute—whether it be corporate talking points, a controversial news story or photo, or a marketing campaign—and simultaneously think hard about potential harm it may pose. This includes thinking about what exactly we mean by harm, what levels of harm may be posed to story subjects, publics, and customers, and whether those levels merit changing our course of action.

For Discussion

1. Most moral philosophers argue that we should avoid "paternalistic" decision making—that is, assuming that we know what's best for others and making judgments or policies with an eye toward protecting others even if they may not want to be protected. Yet such concerns often underscore legislative work and policy making. And media professionals make such paternalistic decisions all the time. Describe some specific kinds of harm that could arise from media content or behavior that you feel would merit this sort of media paternalism.

2. What are some key elements of an effective public relations crisis communication plan? Make a detailed list of all the potential harms that such a plan could limit or prevent.

3. List some specific generalizations about "harmful" media content and how audiences may be harmed by it that Mill's utilitarian theory invites us to make.

4. Think of a recent news story or graphic image that disturbed or offended you. Should it be considered harmful under Feinberg's definition? How would you say your response to the disturbing content may be culturally based?

5. When the subject of a news story claims that the news media have violated her privacy, should we always understand her claim to mean that she has been harmed? Can you think of an example when involuntary reporting of private facts may be justified and should not be considered harmful?

6. Do you think widespread use of new media technology—blogging, electronic bulletin boards, customized news from Internet providers, virtual interfaces—has affected the way we understand the concept of harm? Why or why not?

REFERENCES

Arneson, R. J. (1997). Paternalism, utility and fairness. In G. Dworkin (Ed.), *Mill's "On Liberty": Critical Essays* (pp. 83–114). Lanham, MD: Rowman & Littlefield.

Audi, R. (2004). *The good in the right: A theory of intuition and intrinsic value.* Princeton, NJ: Princeton University Press.

Beeson, P. (2005, April). The ethical dilemma of blogging in the media. *Quill,* 18–19.

Bivins, T. (2006). Responsibility and accountability. In K. Fitzpatrick & C. Bronstein (Eds.), *Ethics in public relations: Responsible advocacy* (pp. 19–38). Thousand Oaks, CA: Sage.

Brewers can help fight sexism. (1991, October 28). *Advertising Age,* p. 28.

Brown, D. G. (1972). Mill on liberty and morality. *Philosophical Review, 81,* 133–158.

Coleman, R., & May, T. (2004). Professional-client relationships: Rethinking confidentiality, harm and journalists' public health duties. *Journal of Mass Media Ethics, 19*(3–4), 276–292.

Comstock, G., & Scharrer, E. (1999). *Television: What's on, who's watching, and what it means.* San Diego, CA: Academic Press.

Consumers Union. (1998). *Selling America's kids: Commercial pressures on kids of the '90s.* Retrieved from http://www.consumersunion.org/other/selling kids/summary.htm

Duhigg, C. (2012, February 16). How companies learn your secrets. *New York Times Magazine.* Retrieved from http://www.nytimes.com/2012/02/19/magazine/shopping-habits.html?pagewanted = all&_r = 0

Dworkin, G. (1997). Paternalism. In G. Dworkin (Ed.), *Mill's "On Liberty": Critical Essays* (pp. 61–82). Lanham, MD: Rowman & Littlefield.

Ellul, J. (1965). *Propaganda: The formation of men's attitudes.* New York, NY: Knopf.

Evan, T. J. (1999, Summer). Odwalla. *Public Relations Quarterly, 15–17.*

Feinberg, J. (1984). *Harm to others: The moral limits of the criminal law.* New York, NY: Oxford University Press.

Grogan, J. (2006, October 4). A gentle paradise, lost: Murder, modernity and the media crash the Amish's gates of Eden. *Philadelphia Inquirer,* p. A15.

Harris, J. (1973). The Marxist conception of violence. *Philosophy and Public Affairs, 3,* 192–220.

Harris, J. H. (1994). The impact of sexually explicit media. In J. Bryant & D. Zillmann (Eds.), *Media effects: Advances in theory and research* (pp. 247–272). Mahwah, NJ: Lawrence Erlbaum.

Holtug, N. (2002). The harm principle. *Ethical Theory and Moral Practice, 5,* 357–389.

Kant, I. (2002). *Groundwork for the metaphysics of morals* (A. W. Wood, Ed. & Trans.). New Haven, CT: Yale University Press. (Original work published 1785)

Kuhn, M. (2005, August). *Interactivity and prioritizing the human: A code of blogging ethics.* Paper presented to the Media Ethics Division at the annual conference of the Association for Education in Journalism and Mass Communication, San Antonio, TX.

Lipinski, T. A., Buchanan, E. A., & Britz, J. J. (2002). Sticks and stones and words that harm: Liability vs. responsibility, section 230 and defamatory speech in cyberspace. *Ethics and Information Technology, 4,* 143–158.

Lovett, I. (2010, November 9). Teacher's death exposes tensions in Los Angeles. *New York Times,* p. A21.

Lyons, D. (1997). Liberty and harm to others. In G. Dworkin (Ed.), *Mill's "On Liberty": Critical Essays* (pp. 115–136). Lanham, MD: Rowman & Littlefield.

Marshall, J. (2007, September 16). Springing the trap: Law enforcement sting operations—and the public's apparent enjoyment of watching victims squirm in humiliation (whether guilty or not)— are crossing the ethical line. *Newsday,* p. A56.

McNaughton, D., & Rawling, P. (2006). Deontology. In D. Copp (Ed.), *The Oxford handbook of ethical theory* (pp. 424–458). New York, NY: Oxford University Press.

Meyers, C. (2003). Appreciating W. D. Ross: On duties and consequences. *Journal of Mass Media Ethics, 18*(2), 81–97.

Mill, J. S. (1991). *On liberty* (J. Gray & G. W. Smith, Eds.). London, England: Routledge. (Original work published 1859)

Montgomery, D., Horwitz, S., & Fisher, M. (2013, April 20). Police, citizens and technology factor into Boston bombing probe. *Washington Post.* Retrieved from http://www.washingtonpost.com/world/national-security/inside-the-investigation-of-the-boston-marathon-bombing/2013/04/20/19d8c322-a8ff-11e2-b029-8fb7e977ef71_story.html

Myers, P. N., & Biocca, F. A. (1992). The elastic body image: The effect of television advertising and programming on body image distortions in young women. *Journal of Communication, 42,* 108–133.

Raz, J. (1986). *The morality of freedom.* Oxford, UK: Clarendon Press.

Romer, D., Jamieson, P. E., & Jamieson, K. H. (2006). Are news reports of suicide contagious? A stringent test in six U.S. cities. *Journal of Communication, 56,* 253–270.

Ross, B., & Walter, V. (2008, February 27). Judge OKs trial in Dateline "Predator" suicide case. *ABC News.* Retrieved from http://www.abcnews.go.com/print?id = 4353781

Ross, W. D. (2002). *The right and the good* (P. Stratton-Lake, Ed.). Oxford, UK: Clarendon Press. (Original work published 1930)

Sheehan, K. (2004). *Controversies in contemporary advertising.* Thousand Oaks, CA: Sage.

Silverstein, N., Perdue, L., Peterson, B., & Kelly, E. (1986). The role of mass media in promoting a thin standard of bodily attractiveness for women. *Sex Roles, 14,* 519–532.

Smiley, M. (1992). *Moral responsibility and the boundaries of community: Power and accountability from a pragmatic point of view.* Chicago, IL: University of Chicago Press.

Smith, R. (2008). *Ethics in journalism.* Malden, MA: Blackwell.

Snyder, W. (2007, December 12). *Advertising ethics: An introduction.* American Advertising Federation. Retrieved from http://www.aafblog.org/blog

Snyder, W. (2008, January 7). *Attention, but at what cost?* American Advertising Federation. Retrieved from http://www.aafblog.org/ blog

Stelter, B. (2007, August 27). "To Catch a Predator" is falling prey to advertisers' sensibilities. *New York Times,* p. C1.

Thomsen, S. R., & Rawson, B. (1998, Fall). Purifying a tainted corporate image: Odwalla's response to an E. coli poisoning. *Public Relations Quarterly,* 35–46.

Tompkins, P. S. (2003). Truth, trust and telepresence. *Journal of Mass Media Ethics, 18*(3–4), 194–212.

Traudt, P. J. (2005). *Media, audiences, effects: An introduction to the study of media content and audience analysis.* Boston, MA: Pearson Education.

Vernon, R. (1998). Beyond the harm principle: Mill and censorship. In E. J. Eisenach (Ed.), *Mill and the moral character of liberalism* (pp. 115–129). University Park: Pennsylvania State University Press.

CHAPTER 8

Autonomy

F*reedom, liberty, autonomy*—these terms are broadly used to refer to a wide range of thoughts and ideas. For many people, freedom is the highest good, the first value from which all others flow. Patrick Henry's famous proclamation, "Give me liberty or give me death," embodies the Western Enlightenment ideal of freedom as that which makes life worth living. Freedom, as the weapon of choice in much of our political rhetoric, is simultaneously supercharged and shopworn, wielded with passion by American presidents as well as the likes of Fidel Castro and those of every political stripe in between.

We understand that we don't enjoy absolute freedom. A web of government laws and social customs restrict our freedom, and chaos would likely ensue without them. We usually assume freedom to mean a state of being that is reasonably unconstrained from external forces and that allows us to pursue our own interests, life plans, and visions of happiness. In his 1859 essay, *On Liberty,* John Stuart Mill provided among the most eloquent arguments for freedom by saying that unless individuals are allowed to live autonomously and unless each of us is allowed to pursue "our own good in our own way" (Cahn, 2002, p. 933), civilization as we know it will likely not advance; our search for truth will be thwarted for lack of a viable "marketplace of ideas," and there would be little hope for the development of spontaneity, genius, originality, or even moral courage. John Locke said "laws of reason" invited us to accept a "social contract" that gave some institutions power to impose restrictions on us. We are willing to give up some of our liberty, he said, to make the conditions of our lives less dangerous and more predictable. Jean-Jacques Rousseau cautioned us against the temptations of unrestrained freedom, and went so far as to warn, in his 1762 essay *On the Social Contract,* that humanity would surely "perish" unless we bound ourselves together; people, he said, "have no other means of self-preservation than to form by aggregation a sum of forces . . . and to make them work in concert" (Cahn, 2002, p. 534).

Some "libertarian" theorists, however, reject such warnings and insist that it is humans' nature to live as free as we please, and we inevitably lose much more than we might gain in restricting that freedom. Robert Nozick (1974), Murray Rothbard (1982), and others argued that absolute freedom is something to which we all should aspire and that the legal and moral justifications for most civil and political restrictions are either suspect or entirely without merit. And at least one theorist has suggested that only the most resolute anarchists among us appreciate the sobering implications and the true meaning of claims to absolute freedom.

It should be clear, even at this point, that the concepts of freedom, liberty, and autonomy are deceptive in their apparent simplicity. And, philosophers have argued, the words don't even necessarily refer to the same thing. While *freedom* and *liberty* can be used synonymously, *autonomy* is a different animal. Locke (1689/1988) used the example of the person who is put into a cell with several doors and told that all of them are locked when in fact one is left unlocked. So the "prisoner" is actually free to leave the cell, but the "deception" of his "captors" prevents him from doing so. The prisoner has lost his autonomy, or capacity for self-determination, but not, strictly speaking, his liberty. As we will see, our common understanding of freedom usually serves as a rather superficial marker, or signpost, for the much more complex—and interesting—concept of autonomy. But anyone who is serious about grappling with ethical dilemmas must have a clear understanding about what it means to be an autonomous agent. While our freedom-loving selves may be solely interested in which restrictions are just or unjust, our autonomous selves, philosophers say, are concerned with the moral implications of what we do. Many even insist, as we will see, that true "moral autonomy" has little to do with liberty or freedom and much more to do with consciously, and freely, *limiting* oneself to upholding moral principles and doing "the right thing." Autonomy, renowned philosophy historian Isaiah Berlin said, "Is not freedom to do what is irrational, or stupid, or wrong" if we truly understand ourselves as moral beings (1969, p. 148).

Kant on Autonomy

Philosopher and Kant expert Herbert James Paton (1971) said that we cannot fully understand the German philosopher "unless we see him as the apostle of human freedom and the champion of the common man" (p. 171). Even before Kant's two landmark works—*Groundwork for the Metaphysics of Morals* and *Critique of Pure Reason*—were published, Kant was explicit in claiming that "freedom" is the source of all value in his moral philosophy. All things that we claim as moral imperatives, he argued, ultimately must derive their value from freedom. In most cases, when Kant talks of freedom, he is usually describing what has come to be known as *moral autonomy:* not the notion of freedom to do whatever we want, but our ability to exercise our free will to fully realize our existence as rational beings with moral duties. In a lecture on ethics that Kant gave in the early 1780s, he summarized why his notion of freedom must be central to any moral framework:

> Freedom is, on the one hand, that faculty which gives unlimited usefulness to all the other faculties. It is the highest order of life, which serves as the foundation of all perfections and is their necessary condition. All animals have the faculty of using their powers according to will. But this will is not free. It is necessitated through the incitement of *stimuli,* and the actions of animals involve a *bruta necessitas.* If the will of all beings were so bound to sensuous impulse, the world would possess no value. The inherent value of the world, the *summum bonum,* is freedom in accordance with a will that is not necessitated to action. Freedom is thus the inner value of the world. (Kant, 1930, pp. 121–122)

Media ethics students also must be aware of the damage that can occur when someone's autonomy is thwarted or undermined. When considered in the context of media, respect for autonomy is critical on both sides of the communication equation—among both those involved in producing media messages and those receiving the messages. Journalists whose news decisions are overly influenced by interests of their sources, their corporate media owners, or any other group can quickly find their credibility severely damaged. Public relations officials who are reduced to mere mouthpieces in the service of narrow client interests face similar credibility threats. Advertising raises questions of autonomy by trading on and reinforcing various stereotypes that can undermine individuality and force people into rigid categories. Inappropriate pressure from advertisers also threatens editorial independence of newspapers, magazines, and television programming. Media messages that fail to fully treat audiences as independent, rational beings violate Kant's charge that we all, as moral beings, have a primary duty to respect the human capacity for reason.

Case in Point: Drug Ad Overdose: From Cholesterol to Erectile Dysfunction

College students today take it for granted, but pharmaceutical companies were only allowed to begin advertising prescription drugs on television in 1997. The earliest drug ads included a magazine ad in the late 1980s for Rogaine, a hair-growth product. Sales of Rogaine ballooned from $87 million in 1988 to $143 million in 1991. Since then, the pharmaceutical industry has become one of the largest advertisers in the United States. Drug ads are known as DTC, or "direct-to-consumer" advertising, and they are allowed only in the United States and New Zealand. Federal regulatory officials and drug companies say DTC advertising—for brands such as Zyrtec, Claritin, and, of course, Viagra—has benefited consumers by empowering them with more information regarding their health care. Many doctors, after initially opposing drug ads, realized they raised awareness of health treatments and actually prompted people to visit physicians more regularly. Drug ads also have been proved to serve as reminders for people to refill their prescriptions and to take their medicine as directed. But drug advertising continues to have its critics who say pharmaceutical companies routinely overemphasize drug usefulness and minimize negative side effects. A TV ad for Claritin, for example, was criticized by federal officials for having risk information read so quickly that it was difficult to understand. Others worry that the ads create a culture in which people are encouraged to turn to drugs for nearly every possible condition, even when physicians would not recommend doing so. Surveys have shown that many Americans mistakenly assume that the government "approves" DTC ads before they are broadcast, and that it only allows ads for "completely safe" drugs. Critics also argue that DTC advertising has increased the cost of drugs and contributed to soaring health care costs in the United States.

This chapter examines how classical and contemporary philosophers help us understand what autonomous agency means, how it is related to freedom, and why it is so critical to have from a moral point of view. The chapter explores the relationship between autonomy and the principle of freedom of expression and suggests ways to apply the concept of autonomy to help in our deliberations over questions about media behavior. Many of these questions come in the form of *conflicts of interests*. And finally, it discusses how the value of autonomy is expressed in actual media work—why journalistic independence is so critical in news and why the ability to manage competing interests is so crucial for public relations practitioners when carrying out their obligations of public service.

FREEDOM AND AUTONOMY

As noted earlier, philosophers and theorists caution us not to confuse the vague, conventional notion of freedom with autonomy. *Freedom* or *liberty* often refers to a desired state of the *absence* of constraints or restrictions on what we can do. Berlin (1969) offered this definition of freedom:

> Freedom is self-mastery, the elimination of obstacles to my will, whatever these obstacles may be—the resistance of nature, of my ungoverned passions, of irrational institutions, of the opposing wills or behaviour of others. . . . The essence of the notion of liberty . . . is the holding off of something or someone—of others who trespass on my field or assert their authority over me, or of obsessions, fears, neuroses, irrational forces—intruders and despots of one kind or another. (pp. 146, 158)

Autonomy, on the other hand, refers to our *deliberative* nature. Truly autonomous individuals, philosopher Gerald Dworkin (1988) concluded, can "define their nature, give meaning and coherence to their lives, and take responsibility for the kind of person they are" (p. 20). Political theorist Joel Feinberg (1989) argued that the word *autonomy* actually has four closely related meanings: the "capacity" to govern oneself, the "actual condition" of self-government, the ideal of virtue stemming from that state, and the "sovereign authority" to govern oneself (p. 28). Philosopher Stanley Benn (1988) said autonomy needs two things to be possible:

> In the first place, it requires that the subject's beliefs be coherent and consistent; secondly, their coherence must be the outcome of a continuing process of critical adjustment within a system of beliefs in which it is possible to appraise one sector by canons drawn from another. (p. 182)

Autonomy, Gerald Dworkin (1988) continued, includes "some ability both to alter one's preferences and to make them effective in one's actions and, indeed, to make them effective because one has reflected upon them and adopted them as one's own" (p. 17).

Freedom and Autonomy: How Are They Defined?

Freedom is understood as a state of being that is reasonably unconstrained by outside forces and that allows us to pursue our own interests and visions of happiness.

Autonomy refers not just to what we *can* do but to what we *ought* to do; *moral autonomy* refers to our ability to control the reasons for our actions in ways that show an understanding of our obligations as moral beings and "a rational grasp of the moral law."

As all these suggest, when we talk about autonomy, we are referring to our singular capacity in the animal world to live and act as moral agents. We are moving beyond the political theory discussions of what kinds of restrictions on our freedom or liberty are acceptable. We are moving beyond talk about what we have the *right* to do as freedom-loving individuals. Instead, questions about what it means to exercise autonomy become questions of ethics. They move us into the normative realm of what we *ought* to do if we are to take our role as moral agents seriously. Autonomy cannot be identical to liberty, philosopher Gerald Dworkin argued. "[W]hen we deceive a patient, we are also interfering with her autonomy. Deception is not a way of restricting liberty" (1988, p. 14). Philosopher John Cristman (1989) provided a way to distinguish between the separate but related concepts of autonomy and freedom, which are often used interchangeably:

> Autonomy is more properly seen as a property of preference or desire formation than a property of whole persons or of persons' lives. One can see this by imagining how people vary, in different aspects of their lives, in the autonomy they manifest. A smoker might be perfectly autonomous in choosing whether to watch a baseball game or read a book, but is virtually powerless against the overwhelming urge for nicotine. . . . Freedom, on the other hand, is a property of human action—a characteristic of the relation among desires, bodily movements, and restraints that may be facing the agent. . . . To be free (in a given context) means there is an absence of restraints (positive or negative, internal or external) standing between a person and the carrying out of that person's *autonomous* [author's emphasis] desires. (p. 13)

Do We Have Free Will?

Kant, whose work was discussed in previous chapters, has been described by one scholar as "the apostle of human freedom and the champion of the common man" (Paton, 1971, p. 171). To exercise our moral duties as Kant calls on us to do, and to enjoy ourselves as autonomous beings, it would follow that having autonomy means also having free will. But do we really? Recent research has prompted neuroscientists and others to enter the debate, which reaches all the way back to Plato and Aristotle, over whether there is such a thing. "Free will does exist, but it's a perception, not a power or a driving force," according to Mark Hallett, a researcher with the National Institute of Neurological Disorders and Stroke. "People experience free will. They have the sense they are free. [But] the more you scrutinize it, the more you realize you don't have it" (Hallett quoted in Overbye, 2007, p. D4). In his landmark work of 1740, *A Treatise of Human Nature,* philosopher David Hume argued that the idea of free will was a myth. While we have strong motivations as rational agents to argue that our capacity for reason rules our passionate and emotional selves, Hume suggested it's the other way around—that desire or repulsion, not reason, drive our conduct. Brain research appears to be catching up with Hume. A burgeoning body of neuroethics research has explored how different parts of the brain "light up" or exhibit increased blood flow when subjects are presented with different types of ethical dilemmas using magnetic imaging techniques such as fMRI. What researchers have found raise fundamental challenges to our conventional understanding of free will: Rather than "rationally" deliberating our way to moral responses, the emotional centers of our brains respond first and appear to influence, or even determine, the reasons we come up with later. Neuroscience researcher and scholar Sam Harris dramatically claimed that free will "is an illusion. Our wills are simply not of our own making. Thoughts and intentions emerge from background causes of which we are unaware and over which we exert no conscious control. We do not have the freedom that we think we have" (2012, p. 5) Science journalist Dennis Overbye writes, "A bevy of experiments in recent years suggest that the conscious mind is like a monkey riding a tiger of subconscious decisions and actions in progress, frantically making up stories about being in control" (2007, p. D1). Needless to say, such research has potentially explosive implications for what constitutes the moral life. And it places even greater urgency on the need for us to determine the ethical obligations of autonomy.

Autonomy as the Highest Good?

In a way, the claim of Gerald Dworkin and others that autonomy doesn't always mean "retaining control" of our actions flies in the face of our cultural value of rugged individualism. Through news media, Hollywood films, advertising, and other institutions, our society is relentlessly bombarded with both subtle and explicit messages proclaiming the value of self-sufficiency. We can be rich, successful, famous, beautiful, and attractive—if we work hard enough. One of the most revered images in our culture is that of the self-made man. Freedom is all we need to be all we can be. Or so we're led to believe. Dworkin and others have warned against our Western tendency to put the idea of autonomy on a pedestal, to claim that it must be considered somehow fundamental to all other values. Our singular cultural focus on self-betterment and our right to live our lives as we see fit may satisfy our egos, but it also threatens to distort our understanding of ourselves as moral beings. Philosopher Alisdair MacIntyre (1984) argued, "The self has to find its moral identity in and through its membership in communities"; otherwise, he said, any claim of having a moral framework makes no sense (p. 221). Having a clearer, limited definition of autonomous agency that doesn't simply mean "retaining control" allows for a more sophisticated accounting of our obligations as moral agents and as members of communities. "What is valuable about autonomy is that the commitments and promises a person makes be ones he views as his, as part of the person he wants to be, so that he defines himself via those commitments," according to Gerald Dworkin (1988, p. 26). He went further and suggested that placing too much importance on autonomy can be as harmful as any other kind of absolutism:

There is an intellectual error that threatens to arise whenever autonomy has been defended as crucial or fundamental: This is that the notion is elevated to a higher status than it deserves. Autonomy *is* important, but so is the capacity for sympathetic identification with others, or the capacity to reason prudently, or the virtue of integrity. Similarly, although it is important to respect the autonomy of others, it is also important to respect their welfare, or their liberty, or their rationality. Theories that base everything on any single aspect of human personality, on any one of a number of values, always tend toward the intellectually imperialistic. (p. 32)

Anne Colby and William Damon spent years studying "moral exemplars"—people who were widely perceived for their commitment to moral principles and for their ethical leadership. They, too, saw that American culture seemed to place individualism and "commitment" at odds, yet in their exemplar subjects, they observed an ability to define one through the other. Their conclusion was that, as the exemplar subjects did, we all must recognize that a simplistic individualism divorced from commitment causes more problems than it helps solve:

We start with the assumption that fully developed individualism includes a dedication to the common good. Moral development is a fundamental part of any person's development as an individual. Moreover, mature individualism implies fully articulated links with others and with society as a whole. Even as individuals seek their own unique destinies, they do so in the context of relations with family, friends, and others in their communities. Strong social relations, in fact, provide a setting in which the exploration of the self flourishes. So, in the course of human development, socialization and individuation are really opposite sides of the same coin. (Colby & Damon 1992, p. 297)

Feminists make a similar argument when they claim that the premium our culture places on freedom stems from our privileging the "public"—and traditionally male-dominated—domain over the domestic (read: female) sphere (Benhabib, 1992; Gilligan, 1982; Noddings, 1984; Steiner, 1989). German theorist Jürgen Habermas (1993), who is widely respected among many media ethicists, echoed a similar concern when he referred to our "dual" moral imperatives of "justice" and "solidarity." "Every autonomous morality has to serve two purposes at once: it brings to bear the inviolability of socialized individuals by requiring equal treatment and thereby equal respect for the dignity of each one; and it protects intersubjective relations of mutual recognition requiring solidarity of individual members of a community, in which they have been socialized," Habermas wrote (1993, p. 98). In other words, our existence as autonomous beings requires us to honor the ideas of equal treatment and give due respect to the dignity of every individual while it simultaneously requires us to recognize our dependence on our relations with others as a central value. "*Justice* concerns the equal freedom of unique and self-determining individuals, while *solidarity* concerns the welfare of socially connected individuals who are ultimately linked in [a] . . . shared form of life" (p. 98).

Autonomy: It's in the Code of Ethics

In most codes, autonomy is not explicitly mentioned but is implied in statements that emphasize professionalism as rooted in an understanding of our moral obligations and in the responsible use of power. In the code of the Society of Professional Journalists, independence is the third of four key directives.

From the Society of Professional Journalists Code of Ethics

Journalists should be free of obligation to any interest other than the public's right to know.

Journalists should do the following:

- Avoid conflicts of interest, real or perceived.
- Remain free of associations and activities that may compromise integrity or damage credibility.
- Refuse gifts, favors, fees, free travel and special treatment, and shun secondary employment, political involvement, public office and service in community organizations if they compromise journalistic integrity.
- Disclose unavoidable conflicts.
- Deny favored treatment to advertisers and special interests and resist their pressure to influence news coverage.
- Be wary of sources offering information for favors or money; avoid bidding for news.

The complete code can be found at http://www.spj.org/ethicscode.asp.

From the Public Relations Society of America Member Code of Ethics

A member shall do the following:

- Preserve the free flow of unprejudiced information when giving or receiving gifts by ensuring that gifts are nominal, legal and infrequent.
- Avoid actions and circumstances that may appear to compromise good business judgment or create a conflict between personal and professional interests.
- Disclose promptly any existing or potential conflict of interest to affected clients or organizations.

The complete code can be found at http://www.prsa.org/aboutUs/ethics/preamble_en.html.

AUTONOMY AS POSITIVE FREEDOM

Isaiah Berlin (1964) urged us to distinguish between what he called "negative" and "positive" freedom. Negative freedom, he suggested, is the common understanding of liberty as being free of undue restrictions or interference. It is the idea of being free *from* constraints that might unreasonably limit our movement, activity, or thoughts. The arguments of John Locke as well as John Stuart Mill's theory of utility are largely aimed at providing justifications for limiting such restrictions except for cases in which one person's exercise of freedom poses the threat of harm to others. All individuals, Mill argued, have the inalienable right to be free *from* restrictions unless such limits explicitly protect the welfare of others.

But Berlin (1964) argued that this conception of freedom only explained half the story. Not only do we have a fundamental need to be free *from* things to act as we wish; we also have a need to be free *to* define ourselves as we wish. We want to "own" our desires, ambitions, and motivations. We don't just want the freedom to act; we want to control the reasons for our acts. A later philosopher suggested that Berlin was saying we must understand autonomy as the self divided against itself: "A true, higher, sovereign self, and an impulsive, lower self that occasionally needs to be brought into line. An autonomous person is able to control herself—to choose which desires to act on" (Brison, 1998, p. 330). Berlin tried to further distinguish this "positive" sense of freedom as a feature of our self aspiring to be "at its best":

> I wish to be a subject, not an object; to be moved by reasons, by conscious purposes, which are my own, not by causes which affect me, as it were, from outside. . . . This is at least part of what I mean when I say that I am rational, and that it is my reason that distinguishes me as a human being from the rest of the world. I wish, above all, to be conscious of myself as a thinking, willing, active being, bearing responsibility for my choices and able to explain them to references to my own ideas and purposes. (Berlin, 1969, p. 131)

Berlin's notion of positive freedom has been hijacked and transformed by the most brutal communist and fascist movements of our history, when the tyrants imposed a single political definition of goodness that they said all citizens should aspire to in their efforts to define themselves. Our understanding of freedom has been shaped and often distorted because different political groups, in efforts to gain power, have sought to link freedom as closely as possible to their agendas. "This history of the matter goes far to explain how freedom came to be identified with so many different kinds of social and individual benefits," philosopher Gerald MacCallum said, "and why the status of freedom as simply one among a number of social benefits has remained unclear" (1967, p. 313). Berlin acknowledged that history has shown how this "positive" conception of liberty has been corrupted and manipulated by despots and dictators, but he insisted that this sense of "positive" freedom through self-realization opened the way to true freedom. He argued that sole dependence upon the concept of "negative" freedom was dangerous by extending it to its logical—and absurd—conclusion:

> [The Stoic doctrine of denying one's desires] maintains that what I cannot have I must teach myself not to desire; that a desire eliminated, or successfully resisted, is as good as a desire satisfied. . . . This makes it clear why the definition of negative liberty as the ability to do what one wishes—which is, in effect, the definition adopted by Mill—will not do. If I find that I am able to do little or nothing of what I wish, I need only contract or extinguish my wishes, and I am made free. . . . But what [this] has created is the very antithesis of political freedom. (1969, pp. 139–140)

MORAL AUTONOMY

So this idea of "positive" freedom, or autonomy, as taking ownership of our reasons for doing things as opposed to simply having the freedom to do them, takes us into a moral dimension. The autonomous being, then, has a *responsibility* to use freedom wisely and in the interest of "doing the right thing." "It is the notion of freedom in its 'positive' sense that is at the heart of the demands for national or social self-direction which animate the most powerful and morally just public movements of our time," Berlin argued (1969, p. 169). Both Plato and Augustine expressed this central feature of autonomy when they wrote about the governing part of the soul being "the highest self" and that part of ourselves as rational beings that acts on the basis of our reason. Montesquieu, Berlin noted, spoke of political liberty as being not freedom to do whatever we want, but only "the power of doing what we ought to will" (Berlin, 1969, p. 147). This also is Kant's idea of "moral autonomy": We enjoy autonomy only insofar as we make our choices not just for self-satisfaction, but, as one philosopher put it, "out of respect for the demands of morality" (Finnis, 1987, p. 441).

Kant: Autonomy in the Service of Duty

Ever since Kant published his work on moral philosophy in the late 18th century, it has shaped how we talk about moral duty. And more than one writer has noted that no one took the literal idea of autonomy—from the Greek *auto* ("self") and *nomos* ("law")—more seriously than Kant did. But Kant makes clear in his *Groundwork for the Metaphysics of Morals* (1785/2002) that our autonomy is very different than mere freedom of movement. It exists to reflect our moral being. Kant most forcefully harnessed the idea of autonomy with moral duty by arguing that "moral law" simply reflects what's in our nature. Using our capacity for reasoning, we cannot help being compelled by the idea that doing the right thing by others and our existence as autonomous, responsible beings really amounts to the same thing. Kant argued in his *Groundwork for the Metaphysics of Morals* that humans, having a rational will and considered "ends" in themselves and never to be used as a mere means by others, are indeed obligated only to obey their own wills. A rational will has absolute value—it is an end in itself. Thus, Kant argued that a man "was obligated only to act in accord with his own will" (1785/2002, p. 50). But Kant also is specific in rejecting any suggestion that such freedom frees us from duties to act in certain ways because "the will of every rational being [is] a will giving universal law"—our free will, he says, is *designed* to favor behavior that could be applied as a universal standard for everyone, not simply for one's own gratification at the expense of others (p. 49). The enjoyment of autonomy for its own sake, oblivious to any sense of moral duty, is no freedom at all, in other words. As Benn (1988) explained, "Someone who is unencumbered by external impediments but acts unreflectingly in response to the desire of the moment is still unfree because he is in bondage to internal pressures he cannot control but which control him" (p. 173).

Autonomy, then, in the Kantian sense, is not a "right." It is a "property of all rational wills," according to philosopher Thomas Hill (1989):

[It is] a property implying the possessor's recognition of rational principles other than desire-satisfaction but not by itself implying the wrongness of specific forms of coercion, manipulation, and control that modern appeals to autonomy typically condemn. (pp. 93–94)

So according to Kant, autonomy for individuals who take seriously their existence as moral agents means acting in harmony with our duties to respect people as ends in themselves with the capacity for reason—it means, as philosopher Robert George (1993) noted, "living in conformity with a rational grasp of the moral law" (p. 148). "In fact," George continued, "Kant allowed for governmental enforcement of 'duties to oneself,' seeing moral laws not as violations of the principle of autonomy but as means to teaching and encouraging people to act autonomously" (p. 149). Wolff (1970) noted that Kant's idea of moral autonomy "is a combination of freedom and responsibility; it is a submission to laws that one has made for oneself" (p. 14). And John Rawls (1971/1999), too, uses this sense of autonomy as fulfilling one's duty: Autonomous action, he said in *A Theory of Justice,* refers to people "acting from principles that they would acknowledge under conditions that best express their nature as free and equal rational beings" (p. 452). In this context, it is no accident that Kant phrases his categorical imperative at one point in his *Groundwork of the Metaphysics of Morals* (1785): "Act in such a way that you treat humanity, *whether in your own person* [emphasis added] or in the person of another, never merely as a means, but always at the same time as an end" (p. 429).

Case in Point: The Gun Owner Next Door: Rage Over an Interactive Map

Shortly after the tragedy of the Sandy Hook school shootings in Newtown, Connecticut, in December 2012, in which 20 first-graders were killed, the *Journal News,* a paper serving the suburban counties of Westchester and Rockland, north of New York City, took a novel approach to the heated national debate over gun control. As in many states, local governments that issue handgun permits keep records that are open to the public. Journalists at the *Journal News* collected the names and addresses of all 33,614 permit holders in those counties, and produced an interactive map on the paper's Web site that identified each one of them. Gun-rights supporters were outraged, arguing that the newspaper unfairly stigmatized legal gun owners, violated their privacy, and turned them into targets by needlessly publishing names and addresses. Others suggested the map, while possibly disturbing, effectively personalized the gun debate by graphically showing how widespread gun ownership is. The newspaper received numerous threats, prompting the editor to hire armed guards and to pay for some staffers to stay in hotels for several nights to avoid attacks at their homes. "The people have as much of a right to know who owns guns in their communities as gun owners have to own weapons," said *Journal News* reporter Dwight Worley (Haughney, 2013, p. A15).

AUTONOMY AND NATURAL LAW

Is there such a thing as a legitimate moral law? Is it always true that a key purpose of government is to promote a greater level of morality, however that is defined? Or does the very notion of using the law to promote morality violate a fundamental human freedom? If autonomy is the core of "moral personality," as several philosophers have argued, then morality itself requires respect for autonomy. Failure here reduces humans and violates their human essence, they say. This is why libertarians and other sympathetic theorists argue that freedom must always be considered the first virtue of society. Some have taken the case for freedom to its extreme. Philosopher David A. J. Richards (1982, 1987) even went so far as to argue that social and legal prohibitions against drug abuse, prostitution, pornography, and even suicide are unjust because they are paternalistic and that they fail to respect the "value" that individuals reasonably and legitimately find in those activities. Another philosopher, Ronald Dworkin (1985), put this argument more eloquently. In his argument that restrictions on access to and ownership of pornography violate our value of autonomy, he said we all have a right to "moral independence":

> People have the right not to suffer disadvantage in the distribution of social goods and opportunities, including disadvantage in the liberties permitted to them by the criminal law, just on the ground that their officials or fellow-citizens think that their opinions about the right way for them to lead their own lives are ignoble or wrong. (p. 353)

But other philosophers have long argued not only that good laws should aspire to make people safe, but that they also should help make them virtuous—that law and politics are "rightly concerned with the moral well-being of members of political communities" (George, 1993, p. 20). This argument has been called the "natural law" theory and goes back to Aristotle, who insisted that the law of the political community, or *polis,* cannot limit itself to merely "a guarantor of men's rights against one another," but must "devote itself to the end of encouraging goodness." "What constitutes a polis," Aristotle said, "is an association of households and clans in a good life, for the sake of attaining a perfect and self-sufficing existence. . . . It is therefore for the sake of good actions, and not for the sake of social life, that political associations must be considered to exist" (as quoted in George, p. 21). George and other natural law philosophers argue there is nothing "unjust" about the legal enforcement of morals in various legal forms. If our laws have no moral basis, they are meaningless, they argue. But natural law theorists have plenty of critics. Using political power and legal tools to enforce someone's or some group's vision of morality is inherently unjust and violates our autonomy, they say. And the debate continues.

AUTONOMOUS AGENCY AND THE MEDIA

As a key institution in our democratic system, the media are largely defined by their openness, or relative freedom. But how should the idea of autonomy, and in particular *moral* autonomy, as philosophers have defined it, be applied to media practice? How should journalists and public relations practitioners understand the duties that their professional autonomy obligates them to carry out? By now, it should be clear that for anyone to claim to have the "right" of autonomy to do anything they please betrays a simplistic and possibly irresponsible understanding of the concept. Kant and others forcefully argue that autonomy is intricately bound with responsibility. In the media, responsible practice often translates into *credibility*. And that is the goal of all serious media workers.

In public relations, autonomous agency often means being able to manage issues and communication campaigns without unreasonable interference or restrictions from interests that may not place high value on disclosure or on building relationships with publics. This means that the question of autonomous agency in public relations work often is related to issues of *power* within an organization and to what extent public relations is considered a player in the decision-making levels. In a study of "issues management" at one major national firm, public relations ethicist Shannon Bowen (2005) noted that the public relations executive was not included in the issues management team. "The access and contribution of public relations personnel are therefore hindered because the top issues manager might not always have the autonomy necessary to make ethical decisions," Bowen concluded (p. 204).

In the news media, the principle of autonomy is intricately bound with the mission of journalists to convey the news "without fear or favor," as *New York Times* owner Adolph S. Ochs said in 1896 (Salisbury, 1981), and in the service of the professional ideals of impartiality and fairness. This idea of journalistic independence "is a lynchpin in what journalists should stand for," wrote Bob Steele (2003), a prominent media ethicist. "Independence is at the heart of journalism's unique and essential role in a society." Most threats to journalistic autonomy, or independence, come in the form of *conflicts of interests*—in other words, cases when the journalistic mission runs counter to or conflicts with other interests or stakeholders. Depending on how conflicts of interests are handled, they can inflict real damage on journalistic credibility. If audiences, for example, learn that a news organization or an individual journalist is profiting directly from the subject of a news story and, thus, begin to wonder whose *interests* are

> ### Conflict of Interest: How Is It Defined?
>
> *Conflicts of interests* can take many forms, but they generally arise when we experience a clash between our professional duties or loyalties (that is, to serve the public or to pursue the truth) and other personal or external interests (that is, helping a friend or boosting profits). Not all conflicts of interest are avoidable; all should be disclosed. Any such conflicts, whether they are *actual, potential,* or *perceived,* should be avoided if they threaten our credibility or our ability to act as responsible moral agents.

being served by such a relationship—the public's interest in impartial reporting or the subject's interest in positive exposure—the journalistic credibility of the media outlet or person may quickly be called into question. For example, an investigation of the magazine *Self* in the 1980s showed that its featured stories referred only to the products of companies that advertised in the magazine. When this practice was publicized, the editor was fired and the magazine changed its policy.

Freedom of Expression

Any discussion of autonomy and the media must address the fundamental free speech rights enjoyed under our democratic system. First Amendment theory is a major topic of analysis and debate among legal scholars. But it is worth noting that the likes of Montesquieu, Thomas Jefferson, and James Madison by no means have the last word on the philosophical underpinnings of our free speech rights. Contemporary philosophers continue to explore the nature of these rights and their implications on moral life. They have debated, for example, how restrictions on hate speech can be philosophically justified (Brison, 1998). They also have debated how we might justify policies restricting other potentially offensive speech in a way that would not trample on basic First Amendment freedoms. Philosopher Thomas Nagel (1995) said the principle of autonomy, if we are serious about free speech, prevents us from being able to claim any "right" *not* to be offended. He refers to our mental autonomy:

> The sovereignty of each person's reason over his own beliefs and values requires that he be permitted to express them, expose them to the reactions of others, and defend them against objections. It also requires that he not be protected against exposure to views or arguments that might influence him in ways others deem pernicious, but that he have the responsibility to make up his own mind about whether to accept or reject them. Mental autonomy is restricted by shutting down both inputs and outputs. (p. 96)

Other philosophers go even further. If autonomy is the core of moral personality, as several have argued, then morality itself requires respect for autonomy. Failure here reduces humans and violates their human essence, they say. However, Thomas M. Scanlon, author of a book titled *What We Owe to Each Other* (1998), said we should not throw freedom of expression around as an absolute right. It should be understood, he said, primarily in terms of the interests it aims to protect. Those interests include the following:

- Interests we all have as potential speakers and writers in having the opportunity to communicate, especially in political life.
- Our interests as potential audiences in having access to expression.
- Our interests as bystanders (including the benefits of living in a society that enjoys cultural/political/technological benefits of free expression).
- Having fair and effective democratic political institutions: their legitimacy is based on free and open public debate. (Scanlon, 1990, pp. 335–336)

So the goals of freedom of expression should be described in the *values* attached to various interests, or "categories of activity and opportunity," according to Scanlon (1990, p. 336). Some interests, however, have no such value attached, such as teaching and learning how to make bombs or fraudulent mail-order schemes. So we can formulate "widely shared judgments of value on which arguments in favor of freedom of expression can be based, and they do this by abstracting from more specific value judgments that we use our freedom of expression to argue about" (p. 337). In other words, we must be suspicious of broad, overarching claims for free speech to be able to say anything we want, and instead should look closely at the *interest* a claim of free speech is aimed at promoting.

Others have argued that in our patriotic or moralistic zeal, we often overemphasize the value of free speech. Philosopher Glenn Tinder (1979) said it is true that "denying freedom of expression brings about a fundamental derangement in our relations with one another and with the primary values" (p. 170), but that "the moral authority of the principle of freedom of expression is undeserved" (p. 165). Alexander Meiklejohn (1960), a prominent First Amendment theorist, said, "What is essential is not that everyone shall speak, but that everything worth saying shall be said" (p. 26) Another theorist, Owen Fiss (1996), also argued that free speech is not useful to a democracy in the way that we often assume it is, and in fact, it can subvert or undermine the very things we want it to help us achieve—freedom of expression may actually pose a threat to itself, he said.

Case in Point: Clear Channel and the Fate of Autonomous Local Radio Programming

The continuing trend of corporate media consolidation—of more and more media outlets concentrated in fewer and fewer hands—is evident across most media sectors, including TV affiliates, newspapers, music record labels, and publishing houses. But few sectors have been as deeply affected by this trend as commercial radio, where corporate consolidation has fundamentally transformed the listening landscape, even as the industry remains largely unconsolidated. Relaxation of media regulatory policies in the 1980s and 1990s triggered a buying spree in which thousands of stations, worth a total of $100 billion, were sold. The result, two conglomerates, Clear Channel and Viacom's Infinity Radio, now control about one-third of all radio advertising revenue, and up to 90% in some markets. Clear Channel, with its aggressive business practices and conservative political connections, has become a lightning rod for criticism ever since and has been accused of trampling the "public service" obligations for license holders' use of public airwaves and of gutting local news and music programming and replacing it with computer-controlled, "cookie-cutter" programming. In January 2002, an early morning train derailment released a huge cloud of ammonia-based fertilizer, killing one person, in Minot, North Dakota. Local emergency officials were unable to reach anyone at local radio station KCJB, the designated emergency broadcaster in the area and one of six local stations, all owned by Clear Channel. The company had consolidated operations and no longer had anyone staffing the station, which instead was receiving a satellite feed. Local officials, after some delay, roused station employees from their homes (Lee, 2003).

Most Americans believe—wrongly, Fiss (1996) suggested—that the First Amendment exists to protect individual self-expression, when in fact, it is a means to a larger end: providing conditions in which everyone can participate in collective self-determination. Tinder (1979) agreed, saying that using our free-speech rights to justify every kind of self-expression undermines its real value:

> Freedom of expression is not spontaneously self-reinforcing. If it is used to
> obscure the truth or create conflict—and in any large society there are bound to
> be those with an interest in using it in this way—it may be self-destructive. Where
> it is used, as in America, mainly for commercial ends, it may be gradually

weakened by trivialization—by undermining a society's respect and capacity for rational discourse. (pp. 164–165)

JOURNALISTIC INDEPENDENCE

There is nothing so precious to professional journalists as the idea of their credibility. If they are not perceived as reliable and impartial sources of information by their audiences, they know that their jobs are in peril. And one of the easiest ways of undermining journalistic credibility is to compromise a journalist's *independence.* There is of course a subjective element of news judgment, but when decisions about news are influenced by factors outside the bounds of professional perceptions of newsworthiness or are shaped by something other than the journalistic commitment to a broad public interest, we say that journalistic independence has been compromised. That is why people in the news business talk about the "fire wall" between the newsroom and the business or advertising operations. News content can quickly suffer a loss of credibility if audiences perceive it is presented for the benefit of advertisers or other special interests. Making decisions about what gets covered and what does not based on promoting an advertiser, a lobby group, or other special interest *conflicts* with the journalistic ideal of serving the public interest "without fear or favor"—in a spirit of independence from people or groups that would want to use the news for their own benefit. Politicians, public relations practitioners, government agencies, and other powerful individuals and institutions try to influence journalists' news decisions all the time. As professionals, journalists strive to sort through the spin, balance competing voices on an issue, and produce impartial news accounts that they hope will rise above the fray. Jockeying to influence, shape, or even control the news is understood by most media-savvy parties as how the game is played. But most journalists are quick to call foul on more aggressive attempts to unduly influence news content for political, personal, or commercial reasons because they threaten to conflict with their mission to serve a broader public interest. These conflicts of interest can take many forms.

Individual-Level Conflict of Interest

Maria Bartiromo emerged as the glamorous face of the struggling CNBC cable channel in 2005 and 2006, combining a polished, confident studio presence with what was described as "Sophia Loren" looks. Broadcast executives credited Bartiromo for CNBC's steadily increasing ratings through 2006. However, the broadcast anchor raised eyebrows in other ways. More than most TV news personalities, Bartiromo socialized with executives of several companies that she covered on the air. Business leaders sought her presence at black-tie events and corporate retreats. Bartiromo raised eyebrows among journalists with her close, frequent association with a powerful Citigroup banking executive, including shared overseas airline flights and an ill-fated joint business arrangement that involved a program on the Sundance Channel cable network. All the while, Bartiromo reported on Citigroup as CNBC's self-described "Money Honey" anchor.

Several media observers questioned Bartiromo's high-profile socializing with her sources, asking whether it was simply the case of a savvy journalist cultivating sources or a more serious case of conflict of interest. "The succession of events has focused media scrutiny on Bartiromo, who, like any reporter, is expected not to get too close to, or accept favors from, the people and companies she covers," according to an Associated Press account (Moore, 2007). Most news organizations require their journalists to abide by explicit conflict-of-interest policies, many of which require them to disclose any business, financial, or personal involvement they may have with people or groups in the communities they cover. Many journalists are even more aggressive in steering clear of any symbols or associations that could lead others to question their autonomy. Many news organizations limit civic activities of journalists if that work might involve groups or issues that the journalist might cover. Political journalists refrain from adorning their cars with partisan bumper stickers. Others even refuse to register to vote for fear of being suspected of advocating an agenda in their work. In the weeks following the terrorist attacks of September 11, 2001, while many anchors at TV affiliates across the country started wearing American flag lapel pins in a show of patriotic sympathy, some executive producers imposed policies prohibiting their on-air personalities from wearing the pins because they thought it an inappropriate partisan symbol for any journalist.

It is important to note that not all conflicts of interest pose a serious threat to a journalist's integrity. Some associations are harmless. But at the very least, it is important for journalists to avoid even appearances of conflict that could compromise their credibility with sources and audiences. Fully disclosing any such associations is usually expected. Journalists must apply Sissela Bok's "publicity" test to themselves: If the journalist's link to a group or organization became a story in itself, would that feel compromising in some way? If so, the threat it poses to one's credibility as an independent journalist probably is not worth it (Bok, 1999, pp. 89–94).

Corporate-Level Conflict of Interest

The trend of corporate media consolidation—of more and more media outlets concentrated in fewer and fewer corporate hands—is arguably the most pressing issue in news media ethics today. Corporate owners of newspapers, radio stations, record labels, publishing houses, and TV affiliates are increasingly demanding more profits from their news-oriented subdivisions and also are tempted to use those news outlets as a promotional tool for other corporate products. This is a corporate conflict of interest—when the parent company's efforts to deliver high performance to stockholders may conflict with the public service mission of the company's news subdivision—that critics have argued contributes to the dilution of news into "infotainment" and blurs the line between journalism and promotion. In one study, 40% of magazine editors surveyed said that they had been ordered by either an ad director or a publisher to take action on behalf of an advertiser—to kill a critical story or tone down coverage that might put a client in a bad light—that they believed would damage the publication's editorial integrity. Only half said they refused the request (Howland, 1989). As a result, "market-driven" journalism increasingly influences what audiences see and what they don't. Bartiromo's personal associations with a Citigroup executive raised questions of a possible conflict of interest, but CNBC also encouraged its anchor's public appearances with executives of the banking giant—which also happened to be a major advertiser on the network. Critics blasted CBS executives in

2003 and 2004 when the ratings-starved network arranged for pop icon Michael Jackson to appear in an exclusive interview on *60 Minutes*—just when the network was about to air a glowing retrospective on Jackson's career highlights. Corporate parents also may "cross-promote" a product by presenting it as news. In 2000, CBS broadcast frequent "news" reports about developments and tidbits from its "reality" entertainment program, *Survivor.* In 2001, AOL Time Warner's *CNN Headline News* was criticized for plugging other AOL Time Warner products in news packages (McChesney, 2004, p. 85). Shortly after *Washington Post* celebrity journalist Bob Woodward of Watergate fame published his book *Plan of Attack* in 2004, he also appeared as a guest on the same *60 Minutes* program at CBS. The network is owned by the media giant Viacom—which also happens to own Simon & Schuster, the publishing house that came out with Woodward's book. There is no doubt that most of Woodward's published works are legitimate news events in themselves, and Viacom's corporate intent is impossible to know. But the corporate connection and the temptation to harness the "synergy" made possible by both the publisher and the news outlet cannot be dismissed.

Corporate advertisers also can be aggressive in insisting on "friendly" editorial environments in the media outlets they do not own. In 1993, Chrysler announced a new policy to all the magazines in which it bought ads: Editors would have to tell Chrysler what kind of stories would appear in magazines with Chrysler ads. The company was concerned about having its cars featured next to stories on controversial sexual or political issues. If the editorial content wasn't friendly enough, Chrysler said it would pull its ads. Of the 100 or so magazines that Chrysler notified, about half agreed to the policy. Four years later, however, Chrysler dropped the policy after the Magazine Publishers of America denounced it as "economic censorship" (Sheehan, 2004, pp. 41, 43).

The influence of corporate pressure to determine the news, with the enormous profit margins at stake and the pressure for ratings and market share intensifying, is likely to get worse, critics have said. "The drive to achieve synergy is often journalism's poison," said media analyst Ken Auletta (2002). And it is this corporate influence, much more than any political bias, that increasingly threatens to dominate journalism culture. Individual journalists do retain a degree of control and autonomy in their day-to-day work—they decide how to write and package stories, who gets quoted and who doesn't—but personal identities are often subsumed by newsroom socialization and by professional norms (Shoemaker & Reese, 1996). And they historically have remained "segregated" from the real centers of power in journalism: the executive levels that determine hiring, long-term business goals, and resource allocation (Glasser & Gunther, 2005, p. 391). Self-censorship of journalists often results. In a recent survey of journalists by the Pew Research Center for the People and the Press, only 25% of the respondents indicated that their news organizations "never" avoid stories that could threaten or embarrass their parent company (Kohut, 2000, p. 43).

AUTONOMY FOR PUBLIC RELATIONS PROFESSIONALS

While the value of journalistic independence emphasizes *freedom from* undue influences in its insistence on a mission of impartial public service, the meaning of autonomy among public relations practitioners is very much in line with Berlin's notion of "positive" freedom: the ability to define oneself according to a professional ethic rather than being relegated as a blindly loyal mouthpiece for narrow client interests. For public relations professionals, true autonomy means not being subject to undue restrictions, but it also has a much more proactive meaning: Autonomous public relations professionals must have a seat at the decision-making table. "In public relations," Bowen (2005) wrote, "autonomy can take the form of freedom from encroachment or sublimation to other organizational functions as well as the individual issues manager's freedom to make moral choices" (p. 194). But while public relations professionals continue to ensure that corporate executives understand public relations as a key component of policy making, they also must be mindful of the ethical questions implicit in the "two-way symmetrical" model of communication so popular among clients' media representatives.

Wanted: A Public Relations Seat at the Executive Table

Too often, public relations is perceived by outsiders as shameless spin doctoring or cynical image management or both. However, public relations theorists have long argued that public relations professionals can and should situate themselves with their clients in ways that allow them to do something quite different: give voice to conscience. Professional public relations, properly understood, "introduces the values and problems of stakeholders into strategic decisions and . . . introduces a moral element to those decisions," according to prominent public relations theorist James Grunig (2000, p. 28). Bowen (2006) echoed this point:

> The structure of an organization should include enough autonomy for the public relations function to contribute to decision-making in an unconstrained manner. . . . To make well-considered decisions, it is vital that the top communicator be a part of organizational leadership. (pp. 332, 336)

This executive "positioning" of public relations implies a critical need for autonomy in the "positive" sense: Full exercise of the public relations practitioner's moral agency requires her to be fully integrated into the decision-making process. Anything less reduces her role to corporate lackey status and denies her an opportunity to exercise her professional ethical duties. Management consultant Christopher Spicer (1997) described the tendency for corporate management to perceive public relations as a strictly subservient or technical function as "organizational arrogance." This often happens when public relations is perceived as a function of marketing offices, and as a result, public relations receives fewer resources and is considered by executives to be less valuable (Grunig & Grunig, 1998). Smart executives avoid this mind-set, public relations theorists say, because they understand that as "boundary spanners," public relations professionals "[deal] with the public most likely to constrain or enhance organizational effectiveness" (Bowen, 2006, p. 332). Often, that understanding emerges from an experience of a crisis in which public relations "proves" itself to be a valuable component of the organization's "dominant coalition" (Plowman, 1998).

> ### Case in Point: NASA's Public Relations
> ### Crises of *Challenger* and *Columbia*
>
> In January 1986, the space shuttle *Challenger* exploded less than two minutes after takeoff as the nation watched in disbelief. The disaster that killed all seven astronauts quickly grew into a public relations nightmare for the National Aeronautics and Space Administration (NASA), which was accused of trying to impose a "news blackout" and whose handing of the event was described as "troubling," "high-handed," "ill-advised," and a "failure" (Martin & Boynton, 2005, p. 258). But 17 years later, in February 2003, when the space shuttle *Columbia* disintegrated while reentering the Earth's atmosphere at 12,500 miles per hour, it was a different story. After mishandling the *Challenger* disaster, the embattled agency appeared to have learned the first rule of crisis communications: control the flow of information. NASA officials "seized control of the public communication high ground and . . . maintained it," according to NASA administrator Sean O'Keefe; the agency began holding news conferences twice a day, strove to answer all questions promptly, made key NASA officials available for interviews, and released information "whether it seemed to benefit the Agency or not" (Kauffman, 2005, pp. 266, 268). The result was widespread praise for NASA's handling of the *Columbia* disaster from investigators, the news media, and members of Congress. A central component of this turnabout was an important revision of NASA's updated "crisis plan" that more fully integrated public affairs staff in how emergencies were to be handled, effectively giving NASA public relations officials the necessary autonomy to help respond to a crisis in proactive ways. Just three months before the *Columbia* accident, O'Keefe noted a "glaring deficiency" in the agency's crisis plan: NASA's public relations officials were not part of emergency practice runs. "We revised the plan immediately to correct this oversight," O'Keefe reported (Kauffman, p. 265).

AUTONOMY IN CYBERSPACE

The exhilarating freedoms and potential of the World Wide Web are posing special, ongoing challenges to our understanding of what constitutes our moral autonomy. This is true not because of any threat that it may limit what we can and cannot do, of course. Quite the opposite. The virtual limitlessness of what we *can* do in our online communication makes the question of what we *ought* to do more pressing than ever. For the most part, there are no Internet editors to check Web pages and postings for fairness, balance, and accuracy. While the vitality of the Internet gives new meaning to the "marketplace of ideas" concept and the belief that the truth is more likely to emerge from it, it also presents new opportunities for deception, duplicity, and controversial conflicts of interests. "Buyer beware" should be a label posted at nearly every Internet portal. If we understand autonomy as acting according to our moral responsibilities, then the tactics for persuasion that we use on the Web also must reflect our ethical standards applied to communication in every other medium.

Public Relations Blogging: Not for the Faint of Heart

Public relations professionals who are preoccupied with managing stakeholder relationships have watched their jobs become rapidly more complex as consumers, customers, and public interest groups have harnessed the Web to bolster their voice, their reach, and their influence on public relations clients. This "Internet induced stakeholder power" (van der Merwe, Pitt, & Abratt, 2005) means public relations efforts must be more nimble and, when possible, more proactive in addressing complaints and concerns. It also means that public relations offices must come to understand that "managing" relationships is not the same as *controlling* the dialogue with stakeholders, which is futile on the Web. In a 2005 report on how to harness the potential of blogs as a communication tool, Bacon's Information, Inc., cautioned that bloggers covet their independence, and that public relations strategies that attempt to undermine this autonomy can backfire. "They will publish their unvarnished opinion of a product—warts and all," according to the report. "Keep in mind that the risks associated with blogs need to be accepted along with their potential benefits" (Bacon's Information Inc., 2005, p. 4). There's an inherent perceived bias of any blog that is public relations-motivated, public relations executive Peter Smudde cautioned, and yet "those responsible for public relations blogs must 'walk the talk' about being virtuous professionals who do what's right and not just for an organization, its stakeholders, society, and themselves as citizens" (Bacon's Information Inc., p. 38).

PR communicators are being forced to adapt in other ways. For those who work with journalists, the traditional "pitch" for stories or quotes featuring clients is giving way to a phenomenon known as "media catching," where social network or listserv formats are used to link single journalists with a broad group of PR "subscribers." Journalists in search of answers or content ideas broadcast their queries, and the PR members can respond. One of the more popular of these is the Help A Reporter Out (HARO) e-mail list, and another is ProfNet, an online service of PRNewswire. While media catching may appear to diminish the ability of media relations communicators to be proactive by reversing the journalist-PR relationship, others suggest the trend reinforces calls for the PR industry to "be willing to participate in accurate dialogue" and places greater emphasis on honest engagement (Waters, Tindall, & Morton, 2010). Media catching may curtail PR "spin-doctoring" tendencies.

Intense criticism has followed "buzz" marketers who use word-of-mouth tactics to plug a product or service without disclosing that the "buzz" is actually being paid for. Even the Federal Trade Commission stepped in to announce that bloggers who receive money from advertising firms and publicists need to disclose the relationship for readers. "The problem is the advertisers are trying to buy a blogger's voice, and once they've bought it they own it," said Jeff Jarvis, a City University of New York journalism professor who writes about technology (Friedman, 2007, p. C1). The same framework applies to public relations efforts to harness online forums to advocate for a client. Many public relations firms and corporate communications officers have waded into the blogosphere themselves in a proactive attempt to control or shape the public information about clients and companies. While the sense of autonomy found in blogging for public relations purposes may be attractive, some warn that public relations blogging can be both "a blessing and a curse" (Smudde, 2005, p. 35) because the Web greatly expands opportunities for communication channels yet prevents control of the channels by any one party.

Journalists Find Their "Voice" in the Online Frontier

In many ways, the Web provides exciting opportunities for journalists to extend their reach by tapping new audiences and encouraging more reader engagement and participation. While blogging allows journalists to connect with readers in a new way, news organizations are struggling with the dangers of the new medium. Media lawyers are cautioning that libel laws are still likely to apply to the more informal, rough-and-tumble exchanges characterized by blog discussions, particularly if the blogger is affiliated with a news organization. Journalists have complained that Internet users don't always distinguish between news bloggers committed to journalistic standards and "pajama" bloggers who don't produce their own material but who merely comment on the news and often trade on rumor or speculation. Perhaps the most famous case of this is Matt Drudge, a blogger who was first to mention White House intern Monica Lewinsky's semen-stained dress and who prompted mainstream news reporters to track down the revelation, leading to impeachment proceedings against President Bill Clinton. Drudge proved to be accurate—that time. "The very nature of the beast seems to encourage carelessly conceived statements and baseless charges," said media critic Eric Alterman. "Matt Drudge brags that he is 80 percent accurate. Well, that 20 percent can do an awful lot of damage" (Alterman, 2003, p. 86).

Journalists must be careful in protecting their independence. Some news organizations, for example, encourage their reporters to express opinions and develop their own "voice" on their blogs, but only so much. A political reporter offering snarky comments about candidates in a race, for instance, would threaten that journalist's credibility as an objective observer. Journalists and blogging, consequently, remain in an uneasy partnership while everyone finds appropriate boundaries. "There's an inevitable clash of values between a newspaper, which has a journalistic reputation and a brand name to protect, and a swiftly changing medium that has grown in power and prestige precisely because it has flouted many of journalism's traditional values," according to one observer (Hull, 2006). Journalists also must take care to protect their credibility. The ease of posting news on the Web means that there's a deadline every minute now, and news organizations are regularly "breaking" stories on their Web sites instead of waiting for the print edition. This has cultivated an audience expectation for immediacy, which tempts news organizations to treat speculation as news and to forgo in-depth reporting for the "quick hit" story.

It should be clear that, particularly for journalists, the Web opens new opportunities as well as new dangers, and yet, the same fundamental ethical concerns of independence and credibility apply to the new technology. In April 2006, editors at the *Los Angeles Times* confirmed this when they suspended a staff blogger after he posted comments using false names, which, the editors said, constituted a form of unacceptable deception. "Over the past few days, some analysts have used this episode to portray the Web as a new frontier for newspapers, saying that it raises fresh and compelling ethical questions. *Times* editors don't see it that way," according to an editor's note on the paper's Web site. "The Web makes it easier to conceal one's identity, and the tone of exchanges is often harsh. But the Web doesn't change the rules for *Times* journalists" (Hull, 2006).

In this era of social media and countless blogging platforms, the news from mainstream journalists often is only part of the story. Independent bloggers now provide a daily diet of information and perspectives on every topic imaginable. But are they independent? In many cases, yes, but increasingly blog voices are being "sponsored" by corporations in mutually beneficial arrangements. McDonald's has linked up with a network of "mommy bloggers" who also are fans of the fast-food chain. Their input has helped shape recent changes in McDonald's menu featuring more fruits and vegetables. In 2010, the company invited 15 of them to the Oak Brook, Illinois, headquarters, flying them and their families in and putting them up in nice hotels. They had tours and meetings with executives. They were asked to write one post about their experience, and all disclosed they were sponsored by the company. "Beyond that, we gave them, and we wanted them to have, free rein," said one executive (O'Brien, 2012, p. 81).

For Discussion

1. In your own words, describe the distinction between freedom and moral autonomy.

2. Think about a situation in which you had to deal with an actual or potential conflict of interest in your life. How did you resolve it, and how did it affect or could it have affected your ability to act autonomously as defined in this chapter?

3. How do individual-level conflicts of interest threaten journalistic autonomy? How do corporate-level conflicts threaten it?

4. Thomas Scanlon and other philosophers said that freedom of speech should not be considered an absolute right, but should instead be judged by various interests served by the speech in question. Explain how this approach differs from the more common understanding of free speech as a "right."

5. In what ways does the "two-way symmetrical" model of public relations communication reflect an Aristotelian model of moderation? How would you say that such a public relations model might help us distinguish between a public relations professional's "positive" autonomy and his freedom?

6. If you were asked to draft a "blogger code of ethics," what guidelines or standards would you suggest to protect or maintain the expectation that bloggers' voices are "morally autonomous"?

REFERENCES

Alterman, E. (2003, Fall). Determining the value of blogs. *Nieman Reports,* 85–86.

Auletta, K. (2002, December 19). *Ken Auletta: "The drive to achieve synergy is often journalism's poison."* www.iwantmedia.com. Retrieved from http://www.iwantmedia.com/people/people22.html

Bacon's Information Inc. (2005). *Introduction to blogs: A quick guide to understanding and maximizing communication efforts in the blogosphere.* Chicago, IL: Author.

Benhabib, S. (1992). *Situating the self: Gender, community and postmodernism in contemporary ethics.* New York, NY: Routledge.

Benn, S. I. (1988). *A theory of freedom.* Cambridge, UK: Cambridge University Press.

Berlin, I. (1969). *Four essays on liberty.* London, England: Oxford University Press.

Bok, S. (1999). *Lying: Moral choice in public and private life.* New York, NY: Vintage.

Bowen, S. A. (2005). A practical model for ethical decision making in issues management and public relations. *Journal of Public Communications Research, 17*(3), 191–216.

Bowen, S. A. (2006). Autonomy in communication: Inclusion in strategic management and ethical decision-making, a comparative case analysis. *Journal of Communication Management, 10*(4), 330–352.

Brison, S. J. (1998). The autonomy defense of free speech. *Ethics, 108,* 312–339.

Cahn, S. M. (2002). *Classics of political and moral philosophy.* New York, NY: Oxford University Press.

Colby, A., & Damon, W. (1992). *Some do care: Contemporary lives of moral commitment.* New York, NY: Free Press.

Cristman, J. (Ed.). (1989). *The inner citadel: Essays on individual autonomy.* New York, NY: Oxford University Press.

Dworkin, G. (1988). *The theory and practice of autonomy.* Cambridge, UK: Cambridge University Press.

Dworkin, R. (1985). *A matter of principle.* Cambridge, MA: Harvard University Press.

Feinberg, J. (1989). Autonomy. In J. Cristman (Ed.), *The inner citadel: Essays on individual autonomy* (pp. 27–53). New York, NY: Oxford University Press.

Finnis, J. (1987). Legal enforcement of "duties to oneself": Kant vs. neo-Kantians. *Columbia Law Review, 87,* 433–456.

Fiss, O. (1996). *The irony of free speech.* Cambridge, MA: Harvard University Press.

Friedman, J. (2007, March 7). Blogging for dollars raises questions of online ethics. *Los Angeles Times,* p. C1.

George, R. P. (1993). *Making men moral: Civil liberties and public morality.* Oxford, UK: Clarnedon Press.

Gilligan, C. (1982). *In a different voice: Psychological theory and women's development.* Cambridge, MA: Harvard University Press.

Glasser, T. L., & Gunther, M. (2005). The legacy of autonomy in American journalism. In G. Overholser & K. H. Jamieson (Eds.), *Institutions of American democracy: The press* (pp. 384–399). New York, NY: Oxford University Press.

Grunig, J. E. (2000). Collectivism, collaboration and societal corporatism as core professional values in public relations. *Journal of Public Relations Research, 12*(1), 23–48.

Grunig, J. E., & Grunig, L. A. (1998). The relationship between public relations and marketing in excellent organizations: Evidence from the IABC study. *Journal of Marketing Communications, 4,* 141–162.

Habermas, J. (1993). Justice and solidarity. In M. Fisk (Ed.), *Justice: Key concepts in critical theory* (pp. 89–100). Atlantic Highlands, NJ: Humanities Press.

Harris, S. (2012). *Free will.* New York, NY: Free Press.

Haughney, C. (2013, January 7). After pinpointing gun owners, paper is a target. *New York Times,* pp. A1, A15.

Hill, T. E. (1989). The Kantian conception of autonomy. In J. Cristman (Ed.), *The inner citadel: Essays on individual autonomy* (pp. 91–105). New York, NY: Oxford University Press.

Howland, J. (1989, December). Ad vs. edit: The pressure mounts. *Folio,* 92–100.

Hull, D. (2006, December 5). Blogging between the lines. *American Journalism Review,* pp. 63–76.

Hume, D. (1888). *Treatise of human nature.* Oxford, UK: Oxford Clarendon Press. (Original work published 1740)

Kant, I. (1930). *Lectures on ethics* (L. Infield, Trans.). London, England: Methuen.

Kant, I. (2002). *Groundwork for the metaphysics of morals* (A. W. Wood, Ed. & Trans.). New Haven, CT: Yale University Press. (Original work published 1785)

Kauffman, J. (2005). Lost in space: A critique of NASA's crisis communications in the Columbia disaster. *Public Relations Review, 31,* 263–275.

Kohut, A. (2000, May/June). Self-censorship: Counting the ways. *Columbia Journalism Review,* 43.

Lee, J. (2003, March 31). In Minot, ND, radio, a single corporate voice. *New York Times,* p. C7.

Locke, J. (1988). *Two treatises on government* (P. Laslett, Ed.), Cambridge UK: Cambridge University Press. (Original work published 1689)

MacCallum, G. C. (1967). Negative and positive freedom. *The Philosophical Review, 76*(3), 312–334.

MacIntyre, A. (1984). *After virtue: A study in moral theory* (2nd ed.). South Bend, IN: University of Notre Dame Press.

Martin, R. M., & Boynton, L. A. (2005). From liftoff to landing: NASA's crisis communications and resulting media coverage following the *Challenger* and *Columbia* tragedies. *Public Relations Review, 31,* 253–261.

McChesney, R. W. (2004). *The problem of the media: U.S. communication politics of the twenty-first century.* New York, NY: Monthly Review Press.

Meiklejohn, A. (1960). *Political freedom: The constitutional powers of the people.* New York, NY: Harper.

Mill, J. S. (1991). On liberty (J. Gray & G. W. Smith, Eds.). London, England: Routledge. (Original work published 1859)

Moore, F. (2007, January 27). Bartiromo did nothing wrong, says CNBC. Associated Press Online. Available at http://www.washingtonpost.com/wp-dyn/content/article/2007/01/27/AR2007012701033.html

Nagel, T. (1995). Personal rights and public space. *Philosophy and Public Affairs, 24*(2), 83–107.

Noddings, N. (1984). *Caring: A feminine approach to ethics and moral education.* Berkeley: University of California Press.

Nozick, R. (1974). *Anarchy, state and utopia.* New York, NY: Basic Books.

O'Brien, K. (2012, May 4). How McDonald's came back bigger than ever. *New York Times Magazine,* pp. 46–48, 78, 81.

Overbye, D. (2007, January 2). Free will: Now you have it, now you don't. *New York Times,* pp. D1, D4.

Paton, H. J. (1971). *The categorical imperative: A study in Kant's moral philosophy.* Philadelphia: University of Pennsylvania Press.

Plowman, K. D. (1998). Power in conflict for public relations. *Journal of Public Relations Research, 10*(4), 237–261.

Rawls, J. (1999). *A theory of justice.* Cambridge, MA: Belknap Press of Harvard University. (Original work published 1971)

Richards, D. A. J. (1982). *Sex, drugs, death and the law.* Totowa, NJ: Rowman & Littlefield.

Richards, D. A. J. (1987). Kantian ethics and the harm principle: A reply to John Finnis. *Columbia Law Review, 87,* 457–471.

Rothbard, M. N. (1982). *The ethics of liberty.* Atlantic Highlands, NJ: Humanities Press.

Salisbury, H.E. (1981). *Without fear or favor: An uncompromising look at The New York Times.* New York, NY: Ballantine Books.

Scanlon, T. M. (1990). Content regulation reconsidered. In J. Lichtenberg (Ed.), *Democracy and the mass media* (pp. 331–354). New York, NY: Cambridge University Press.

Scanlon, T. M. (1998). *What we owe to each other.* Cambridge, MA: Harvard University Press.

Sheehan, K. (2004). *Controversies in contemporary advertising.* Thousand Oaks, CA: Sage.

Shoemaker, P. J., & Reese, S. D. (1996). *Mediating the message: Theories of influences on mass media content.* White Plains, NY: Longman.

Smudde, P. M. (2005, Fall). Blogging, ethics and public relations: A proactive and dialogic approach. *Public Relations Quarterly,* 34–38.

Spicer, C. (1997). *Organizational public relations: A political perspective.* Mahwah, NJ: Lawrence Erlbaum.

Steele, B. (2003, July 3). The value of independence. *The Poynter Institute*. Retrieved from http://www .poynter.org/column.asp?id = 36&aid = 40421

Steiner, L. (1989). Feminist theorizing and communication ethics. *Communication, 12,* 157–173.

Tinder, G. (1979). Freedom of expression, the strange imperative. *Yale Review, 129*(2), 161–176.

van der Merwe, R., Pitt, L. F., & Abratt, R. (2005, Spring). Stakeholder strength: PR survival strategies in the Internet age. *Public Relations Quarterly,* 39–48.

Waters, R. D., Tindall, N. T. J., & Morton, T. S. (2010). Media catching and the journalist-public relations practitioner relationship: How social media are changing the practice of public relations. *Journal of Public Relations Research, 22*(3), 241–264.

Wolff, R. P. (1970). *In defense of anarchism.* New York, NY: Harper & Row.

CHAPTER 9

Privacy

We zealously guard privacy as a fundamental "right," yet gleefully bare our souls, innermost fears, and sexual anxieties on *The Maury Show.* We are drawn to lurid tales of human suffering and embarrassment, yet we are quick to accuse the media of invasion when something makes us uncomfortable. It is no wonder privacy is one of the most vexing media issues of our time. And digital media technology has made things more confusing by providing new ways to break through barriers that traditionally have protected privacy while simultaneously transforming what we think of as private in the first place. The topic of privacy tends to highlight a dualistic—even hypocritical—feature of our culture: We are absolutist about our right to privacy, except when we are eager to carelessly fling it away— for publicity, for money, or for the chance to win an Xbox 360 game console. "An American has no sense of privacy," commented George Bernard Shaw. "He does not know what it means. There is no such thing in the country." The famous Irish dramatist and social critic made that observation in 1933. What would he say about our 21st-century World Wide Web culture, in which private citizens install 24-hour Web cams in their bedrooms and offer any and all strangers viewing access for an annual fee?

So far, most key principles discussed in this book have been *intrinsic* features of solid ethical practice. They are, in other words, important values that help define what it means to behave as responsible professionals in the media. Ideas of transparency, justice, minimizing harm, and autonomy should guide the way we conduct ourselves. But the idea of privacy, like that of community, is a bit different. Privacy doesn't guide our behavior in the same way since, as communicators, we aren't expected to "embody" the value of privacy like we're expected to embody these other principles. Privacy is "outside" of media practice, so to speak. It is a key objective concern of media *subjects,* or of people caught in the media spotlight. Yet a full understanding of privacy is critical for responsible behavior. Failure to do so is at the root of many legitimate charges of unethical behavior.

We don't question whether privacy is important to us. Of course it is. But *why* exactly is it important? How does the concept of privacy function? How should we understand privacy, and how should that understanding guide the judgments we make as both media practitioners and media consumers? Simplistic claims about privacy lead many to unfairly accuse the media of crossing the line. Both media professionals and audiences commonly misconstrue the concept of privacy in ways that obscure, not enlighten, ethical deliberation. This chapter aims to clarify the concept of privacy and challenge students to get beyond jingoistic claims of the "public right to know" versus our "right to be left alone." Such claims, according to one prominent privacy theorist, can be "incomplete and misleading" (Schoeman, 1992, p. 8).

Paradoxical as it may sound, a strengthened respect for the concept of privacy is critical for any media system to be able to successfully serve its community-based functions. Jeffrey Rosen (2000, 2011) persuasively argued that digitally based media is eroding our sense of privacy by gradually removing the ability of individuals to control the information about them that is made public. This development leaves individuals less able to shape and control their identity, Rosen said. Moreover, it could eventually serve to further cheapen the "public sphere" that the journalistic enterprise ought to be cultivating. If the distinctions between the public and private spheres are blurred, useful social divisions will make it harder to cultivate a more participatory democracy, he argued. Maintenance of a clearly defined sense of privacy is essential to preserving the value of community participation; individuals who feel they have little control over their public identities because of an overbearing media system are less likely to attach themselves to such a community or to participate in it if that means potentially unlimited and unrestrained media exposure.

Rawls on Privacy

Maximizing everyone's privacy often is assumed to be the ultimate goal in much political thought. The "private society" praised by Plato, Hegel, and others is built on the claim that individuals all have their private ends and that they participate in society and engage in relationships solely as a means to accomplish those ends, and not out of a belief that such social engagement is a good in itself. The hard reality of this private society is that "no one takes account of the good of others, or of what they possess; rather, everyone prefers the most efficient scheme that gives him the largest share of assets," as John Rawls described it (1971/1999, p. 457). But Rawls argued against viewing this private society as an ideal to which we should aspire because it fails to take into account the true value of social engagement. Rather than assuming privacy is an "end" that should be maximized for its own sake, we should understand it as a "means" to the successful realization of our social nature. The real value of privacy lies in what it allows us to accomplish. "The social nature of mankind is best seen by contrast with the conception of private society," Rawls said. "We need one another as partners in ways of life that are engaged in for their own sake, and the successes and enjoyments of others are necessary for and complementary to our own good" (p. 458). He went on to argue that privacy should be understood as a means to realize our personal strengths, which we then contribute to society. Considered this way, the value of privacy, Rawls claimed, is that it helps us realize the unique potential for excellence in ourselves and in others. This value is inherently *social* in its nature and is not focused on the individual, as our culture often leads us to think. "It is through social union founded upon the needs and potentialities of its members that each person can participate in the total sum of the realized assets of others. . . . Persons need one another since it is only in active cooperation with others that one's powers reach fruition. Only in a social union is the individual complete" (pp. 459–460). This is one of the central insights into human nature that he suggests emerges when people imagine themselves to be in the "original position," which is created by the veil of ignorance.

Ethical journalism requires a solid understanding of the philosophical justifications for privacy. It respects private spaces and information when there is not an overriding public interest—particularly if journalists are serious in cultivating community or civic engagement. Ethical journalists understand that people's success and effectiveness as social beings *require* them to maintain a private sphere that is not subject to public scrutiny. This may seem paradoxical. How can journalists credibly carry out their primary function of pursuing the truth if they are preoccupied with respecting others' privacy? Yet journalists who fail to appropriately understand the nature of privacy can cause both unethical intrusions into private lives and an erosion of journalistic credibility. And without credibility, the professional journalist has little else.

Privacy is a major concern in the news media. Yet it also can be a concern for public relations professionals while taking several different forms. Most immediate is the priority given to the idea of confidentiality in the service of a client. Indeed, "safeguarding confidences" is among the six "core principles" listed in the code of ethics of the Public Relations Society of America. Another way that public relations professionals need to think about privacy is in control of information. While the work of client advocacy may tempt public relations professionals to seek ways to increase control of third-party content and commentary, such efforts also can increase liability in the event of invasive or defamatory claims. As lawyer and public relations professor Michael Parkinson and his research colleagues note, "The more we attempt to control, edit or manage the contents of our employee chat rooms, bulletin boards or other Internet postings, the more likely we are to be liable for anything placed in the database, even by an anonymous user" (Parkinson, Ekachai, & Hetherington, 2001, p. 253). Accessing and using personal data when conducting public opinion research also requires public relations professionals to consider privacy concerns. And finally, questions about the security of a company's database with client or customer information can quickly become a public relations issue when that security is breached. Several laws and regulations require companies to notify clients or consumers when their personal data may be stolen or compromised, which can quickly trigger "bad press and worse customer relations for the company announcing the breach" (Kelly, 2005, p. 25).

"Privacy is important largely because of how it facilitates association with people, not independence from people."

—F. D. Schoeman (1992)

PRIVACY DEFINED

At its most basic level, privacy is understood to be the ability to do things in our lives without public scrutiny. We often talk about our "right" to be left alone, to refuse to let everyone have access to us. The word *privacy* appears nowhere in the U.S. Constitution or Bill of Rights, yet Supreme Court rulings over the decades have found an implicit "right" to privacy in the First, Third, Fourth, and Fifth amendments. The term *right to privacy* was not widely used until 1890, when two prominent lawyers—one, Louis Brandeis, went on to become a Supreme Court justice—used it as a title to their law review article that complained about an out-of-control press using the new technology of photography to peer into the windows of houses. "Privacy," one theorist said, "is the condition of not having undocumented personal knowledge about one possessed by others" (Parent, 1983, p. 269). The case of *Griswold v. Connecticut* in 1965 is commonly credited as establishing a general constitutional right to privacy. The Supreme Court ruled that a Connecticut statute forbidding the use of contraceptives violated a right of marital privacy. Law professor Jeffrey Rosen (2000) wrote about privacy as having control of information that other people have about you. Our modern, liberal view of privacy comes largely from the claims of Thomas Hobbes and John Locke. For Hobbes, the "private world" served to protect individual security. For Locke, it helped ensure autonomy by protecting anything an individual "hath mixed his labour with" (cited in Swanson, 1992, p. 5). In this view, the public and private spheres were mutually exclusive, with whatever is considered to be in the public sphere as having the potential to "intrude" on the people's privacy.

But privacy is more than some individual "right" to be left alone just for the sake of avoiding public scrutiny. It paradoxically serves particular social functions. Theorists have identified four privacy-related cultural features that seem to be universal:

1. Individuals tend to rely on an idea of social distance as part of their social interaction.

2. People believe they are never fully alone, which mostly likely stems from a primal fear of isolation.

3. Individuals will tend to invade others' privacy for a perceived social benefit or to prevent antisocial conduct.

4. As a society becomes more complex, the opportunities for physical and psychological privacy tend to increase (Westin, 1984).

As some of these features suggest, there is something important about the concept of privacy that goes far beyond merely having the "right" to do what we want. It serves a broader purpose. Hannah Arendt (1958) said the private realm, in both ancient Greek and Roman cultures, was where people managed their "material dependencies" but not their creative, rational, and other higher-level activities, which were considered part of one's "public" life. Indeed, while we may view privacy as special or somehow privileged, the Latin root of the word suggests something very different. The word *private* derives from the Latin *privatus* meaning "withdrawn from public life" or "deprived of office," and stems from the verb *privare*, meaning "to deprive" or "bereave." This root suggests that any claim of privacy as an absolute right to be left alone is based on a rather limited understanding of why humans, as social creatures, need privacy in the first place. "Privacy," according to a key theorist on the topic, "is important largely because of how it facilitates association with people, *not independence from people* [emphasis added]. This approach suggests that the identification of the right to privacy with the right to be left alone is an incomplete and misleading characterization" (Schoeman, 1992, p. 8).

Deconstructing the "Right" to Privacy

How can privacy be considered important in a way that doesn't simply mean the "right" to be left alone? The very idea may seem ridiculous in our individualistic, technology-enabled, whatever-feels-good culture. But philosophically, privacy is important not just for its own sake, as we conventionally think about it, but for what it enables us to do. It's not an absolute value, but an instrumental value. Privacy is important because of the way it enables us to be fully moral and social beings. Aristotle was clear on this: Privacy was essential for individuals to pursue virtue by "turning away" from the masses. Unlike Locke or Hobbes, claiming privacy to do whatever one wants made no sense to Aristotle. "In Aristotle's account, privacy is not a right to do as one pleases, but an opportunity to do as one ought," according to one scholar (Swanson, 1992, p. 207). Its value is paired with its philosophical opposite: accountability. Privacy is important, but it "is not everything," said Anita Allen, a law professor who specializes in privacy issues. "Privacy and accountability each in their own way render us more fit for valued forms of social participation" (Allen, 2005, p. 399). Both, she said, serve as ways to protect not just our freedoms, but our moral lives:

> Accountability dignifies. The society that holds individuals to account dignifies them by presupposing intelligence, rationality, and competence. . . . No one expects hamsters and centipedes to give account. That is one of the reasons they get squished and locked into little cages. The fact that we expect accountability of fellow humans is a measure of the seriousness with which we regard them. (p. 410)

> ### Privacy: Why Is It Valuable?
> According to many theorists, privacy
>
> - Is "a system of nuanced social norms [that] modulates the effectiveness of social control over an individual" (Schoeman, 1992).
> - Gives us the "ability to protect ourselves from being judged out of context" (Rosen, 2000).
> - Is critical to allow the development of the self and the pursuit of a virtuous life (Aristotle).
> - Allows us to maintain social relationships and serve multiple social roles (Nagel, 1998).

"Taken to the extreme, privacy results in total isolation and denies the social bases of human existence. At the other extreme, unlimited communication and the end of privacy, leaves the human subject depleted of self, of personality. Both unbridled solipsism and pure collectivism are forms of spiritual decay and ultimately death."

—I. L. Horowitz (1999)

The "instrumental" value of privacy—that is, the value that it holds in helping us carry out bigger moral objectives and not just for its own sake—takes many forms. Most people are familiar with John Stuart Mill's oft-quoted line from his famous essay, *On Liberty:* "The individual is not accountable to society for his actions, insofar as these concern the interests of no person but himself." But this is only partially correct, as Mill himself later acknowledged. The "right to control information about oneself," though often invoked in absolutist terms, has never been among the "foundations of our moral universe" in the same way that concepts such as justice, utility, rationality, and respect have for theorists as diverse as Mill and John Rawls. Several thinkers suggest that privacy should be considered a "secondary" right—that is, it is something that can be invoked as a right only in the service of a larger, more compelling "primary" right. This is how, for example, many First Amendment experts suggest that free speech is recognized and protected not merely for its own sake as an absolute right, but because it advances a broader good: enabling the best public policy to emerge from a vibrant exchange of ideas. The same can be said regarding privacy. As one privacy theorist concluded, "We understand what is being said when privacy is described as an aspect of human dignity, but we also understand why it is understood that dignity is the moral primary of which privacy is only a component part" (Schauer, 2003, p. 6).

Case in Point: Covering the Moment of Death in War

In 2009, a squad of Marines was ambushed by Taliban fighters in Afghanistan. One of the Marines, 21-year-old Lance Cpl. Joshua M. Bernard, was struck in the legs by a rocket-propelled grenade. Julie Jacobson, an Associated Press photographer, had been on patrol with the soldiers, and had just taken photos of Bernard. She instinctively photographed Bernard as he lay dying, surrounded by his comrades. After the Pentagon released Bernard's identity, AP released a photo essay and a video narrated by Jacobson to member newspapers, even though Bernard's father asked the AP not to use the graphic photo showing his son mortally wounded. AP's decision to do so created a firestorm of protest, with U.S. defense secretary Robert M. Gates denouncing the agency: "Why your organization would purposefully defy the family's wishes knowing full well that it will lead to yet more anguish is beyond me," he wrote. Journalists defended the decision. "What it does is show—in a very unequivocal and direct fashion—the real consequences of war," said Santiago Lyon, AP's photography director. Jacobson noted that Bernard's fellow Marines saw her photos before she transmitted them and had no complaints. "An image personalizes that death and makes people see what it really means to have young men die in combat," she wrote. "It is necessary to be bothered from time to time" (Dunlap, 2009, para. 28, 29). While many U.S. news organizations printed the photo in their pages and on their Web sites, several did not, including the *Portland Press Herald*, near Bernard's hometown in Maine.

Privacy should be seen as a secondary or instrumental right for another reason: The concept itself is socially and culturally constructed. In a landmark 1971 case in which the Supreme Court limited the extent to which people could be shielded against media attention by claiming privacy rights, Justice William Brennan said, "Exposure of the self to others in varying degrees is a concomitant of life in a civilized country." Writing for the majority, he continued, "The extent to which people are expected to expose their lives, their personalities, their attributes, and their behavior to public scrutiny is not for them to control, but is instead a function of the external understanding—the social construction of the world they and we inhabit" (*Rosenbloom v. Metromedia,* 1971, p. 47). Take the example of anonymity and lawsuits. In the United States, since the court system has so much state power affecting people's lives, its "publicness" is a built-in feature of our culture. A cornerstone of our democratic system is that the rule of law applies to everyone equally. To ensure that, no one (except for cases involving particularly vulnerable parties such as juveniles) can be anonymous. No one can be "secretly" sued, and no one can be "secretly" imprisoned. We cannot shield our identities if we file a civil lawsuit against another person. But in Germany, such an idea of involuntary exposure is believed to unlawfully *discourage* people from exercising their right to use the courts, and anonymity is *protected* for anyone filing a lawsuit or being sued. The two widely conflicting notions of what should be "private" are based on very different cultural constructions. As this example shows, we should be cautious about claiming any right to privacy as "absolute." Privacy ethicist Frederick Schauer (2003) uses another example to illustrate the shifting nature of what we—and the law—consider as private:

> When I attend a sporting event and then see my picture in the newspaper as part of a large crowd, I have no legal remedy—not because of some defense or constitutional side constraint, but because the law refuses to recognize that I have been harmed at all. The harm . . . is not a function of my own preferences and my own feelings, but is instead a function of and socially constructed by the understandings of the larger world I inhabit. (p. 8)

THE MORAL VALUE OF PRIVACY

Obviously, exercising our right to privacy is an important way to express our *freedom*. And in our individualistic culture, it's not surprising to see how, by attaching it to the idea of freedom, we have come to consider privacy as an absolute right that trumps all else. "Some minimal right to immunity from uninvited observation and reporting is required by certain basic features of our conception of a person," said Stanley Benn (cited in Byford, 1998, p. 5). Yet from a philosophical perspective, freedom, per se, has little to do with the justifications for valuing privacy. Instead, most theorists agree that privacy is critical both for the development of the self and for social cohesion. We develop our own sense of self through privacy. But at the same time, odd as it may sound, protecting zones of privacy maintains the social fabric. Privacy is important "to both the maintenance of self and person and to the processes by which we create social relations and negotiate social power," according to one theorist (Byford, 1998, p. 3).

Development of the Self

If someone were to post compromising photos of you online, doing so would likely be considered a gross violation of your privacy. But would you have the right to order them taken down? Not necessarily. Often, the same federal laws that say online service providers can't be held liable for offensive content that appears on their sites also, indirectly, protect the "trolls" who post it. In 2009, one young woman, whose nickname is Lani, became a flashpoint for this tension when someone, perhaps an ex-boyfriend, posted nude photos of her on a Web site called Private Voyeur under the title "Jap Slut." She went to the police, but was told they could do nothing. Eventually, Private Voyeur agreed to take the photos down. But such cases put victims such as Lani in a tough situation. She could sue in court for defamation or invasion of privacy, but that would likely result in forever linking her with the photos since they inevitably would resurface in court and be broadcast on the Web. And most judges won't allow Lani and others like her to sue anonymously. So we seem to be stuck with trolls. The most direct solution, holding online sites liable for defamatory content, "would mean choking off other critics, which obviously has undemocratic implications," wrote legal scholar Emily Bazelon (2011). "After all, anonymity is a trusted tool of dissidents and whistleblowers. . . . [S]ome posts would be deleted not because they actually defame or violate privacy but because someone *complains* that they do. The heckler's veto, as it's called, is anathema to free-speech advocates" [author's emphasis] (2011, pp. 9–10).

In his book *The Unwanted Gaze: The Destruction of Privacy in America,* Jeffrey Rosen defined privacy as "the ability to protect ourselves from being judged out of context" (2000, p. 210). This is why Monica Lewinsky felt violated after independent prosecutor Kenneth Starr gained access to details of her life—including the records of which books she bought at a local bookstore—during his effort to build a case against President Bill Clinton. "I felt like I wasn't a citizen of this country anymore," the famous former White House intern said. Jeffrey Reiman (1976), a prominent privacy theorist, said privacy serves as "a social ritual by means of which an individual's moral title to his existence is conferred" (p. 39). Through privacy, a society recognizes and acknowledges the individual as an autonomous agent with a moral right to exercise that agency. Even while privacy expert Anita Allen (2003) argued why journalists cannot protect privacy (which is discussed later), she acknowledged that opportunities for privacy "are preconditions for the kind of individuality—moral independence—and repose presupposed by free, meaningful participation in civic life" (p. 76). These claims all have one thing in common: While we need privacy to understand and develop our own sense of self, privacy also serves a very *social* function, which we often ignore in our insistence to define privacy as simply the right to be left alone. Forces on the Web that invite people to act as trolls and post details of people's lives worry privacy advocates, who fear this creeping erosion of privacy online for people who have very real reasons to withhold personal details. "It may be victims of domestic abuse who don't want to be stalked or tracked, or it could be dissidents in Syria, or someone who has weird opinions and could mistakenly end up on a watch list when they don't deserve it,"

> **"Narrow" and "Broad" Senses of Privacy**
>
> "On the narrow end of the spectrum privacy relates exclusively to personal information and describes the extent to which others have access to this information." The broader conception refers to privacy as "the measure of the extent an individual is afforded the social and legal space to develop the emotional, cognitive, spiritual and moral powers of an autonomous agent" (Schoeman, 1992).

said Rebecca MacKinnon (2012, p. SR7), who wrote a book about digital freedom and privacy. "If you have a democratic society, the point is not to say whatever is good for the majority is all we need" (p. SR7).

Maintenance of the Social Fabric

In her famous 1943 novel, *The Fountainhead,* which spreads the gospel of American rugged individualism, Ayn Rand has her hero make a provocative claim about privacy: "Civilization is the progress toward a society of privacy. The savage's whole existence is public, ruled by the laws of his tribe. Civilization is the process of setting man free from men" (p. 715). This absolutist view of privacy is seductive in its simplicity, but it has little to do with the reality of human existence, and it even denies a fundamental feature of the human character: that we are social animals. Sociologists and philosophers have long since documented how our self-knowledge is largely based in how we see ourselves in relation to others. George Herbert Mead (1934/1967) said we cannot fully exercise our rationality until we can get beyond seeing ourselves as "subjects" and can instead impersonally examine ourselves as "objects" and see ourselves as others do:

> For he enters his own experience as a self or individual, not directly or immediately, not by becoming a subject to himself, but only in so far as he first becomes an object to himself just as other individuals are objects to him or in his experience; and he becomes an object to himself only by taking the attitudes of other individuals toward himself within a social environment of context of experience and behavior in which both he and they are involved. (p. 138)

A prominent sociologist, Erving Goffman (1973), talked about how society has organized itself to allow for "backstage" spaces and "frontstage" spaces. *Frontstage* spaces are those in which we must "perform" publicly in various roles that require relatively formal presentation of ourselves—as students, teachers, colleagues, coworkers. But Goffman said we all need more informal *backstage* areas in which we can bond through more relaxed—even a bit raucous or lewd—behavior that would be considered unacceptable on the frontstage. Our backstage conduct, he said, "is one which allows minor acts which might easily be taken as symbolic of intimacy and disrespect for others present . . . while front region conduct is one which disallows such potentially offensive behavior" (p. 128). He also suggests that we experience stress when we have no backstage space that we can control.

Case in Point: Do Geofences Corral Customer Loyalty?

It's called "showrooming," and retailers hate it: Increasingly, smart-phone users are getting in the habit of comparing prices online while shopping in a store. To fight back, companies are joining up with GPS-based mobile networking apps and inviting their customers to join. When they do, retailers

(Continued)

(Continued)

can text them with discounts and sales offers when they come, say, within a certain radius of their store. North Face, the outdoor gear manufacturer, not only uses a geofencing system to text users who come near their stores; it has also set up geofences around national parks and ski resorts. A promising microtargeting strategy, perhaps, but geofencing also may invite ad clutter on mobile phones, even turning off customers signed up for the service. "Texting is a very personal medium, and it can annoy people," one retail executive said (Mattioli & Bustillo, 2012).

Just as we need more private, backstage space to maintain social harmony, our privacy serves as an important mechanism to enforce moral standards in society. "Privacy is just as important for the group to maintain its integrity and independence as it is for the individual to maintain her integrity and independence," according to Schoeman (1992, p. 111). Philosopher Thomas Nagel (1998) said that the right to conceal things about our lives from the public does nothing less than prevent "constant social breakdown" and "interpersonal chaos." The time and space in our lives in which we interact with others, he said, is pretty limited—and, thus, we must continually make serious efforts to control the content of our interaction. "Human beings are highly complex and very diverse," Nagel said, and "the full range of what any number of them feel, want and think would not fit into a common space without generating uncontrollable conflict and offence" (p. 15). We each have a system of moral beliefs that we have internalized and that we use to make judgments and decisions. But we must remember that it doesn't make sense to talk of ethics as something that only has to do with an individual. Ethics by definition deals with *relations*—determining the best course of action by acknowledging almost everything we do affects other people. Our moral selves are actually rooted in our *interdependence* with others. Schoeman, the prominent privacy theorist, drove this point home eloquently:

> In fact, it is our dependence on others—our cognitive, emotional, cultural and material dependence—that accounts for most of our moral qualities. . . . Our dependence on others also accounts for most of what we are and can hope to become. . . . It is good, in sum, that we are subject to forces and pressures we do not monitor and judge. It is good that we are driven to be like others and care what they think about how we behave and about what we are like. (1992, pp. 6–7)

THE HISTORY OF PRIVACY

Our Western culture, based on Enlightenment thinking that emphasizes the centrality of the individual, has led us to assume that our popular view of privacy—the right to be left alone—is a fact of life, a universal truth. As we have seen, this view doesn't help us much. A brief look at how notions of privacy have evolved historically is both instructive and fascinating. It's instructive because it helps us examine our cultural assumptions and improves our understanding of the concept. It's fascinating because it can open our eyes to just how alien our contemporary claims of privacy would be to people living in just about every other time period. What we now assume is the sphere of privacy and of the "individual" began emerging as economic forces opened new opportunities in the 19th century for people to make a living in urban centers, which weakened the power of kin. But even then, individual "freedom" did not suggest a social disengagement that it suggests today, but only that a person has increased influence over which social associations can influence personal decisions. And constitutional historians are quick to point out that our ideal of "tolerance" was not initially based on some grand notion of respecting the private lives of others, but was "the result of a political compromise between intolerant groups who feared for their own security" (Schoeman, 1992, p. 126).

Plato was openly dismissive of the idea of privacy, deeming it unnecessary and counterproductive in the pursuit of the ideal state. He did not recognize any psychological, sociological, or political need for individuals to be able to control their conduct or their social relations. But Aristotle emphasized the importance of the public/private distinction in two ways, separating the sphere of the *polis,* or political community, from the sphere of the *oikos,* or personal realm. Anyone who aspired to the virtue of the contemplative life required solitude and space, he argued. Leading a virtuous life *required* a turning away from the masses. In Roman culture in particular, things that we consider private now did not receive much respect. There was no "privacy" in death or grieving, for example. Roman tombstones along highways often featured announcements such as one by a father saying the girl buried in one spot was disinherited. "The private-public dichotomy in ancient times was not associated with respect for privacy," Schoeman said. "Nor was it the domain of self-expression. Rather the reverse was the case" (1992, p. 117). Throughout medieval Europe, solitary travel or wandering was regarded as a symptom of insanity: "It was pious work to place them back in some community, regardless of what they might say" (Duby, 1988, p. 510).

A more modern notion of privacy only began to develop when political, economic, and social life became more complex and required people to regulate their conduct to allow them to perform multiple social roles. Consider this description of "intimacy" in the Middle Ages and how jarring it is to our contemporary expectations:

> [In the early Middle Ages], there were few functional relationships between people outside their local community. Although people had reason to fear starvation or slaughter, they had little need to restrain themselves in their expression of their impulses, passions and emotions. What we think of as inner life, they lived openly. Life was characterized by belligerence, joy in tormenting others, hatred, gaiety—all spontaneously following upon one another. Social customs and sensibilities were radically different. During the Middle Ages attitudes toward sex were quite different: In order for a marriage to be valid, the bride and groom, after being disrobed by their attendants, had to be placed naked on the bridal bed together in the presence of witnesses. This practice evidences the degree to which virginity and consummation were key elements of marriage practices. But they also illustrate the extent to which social structure was incorporated into the marital

relationship. Marriage as an institution was not an escape from social control. (Schoeman, 1992, p. 118)

But this all began changing when previously isolated, small communities developed as economically linked networks. Natural impulses, bodily functions, and desires were "banished" to a new private sphere as social interaction increased. Through the 16th and 17th centuries in England, neither personal autonomy nor privacy was respected as a social ideal. Freedom of choice in just about every aspect of life—marriage, sex, work—was subordinated to the interests of lineage, parents, church, or state. Even in colonial America, a "right to privacy" was nonexistent. "What to labor at, when to labor, with whom, whom to marry, whether to have children, whom to have in one's house, whom to associate with—none of these areas provided people with socially shielded options" (Schoeman, 1992, p. 126). Social control of marriage and sexual activity began to loosen in the 18th century—but only a little:

> It was common practice for midwives to interrogate the expectant unwed mother about the identity of the father during the agony of labor, offering her assistance only after she supplied a name. The midwives' oath of 1726 imposed this duty upon them. It would be hard to think of behavior more intrusive into an individual's privacy than this. (Schoeman, 1992, p. 127)

The Reformation undermined the authority of the church and allowed people more options. Scientific and technological developments also encouraged the idea that individuals could control their fate and actively seek advancement beyond their family station.

Enlightenment thinkers famously rebelled against arbitrary social controls by church and state. Emerging from the Age of Reason, when social structures based on religion were challenged, John Locke, Montesquieu, Adam Smith, Thomas Jefferson, and others championed the right to self-government based on "inalienable" rights of liberty and the exercise of reason. State power was illegitimate unless it served to protect and promote individual liberties.

Fast-forward to 1890. Two American lawyers, Samuel Warren and Louis Brandeis, wrote an article spelling out what they saw as a "right to be left alone." They were reacting angrily to what they saw as an increasingly invasive press. "The press is overstepping in every direction the obvious bounds of propriety and decency," they declared. "Instantaneous photographs and newspaper enterprise have invaded the sacred precincts of private and domestic life; and numerous devices threaten to make good the prediction that 'what is whispered in the closet shall be proclaimed from the house-tops'" (Warren & Brandeis, 1890, p. 195). Despite their claim, there was very little that was "obvious" about when aggressive journalism became "indecent" and invasive. Through the 1960s and 1970s, the Supreme Court issued several rulings that staked out clearer and expanded "zones" of privacy, including *Roe v. Wade,* the 1973 decision that established a woman's right to abortion services. With these rulings, some theorists have argued that the protection of individual privacy had become nearly absolute in the United States. But in many ways, decisions about how privacy concerns should influence the media have become more complicated than ever.

PRIVACY IN THE MEDIA

Despite some powerful cultural forces, claims of privacy do not necessarily override other values or interests when it comes to media practice. As we have seen, our ability to maintain privacy is critical so that we can have the space we need for self-development and to maintain important social relations. Rather than emphasizing a public "right" to know, journalists are on more solid ethical ground by assessing whether personal information would serve a "need" to know. Acts by the media that infringe on that space, in the form of unsanctioned disclosures of personal information or photos, or unwelcome media news coverage, must be justified by arguments that a broader, vital public interest is being served. Such disclosures or use of personal information merely to increase market share, to polish a corporate image, or to increase the sexiness of news coverage are not ethically justifiable, since those narrow interests do not override the reasons we have to protect privacy. Too often, the degree of personal information we see in the media is driven by a sensationalistic attitude about what the public "wants" to know and, thus, delivering what it wants as a matter of business. But we also have seen that invoking a "right" to be left alone for its own sake has little merit as an ethical justification if doing so does not recognize the broader reasons why privacy is valuable to us in the first place. The "right" to privacy can be distorted and misappropriated if we fail to recognize our roles and responsibilities as social actors and members of communities.

Case in Point: NASCAR and Dale Earnhardt's Autopsy Photos

In February 2001, while traveling about 160 miles per hour on the last lap of the famed Daytona 500 race, a car bumped another one driven by the legendary NASCAR driver Dale Earnhardt. Earnhardt lost control and slammed into the side wall, and he died instantly. Less than a week later, a reporter for the *Orlando Sentinel* filed a request to access the autopsy photos of the beloved NASCAR driver, touching off a torrent of angry letters, calls, and e-mails from fans. In Florida at the time, state law allowed public access to autopsy files. *Sentinel* editors repeatedly said the paper had no intention of publishing the grisly photographs but instead planned to show them to a head trauma expert to make an independent determination of the cause of death. NASCAR is notoriously secretive about the details surrounding the deaths of drivers, conducting its own investigations without the involvement of local police. Questions also surfaced about whether Earnhardt had been allowed to change his seat belt mounting. NASCAR's refusal to release information about the Earnhardt crash—and the deaths of several other drivers—created a cloud of suspicion. Teresa Earnhardt, the driver's widow, asked a state judge to block access to the autopsy photos, arguing such coverage would inflict needless added pain on the family. But *Sentinel* editor Tim Franklin argued that the Earnhardt story represented a public issue that was bigger than the family's desire to keep the autopsy photos private. "While we feel sorry for the Earnhardt family and what they're going through, there's a big issue here about NASCAR safety, and we're simply trying to provide more information about how Dale Earnhardt died," he said. The judge agreed with the widow, blocking access and saying the photos had no "bona fide newsworthiness." Less than two months later, Florida governor Jeb Bush signed a measure into law that prohibited public access to autopsy photos unless a judge approves.

The Role of Privacy in the News

The 19-year-old Colorado woman who accused basketball superstar Kobe Bryant of rape in June 2003 set off an explosion of news coverage as state prosecutors tried to put together their case and as Bryant's defenders attacked the woman's credibility and motives. Throughout the intense national coverage, mainstream news outlets never revealed the woman's name, following long-standing journalistic policies to protect actual and suspected rape victims from unfair public scrutiny and the continuing social stigma attached to sex crimes. The media circus began to subside when the woman decided against testifying, thus forcing prosecutors to drop the charges. But the game changed in late 2004, when the woman filed a civil lawsuit against Bryant seeking monetary damages. A federal judge refused her request to file her suit anonymously. Now, her identity was part of the public record. Journalists were stuck in a quandary: Do they name her in their news stories about her civil lawsuit? In Denver, where she filed her complaint, journalists did both. The competing metro daily papers in town, the *Denver Post* and the *Rocky Mountain News,* reached opposite conclusions, largely based on how much weight each assigned to the woman's right to privacy once she sued Bryant for money. For editors at the *Denver Post,* just because her name was in a court record didn't mean the underlying reasons for protecting her identity—the tendency of the public to "blame" victims of sex assault crimes—had changed. They said the *Post* would continue covering the case without using her name. "Though her identity will be available to anyone who attends the federal trial or reads court documents, and many in her community know her name, it is not the same as publishing her name and photograph day after day in hundreds of thousands of newspapers," the editors wrote (Moore & Clark, 2004). The *Rocky Mountain News* publisher, however, argued just the opposite: The woman, by filing suit to get money, *had* changed the game and had relinquished her prior entitlement to anonymity. For him, the question became less one of privacy and more about fairness: On what basis should the accuser be given special treatment denied to everyone else who files a civil claim? "In the criminal case, we did not name the accuser because it was the state of Colorado prosecuting the case," said *Rocky* publisher John Temple in an interview. "The state . . . was attempting to vindicate a state interest. . . . In a case where there is no state interest involved and the complaint doesn't address a larger public interest, it's unfair for the accused to be treated differently from the accuser" (Mitchell, 2004).

While the woman dropped her lawsuit in 2005 after reaching a monetary settlement with Bryant, the case illustrates how widely journalists may disagree over how much weight to assign claims of privacy when covering controversial events. It also illustrates how news coverage has shifted over the past few decades from an emphasis on *issues* to an emphasis on *individuals* who are key players in a debate or whose stories are used to symbolize a larger human drama. People in the news and entertainment business know that audiences are attracted to personal stories. "The public is a two-faced beast: It deplores television reporters who exploit tragedy, poking microphones at the mothers of crash victims; but people watch the programs," wrote veteran journalist Anthony Lewis (2003, p. 66). Most people also want to limit or control their exposure by the media. Thus, there is a constant clash between privacy interests and the mission of journalists to serve community needs by pursuing the news and reporting as much "truth" as possible. Doing so inevitably requires delving into individual lives, even when it is unwelcome. Privacy arguments become especially heated with stories involving graphic images; the public often reacts to the use of such images as inherently intrusive and without redeeming value. But many theorists question this response. Susan Sontag famously argued that photos of atrocity and death are important precisely because of their disturbing qualities: "Let the atrocious images haunt us. Even if they are only tokens, and cannot encompass most of the reality to which they refer, they still perform a vital function. The images say: this is what human beings are capable of. . . . Don't forget" (2003, p. 115). Of course, whether and how to publish or distribute disturbing images "always involves an ethical crisis of representation," as one theorist says (Prosser, 2012, p. 9). But the solution is not necessarily to sanitize the news or to "protect" the sensibilities of audiences. Veteran photojournalist John Long speaks to the broader mission of photojournalism that often gets overrun by privacy claims:

> A great photo is a window into history. It allows us to be present as history is happening, to see for ourselves the moment Martin Luther King Jr. was shot at the Lorraine Motel, to see Lee Harvey Oswald crumple with a bullet in his abdomen, to see the effects of war on a little Vietnamese girl burned by napalm, to see the invasion on D-Day. And also to see history in much less spectacular fashion as it happens in our local town councils, or school sporting events, or any of the events that make up our daily lives. The honest photograph has power because it is real. It has power because it shows us exactly what the photographer saw and what the camera captured at the moment the shutter was tripped. History demands accuracy. (2011)

Many people unaccustomed to dealing with the media assume that journalists must get permission to identify someone in a news story. For most stories that are deemed newsworthy and of public interest, this is *not* the case. Allowing potential news subjects to have such power thwarts the professional journalists from fulfilling their duty to serve the public. For this reason, Anita Allen (2003) argued that as a matter of professionalism, journalists *cannot* be guided primarily by concern for privacy in most of their work. For one thing, journalists' first priority is *public* service and holding people with power accountable for their actions, and they must be vigilant about attempts that abuse privacy claims to dodge accountability. This ethical obligation is key to journalistic professionalism. "Should a journalist ever report a true fact about a person when the journalist knows the person prefers privacy respecting that fact? The answer to this question is clearly yes," Allen argued. "We should be more accountable than we want to be" (2003, p. 81). Second, Allen said that we don't actually have a universally accepted definition of what privacy is. People, she said, "value privacy inconsistently or idiosyncratically," making it impossible for journalists to assess what individual story subjects would define as potential invasions of their privacy at any given time. "People expect what they consider privacy yet embrace certain kinds of mass publicity," she said (p. 74). And not only does information that people consider private vary widely based on age, ethnicity, and other background factors; Allen also noted that what's private is also constantly changing:

Shouldering the burden of respecting privacy grows increasingly impractical as the information demands of our complex society multiply and as diverse, pluralistic conceptions of "private" flourish. . . . It is difficult for journalists acting in good faith to comprehend what respecting privacy is supposed to entail concerning individuals in a diverse population. . . . Once fairly uniformly deemed personal and private, today sexual matters, medical matters, family matters, finances, and criminal histories are commonly shared with mass-media audiences. . . . People who share medical information point out the benefits to individual and public health of shedding traditional shame and modesty about illness. (2003, pp. 69, 73)

Families and victims who are involuntarily thrust into the public spotlight through crime stories often bitterly complain that the decisions of journalists to write stories without their consent are invasive. But while journalists can often do a better job of reporting and presenting crime news in more compassionate and sensitive ways, arguing that such news is in itself invasive is often based on a mistaken assumption that privacy trumps the public interest—that privacy is an absolute right. "Although it deeply affects the persons directly involved, it is, nevertheless, a crime against the state, and therefore, a public concern," wrote two ethicists in their analysis of ethics and news of murder cases. "Such publicly told stories connect the readers to the lives and experiences of persons who might otherwise remain foreign and strange to them" (Fullerton & Patterson, 2006, p. 305).

Privacy in the Law

Courts have specified several allowable claims, or torts, regarding privacy interests:

- Intrusion: The intentional invasion of the solitude or seclusion of another in his or her private affairs or concerns through either physical or electronic means
- Disclosure: Revelation of private facts guided by judgments on whether the information serves a compelling public interest that outweighs an individual's right to remain out of the public eye
- Appropriation: The use of someone's name or likeness without his or her consent for commercial purposes

Legal Aspects of Privacy

Even so, journalists concerned about acting responsibly must understand the two more technical elements of privacy: intrusion and disclosure. Most lawsuits in which people claim the media have violated privacy fall under one or both of these categories. And while both elements refer to the legal realm, they also require consideration for ethical behavior as well. *Intrusion* is the "intentional invasion of the solitude or seclusion of another in his or her private affairs or concerns through either physical or electronic means" (Gates, 2000, p. 106). The courts have been clear that the media *do not* enjoy a general news gathering "immunity" from intrusion claims—that is, reporters have no special status that allows them to gather information differently than any other citizen. But elected politicians, community leaders, celebrities, or other "public figures" who have thrust themselves voluntarily into the spotlight are understood to have "given up" some degree of privacy and, thus, have less ability to claim intrusion. The second element, *disclosure,* addresses not how information is obtained, but how and whether it may be used. Questions of ethical disclosure deal with the revelation of private facts guided by judgments on whether the information serves a compelling public interest that outweighs an individual's right to remain out of the public eye. In this area, journalists generally have wide latitude, as described by Gates:

> Even though news reports may be embarrassing to those in the public eye . . . coverage of legitimate news is protected as an exercise of free speech even when it gives offense to some. . . . Newsworthiness is not confined to events and facts of politics, economics and social interaction, but also includes descriptions and portrayals of how people live, work and think within their social milieu. (p. 110)

Privacy: It's in the Code of Ethics

In some codes, such as that of the Public Relations Society of America, privacy is a key concern that is explicitly addressed in the form of safeguarding confidential client information. In others, such as that of the Society of Professional Journalists, the concept is implied in statements throughout the codes that outline what constitutes ethical behavior.

From the Society of Professional Journalists Code of Ethics

Journalists should do the following:

- Show compassion for those who may be affected adversely by news coverage. Use special sensitivity when dealing with children and inexperienced sources or subjects.
- Diligently seek out subjects of news stories to give them the opportunity to respond to allegations of wrongdoing.
- Recognize that private people have a greater right to control information about themselves than do public officials and others who seek power, influence or attention. Only an overriding public need can justify intrusion into anyone's privacy.
- Be cautious about identifying juvenile suspects or victims of sex crimes.
- Identify sources whenever feasible. The public is entitled to as much information as possible on sources' reliability.
- Always question sources' motives before promising anonymity. Clarify conditions attached to any promise made in exchange for information.

The full code can be found at http://www.spj.org/ethicscode.asp.

From the Public Relations Society of America Member Code of Ethics

Client trust requires appropriate protection of confidential and private information.

A member shall do the following:

- Safeguard the confidences and privacy rights of present, former and prospective clients and employees.
- Protect privileged, confidential or insider information gained from a client or organization.
- Immediately advise an appropriate authority if a member discovers that confidential information is being divulged by an employee of a client company or organization.

The full code can be found at http://www.prsa.org/aboutUs/ethics/preamble_en.html.

So despite cultural assumptions about privacy rights as absolute, professional journalists are obligated to weigh privacy claims against their duty to serve a broader public interest. This won't help journalists win many popularity contests. Indeed, a degree of moral courage often is required in pursuing stories important to the public that also may be perceived to be invasive by individuals. This is all the more reason, then, that journalists must be able to articulate exactly *what* public interest is being served and *why,* in a particular case, that interest overrides someone's claim to privacy. As we have seen, suggestions that journalists may be motivated by higher ratings, bigger audiences, or a sexier story will often—rightly—draw charges of unethical conduct and pose threats to journalistic credibility since those motives are certainly outweighed by the legitimate reasons we value our privacy as we've discussed. Responsible journalism requires reporters and editors to have a solid grasp of the complexity of privacy beyond jingoistic claims of the "right" to know, just as audiences and news subjects should understand that privacy cannot be reduced to a simple "right" to be left alone. Journalists should be able to articulate how the use of ordinarily private information serves a greater value, such as justice, and they should be able to demonstrate how their conduct demonstrates an ongoing concern for everyone's human dignity and keeping potential harm to a minimum.

Privacy Concerns in Public Relations

Unlike journalists, public relations professionals rarely face dilemmas involving potential claims of *intrusion* of privacy. But questions over what is appropriate *disclosure* of personal information in the course of different types of public relations–related work often crop up. Such claims may even pose a greater threat to professional credibility than in the news since the public good often sought by public relations practitioners hinges on the perceptions of a public that may choose to see only more immediate client interests being served. As public relations theorist Kirk Hallahan (2006) cautioned, "A breach of privacy . . . that becomes widely known can become an explosive situation that generates negative publicity, a loss of reputation, and direct costs and legal liabilities for an organization" (p. 217). Public relations agents serving corporate clients also must be mindful of how photos of or information about client employees should be used in publicity efforts. There also is a third area of privacy concern that is relevant to public relations professionals: *appropriation.* A company can be liable for "misappropriation of personality" if, to promote an image or conduct a marketing strategy, it uses images or details about employees without their permission. In one notable recent case, Chemical Bank of New York used the pictures of more than three dozen employees as part of a campaign to humanize the bank's image. But no one had asked the employees for permission, and they sued, claiming misappropriation of personality for commercial purposes. For public relations professionals, the lesson is to get permission. This usually means obtaining a signed release or consent form. While journalists don't often face issues of appropriation because newsworthiness is a compelling defense in the courts, using a person's likeness to make money is a different matter. Whether it is an employee photo for a marketing brochure or using personal data as part of a research project, permission should always be obtained to avoid the appearance of impropriety and even possible lawsuits.

Increasingly, as public relations work involves research into marketing strategies, public or audience perceptions, and assessments of message campaign effectiveness, public relations professionals must be mindful of the possibility of unethical exploitation of personal data. Retailers routinely are analyzing collected data on customers to identify narrow profiles of different types of patrons and to tailor pitches to them. While the mining and analysis of this "secondary" data on real or potential customers may not raise many ethical questions, good marketers never forget that all the psychographic and demographic slicing and dicing in the world doesn't replace talking to real people and getting to know their buying habits. And when doing this kind of public opinion or marketing public relations research, it is critical to keep in mind some key ethical obligations. Informed consent is a cornerstone concept of research ethics. This is the idea that individuals asked to participate in research—surveys, focus groups, interviews, or experiments—must be fully informed about the nature of the research, be free from any forms of coercion, and be rationally capable of consent. Research ethics codes also require researchers to allow participants to withdraw at any time from the research project.

PRIVACY IN CYBERSPACE

DoubleClick is an Internet advertising firm that tracks the surfing habits of millions of people by using the "cookies," or digital identification tags, that Internet ads link to visitors' computers. Traditionally, cookies have been anonymous. They only identify a computer, not a person. But in 1999, DoubleClick bought Abacus Direct, a marketing database firm that owned detailed information on millions of Americans, including names and addresses. DoubleClick planned to combine this data to track the Web activity of identifiable Web users. Such information would be a marketer's dream. But DoubleClick was forced to scrap their plans when privacy groups loudly protested. Private people would be under surveillance without their knowledge and in most cases have little ability to "opt out" of such a program. But since then, technology has largely enabled companies to be similarly invasive, and we routinely let them: Many of the mobile apps we download into our phones can and often do scroll through your phone contact list and other data to send it to the app vendor. The DoubleClick and other similar controversies reflect Jeffrey Rosen's argument that privacy means controlling the information that others know about us. This is particularly important regarding digitized bits of information about everyone that are floating about on the Web. Everyone who has used the Internet, whether they realize it or not, has left digital footprints that can be tracked by data mining companies and used to create purchasing profiles, medical summaries, and political pitches. Google now "follows" all of us as we use Gmail, its giant search engine, and all its other properties, including YouTube, to gather data that helps it tailor ads to our interests and tastes. And there is no opting out. "If someone watches an NBA clip online and lives in Washington, the firm could advertise Washington Wizards tickets in that person's Gmail account" (Kang, 2012). There are companies besides Google created solely to collect and bundle bits of information about Internet users and then to sell these bundles to direct marketing companies. These, in turn, use the lists to "call, write, or . . . e-mail us—government agencies, private investigators, or to anyone for any reason" (Moore, 2005, p. 172). This is why Rosen argued we should insist on more control of how these bits of data about us are used: More than ever in our age of digital data, people are increasingly tempted to mistake these "bits" of information about us as knowledge. "True knowledge of another person is the culmination of a slow process of mutual revelation," Rosen (2000) said. "It requires the gradual setting aside of social masks, the incremental building of trust, which leads to the exchange of personal disclosures" (p. 8). This concern has been heightened by cases in which Web sites and companies have been caught collecting data on children without permission. In late 2012, Artist Arena, the company that operates Web sites for fans of Justin Bieber, Selena Gomez, Rihanna, Demi Lovato, and others, agreed to pay a $1 million fine for illegally collecting personal information from children on the sites—including names, e-mail addresses, street addresses, and mobile phone numbers (Singer, 2012). In 2013, Google agreed to pay a $7 million fine when it admitted—after months of denial—that its "Street View" cars mounted with sophisticated cameras and sensors that drive around neighborhoods of the world to collect images for Google's map services had been vacuuming up personal data gleaned from private Wi-Fi networks as it passed homes. Passwords, e-mails, and other family data were routinely picked up by the cars.

The danger posed by the potential to abuse Web-based data should remind us of the important purposes that privacy serves in our public lives—and that those purposes should not receive any less consideration when it comes to Web-based communication. Many Web-based companies, including Microsoft, have paid heed to this danger. At the prompting of federal regulators, they began voluntarily incorporating a "Do Not Track" function into software in 2013 that, once activated by the user, blocks the ability of visited Web sites from using cookie-based data for tracking purposes. As stories of DoubleClick and Google show, technology raises some serious and immediate questions about how privacy concerns should guide its use. The generation that has grown up using the Web is likely to think about privacy differently than previous generations, simply because the technology has transformed communication habits, perceptions of what's "public" in the online world, and how users think about what "communities" they belong to. Many younger users mistakenly treat their Facebook sites as "private," posting photos of themselves partying and drinking with friends. But prospective employers and even college admissions officials have begun going to the sites for "background" checks. Several recruiters have said that they dropped plans for job offers after seeing questionable or unprofessional content on an individual's social media sites (Finder, 2006). Clearly, when it comes to privacy, our relationship with technology is in turmoil. We have eagerly embraced all that the Web allows us to do, and its speed and reach has tempted us to place a greater value on convenience and expediency. Questions of privacy, information control, and the moral implications of our Web use have received relatively short shrift as a result. While treating a Facebook page as a private domain is naive, technology poses some age-old ethical questions about respecting the dignity of others and minimizing harm. On one hand, technology makes it easier to see into other people's lives. On the other, it is fundamentally changing what we consider private. However, this does not mean that the Internet should become an ethical free-for-all. As Schauer (2003) said,

> As technological changes make invasion of privacy easier, the right—itself
> conceptually immune from these changes—is increasingly under threat. Just as

technological changes make racial profiling easier without affecting the moral wrongness of racism, so too do technological changes make privacy invasion easier without affecting the moral wrongness of those invasions, and therefore without affecting the moral necessity of increasing our safeguards so that the right to privacy remains as well protected as it was in the precyberspace age. (pp. 4–5)

One privacy lawyer, Katrin Byford, argued that the function of privacy, consequently, means that we should ensure that people have the freedom to develop online personas without fear of constant observation or unchecked data collection on individuals. If it's true that privacy is crucial for the development of a healthy self, then cyberspace should accommodate our expectations of privacy just as the "real" world does. According to Byford (1998), "Virtual communities which provide an occasion for experimentation with social role formation should not be discouraged simply because the activities of their members may potentially be compromised due to unchecked surveillance and data collection" (p. 9). Knowledge is power, and knowledge about the personal characteristics, strengths, and weaknesses of others is a form of social power that privacy norms aim to regulate. So, as Byford says, because "the very essence of cyberspace is its ability to serve as a repository of information and a conduit for information exchange" (p. 12), our concerns about maintaining our privacy should determine how the Internet should be regulated. Technology continues to raise this issue for us. Consider Google Glass, the wearable computer in the form of glasses. "If you use Google Glass to record a couple whispering to each other in Starbucks, have you violated their privacy?" asked one privacy advocate (Streitfield, 2013).

Journalists and Web Technology

Less than 24 hours after 23-year-old Cho Seung-hui killed 32 others on the Virginia Tech campus in April 2007, editors at the campus newspaper were able to publish a list of about a dozen of the victims—upstaging many national media outlets. The students didn't benefit from special sources on campus. Instead, they systematically scoured Facebook sites for memorials and comments referring to the victims. Then they made calls and online contacts to confirm the deaths through creators of Web postings and through friends and fellow classmates (Bauerlein & Steel, 2007). The episode illustrated the importance of Web technology as a journalistic newsgathering resource—and the value of being able to harness people's use of online "communities" to tell a story. While grief is an intensely private matter, and several people hung up on the reporters trying to confirm victims' identities, others understood that the Virginia Tech shootings transcended the individuals involved. The event became the latest in a string of national traumas that journalists were obliged to convey to hungry, shocked audiences.

Computerized databases maintained by government agencies and private clearinghouses have greatly expanded the ability of journalists to tell stories that once would have been impossible. The National Institute of Computer-Assisted Reporting (NICAR), based at the University of Missouri School of Journalism, provides tips about strategies, databases, and a story archive (http://www.ire.org/training/nettour/). In this and other ways, investigative reporting has been revolutionized by the Web. But the technology also has triggered backlashes and concern among government agencies and privacy organizations over whether access to these sources should be restricted and when permission is needed to use them. Because of the easy and instantaneous exchange of information, access to several important sources of information has been restricted over the years in the interest of protecting privacy. Among the most notable is the federal Driver's Privacy Protection Act of 1994, which restricted access to states' drivers' licenses and vehicle registration records—in the past a treasure trove of personal information for journalists. Similarly, the federal Health Insurance Portability and Accountability Act (HIPAA) of 1996 placed a premium on the confidentiality of patient information. Before HIPAA, reporters covering local auto accidents usually were able to call the local hospital to confirm the status of the people involved as part of the story. Such sharing of routine information has become rare because of privacy concerns.

Even though what's deemed news has shifted in emphasis from issues to individuals, responsible journalists do not exploit the anonymous and largely unregulated world of the Web in ways that invade individuals' privacy unless a clear, compelling broader public interest is being served. That was exactly what editors at the Spokane newspaper, the *Spokesman-Review,* argued when they hired a computer expert to pose anonymously as a young man interested in gay sex in a Web site chat room to document the sexual orientation of longtime Spokane mayor Jim West. The resulting stories in 2005 told of West's efforts to troll the Internet for young men and his use of public office to entice sexual partners with gifts, favors, and promises of City Hall internships. The Spokane stories triggered a heated ethics debate among journalists around the country, as well as a recall election in which West, a prominent state conservative and longtime mayor who had blocked gay rights legislation in the past, was ousted from office. In an editor's note that ran with the stories, Steven A. Smith argued that the questions of sexual misconduct and possible misuse of office overrode the mayor's expectation that his sex life would remain private. "This is not a story about sexual orientation," Smith wrote. "This is a story about alleged sexual abuse of children and misuse of power and authority," he said, calling West "the face of our city whose secret life could open him to blackmail or extortion attempts and compromise his ability to do his job" (Smith, 2005, p. A1).

Public Relations and Privacy on the Web

Since public relations uses of Web technology typically are more narrowly tailored to serve a client objective or to augment a persuasion campaign, public relations professionals are less able to claim a broader "public" mandate in their use of private details or information. This makes it even more critical for public relations professionals to take extra care in the use of data that could potentially be perceived as private. Using such data with little thought to its inappropriateness could easily trigger a backlash of negative publicity and suddenly pose a serious threat to professional credibility. Public relations professionals also must be mindful of security issues surrounding the accessibility of client data that could be considered confidential. "Not surprisingly, public concern about online privacy and security has evolved into a major public issue that public relations practitioners must address on behalf of clients in their dealings with customers, the media and government," Hallahan wrote (2006, p. 128).

Case in Point: Best Buy Hunts Down Bad Customers

Use of marketing-oriented public relations has exploded among U.S. companies that are increasingly questioning the value of mainstream advertising. Marketing public relations, or MPR, has become a part of many corporate structures to harness public relations strategies to achieve marketing objectives. "PR is probably more effective in changing consumer attitudes about products today than advertising," one marketing CEO claimed (Harris & Whalen, 2006, p. 4). One key strategy of MPR is data mining, or gathering and analyzing digital information about the buying habits of consumers. This allows companies to better position products or make pitches in a market. Some retailers have taken this a step further, slicing and dicing data about their customers—a "captive" audience of people who have given the company personal information at the checkout counter. Recently, Best Buy, the electronics retail giant, examined its sales records and demographic data on customers to single out the "angels," high-spending people who snap up DVDs and other gadgets without waiting for markdowns and rebates, and to discourage the "devils"—savvy, bargain-hunting customers who apply for rebates, return purchases to buy them back as discounted merchandise, and "flip" goods for a profit on eBay. To discourage the "devils," Best Buy cut back on promotions and culled them from marketing lists. Best Buy CEO Brad Anderson said as many as 100 million of its 500 million annual customers fall into this "devil" category that he wants to discourage. The strategy of shunning "unprofitable" customers runs counter to the standard retail goal of increasing traffic, and it potentially raises questions about using personal data to discriminate against some shoppers over others. But Anderson argued that these savvy customers were hurting the company's profit margin. "They can wreak enormous economic havoc," he said (McWilliams, 2004).

Hallahan (2006) offered three general points that public relations professionals should consider as part of a broader policy on handling data to avoid any such backlash or even legal liability. The points reflect in a general way the philosophical concerns of respecting the dignity of others, allowing autonomous agency, and minimizing harm.

1. *Notice.* Individuals or groups who intend to gather data from others that could be considered private should clearly notify participants, customers, and clients. This could involve posting a privacy statement on a Web site or sending targeted e-mail notices that address what information might be solicited and how that data would be used. Many organizations are more explicit in promising that the information gathered will be used only for the purpose for which it was obtained and that it will not be provided or sold to outside parties. Many also endeavor to reassure customers and participants that any data collected will be kept confidential.

2. *Choice.* Many organizations that hope to routinely collect data on clients or customers when they visit a Web site offer an "opt-out" option: That is, individuals are given a chance to say no. This opt-out could provide individuals the opportunity to block any collection of data or could allow them to place limits on how such data might be used once it is collected. For example, the Web site may allow individuals to interact even after visitors disable the site's "cookies," or the organization can ask whether visitors would allow the site to "share" collected data with third parties by clicking on a box.

3. *Redress.* When online security is breached or when someone feels their privacy has been invaded by an organization using personal data, quick and full acknowledgment is the best strategy if the public relations professional's first concern is credibility. Organizations should provide a process that allows online visitors and users to correct errors. There are few better ways to invite a public relations nightmare than to offer unresponsiveness to perceived failures to respect privacy or confidentiality of information.

For Discussion

1. What is the difference between a public "right" to know and a public "need" to know?

2. In what kinds of situations do you feel that journalists should be ethically obligated to ask permission to include a person in a news story?

3. What are some examples of some "backstage spaces" in your life over which you feel you have control? How do you feel those spaces are valuable to you?

4. Many privacy theorists say it is important to distinguish the value we place on privacy from our claims about the importance of liberty. How would you define these separately?

5. Consider the controversy over whether to name the woman who accused Kobe Bryant of rape in news coverage. Most news organizations have policies that shield the identity of suspected or actual rape victims due to the social stigma attached to such crimes and due to a concern that publicity discourages other rape victims from going to the police to report assaults. But in 1991, the *Des Moines Register* won a Pulitzer Prize for a series that documented one woman's journey through the court system after her rape, and she consented to be named. Geneva Overholser, editor of the *Register* at the time, has since argued that the practice of withholding the names of rape accusers and victims actually reinforces the social stigmatization of rape victims that journalists claim to be fighting. How should this perceived stigma be considered a factor in the decision whether to name the woman in the Kobe Bryant case?

6. Think about your use of the Web—to learn about news events, to tell other people about yourself, to find out about other people. Do you have a different expectation of privacy regarding information on the Web compared with other media? How so? Should the medium determine the level of privacy that we enjoy, or should the same degree of privacy be expected across the board, regardless of the format?

REFERENCES

Allen, A. (2005). Privacy isn't everything: Accountability as a personal and social good. In A. D. Moore (Ed.), *Information Ethics: Privacy, property and power* (pp. 398–416). Seattle: University of Washington Press.

Allen, A. L. (2003). Why journalists can't protect privacy. In C. L. LaMay (Ed.), *Journalism and the debate over privacy* (pp. 69–87). Mahwah, NJ: Lawrence Erlbaum.

Arendt, H. (1958). *The human condition.* Chicago, IL: University of Chicago Press.

Bauerlein, V., & Steel, E. (2007, April 18). Virtual to actual grief—Confirming victims' names. *Wall Street Journal,* p. B1.

Bazelon, E. (2011, April 24). Trolls, the bell tolls for thee. *New York Times Magazine,* pp. 9–10.

Byford, K. S. (1998). Privacy in cyberspace: Constructing a model of privacy for the electronic communications environment. *Rutgers Computer and Technology Law Journal, 24,* 1–48.

Duby, G. (1988). Solitude: Eleventh to thirteenth century. In P. Ariès & G. Duby (Eds.), *A history of private life: Vol. 2. Revelations of the medieval world* (pp. 509–533). Cambridge, MA: Belknap Press of Harvard University.

Dunlap, D. W. (2009, September 4). Behind the scenes: To publish or not? *New York Times.* Retrieved from http://lens.blogs.nytimes.com/2009/09/04/behind-13/

Finder, A. (2006, June 11). For some, online persona undermines a resume. *New York Times,* p. A1.

Fullerton, R. S., & Patterson, M. J. (2006). Murder in our midst: Expanding coverage to include care and responsibility. *The Journal of Mass Media Ethics, 21*(4), 304–321.

Gates, P. H. (2000). Privacy and access: The inevitable collision of competing values. In C. N. Davis & S. L. Splichal (Eds.), *Access denied: Freedom of information in the information age* (pp. 103–119). Ames: Iowa State University Press.

Goffman, E. (1973). *The presentation of self in everyday life.* Woodstock, NY: Overlook.

Hallahan, K. (2006). Responsible online communication. In K. Fitzpatrick & C. Brontsein (Eds.), *Ethics in public relations: Responsible advocacy* (pp. 107–130). Thousand Oaks, CA: Sage.

Harris, T. L., & Whalen, P. T. (2006). *The marketer's guide to public relations in the 21st century.* Mason, OH: Thomson.

Horowitz, I. L. (1999, Fall). Networking America: The cultural context of the privacy v. publicity debates. *ETC, 305*–314.

Kang, C. (2012, January 24). Google announces privacy changes across products; users can't opt out. Retrieved from http://www.washingtonpost.com/business/economy/google-tracks-consumers-across-products-users-cant-opt-out/2012/01/24/gIQArgJHOQ_story.html

Kelly, C. (2005, Fall). Data security: A new concern for PR practitioners. *Public Relations Quarterly,* 25–26.

Lewis, A. (2003). The right to be let alone. In C. L. LaMay (Ed.), *Journalism and the debate over privacy* (pp. 61–67). Mahwah, NJ: Lawrence Erlbaum.

Long, J. (2011, March). It's a cloudy, liquid world. *News Photographer Magazine.* Retrieved from https://nppa.org/page/8797

MacKinnon, R. (2012, February 5). Should personal data be personal? *New York Times,* p. SR7.

Mattioli, D., & Bustillo, M. (2012, May 8). Can texting save stores? *Wall Street Journal.* Retrieved from http://online.wsj.com/article/SB10001424052702303978104577362403804858504.html

McWilliams, G. (2004, November 8). Minding the store: Analyzing customers, Best Buy decides not all are welcome. *Wall Street Journal,* pp. A1, A8.

Mead, G. H. (1967). *Works of George Herbert Mead: Vol. 1. Mind, self and society* (C. W. Morris, Ed.). Chicago, IL: University of Chicago Press. (Original work published 1934)

Mitchell, B. (2004, October 20). *Rocky*'s editor pegs naming decision to fairness. *Rocky Mountain News.* Retrieved from http://www.poynter.org/content/content_print.asp?id=73133

Moore, A. D. (2005). Intangible property: Privacy, power and information. In A. D. Moore (Ed.), *Information ethics: Privacy, property and power* (pp. 172–190). Seattle: University of Washington Press.

Moore, G. L., & Clark, G. R. (2004, October 15). Letter from the editors. *Denver Post,* p. A2.

Nagel, T. (1998, August 14). The shredding of public privacy. *Times Literary Supplement,* p. 15.

Parent, W. A. (1983). Privacy, morality, and the law. *Philosophy and Public Affairs, 12,* 269–288.

Parkinson, M. G., Ekachai, D., & Hetherington, L. T. (2001). Public relations law. In R. L. Heath (Ed.), *Handbook of public relations* (pp. 247–257). Thousand Oaks, CA: Sage.

Prosser, J. (2012). Introduction. In G. Batchen, M. Gidley, N. K. Miller, & J. Prosser (Eds.) *Picturing atrocity: Photography in crisis*. London, England: Reaktion Books.

Rand, A. (1943). *The fountainhead*. Indianapolis, IN: Bobbs-Merrill.

Rawls, J. (1999). *A theory of justice*. Cambridge, MA: Belknap Press of Harvard University. (Original work published 1971)

Reiman, J. H. (1976). Privacy, intimacy, and personhood. *Philosophy and Public Affairs, 6*(1), 26–44.

Rosen, J. (2000). *The unwanted gaze: The destruction of privacy in America*. New York, NY: Random House.

Rosen, J. (2011, July 21). The Web means the end of forgetting. *New York Times Sunday Magazine,* pp. 1–14.

Rosenbloom v. Metromedia Inc. (1971). 403 U.S. 29 (plurality opinion of Brennan, J.).

Schauer, F. (2003). The social construction of privacy. In C. L. LaMay (Ed.), *Journalism and the debate over privacy* (pp. 3–16). Mahwah, NJ: Lawrence Erlbaum.

Schoeman, F. D. (1992). *Privacy and social freedom*. Cambridge, UK: Cambridge University Press.

Singer, N. (2012, October 3). Fan sites settle children's privacy charges. *New York Times*. Retrieved from http://www.nytimes.com/2012/10/04/technology/fan-sites-for-pop-stars-settle-childrens-privacy-charges.html

Smith, S. A. (2005, May 5). Stories result of 3-year investigation: Note to our readers. *Spokesman-Review,* p. A1.

Sontag, S. (2003). *Regarding the pain of others*. New York, NY: Farrar, Straus and Giroux.

Streitfield, D. (2013, March 13). Google concedes drive-by prying violated privacy. *New York Times,* pp. A1, B6.

Swanson, J. A. (1992). *The public and the private in Aristotle's political philosophy*. Ithaca, NY: Cornell University Press.

Warren, S. D., & Brandeis, L. D. (1890). The right to privacy. *Harvard Law Review, 4* (5), 193–220.

Westin, A. (1984). The origins of modern claims to privacy. In F. D. Schoeman (Ed.), *Philosophical dimensions of privacy* (pp. 56–74). Cambridge, UK: Cambridge University Press.

CHAPTER 10

Community

If you were asked to describe yourself in only a few sentences, chances are that you would start by talking about the primary roles that define you: student, employee, roommate, sorority sister, believer, or sports fan. You might go on to explain your ambitions or where you come from. While all of these could contribute to an understanding of you as an *individual,* note that virtually every role mentioned is fundamentally *relational*—that is, they each describe you in a way that suggests your identity is largely determined by the groups to which you belong. They describe you as a point in a network of relations with others. We often like to think of ourselves as self-sufficient masters of our destiny. We get many messages in our culture that we are free to create ourselves, that we are independent from others, and that this independence and self-sufficiency is something that we should continually try to develop. Our Western capitalist ideology privileges individual over collective interests in all kinds of ways. A high degree of privacy is considered a universal right; cultural narratives in film, television sitcoms, literature, and advertising reinforce the desirability of independence and self-reliance. A central tenet of the American ethic is our prerogative to define, and continually redefine, ourselves.

Yet such seductive portrayals of the individual as untethered and self-governing come at a cost according to social theorist Michael Walzer (2004):

> All in all, we . . . probably know one another less well, and with less assurance, than people once did, although we may see more aspects of the other than they saw, and recognize in him or her a wider range of possibilities (including the possibility of moving on). . . . We are more often alone than people once were, being without neighbors we can count on, relatives who live nearby or with whom we are close, or comrades at work or in the movement. (p. 151)

Notwithstanding the significance and influence of libertarian champions such as Thomas Hobbes and John Locke, many thinkers argue that our ingrained ethic of rugged individualism denies the reality that we are, at bottom, creatures of community. Our livelihood, our self-knowledge, and our self-image stem primarily from our connectedness rather than our detachment. We know ourselves largely through our relations with others and through our multiple roles within social networks. A culture that dismisses or denies this reality in favor of a more self-focused, anything-goes, whatever-feels-good ethic warps our moral outlook and threatens the social fabric, critics have argued. "The probable trend of modern society and of mass media is [toward] a loosening of collective social bonds and a weakening of mutual obligations of a moral kind, including public duties," suggested media theorist Denis McQuail (1977, p. 516). Some researchers have concluded that this loosening of social bonds in favor of "it's all about me" is a generational phenomenon. Psychologist Jean Twenge (2006) has labeled those born in the 1970s, 1980s, and 1990s as "Generation Me": They have "never known a world that put duty before self" (p. 1). In a study of more than 16,000 college students nationwide between 1982 and 2006, Twenge and her colleagues found that today's college students are more narcissistic, or self-involved and concerned with gratifying their desires than their predecessors—they are "more likely to have romantic relationships that are short-lived, at risk for infidelity, lack emotional warmth, and to exhibit game-playing, dishonesty, and over-controlling and violent behaviors" (Crary, 2007, p. A7). This trend is even expressed in our pop songs: Psychologists who conducted a computer analysis of hit songs from 1980 to 2007 found "a statistically significant trend toward narcissism and hostility in popular music." "As they hypothesized, the words 'I' and 'me' appear more frequently along with anger-related words, while there's been a corresponding decline in 'we' and 'us' and the expression of positive emotions," wrote science journalist John Tierney (2011, para. 4).

Many classical and contemporary thinkers have shown how human reality and identity are rooted in the concept of community. Ethicists and political theorists with a wide range of perspectives have long argued that an ethical life and moral decision making are largely based on some kind of concern for community. This also is embodied in the concept of *ubuntu* in several African cultures. The term, from the Zulu language, means "a person is a person through other persons," or "I am because of others" (Christians, 2004, p. 241). Media ethicist Clifford Christians argued that Western culture would do well to counterbalance its hyperindividualism by considering the truth of the *ubuntu* way of thinking. He and others argue that we cannot fully understand the idea of freedom, or autonomous agency, before we fully appreciate the community-based moral framework in which personal identity operates. If we do not do so, we can end up putting the personal identity cart before the moral horse, so to speak—we end up making claims about what we can or should do as individuals without a proper social, relational context. Without this context, our ethical thinking becomes muddled, and the moral claims we make threaten to become merely self-serving excuses. Cultural critic Benjamin Barber argued that "we sow as individuals what we would not necessarily choose to reap as a community. We are trapped in an individualistic consumer culture in which the public goods that belong to us as citizens are no longer part of the accounting" (2007, p. 18).

"The ideal picture of autonomous individuals choosing their connections (and disconnections) without constraints of any sort is an example of bad utopianism."

—Michael Walzer (2004, p. 1)

Our culture places a premium on the virtues of individual action and autonomy—personal privacy, freedom, self-sufficiency, being in control of our destinies, and so on—in ways that often minimize or ignore the importance of community. This chapter explains the philosophical underpinnings of the concept of community and suggests how a solid understanding of the concept should inform our ethical decision making. It explores the central claims of a body of theory known as *communitarianism*. It summarizes the work of philosopher John Dewey, who thought deeply about the nature of human community and of how it should shape both our communication systems and our democratic life. It discusses the idea of the "public sphere" and its implications for media practice. It considers feminist perspectives that challenge many assumptions about treatment of others, about questions of social power, and about the nature of communication itself.

It also explores what kind of role the concept of community should play in media practice. In communication, ethical behavior *requires* that we put a significant value on both the ideal of community service and the more concrete notion of "community" as a key stakeholder. Communication and community are intimately interwined: "A community exists not through agreement, but through communication," according to one perspective (Anderson, Dardenne, & Killenberg, 1994, p. 10). In nearly all media sectors—public relations, journalism, and even advertising—practitioners claim that public or community service is an important professional value. But what does that look like? And what does it mean when the value of community service collides with other professed values such as journalistic independence, client loyalty, or the financial health of a media company? While the idea of community service often is given lip service, it more often takes a backseat to more individualistic themes of freedom, personal ambition and responsibility, and privacy. However, this chapter shows that failure to fully appreciate the roles and dimensions of community in our human existence leaves both media practitioners and consumers with a stunted view of their responsibilities. Furthermore, failure to take into account the implications that our basic human connectedness have for communication can limit our ability to make ethical judgments about the media system.

Bringing Kant to Bear on Advertising Practices

The targeting of vulnerable and impressionable groups such as children and young people by advertising and marketing is effectively using the members of these groups merely as means to the end of promoting the sale of consumer products whose consumption is potentially harmful to those targeted groups. Even if the exploitation of vulnerable groups of people is allowed by the role morality (i.e., one's moral duty not in a broad, public sense, but in a narrow sense of one's obligation to capably carry out a particular function or role) of advertising, universal public morality that trumps role morality when the two come into conflict precludes the exploitation of people as means merely for the end of promoting the sale of consumer goods. Because people are clearly inherently more valuable than commodities, advertisers as members of the community should desist from exploiting the vulnerabilities of their fellow citizens merely for their own financial self-interest. Moreover, the exploitation of

(Continued)

(Continued)

people by advertisers through targeting that can potentially harm them can also harm the instrumental interests of the advertisers themselves by creating an image of corporate moral irresponsibility in the public mind. Insofar as the exploitation of the targeted groups is designed to enhance the instrumental interests of the advertisers engaged in these types of potentially harmful targeting, this is a self-defeating and thus an instrumentally undesirable strategy that is best avoided both for instrumental and for ethical reasons. (Spence & Van Heekeren, 2005, p. 40)

DEFINING COMMUNITY

There are clearly many different ways to understand or interpret the idea of community. We talk of it in terms of communities that are defined geographically—a group with a physical headquarters, a fraternity house, a church, a town, a state, or a nation. We talk of communities that exist beyond spatial considerations. The Internet has allowed the cultivation of new, interest-based communities that transcend geography in unprecedented ways. The term itself evokes a wide range of images and associations; people can hear many different things when they hear "community." It is often a loaded concept. Some think of community as implying a glow of harmonious association, of referring to some dreamy and elusive environment full of love and support and spiritual fulfillment—a utopian myth. Sociologist Charles Horton Cooley (1962) described this ideal state of communal life:

> In so far as one identifies himself with a whole, loyalty to that whole is loyalty to himself; it is self-realization. . . . One is never more human, and as a rule never happier, than when he is sacrificing his narrow and merely private interest to the higher call of the congenial group. (p. 38)

In fact, American utopian settlements over the past two centuries placed a premium on just such a vision of the ideal, complete, and spiritual or religious community. Here, from Mark Holloway's book, *Heavens on Earth* (1951), is a stanza from a song sung by members of the Oneida community in New York, one of the more notable and enduring utopian settlements of the 19th century:

> We have built us a dome
>
> On our beautiful plantation,
>
> And we all have one home,
>
> And one family relation. (p. 179)

Others hear the word *community* and, instead of envisioning an ideal of a harmonious society, think of a discredited, hippie-style mode of communal living. "When the hippie thing came along, we saw a better way to live," one self-styled San Francisco hippie was quoted as saying. "Now in a tribe, a commune, you're with people that relate to each other, and it's a much groovier experience. Communal living is beautiful. It's the structure of the new age" (Wolfe, 1968, p. 85). Still others hear the word *community* and they envision the ghost of Jean-Jacques Rousseau: They perceive its meaning as much more subversive and perhaps even malicious. It is associated with Communism, with a Stalinist social order imposed from above, a system that, intentionally or not, stifles individual rights and creativity. A large amount of distrust at any emphasis on the notion of community that may threaten to curb individual freedom can be traced back to the 18th-century writings of Rousseau, who sought to justify the "chains of dependence" (Yack, 1986, p. 63) that we must bear in civil society by arguing that submission to the power of the state is the only way man can rise above his "savage" nature. The individual gains political freedom only by subordinating himself to the "general will," Rousseau wrote. In his 1761 treatise *Of the Social Contract,* he called for the "total alienation of each associate, with all of his rights, to the whole community" (Rousseau, 1762/1997, p. 53). Rousseau continued, "Each of us puts in common his person and his whole power under the supreme direction of the general will; and in return we receive in a body every member as an indivisible part of the whole" (p. 53).

"The end of the community is the self-development of the individual. Without community, individual growth is impossible. The self, in order to rise above the merely trivial and inauthentic, must be constructed within a context of meanings and valuations that transcend merely personal preferences."

—D. M. Savage (2002)

The idea of community should be understood broadly because part of its value lies in the range of lives, interests, and cultural factors that it can encompass. At the very least, *community* refers to a network of individuals in social relations with one another that helps us define who we are as well as provides the basis for action and expression regarding shared values and goals. It is something that we invest in, and in turn, it provides the basis for what Walzer (2004) calls "a culture of individuality" through which we build our lives as social creatures. He reminds us that we can never dismiss what he refers to as four primary "involuntary" constraints—that is, circumstances of our lives not of our own making but that largely shape who we are and who we will be:

1. *The familial or social.* "We are born member of a kin group, of a nation or country, and of a social class; and we are born male or female. These four attributes go a long way toward determining the people with whom we associate for the rest of our lives," according to Walzer (2004, p. 3).

2. *The cultural.* "Associates may choose one another, but they rarely have much to say about the structure and style of their association. Marriage is an obvious example: the match may be a true meeting of minds, but the meaning of the match is not determined by the minds that meet" (pp. 5–6).

3. *The political.* "We are born citizens (unless we are very unlucky) and are rarely invited to agree to our citizenship" (p. 8).

4. *The moral.* "Living together with other people just *is* a moral engagement. It ties us up in unexpected ways" (p. 11).

Our individualistic attitudes can blind us to the roles community plays in our lives and to the centrality of community as an ethical concern.

While a sense of belonging and fraternity can be important, the two can be used to define *community* in negative, exclusionary, and destructive ways. Community in these senses can become little more than indoctrination or a justification to shut out anyone different. Mapel (1989) said a more significant sense of community is based on the fact that "we are united not simply by a sense of belonging, but by emotional ties to a democratic way of life that itself encourages the airing and toleration of differences" (p. 143). True community allows for both diversity and individuality yet depends on the recognition of all members that they share interests and fates. "Even in communities torn by conflict, bonds remain as long as people communicate, whether in polite talk or heated argument," Anderson, Dardenne, and Killenberg wrote (1994, p. 10). As Yack (1993) described Aristotle's view,

> Aristotle differs from most modern social theorists in that he treats community as a generic rather than a specific social category. He uses it to characterize *all* social groups rather than to characterize one especially close and highly integrated form of social life. . . . Aristotle's understanding of community captures . . . the way in which all forms of social interaction help shape individual character and identity. But it also leaves open questions about the nature and value of any particular form of communal life that one might advocate. It allows us to give full weight to the social constitution of individual character and actions without suggesting the necessity of any specific form of communal life. (pp. 26, 50)

While the actual makeup of what is "community" will differ among cultures and demographic strata, there is little debate over whether it exists. As this chapter indicated earlier, the issue often is how much weight to assign the concept in our decision making. This is an ethics issue because we are faced with a dilemma in which individual interests clash with broader social or community interests. In these cases, we often are culturally predisposed to side with the individual interests, and in many of these cases, such a position can be compellingly defended. But as this chapter shows, our individualistic attitudes can blind us to the roles community plays in our lives and to the centrality of community as an ethical concern. We often talk about relying on our inner "moral compass" for guidance on ethical questions, unaware what we really mean is that we rely on socialization for our internalized norms and values. Many theorists, from a wide range of approaches, have issued warnings about how our individualistic predispositions can warp our moral thinking. Here are a few:

- "There is no two-step process in which sovereign individuals are first true to themselves and then calculate the risk and benefits of their actions for others. Responsibility is not accountability to oneself while acting out one's preferences, some of which intersect with others. Judgments about being responsible arise from the interpersonal character of our lives together. The I-Thou relationship is both the beginning and the end of responsibility. It is determined in community formations, not first of all in the inner sanctum of individuals insisting on their rights while they decide what duties they might have to others." (Christians, Fackler, & Ferré, 2012, p. 103)

- "Failing to recognize the way in which human beings can be and are constitutively attached to their communities entails an inability to give a coherent account of the circumstances necessary to achieve *any* kind of human good (whether communal in content or not), for in the absence of such constitutive communal frameworks, the very idea of morality as a rational or intelligible enterprise drops out." (Philosopher Alisdair MacIntyre, quoted in Mulhall & Swift, 1992, p. 93)

- "[Problem solving, or moral growth, is a social, not an individual task.] The individual by himself can do little to regulate the conditions which will render important values more secure." (Philosopher John Dewey quoted in Damico, 1978, p. 31)

- "Individuals are interdependent. No one is born except in dependence on others. . . . The human being is an individual because of and in relation with others. Otherwise, he is an individual only as a stick of wood is, namely, as spatially and numerically separate." (Dewey, 1932/1985, p. 227)

- "The self has to find its moral identity in and through its membership in communities." (MacIntyre, 1984, p. 221)

- "[Basing decisions on concern for community is a primary feature of being ethical; it is based on] a conception of oneself as a moral agent among others. It is therefore the conditions of human agency and not the satisfaction of desire that set the object of moral requirement." (Philosopher Barbara Herman, 1993, p. 86)

- "[Western society] lives on the mistaken assumption that our personal identity exists independently of socially given ends; it confuses an aggregate of individual goods with the common good." (Christians et al., 1993, p. 46)

- "We cannot adequately understand human moral nature by disregarding our cultural dependencies and our social vulnerabilities. . . . In fact, it is our dependence on others—our cognitive, emotional, cultural and material dependence—that accounts for most of our moral qualities. . . . Our dependence on others also accounts for most of what we are and can hope to become." (Schoeman, 1992, pp. 5–6)

- "The individual alone is not regarded as a mature state. The word for a mature individual translates as 'person-among-others.' In the beginning is the group: How can I as an individual serve the group better? From that competence I derive my status." (Trompenaars & Hampden-Turner, 2002, p. 64)

How might the distorting effect of our individualistic culture be seen in our decisions on questions about media ethics? As marketers or advertisers, we might be quick to dismiss the potential harm caused by a type of advertising to society as a whole or to certain groups, and, thus, be more likely to place greater weight on free speech claims of individuals. As journalists, we might be more ready to focus on individual responsibility or culpability and be less interested in exploring or documenting the community or social roots of a problem. As public relations professionals, we might feel more justified in pursuing client objectives and be less concerned with long-term community interests. As a value, the idea of community service or connectedness can regularly clash with other values of independence, privacy, personal gain, and corporate profitability. We will focus more specifically on implications of the idea of community in media practice, but first, consider how key theorists have talked about community and why they placed so much emphasis on it.

"The self has to find its moral identity in and through its membership in communities."

—Alisdair MacIntyre (1984, p. 256)

Aristotle on Community

The idea of community, as Aristotle used the term, has four primary features: (1) A community consists of individuals who differ from each other in some significant way; (2) these individuals share something—some good, activity, feature of their identity, or any combination thereof; (3) they engage in some interaction related to what they share; and (4) they are bound to each other, to a greater or lesser extent, by some sense of friendship (*philia*) and some sense of justice (Yack, 1993). Aristotle wrote about community in a sense that is very different from the harmonious visions of later writers. For him, community was as much about conflict as it was about cooperation. Aristotle insisted in his *Politics* that, as "communal animals," we are naturally disposed to share a wide variety of communal goals and activities, not just those that hold political value. "Men strive to live together even when they have no need of assistance from one another, though it is also the case that the common advantage brings them together," Aristotle wrote. Aristotle criticized Plato's idea of collective identity because it pushes a goal of eliminating social tension created by heterogeneity. For Aristotle, such tension was precisely what a true community meant. "The creative—and sometimes destructive—tension that emerges from combinations of sharing and difference is one of the most important features of community, as Aristotle conceives of it. Eliminate differences in social identity in the name of easing this tension and you destroy community itself" (Yack, 1993, p. 30).

PHILOSOPHICAL ROOTS OF COMMUNITY

Most classical philosophers address the concept of community in some way. But two in particular are useful in the effort here to explore community as a key concept in ethical thinking in general and a central idea in media ethics more specifically. Aristotle was mentioned earlier. In his *Politics,* he insisted that we are "communal animals" as well as "political animals," and he made some important distinctions that help us clarify what community is as well as what it is not. Immanuel Kant also suggested why we ought to see community not simply as one among several alternative values or approaches but as the basis for reality itself and, thus, as a key justification for ethical action. Aristotle used the term *koinonia* as a generic term for all social groups. In his study of Aristotle, Yack (1993) explained that such communities

> emerge out of almost every kind of social interaction. *Koinonai* can be as fleeting as a business deal or as enduring as religious customs, as small as a nuclear family or as large as a nation. Wherever individuals hold something in common (*koinon*), be it a household, a contract, a destination or a political regime, they participate in a *koinonia*. (p. 27)

Aristotle also made an important distinction between a community of "sharing" and what Rousseau and other later thinkers referred to as a collective identity or "general will." The idea of community is very different from an intense sense of belonging to a group, or the idea of "communion." Community members rarely have an awareness of collective identity—it's just how they live. It's almost unconscious, a fact of life not even worthy of contemplation. Yack explained the difference between this and communion, which he argued was unimportant to Aristotle:

> Those who experience "communion," in contrast, consciously experience the loss of separate identity that often comes with an intense sense of belonging to a group. This experience can arise in many different kinds of groups and situations—for example, among soldiers sharing adversity in the trenches, [or] among travelers on a ship who share the pleasures of a cruise. . . . Those who participate in communion lose their sense of distinction from one another and are, if only for a brief time, disposed toward high levels of mutual trust and relatively rare forms of cooperation. Those who participate in community, in contrast, do not lose this sense of distinction from one another, even if they share important elements of their identities. . . . Once we distinguish community from communion and collective identity, it becomes clear that for Aristotle community is a structural feature of everyday social interactions rather than an ideal of solidarity and harmonious living. (Yack, 1993, pp. 31–33)

Isocrates, Community, and Symmetry

While Aristotle advocated a notion of community that served as a robust forum for persuasion and argumentation, another ancient Athenian was teaching a radically different approach. Repelled by the popular notion that rhetoric was simply a tool to win cases regardless of the moral righteousness of the position argued, Isocrates taught a "rhetoric of unification" (Poulakos, 1997, p. xii) that emphasized engagement, cohesion, and collaboration. (Isocrates, a successful teacher of rhetoric whose Athens school in the 4th century was a precursor to today's liberal arts curriculum, is not to be confused with his famous contemporary, Socrates, the more popular skilled rhetorician and teacher of Plato who was forced to drink poison after becoming ensnared in Athenian politics.) In contrast to the adversarial strategies of argumentation and discourse taught by Aristotle and Plato,

Isocrates emphasized consensus and a form of interaction that placed a premium on attaining the broadest public good instead of winning arguments based on self-interest. Scholar Charles Marsh (2001, 2003, 2008) has detailed how Isocrates' method of communication is arguably more effective than those of the better-known Greeks because of his emphasis on community cohesion. Marsh also argued that Isocrates' rhetorical philosophy was "assuredly symmetrical"—that success in persuasion depended as much on listening and compromise as it did on persuasion. Because of this, Marsh argues persuasively that Isocrates provides an important framework for effective public relations. As Isocrates stated in one of his writings, political leaders "ought to be as much concerned about the business of the commonwealth as your own" (Marsh, 2003, p. 238). What makes the approach of Isocrates valuable for us is his unprecedented melding of rhetoric with morality: For the first time, the integrity of the speaker, not the cleverness of the speech, was the measure of success. "In the hands of Isocrates rhetoric is gradually transformed into ethics," claimed one theorist (Marrou, 1956, p. 89). While Aristotle is commonly understood to have emphasized the quality of one's character as the measure of morality, Isocrates was arguably even more emphatic:

> The man who wishes to persuade people will not be negligent as to the matter of character; no, on the contrary, he will apply himself above all to establish a most honourable name among his fellow-citizens; for who does not know that words carry greater conviction when spoken by men of good repute than when spoken by men who live under a cloud, and that the argument which is made by a man's life is of more weight than that which is furnished by words? Therefore, the stronger a man's desire to persuade his hearers, the more zealously will he strive to be honourable and to have the esteem of his fellow citizens. (Isocrates, 1986–1992, p. 278)

Marsh (2001, 2003, 2008) persuasively makes the case that the Isocratean model of communication is the strongest basis for public relations ethics and an emphasis not on mere lobbying skills, but on cultivating "symmetrical" communication with publics and with stakeholders. This is discussed in more detail next.

Case in Point: Attack Ads and a Healthy Body Politic

When asked about the political advertising they see on television, people routinely complain about the negative ads by campaigns and private interest groups. But there are reasons why politicians "go negative" in the run-up to Election Day. Negative information tends to have more of what social psychologists call "salience"—that is, it tends to more easily capture our attention and register in our brains, and it is more easily recalled later than benign, "positive" information. Attack ads can also generate "free" news coverage and are considered effective ways for challengers without much of a track record to contrast themselves with established incumbents. Federal campaign laws regulating how special interest groups can run ads in support of a candidate (without explicitly promoting a single person) also allow politicians to take the "high road" while advocacy groups do the dirty work. In the 2000 presidential elections, for example, only 16% of the advertising by the actual candidates were attack ads; but a whopping 72% of ads aired by advocacy groups were negative (Goldstein & Freedman, 2002). And while attack ads may not be effective in persuading independent or undecided voters, they are considered effective in mobilizing one's base of core supporters to go to the polls. But while attack ads may be useful in the short term for individual politicians, many critics have argued they are irresponsible because they inflict long-term damage to the political process by increasing cynicism among voters and contributing to a decline in civility in politics. Many voters don't distinguish whether the attack ad comes from the candidate or from an independent support group (Magleby, 2002). Attack ads also may discourage voting. One study found that campaigns with high numbers of attack ads had voter turnouts that were 5% smaller than elections with less negative advertising (Ansolabehere & Iyengar, 1995). Another study found that attack ads may backfire on the attacking candidate if the ads are perceived as false or unjustified (Smith & Kidder, 1996). Advertising professionals also have worried that the increasing trend of slick political campaigns to "go negative" may damage the credibility and, perhaps, even the persuasiveness of traditional commercial advertising.

Drawing on Isocrates' model of communication as collaboration, we are less likely to make claims that presume an unconnectedness or detachment of individuals. We are more likely to feel our decisions should take into account a pervasive state of interdependence. Another philosopher, Norman Fischer, explained that our focus on the idea of community in ethical considerations is simply an extension of this "community" of objects in the world: "Community in nature is bound up with simultaneity and reciprocity, the latter involving the concept of the interdependence of parts. . . . This interdependence of parts is also suggested in ethical community" (1978, p. 376). If we understand this link between metaphysical and practical relatedness, it should be easy to see why this matters in our ethical decision making—and how it should influence media practice. Rather than striving for moments of communion, journalists and public relations practitioners might spend more time, energy, and resources on cultivating a deeper, more lasting sense of community engagement among audiences and clients. Rather than aspiring to create an artificial sense of social harmony, they might embrace conflict as a sign of healthy community. Rather than relying on an atomistic view of individuals and events, news might focus on uncovering patterns, trends, and associations as a better way to understand the world. As we will see, American philosopher John Dewey and other communitarian thinkers have sought to demonstrate why this was so important in communication and what it might look like in practice.

COMMUNITARIAN THEORY

The start of this chapter included some references to the American utopian movement, in which groups of people turned their backs on Western liberal society to pursue the ideal of communal living. Such communal utopianism often has been the butt of jokes and ridiculed by caricature. But for those from what is loosely called the "communitarian" school of thought, the joke is on everyone else who lives out delusional lives of independence—on people who claim to be free but who merely choose to ignore how radically they are indebted to their community roots. "The ideal picture of autonomous individuals choosing their connections (and disconnections) without constraints of any sort is an example of bad utopianism," Michael Walzer argued (2004, p. 1). This school of thought should not be confused with Communism, the Soviet-era political doctrine of Marxist revolution that in reality cloaked a brutal totalitarianism in which individual rights were not only subordinated to state interests but were almost completely annihilated. Communitarianism, in contrast, is a theoretical approach that emphasizes the moral implications of understanding the self as deeply rooted in a sense of community. Nor should communitarian references to the "liberal state" be associated with the progressive spectrum of today's politics usually linked to the American Democratic Party. Classic liberalism refers to the Enlightenment movement that struggled against the aristocracies and authoritarian states of 16th-century Europe. Liberalism in its original sense referred to governments and political systems that promoted individual rights and egalitarianism and was reflected in the writings of John Locke, Montesquieu, and Thomas Jefferson. Communitarian thinkers believe that the community and the individual are inextricably intertwined and that, while it may make us more comfortable and feel more empowered by emphasizing individual freedom, it makes little sense philosophically or morally. They question central assumptions of Western society, based on classical liberal notions that government and society must above all protect and promote individual freedom. They suggest that our political and social model, which overwhelmingly places more value on individual rights than on ideas of the public good, distorts our moral thinking. Western liberal society, according to a group of key communitarian media ethics theorists, "lives on the mistaken assumption that our personal identity exists independently of socially given ends; it confuses an aggregate of individual goods with the common good" (Christians, Ferré, & Fackler, 1993, p. 46).

This "mistaken assumption" is based on an inadequate or uninformed conception of the self. We cannot truly know autonomous human identity, these thinkers argue, before appreciating the moral framework in which that identity exists. In our society, it is common to assume that our ability to serve the broader public interest or pursue goodness or virtue stems from the rights and freedoms we have as individuals. But this gets it backward, communitarian thinkers say. If we were serious about our roles as moral agents, our system of rights would be in the service of human virtue, not the other way around. They argue that the notion of the "good," or the most virtuous of human endeavors, should take priority over our rights-based system. If we fully

Communitarianism: What Is It?

According to different theorists, the approach of communitarianism

- Challenges the assumption in our individualistic culture that our identity is derived primarily from personal action and exercise of freedom.
- Seeks to provide more balance between individual interests and valuing the public good.
- Should not be confused with Communism or communal "hippie" lifestyles.
- Argues that our moral life is rooted in our community ties, not an independent internal "compass."

realize this moral context, communitarians say, we come to know why the notion of the human good as a moral claim must be given priority over rights. "The good is always primary to the right," said philosopher Charles Taylor (1990). "The good is what, in its articulation, gives the point of the rules which define the right" (p. 89). Amitai Etzioni (1999), another key communitarian thinker, saw our rights-based society as the flawed product of an inevitable historical process in which classic liberal thinkers such as John Locke, Adam Smith, and John Stuart Mill championed individual rights in response to "authoritarian and excessively communal historical periods."

> Not surprisingly, social philosophers whose societies experienced these highly restrictive conditions did not concern themselves with the danger of legitimizing individual rights to excess—no more than one is concerned about overusing a town's water supply in the depths of the rainy season after decades of more than ample rainfall, indeed flooding. . . . What started as an individualistic correction of excessive communalism led to excessive individualism, wanton manufacturing of presumed rights (such as a right to a credit card or a right to use the men's room if there is even a small line in front of the women's room), neglect of social responsibility, and the waning of commitments to the common good. (Etzioni, 1999, pp. 194, 198)

The central moral claim of communitarianism, then, is that we cannot fully carry out our moral duties until we understand that much of who we are does not stem from the exercise of our rights as individuals but rather is socially constructed. At the very least, this communitarian approach should help us reconsider some of our basic assumptions about how we perceive ourselves—or any single individuals, for that matter—in relation to community needs or goals or in relation to the public good. This approach is not without its critics, of course. While most communitarian theorists talk about striking the proper balance between the individual and the community, opponents see only a thinly veiled assault on personal freedom in the name of some vague notion of the public good. In his influential critique of communitarianism, Walzer (2004) said it was often contradictory and unlikely to ever replace our rights-based society. But that doesn't mean it isn't useful as a constant reminder about the shortcomings of the classic liberal, rights-based state, which he said instills in each generation "renewed hopes for a more absolute freedom from history and society" (p. 153). Communitarianism, he said, serves as a regular, valuable reminder that those hopes are delusional and in fact self-defeating:

> Nothing is waiting; American communitarians have to recognize that there is no one out there but separated, rights-bearing, voluntarily associating, freely speaking, liberal selves. It would be a good thing, though, if we could teach those selves to know themselves as social beings, the historical products of, and in part the embodiments of, liberal values. . . . Liberalism is plagued by free-rider problems—by people who continue to enjoy the benefits of membership and identity while no longer participating in the activities that produce those benefits. Communitarianism, by contrast, is the dream of perfect free-riderlessness. (2004, pp. 154–155))

What does this mean for media ethics? In 1990, James K. Batten, chief executive of Knight Ridder, which had owned many newspapers across the country, including the *Philadelphia Inquirer* and the *San Jose Mercury News,* embodied this communitarian focus in journalism when he challenged journalists to promote what he called "community spirit," which he described as "the willingness of people to care about where they live and to wade in to help solve its problems." He said that sense of community was eroding, and added, "If communities continue to erode, how can we expect newspapers to continue to prosper, over the long term?" (Rosen, 2005, p. 117). In their landmark 1993 book, *Good News: Social Ethics and the Press,* Clifford Christians and his colleagues argued that a communitarian-minded news media would give up its obsession with stories about individual gratification and resist its tendency to reinforce the status quo in society. It would instead be an advocate for social justice. It would not fawn over those with wealth and power but stop allowing big, public egos to determine what's news and be a true watchdog primarily interested in "stories of justice" (p. 93).

Case in Point: Journatic: Hyperlocal Value or Sweatshop Journalism?

Faced with dramatically shrinking budgets and forced to slash newsroom staff, news organizations have scrambled to do less with more during the recent economic downturn. Some have outsourced newsgathering and editing work to contractors while also realizing that providing hyperlocal content—town council agenda items, high school swim meet stats, police blotter entries—can be a good way to increase readership. Enter Journatic. What started as a real estate listing service became a journalistic content provider when CEO Brian Timpone contracted with the *Chicago Tribune* in 2013 to take over TribLocal, its online news service. While the *Tribune* laid off 20 staffers under the deal, Journatic hired "writers" in the Philippines and elsewhere to comb through online listings and put together stories about community happenings in Chicago suburbs such as Naperville and Oak Park. The *Tribune* suspended the deal, however, after journalists at the NPR program *This American Life* revealed Journatic was lifting material from others without proper credit and using fake bylines. After several months, the *Tribune* resumed the contract with Journatic, but editors said the company would only provide "listings and other informational items" and not actual news stories. Soon afterward, Journatic began offering the same services for Hearst newspapers in Seattle and San Antonio. While *Tribune* editors argued that Journatic provided a valuable service that supplemented the work of their reporters, others were more cynical, given the history of profit-protecting budget cuts by *Tribune* and other media giants. "It's a short-term cost-cutting measure, and that's all it is," said Tim McGuire, former editor of the Minneapolis *Star Tribune* (Folkenflik, 2012).

COMMUNITY: A FEMINIST PRIORITY

While there are many different feminist critiques of society, a few in particular are helpful to explore the nature and value of community as well as to consider the media's role in serving and cultivating community. Many feminist theorists have long argued that our individualistic culture, by its nature, privileges a masculine outlook. Feminist ethics is concerned with identifying and challenging social and political sources of gender, racial, and class oppression. Thus, feminism often has claimed to promote a particular kind of social ethic; as media theorist Linda Steiner (1989) noted, "It wants to account not only for how individuals might act morally (and why they should), but also for how society might be transformed so that social institutions and social processes are more moral" (p. 159). This social ethic challenges the ways in which the dominant social culture— associated with masculine, capitalist centers of power—routinely trivializes and excludes more "communal" values such as nurturance, empathy, and collaboration. Indeed, feminist theory questions the assumption that the "rational autonomous individual" should be considered a model of moral life since by definition this model denies the profound connectedness that largely defines what it is to be human. A feminist ethics insists that the obligation of "care" implicit in all social relationships, rather than an abstract ideal of rationality or aspiring to a universal norm, should be given priority (Noddings, 1984; Seigfried, 1996). "Feminists propose an ethic that acknowledges the moral self as embedded in a web of family and communal relationships, that regards caring and empathy as morally significant and legitimate virtues" (Steiner, 1989, p. 166). Political philosopher Seyla Benhabib (1992, 1995) has promoted a more "conversational model" that features the idea of a "collective practical reason" as a middle way between a Kantian universalist ethic and questionable relativism. Rather than having an ethical system based on rational agreement, she proposed a way of "sustaining those normative practices and moral relationships within which reasoned agreement *as a way of life* [author's emphasis] can flourish and continue" (1992, p. 38). She and others challenge the traditional division between the public sphere (which is male dominated) and the domestic sphere, which is trivialized. Consequently, a feminist approach calls for changes in our media system to more realistically reflect and promote this communal web. Donna Allen, the president of the Women's Institute for Freedom of the Press, argued that the media "need to be more caring and more sharing, less violent, less hierarchical, and more equal in extending to the whole public the outreach efforts of people speaking for themselves" (Steiner, 1989, pp. 168–169).

JOHN DEWEY AND COMMUNITY

Many of the concerns of communitarianism can be traced back to American philosopher John Dewey (1859–1952), who wrote extensively about how we should understand ourselves as community members and how this understanding is critical to the survival of democracy. Dewey was a champion of participatory democracy, which he saw as an ethical ideal that called on everyone to help build communities with the aim of allowing every individual to blossom and develop his or her talents. Thus, the value of the individual and the priority of community building were not mutually exclusive. People realize their common interests, he argued, through two things: education and communication. With these two ongoing processes, society uncovers the common good. But by "common good," Dewey did not have a specific end in mind; he meant, as Damico (1978) described, "a society which measures moral progress by the continuing growth and development of individual personality" (p. 29). This vision of society was greater as a whole, according to Dewey, than the private person because, as Horowitz (1999) noted, "The need for public interaction pre-empts the issue of privacy, by permitting each individual to contribute his or her specific qualities and talents to make the society function properly" (pp. 306–307). In his wide-ranging writings, Dewey proposed an ethical theory grounded in the belief that only social ends are reasonable since they, by definition, enhance the individual's life by developing and enriching his relationships with others. Alfonso Damico (1978), a Dewey scholar, summarized this approach:

> [Dewey] objects to any explanation of political issues in terms of opposition between the individual and the social and between authority and freedom. He believes that such analyses distort the true nature of experience. The individual and the collective are not in opposition; rather, he says, they are different parts of an experience that finds its fulfillment in community life. The good community is one where men are aware of their common interests in the progressive growth of each individual. (p. 5)

Dewey's thought has had a significant impact on how we think about the role of media in our society. The call by some media ethicists for the news media to undertake the mission to cultivate a "revitalized citizenship" (Christians et al., 1993, p. 89) mirrors Dewey's argument that the good of the individual and the good of the community are the same goal, and creating a "public experience" for everyone is the true means for individual self-realization. In his 1927 book, *The Public and Its Problems,* Dewey questioned the prevailing view that society was getting too complex and technical for the average person to make competent decisions about public policy. This view, promoted by newspaper columnist Walter Lippmann, argued that public opinion was a poor basis for good government and that modern society is best served by a sort of democratic elitism—an executive level of experts and technicians elected and appointed to make decisions— rather than relying on a more participatory version of democracy. Lippmann suggested that journalism was a critical part of this governing elite: Its job was to work closely with the policy experts and disseminate their conclusions to the largely uneducated masses. In other words, the news media needed to be a shaper of public opinion and not merely reflect it. Dewey, however, said this call for elitism relied on a false understanding of the individual as isolated and without any social context. For one thing, Dewey said, people living and working *in association* with each other constitute a whole that becomes greater than the individual parts. It is the interaction among individuals that forms meaning, intelligence, and knowledge, and this "public opinion" constitutes something more effective and compelling than a mere aggregate of individuals. For another, society ruled by a governing class of elites ceases to be a true democracy but instead becomes an oligarchy. "In the degree in which they become a specialized class, they are shut off from knowledge of the needs which they are supposed to serve," Dewey wrote (1927, p. 206). And finally, the fact that people seem increasingly uninterested and disengaged may be in large part the fault of the media that can appear to talk *at* them rather than with them.

Journalists are part of the problem, some have claimed. They are "contributing to a mood of fatalistic disengagement" (Fallows, 1997, p. 243). The concern that the news media were contributing to the alienation of the people from public life through "horse race" coverage and focus on the most extreme or entertaining views bothered many journalists, and, thus, the "public journalism" movement was born in the 1990s. This form of journalism, which also is called "civic journalism," sought to engage communities in more of a dialogue about the issues of the day rather than presenting news of politics or policy decisions that didn't seem relevant to the lives of average people. Supporters of public journalism initiatives around the country say that their work merely gets back to good news work that focuses on community concerns. "Public journalists want public life to work," wrote Jay Rosen, who has long advocated the form.

> In order to make it work they are willing to declare an end to their neutrality on certain questions—for example: whether people participate, whether a genuine debate takes place when needed, whether a community comes to grips with its problems, whether politics earns the attention it claims. (Rosen, 1999, p. 75)

But there are plenty of critics, too, who say that this "movement" is actually just journalism done right. Others warn that public journalism, with its focus on promoting civic engagement, can verge on an abandonment of the traditional notion of journalistic objectivity and instead produce "community cheerleader" journalism. Some warn that just because people may be brought together to talk about public issues does not mean that they will acknowledge that they have common goals or shared interests. Many communities are deeply fragmented, which no amount of public journalism will change. Researchers also have suggested that sometimes consensus may not be inherently desirable (Hackett & Zhao, 1998), and the actual face-to-face dialogue is not always productive (Glasser & Craft, 1998).

Case in Point: Activist Coverage of Racial Problems in Akron

In May 1992, racially charged violence erupted in cities across the nation upon the news that white Los Angeles police officers were acquitted of assault charges in the videotaped beating of Rodney King. News organizations sought to get beyond the daily reports of events and examine local race relations. In Akron, Ohio, the *Akron Beacon Journal* published a dramatic, yearlong series called "A Question of Color" that explored the different "realities" of black and white residents. But then the paper went much further. It began actively encouraging groups to meet to discuss race relations. It ran a front-page "coupon" in December 1993, asking people to do something to try to improve race relations. The paper established a nonprofit group, Coming Together, which sponsored study groups, workshops, and even a radio show. Professionally, such activism paid off: In 1994, the *Beacon Journal* won the Pulitzer Prize for Public Service. But many critics were disturbed that the paper crossed a line by abandoning its role of impartial observer and disseminator of news. Was this kind of community activism really the job of journalists? What effect might it have on their credibility?

(Continued)

(Continued)

What's the difference between such activism and "cheerleader" journalism? If news organizations start using news pages to advocate on social issues, how will journalists know they're on the side of the angels? One critic, writing in a politically liberal opinion magazine, asked what if American southern newspapers, which, during the civil rights unrest in the 1960s were overwhelmingly segregationist, had taken a similarly activist stand: "Would they have taken a more accommodating attitude toward the white establishment? Would they have searched for the 'common ground' of separate but equal?" (Cohn, 1995, p. 16).

Case in Point: For Businesses, No Way Out of Facebook Hell

Companies eager to increase brand presence and engage directly with customers have flocked to Facebook and other social networking sites. Yet by doing so, they relinquish control, which is often so important to marketers. Brands can be supported or buried by vitriolic posts in the blink of an eye—especially if the company wades into a social or political controversy. When is it beneficial for a company to continue engagement through social media, even if things get nasty? Many a company has found its brand scorched in a Facebook hell, where critics and boycotts can be quick to pile on at the slightest misstep. One recent victim was Lowe's, the home-improvement retailing giant. The company was a regular sponsor of a popular television series spotlighting unusual, nontraditional, and marginalized Americans produced by The Learning Channel (TLC). In 2011, the series featured Arab Americans in the segment called *All-American Muslim*. When conservative Christian groups lobbied against advertisers supporting the show, Lowe's pulled out, and the social-media firestorm erupted. "#LoweshatesMuslims" spread widely on Twitter, and its Facebook page was overwhelmed with negative, often racist posts (Popken, 2011). Eventually, Lowe's executives deleted all comments from the site.

THE IDEA OF THE PUBLIC SPHERE

Dewey was among the first to write about what is meant by the "public" as something that exists largely in *communication*—that is, what we refer to as public opinion being the result of interaction and expression of values and goals. Others, most notably a German philosopher named Jürgen Habermas (1989, 1996), sought to refine this idea into something called the "public sphere." Think of the concept of the public sphere as a huge arena with countless kiosks, computer terminals, information booths, and conference tables where people come to talk about issues, get information, exchange ideas, and form opinions. It is a zone of exchange that is "free from both the cares of private life and the violence of raw state power" (Peters & Cmiel, 1991, p. 200). But writers through the ages disagreed on what the public sphere should look like and what interests it should serve. For John Stuart Mill (1859/1975), the public sphere was a political arena in which people could express their individuality, and it was protected by individual rights to private property and individual opinions. It was very much separate from the state. But others, such as Hannah Arendt (1958), argued that it was where people went to engage in politics that was in essence self-government. It is what allowed people to become full-fledged human beings; individuals who were solely concerned about their private matters were stunted creatures, a claim that reflects the ancient Greek notion of public life as an embodiment of virtue. A useful definition of the public sphere was provided by media theorists Lance Bennett and Robert Entman (2001):

> Put simply, the public sphere refers to the areas of informal public life—from cafes, to Internet chat rooms, to the exchange of opinion in magazines and television talk programs—where citizens can go to explore social interests and conflicts. In this sphere, individuals have the freedom to judge the quality of their government decisions independently of censorship. The public sphere is comprised of *any and all locations, physical or virtual, where ideas and feelings relevant to politics are transmitted or exchanged openly* [authors' emphasis]. . . . Of course, this ideal has never been achieved, and probably never will. . . . Yet the public sphere serves theorists well as an ideal type—that is, as a construct against which different real-world approximations can be evaluated. (Bennett & Entman, 2001, pp. 2–3)

Habermas (1989, 1996) and others argued that though Western societies place a premium on the right of everyone to have a clear zone of privacy, a public sphere is critical for human development and self-government. And the media play a critical role in fostering and maintaining the public sphere. But Habermas's vision of the public sphere is not the same as the idea of a competitive, commercially driven media system whose main function is not engagement or dialogue, but selling and persuading. He called the latter "strategic action," which is goal oriented and often manipulative. A true public sphere, in contrast, is based on what Habermas called "communicative action"—it is based on "mutual understanding, trust and shared knowledge" (Dahlgren, 2001, p. 40). It is where what Habermas called the public "will formation" takes shape. But other theorists, including Nancy Fraser, argued that it isn't enough. The way most people envision the public sphere, she said, remains male dominated and shaped by the most powerful interests. Better, she said, to think of a "multiplicity of publics" organizing and talking to each other and negotiating over the allocation of power (Fraser, 1990). She challenged the assumption that the goal of the public sphere should be "consensus" and instead argued the goal should be to acknowledge and deal with the legitimate conflicting interests of various publics.

This debate over the public sphere continues, but nearly all agree that, in reality, the public sphere is in "dismal" shape because a nonmanipulative, nonpartisan sharing of information is increasingly rare in our commercial media system. That system also undermines a key requirement that the public sphere be *universally* accessible and representative. But in fact, the media system regularly shuts out voices and perspectives that are not mainstream or profitable. A true public sphere has become "all the more challenging in an era when market forces have such a strong influence" (Dahlgren, 2001, p. 36). This inability to help build a public sphere is a central ethical failure of the media, according to some theorists. Journalists, they say, are too concerned about establishing their own professionalism—being detached, dispassionate deliverers of news content—in ways that don't help people become active citizens. "Media ethics, in its preoccupation with the practices of the professional few rather than the participation of the many, is one sign of the lack of a clear public sphere in both our society and our imagination" (Peters & Cmiel, 1991, p. 210).

Community and Journalism

There are many different ways in which journalists have sought to connect with their communities and make sure that a focus on community as a news value drives decision making in newsrooms. The development of public journalism has already been mentioned. Jay Rosen, among public journalism's most prominent champions, wrote admiringly of the editor of the paper in Columbus, Georgia, that sponsored town hall meetings after running a series of articles on racial and financial problems in the city. The paper's editor held barbecue dinners in his backyard that brought black and white citizens together. While this example of public journalism sought to increase community involvement, plenty of critics wondered whether the paper had taken on an activist role it should not have (Rosen, 1999, pp. 27–33). The debate over how best to relate journalism and community continues. This debate becomes a matter of ethics when it requires journalists to justify treating their communities in certain ways and when other priorities, such as economic interests, begin influencing what becomes news. It also requires journalists to examine some fundamental duties involved in "serving the public" that may invite some hard questions about the nature of news itself. Is the news presented in ways that discourage people from getting involved, that invite apathy? Some say yes. Anderson and colleagues, in their book, *The Conversation of Journalism* (1994), represented a common view that the way journalists define news—often treating audiences as consumers instead of citizens and covering only that which is entertaining—is part of the problem:

> As news pages fill with theme sections, features, listings, and the other things that editors and publishers think consumers want, the information that people *need* in order to be communicators within the community gets squeezed into smaller and smaller spaces. The more papers attempt to make news items shorter and more accessible, sometimes stripping all but the most exciting facts, the more life they remove from them and, therefore, the easier they make it for people to disengage and distance themselves from the news (and, perhaps, their own communities). People are not passive readers and viewers who ultimately prefer empty entertainment over a news that serves them as citizen-communicators, but they have been invited—in part, by journalism itself—to assume just such a passive role. (p. 7)

When considering community interests as an ethical value, journalists have a duty to resist or at least question the cultural tendency to privilege individual interests over a sense of serving a public good. Members of "Generation Me" may have specific assumptions about how they want their news tailored to advance their personal and consumer interests, but journalists would do well to understand that, in an Aristotelian sense, any community-oriented service embraces conflict as well as acknowledges shared values and goals. According to this approach, good journalism does not merely mean transmitting "the truth" to audiences. Christians and colleagues argue that truth, in our multicultural world, cannot merely mean accuracy, but must strive for comprehensiveness:

> [The] view of truth as accurate information is too narrow, given today's political and social complexities. Truth's deeper meaning for international news is authentic disclosure, to get at the heart of the matter, to explain the context behind the facts. The ethical principle of truth, as communitarianism defines it, means comprehensiveness. The term "interpretive sufficiency" is one way to describe it. A newsworthy account that is truthful represents complex cultures and religions adequately. The people involved at all levels are portrayed authentically without stereotype or simplistic judgments. (Christians et al., 2012, p. 33)

Community and Public Relations

A deep understanding of the concept of community is obviously essential in public relations—the term *community* itself implies a host of qualities discussed in this chapter, such as social identity, communal interests, and connectedness. Public relations theorists Dean Kruckeberg and Kenneth Starck (1988) and later Laurie Wilson (1996) make the case that the mission of public relations, first and foremost, ought to be understood as a sustained effort to cultivate and maintain a sense of community. Wilson, as well as others (Culbertson & Chen, 1997), advocated a communitarian framework for corporate communications that emphasized "the interdependent relationship and role of business as a participant in [communities] that consist of a variety of actors, individual and organizational, all cooperating for a common good that extends far beyond solely financial factors" (Wilson, 2001, p. 522). Such emphasis on the need to professionalize the value of care for others mirrors the ethical frameworks of Dewey and Benhabib discussed earlier in this chapter. But as we have seen, the roots for this emphasis on community go much deeper, to Isocrates. At times, the ancient Greek seems to be speaking directly to today's PR practitioners in his emphasis on communication for the common good: "I myself should be ashamed if, while offering counsel to others, I should be negligent of their interests and look to my own advantage" (1986–1992). Charles Marsh, who explains how Isocrates' model of "symmetrical" communication is the true precursor of modern PR, argues that "a 21st-century version of Isocratean public relations . . . would champion the virtues of moderation and justice and would seek relationships that constantly build on discourses of many voices" (2008, p. 242). In fact, at least one public relations theorist suggested the field might be better called "community relations," arguing that the term was more accurate than the problematic concept of what we mean by a "public" (Hallahan, 2004, p. 235). "Unlike an ephemeral public that emerges around a particular issue and then dissolves, a community can be located, and its interests, values, history, power and political structure understood," he wrote (p. 235).

Community: It's in the Code of Ethics

While few media ethics codes explicitly refer to the concept of community as a practical value, the concept is implied in statements that address the mission of public service and the duty to cultivate and maintain a healthy marketplace of ideas.

From the American Marketing Association

- Marketers must: Recognize that they not only serve their enterprises but also act as stewards of society in creating, facilitating and executing the efficient and effective transactions that are part of the greater economy.
- Acknowledge the social obligations to stakeholders that come with increased marketing and economic power.

The complete code can be found at http://www.marketingpower.com.

From the Society of Professional Journalists Code of Ethics

Journalists should do the following:

- Strive to serve the public with thoroughness and honesty.
- Diligently seek out subjects of news stories to give them the opportunity to respond to allegations of wrongdoing.
- Tell the story of the diversity and magnitude of the human experience boldly, even when it is unpopular to do so.
- Avoid stereotyping by race, gender, age, religion, ethnicity, geography, sexual orientation, disability, physical appearance or social status.
- Identify sources whenever feasible. The public is entitled to as much information as possible on sources' reliability.
- Support the open exchange of views, even views they find repugnant.
- Give voice to the voiceless; official and unofficial sources of information can be equally valid.
- Clarify and explain news coverage and invite dialogue with the public over journalistic conduct.

The complete code can be found at http://www.spj.org/ethicscode.asp.

From the Public Relations Society of America Member Code of Ethics

A member shall do the following:

- Serve the public interest by acting as responsible advocates for those we represent.
- Provide a voice in the marketplace of ideas, facts and viewpoints to aid informed public debate.
- Adhere to the highest standards of accuracy and truth in advancing the interests of those we represent and in communicating with the public.
- Build mutual understanding, credibility and relationships among a wide array of institutions and audiences.
- [Honor] our obligation to serve the public interest.
- Respect all opinions and support the right of free expression.

The complete code can be found at http://www.prsa.org/aboutUs/ethics/preamble_en.html.

Public relations theorists continue to propose competing frameworks that would explain public relations purposes, effects, and ideals. Many seek to address ethical practice. One dominant model, however, features a particularly important ethical dimension. Most public relations professionals understand that to be effective in cultivating relationships among clients and various publics with which those clients interact, public relations should emphasize what has been called a "two-way symmetrical" model of communication. This model, first put forth by public relations theorists James Grunig and Todd Hunt (1984), says that public relations serves client interests best when it tries to engage the public in a dialogue, to cultivate mutually beneficial relationships, and *listens* to others as much as it advocates on a client's behalf. The model also acknowledges that business or organizational clients cannot assume that they are more "powerful" than the publics they deal with. These publics, or stakeholders, can include customers, the news media, marketing audiences, suppliers, policymakers, labor groups, and consumer advocacy groups. Ideally, public relations uses communication "to bring about symbiotic changes in the ideas, attitudes and behaviors of *both* [emphasis added] their organizations and their publics," according to Grunig (2001). "Symmetry in public relations really is about balancing the interests of organizations and publics, of balancing advocacy and accommodation" (pp. 12, 16). In contrast, an "asymmetrical" model of communication assumes public relations' main job is simply to persuade publics of the "rightness" or primacy of the client's interest and to exercise client power.

Grunig has said that the symmetrical model is "inherently ethical" (2001, p. 29) because it calls for organizations to resist being exclusively focused on self-interest and to take their moral agency seriously by embracing a concern for the welfare of other stakeholders. Public relations should be more than single-minded persuasion efforts; the concept of symmetry incorporates a process that "embeds" ethical concerns into the very process of communication. This is Kantian in its framing of autonomy and transparent action:

> Public relations should go beyond the advocacy of self-interest without concern for the consequences of an organization's behavior on others to a balance between self-interest and concern for the interest of others. . . . Symmetry means that communicators keep their eye on the broad professional perspective of balancing private and public interests. Their job consists of more than argumentation or "a wrangle in the marketplace." (Grunig, 2000, pp. 33–34))

However, the symmetrical model for public relations has its critics. Some have called it utopian, unrealistic, and in conflict with public relations' fundamental mission of partisan advocacy. Power imbalances among advocates and stakeholders inevitably result in symmetry despite all efforts (Leitch & Neilson, 2001). And often, the unquestioned norm in much of PR work is that, as a product of capitalism, it tends to reinforce organizational power (Holtzhausen, 2000). Stoker and Tusinski (2006) also have suggested that an "unhealthy infatuation with dialogue" among public relations professionals, while sounding virtuous, actually poses serious ethical problems. Drawing from the work of communication theorist John Durham Peters, who suggested that "dialogue can be tyrannical and dissemination can be just" (1999, p. 34), they argued that dialogue can actually subvert true communication and "saddle" public relations with ethically questionable quid pro quo relationships:

> The demands of dialogue force the organization to become more strategic and selective in its communication and more reliant on homogenous public to achieve mutual understanding. The use of selective communication designed to persuade like-minded publics transforms dialogue into two-way asymmetric communication, which is based on controlling the environment rather than adjusting and adapting to it. . . . The sender's motivation for entering dialogue is not necessarily to hear what the receiver has to say but to make sure the sender's words reach the *right* people and are understood in the *right* way. (Stoker & Tusinski, 2006, pp. 163–164)

This, they said, is the antithesis of ethical communication because it appears to abandon the Kantian persons-as-ends principle and can allow organizations to excuse themselves from true moral responsibility by merely demonstrating a good faith effort to *talk* with various stakeholders. More straightforward, "asymmetrical" dissemination of information, less subject to corrosive selectivity, can be more ethical than dialogue.

COMMUNITY AND ADVERTISING

Ethics researchers who examined advertising principles and standards around the world concluded that, at least on paper, the advertising industry embraced five principles, including "decency, honesty, and truth," "avoidance of misrepresentation," and "fair competition." Foremost among the standards touted by the ad industry, however, was "a sense of responsibility to consumers, community concerns and society" (Spence & Van Heekeren, 2005, p. 26). Advertisers naturally are driven to create positive associations between targeted groups and their brands. They also routinely "segment" populations to receive specific messages. To do both, they must be "tuned in" to the community they're trying to win over.

> Insofar as the professional self-regulating process in advertising involves the community as a key and major stakeholder, as the process ought to, then the community has an ethical responsibility to be part of and contribute actively to that process. . . . Equally, the advertising industry has an ethical responsibility to actively involve the community it its regulative process and be ethically responsive to the community's concerns regarding unethical advertising processes. (Spence & Van Heekeren, 2005, p. 27)

Advertising strategies that target certain segments of a community are morally obligated to balance their advertising objectives with ideas of community well-being. Creating brand loyalty among population segments certainly is a valid business goal. However, ethicists make the important distinction between targeting strategies that respect consumers' reasoning capacities and more exploitative targeting that attempts to take advantage of more vulnerable community members such as children. Advertising strategies of the makers of junk food directed at children is one such issue. Several public health groups have long argued that advertisers knowingly contribute to the world's obesity epidemic by promoting junk food in exploitative ways. "The attempt to elicit the consumers' loyalty to products that may be harmful to them undermines the consumers' interest, and by extension, that of the whole community," Spence and Van Heekeren (2005, p. 37) wrote. "By undermining the children's interest in health, an interest that is not only restricted to children themselves and their families . . . advertising undermines the interest of the whole community" (2005, p. 37).

COMMUNITY IN CYBERSPACE

This chapter referred earlier to "communities of interest" that transcend geography and that have blossomed by the thousands through the Web. Technology has enabled an unprecedented degree of connectivity and interconnectivity, which in turn has fundamentally changed our understanding of what participating in community means. While society has embraced these changes, the changes do pose long-standing ethical concerns in some new forms. The Internet has given interest groups that traditionally received little or no attention in the mainstream media a new and readily accessible profile. Everyone now has a microphone. But one effect has been a "balkanization" of society into separate enclaves, or publics. Technology has raised in more pronounced ways the question of boundary between private lives and public information. It has made it easier than ever for us to limit our exposure to opposing or uncomfortable views. The multiple communities now existing on the Web are actually, some suggest, as much or more insular than geographically based ones. The Web has encouraged a series of "echo chambers," or informational communities who only share like-minded views and deliberately shut out challenging facts and viewpoints. Such "insularity," many fear, only promotes extremism and reinforces ill-founded opinions, resulting in a democratic society less able to recognize shared interests and experiences (Sunstein, 2008).

Participatory Journalism

The Web has made a publisher of everyone who wants to be one. And while that doesn't necessarily make everyone a journalist, it has fundamentally altered the balance of power between news organizations who see themselves as gatekeepers and everyone else who may want to be heard. News organizations around the country have invited nonjournalists to write their information, views, and perspectives to be included in news packages. Ever since some of the more dramatic published images of the 2005 London subway bombings came not from journalists but from the cell phones of commuters, it is almost expected that eyewitness content will be used from people who would never otherwise call themselves journalists. Technology is altering news in many ways, breathing life into Dewey's idea of a news media that fosters community talk. News is becoming "a multidirectional conversation, enriching civic dialogue at the local, national and international levels," said Dan Gillmor, author of *We the Media: Grassroots Journalism by the People, for the People* (2004, p. 111). Others have suggested that what's happening is that, like computer monitoring systems that are always on, the new model of news through quick, short dispatches on Twitter, Facebook, and other social media sites has created a new "awareness system" for people, which in turn is becoming a new model for news itself (Hermida, 2010). There is also an economic incentive to tap this potentially vast new source: It's usually free content. And yet this technology-driven transformation poses some fundamental ethics questions about responsibility, public service, and credibility. When does this strategy truly foster more dialogue and when does it encourage just more unproductive, narcissistic chatter? Collecting fragmented dispatches from eager eyewitnesses who may not have any interest in providing a full picture of an event or issue invites us to mistake data for knowledge. "There is a fundamental difference between reading hundreds of people's stories and understanding the 'real' story," said Weblogger and media critic Simon Waldman (2005, p. 78). News coverage of the 2005 tsunami disaster was a prime example of the pitfalls of this online "citizen journalism." Waldman neatly summarized it:

> With the tsunami coverage, the story was big, complex and continually evolving. . . . Making sense of it all needed the sort of distillation, reduction and, yes, the editing process that happens in traditional media. The disciplines of traditional media aren't just awkward restrictions. Deadlines, limits on space and time, the need to have a headline and an intro and a cohesive story rather than random paragraphs, all of these factors force out meaning and help with understanding. Without the order they impose, it's much, much harder to make sense of what's happening in the world. In the online environment, many of these physical guideposts are removed, but that does not mean that the intellectual processes that result from them should not be maintained. They should. And it was here that traditional media carved out their role—and will continue to do so for years to come. (2005, p. 78)

The same technology that enables more immediacy and more voices also opens up news organizations to more hoaxes, which can damage credibility. The *Times* of India, eager to incorporate blogger dispatches into its coverage, published a picture submitted through the Internet that editors thought was the tsunami. In fact, it was a photo of a tidal bore on a river in China taken two years earlier (Waldman, 2005, p. 79).

Public Relations "Publics" and the Web

Technology has exploded the reach of message campaigns and has transformed information access—both for public relations practitioners disseminating messages and for critics of public relations agents and client behavior. "Through databases, public relations can provide and obtain information," public relations theorist Robert Heath (2001) wrote. "So can critics of an organization. In this regard, the standard elements of public relations communication might not change much but can take on a new look and a cyberspace character through the use of new technologies" (p. 580). Public relations use of the Web can also aid crisis and risk managers in communicating with communities. When a series of tornadoes struck Michigan in 1996, the state Emergency Management Service (EMS) provided an up-to-the-minute Web site for reporters that in turn freed up EMS officials from dealing with phone calls from news organizations (Springston & Brown, 1998). Lordan (2001) also noted that "public relations managers must be extremely sensitive in using information developed for databases because audiences, including consumers and members of the media, are extremely sensitive to privacy issues" (p. 585).

Traditionally, public relations efforts have focused on one-way communication (direct mail campaigns), two-way communication (negotiations with external stakeholders), or multidirectional communication (soliciting involvement in a program on behalf of a sponsor or client). Technology, however, can revolutionize these categories and "effectively shifts the sender-based information model to a receiver-based model," public relations theorist Jeffrey Springston (2001) said. "Traditional notions of informational power and access are fundamentally altered" in ways that force public relations to consider the proliferation of sexual, racist and other politically unpopular content as well as practices of information sabotage (pp. 604, 607). Technology allows public relations practitioners to "narrowcast" messages and increasingly use psychographic data collection to gather information and identify and target niche "publics." This new form of technology-driven "community work" is a two-edged sword: It enables savvier and more efficient selection and delivery, yet also has the potential to undermine the public relations obligations to community that have been outlined by public relations professor Kirk Hallahan (2004) and others.

For Discussion

1. Do you personally perceive the idea of community in a positive or negative sense? Why?

2. How would you respond to the claims of psychologist Jean Twenge, who says that members of "Generation Me"—individuals born in the 1970s, 1980s, and 1990s—are more narcissistic and self-involved than any other generation?

3. Aristotle's sense of community includes the idea that conflict is an inevitable and important reality. Why would "conflict" be an important "value" in the idea of community?

4. According to communitarian thinkers, our individualistic attitudes and assumptions can blind us to the roles community plays in our lives. Can you think of some media-related examples in which this might actually occur?

5. Consider the idea of the public sphere. What would a news media system devoted to its creation and maintenance look like? How might public relations practice devoted to expanding the public sphere differ from current practice?

6. You are charged with drafting a general code of media ethics and asked to write something about balancing individual-oriented interests with community-oriented interests. What would you write?

REFERENCES

Anderson, R., Dardenne, R., & Killenberg, G. M. (1994). *The conversation of journalism: Communication, community and news.* Westport, CT: Praeger.

Ansolabehere, S., & Iyengar, S. (1995). *Going negative: How attack ads shrink and polarize the electorate.* New York, NY: Free Press.

Arendt, H. (1958). *The human condition.* Chicago, IL: University of Chicago Press.

Barber, B. R. (2007). *Consumed: How markets corrupt children, infantilize adults, and swallow citizens whole.* New York, NY: W. W. Norton.

Benhabib, S. (1992). *Situating the self: Gender, community and postmodernism in contemporary ethics.* New York, NY: Routledge.

Benhabib, S. (1995). Cultural complexity, moral independence and the global dialogic community. In M. C. Nussbaum & J. Glover (Eds.), *Women, culture and development: A study of human capabilities* (pp. 235–259). Oxford, UK: Clarendon Press.

Bennett, W. L., & Entman, R. M. (Eds.). (2001). *Mediated politics: Communication and the future of democracy.* Cambridge, UK: Cambridge University Press.

Christians, C. G. (2004). Ubuntu and communitarian media ethics. *Ecquid Novi, 25*(2), 235–256.

Christians, C. G., Fackler, M., & Ferré, J. P. (2012). *Ethics for public communication: Defining moments in media history.* New York, NY: Oxford.

Christians, C. G., Ferré, J. P., & Fackler, P. M. (1993). *Good news: Social ethics and the press.* New York, NY: Oxford University Press.

Cohn, J. (1995, Summer). Should journalists do community service? *American Prospect, 22,* 16.

Cooley, C. H. (1962). *Social organization: A study of the larger mind.* New York, NY: Schocken.

Crary, D. (2007, February 27). Study: College students more narcissistic. *Boston Globe,* p. A7.

Culbertson, H. M., & Chen, N. (1996). Communitarianism: A foundation for communication symmetry. *Public Relations Quarterly, 42*(2), 36–41.

Dahlgren, P. (2001). The public sphere and the Net: Structure, space and communication. In W. L. Bennett & R. M. Entman (Eds.), *Mediated politics: Communication and the future of democracy* (pp. 33–55). Cambridge, MA: Cambridge University Press.

Damico, A. J. (1978). *Individuality and community: The social and political thought of John Dewey.* Gainesville: University of Florida Press.

Dewey, J. (1927). *The public and its problems.* New York, NY: Henry Holt.

Dewey, J. (1985). *The later works, 1925–1953* (Vol. 7, J. Boydston, Ed.). Carbondale: Southern Illinois University Press. (Original work published 1935)

Etzioni, A. (1999). *The limits of privacy.* New York, NY: Basic Books.

Fallows, J. (1997). *Breaking the news: How the media undermine American democracy.* New York, NY: Vintage.

Fischer, N. (1978). The concept of community in Kant's architectonic. *Man and World, 11,* 372–391.

Folkenflik, D. (2012, July 6). Fake bylines reveal hidden costs of local news. National Public Radio. Retrieved from http://www.npr.org/2012/07/06/156311078/fake-bylines-reveal-true-costs-of-local-news

Fraser, N. (1990). Rethinking the public sphere: A contribution to the critique of actually existing democracy. *Social Text, 25/26,* 56–80.

Gillmor, D. (2004). *We the media: Grassroots journalism by the people, for the people.* Sebastopol, CA: O'Reilly.

Glasser, T., & Craft, S. (1998). Public journalism and the search for public ideals. In T. Liebes & J. Curran (Eds.), *Media, ritual and identity* (pp. 203–218). London, England: Routledge.

Goldstein, K., & Freedman, P. (2002). Lessons learned: Campaign advertising in the 2000 elections. *Political Communication, 19,* 5–28.

Grunig, J. E. (2000). Collectivism, collaboration and societal corporatism as core professional values in public relations. *Journal of Public Relations Research, 12*(1), 23–48.

Grunig, J. E. (2001). Two-way symmetrical public relations: Past, present and future. In R. L. Heath (Ed.), *Handbook of public relations* (pp. 11–30). Thousand Oaks, CA: Sage.

Grunig, J. E., & Hunt, T. (1984). *Managing public relations.* New York, NY: Holt, Rinehart & Winston.

Habermas, J. (1989). *The structural transformation of the public sphere.* Cambridge, MA: MIT Press.

Habermas, J. (1996). *Between facts and norms: Contributions to a discourse theory of law and democracy* (W. Rehg, Trans.). Cambridge, MA: MIT Press.

Hackett, R., & Zhao, Y. (1998). *Sustaining democracy? Journalism and the politics of objectivity.* Toronto, Ontario, Canada: Garamond Press.

Hallahan, K. (2004). Community as a foundation for public relations theory and practice. *Communication Yearbook, 28,* 233–279.

Heath, R. L. (2001). Public relations in cyberspace: The frontier of new communication technologies. In R. L. Heath (Ed.), *Handbook of public relations* (pp. 579–581). Thousand Oaks, CA: Sage.

Herman, B. (1993). *The practice of moral judgment.* Cambridge, UK: Cambridge University Press.

Hermida, A. (2010). Twittering the news. *Journalism Practice, 4*(3), 297–308.

Holloway, M. (1951). *Heavens on earth: Utopian communities in America, 1680–1880.* London, England: Turnstile.

Holtzhausen, D. R. (2000). Postmodern values in public relations. *Journal of Public Relations Research, 12,* 93–114.

Horowitz, I. L. (1999, Fall). Networking America: The cultural context of the privacy v. publicity debates. *ETC,* 305–314.

Isocrates. (1986–1992). *Isocrates* (G. Norlin, Trans., Vols. 1–2; L. R. Hook, Trans., Vol. 3). Cambridge, MA: Harvard University Press.

Kruckeberg, D., & Starck, K. (1988). *Public relations and community: A reconstructed theory.* New York, NY: Praeger.

Leitch, S., & Neilson, D. (2001). Bringing publics into public relations. In R. L. Heath (Ed.), *Handbook of Public Relations.* Thousand Oaks, CA: SAGE.

Lordan, E. J. (2001). Cyberspin: The use of new technologies in public relations. In R. L. Heath (Ed.), *Handbook of public relations* (pp. 583–589). Thousand Oaks, CA: Sage.

MacIntyre, A. (1984). *After virtue: A study in moral theory* (2nd ed.). South Bend, IN: University of Notre Dame Press.

Magleby, D. B. (2002). *The other campaign: Soft money and issue advocacy in the 2000 congressional elections.* Lanham, MD: Rowman & Littlefield.

Mapel, D. (1989). *Social justice reconsidered: The problem of appropriate precision in a theory of justice.* Urbana: University of Illinois Press.

Marrou, H. I. (1956). *A history of education in antiquity* (G. Lamb, Trans.). New York, NY: Sheed and Ward.

Marsh, C. W. (2001). Public relations ethics: Contrasting models from the rhetorics of Plato, Aristotle, and Isocrates. *Journal of Mass Media Ethics, 16*(2–3), 78–98.

Marsh, C. W. (2003). Antecedents of two-way symmetry in classical Greek rhetoric: The rhetoric of Isocrates. *Public Relations Review, 29,* 351–367.

Marsh, C. W. (2008). Postmodernism, symmetry, and cash value: An Isocratean model for practitioners. *Public Relations Review, 34,* 237–243.

McQuail, D. (1977). Accountability of media to society. *European Journal of Communication, 12*(4), 511–529.

Mill, J. S. (1975). *On liberty* (D. Spitz, Ed.). New York, NY: Norton. (Original work published 1859)

Mulhall, S., & Swift, A. (Eds.). (1992). *Liberals and communitarians.* Oxford, UK: Blackwell.

Noddings, N. (1984). *Caring: A feminine approach to ethics and moral education.* Berkeley: University of California Press.

Peters, J. D., & Cmiel, K. (1991). Media ethics and the public sphere. *Communication, 12,* 197–215.

Popken, B. (2011, December 13). Lowe's in Facebook hell as racist comments pile up. *AdWeek.* Retrieved from http://www.adweek.com/adfreak/lowes-facebook-hell-racist-comments-pile-137070

Poulakos, T. (1997). *Speaking for the polis: Isocrates' rhetorical education.* Columbia, SC: University of South Carolina Press.

Rosen, J. (1999). *What are journalists for?* New Haven, CT: Yale University Press.

Rosen, J. (2005). Community connectedness: Passwords for public journalism. In R. P. Clark & C. C. Campbell (Eds.), *The values and craft of American journalism* (pp. 116–122). Gainesville: University of Florida Press.

Rousseau, J. J. (1997). Of the social contract. In S. M. Cahn (Ed.), *Classics of modern political theory: Machiavelli to Mill* (pp. 420–484). New York, NY: Oxford University Press. (Original work published 1762)

Savage, D. M. (2002). *John Dewey's liberalism: Individual, community and self-development.* Carbondale: Southern Illinois University Press.

Schoeman, F. D. (1992). *Privacy and social freedom.* Cambridge, UK: Cambridge University Press.

Seigfried, C. H. (1996). *Pragmatism and feminism: Reweaving the social fabric.* Chicago, IL: University of Chicago Press.

Smith, A., & Kidder, R. M. (1996). *Political attack advertising.* Camden, ME: Institute for Global Ethics.

Spence, E., & Van Heekeren, B. (2005). *Advertising ethics.* Upper Saddle River, NJ: Pearson Prentice Hall.

Springston, J. K. (2001). Public relations and new media technology: The impact of the Internet. In R. L. Heath (Ed.), *Handbook of public relations* (pp. 603–614). Thousand Oaks, CA: Sage.

Springston, J. K., & Brown, J. W. (1998, April). *Using public relations field dynamics in risk communication.* Paper presented at the annual meeting of the American Society for Business and Behavioral Sciences, Las Vegas.

Steiner, L. (1989). Feminist theorizing and communication ethics. *Communication, 12,* 157–173.

Stoker, K. L., & Tusinski, K. A. (2006). Reconsidering public relations' infatuation with dialogue: Why engagement and reconciliation can be more ethical than symmetry and reciprocity. *Journal of Mass Media Ethics, 21*(2–3), 156–176.

Sunstein, C. (2008). Democracy and the Internet. In J. vanden Hoven & J. Weckert (Eds.), *Information technology and moral philosophy* (pp. 93–110.) Cambridge, UK: Cambridge University Press.

Taylor, C. (1990). *Sources of the self.* Cambridge, UK: Cambridge University Press.

Tierney, J. (2011, April 25). A generation's vanity, heard through lyrics. *New York Times.* Retrieved from http://www.nytimes.com/2011/04/26/science/26tier.html?_r = 0

Trompenaars, F., & Hampden-Turner, C. (2002). *Riding the waves of culture: Understanding cultural diversity in business.* London, England: Nicholas Brealey.

Twenge, J. M. (2006). *Generation me: Why today's young Americans are more confident, assertive, entitled—and more miserable than ever before.* New York, NY: Free Press.

Waldman, S. (2005, Spring). Arriving at the digital news age: "It is in this fusion of old and new that the future of journalism most probably lies." *Nieman Reports,* pp. 78–79.

Walzer, M. (2004). *Politics and passion: Toward a more egalitarian liberalism.* New Haven, CT: Yale University Press.

Wilson, L. J. (1996). Strategic cooperative communities: A synthesis of strategic, issue management and relationship building approaches in public relations. In H. M. Culbertson & N. Chen (Eds.), *International public relations: A comparative analysis* (pp. 67–80). Mahwah, NJ: Lawrence Erlbaum.

Wilson, L. J. (2001). Relationships within communities: Public relations in the new century. In R. L. Heath (Ed.), *Handbook of public relations* (pp. 521–526). Thousand Oaks, CA: Sage.

Wolfe, B. H. (1968). *The hippies.* New York, NY: Signet.

Yack, B. (1986). *The longing for total revolution: Philosophic sources of social discontent from Rousseau to Marx and Nietzsche.* Princeton, NJ: Princeton University Press.

Yack, B. (1993). *The problems of a political animal: Community, justice and conflict in Aristotelian political thought.* Berkeley: University of California Press.

CHAPTER 11

Conclusion

From such crooked wood as man is made of, nothing perfectly straight can be built.

—Immanuel Kant

This book began by claiming that ethics goes to the heart of who we are as individuals and as a society. Ethics requires us to think deeply about the judgments we make and about the assumptions embedded in those judgments. It requires us to consider our motivations, our relations with others, and what duties we have as a result of those relations. This book also began with the caution that ethics is about asking the right questions rather than reaching the "right" answers, and that this is a reason many find the topic frustrating. The key principles emphasized in Chapters 5 through 10 were chosen and depicted with the aim of reflecting the truth of these two premises. Questions on topics such as justice, autonomy, and privacy are really questions about what constitutes a moral life—about what makes us *human*. They challenge us to think beyond our personal bubbles of self-involvement and gratification and consider the moral claims that others can rightly make on us. They also require us to think more deeply about some important concepts, to get beyond the sloganeering and culturally bound reflexes, and to consider ideas (and ourselves) in a broader social, and global, context. Developmental psychology researchers say that our "moral identities" do not emerge in isolation but from the web of social relationships and institutions in which we live. Similarly, the chapters deliberately avoided offering specific answers about what constitutes harm in a particular case or the moment in media scrutiny when privacy is violated. Instead, the presentation of each of the key principles mirrored the deliberative nature of the ethics. By design, each of the chapters sought to underscore the assertion that the ability to ask the right questions requires a solid grounding in the history and thought behind the principles. We can't very well make compelling arguments about the duty of the media system to serve a public good without a good grasp of concepts such as community, justice, and transparency—both their origins and their contemporary incarnations.

All authors have an "agenda." While this author believes that dispassion is a critical virtue in media ethics education, deliberation does indeed usually culminate in decisions and positions. By choosing to focus on these principles and emphasizing them as they are here, this book inevitably communicates a message of judgment about their proper application for media practice. This author believes that partisan moralizing and expediency too often hijack ethical deliberation, that our postmodern sensibilities require continual reminders that respect for human dignity be a feature in every decision we make, that offensive media content is not usually synonymous with harmful content, that a "me" culture of hyperindividualism tempts us to inflate the value of privacy for the wrong reasons, and that mouthing simplistic claims about freedom hobbles our ability to carry out our duties as members of community. More broadly, this book makes the claim that ethics is not just an esoteric academic exercise. Solid ethical deliberation is hard work that pays off in increased media credibility and respect. Questionable media content and frequent media scandals often are the direct result of far too little thought beforehand of our professional duties and responsibilities. Profitability and deadline pressures, not ethical values, too often end up defining the quality of media content. By challenging the media professionals of the future to think more deeply about key ethical concepts, this book aims to tie the more useful and relevant *philosophy* behind ethics theorizing more closely to actual media practice.

THEORIES OF MORAL DEVELOPMENT

The capacity to deliberate well—to weigh conflicting values, obligations, and duties and consistently come up with rational, ethically defensible decisions—does not develop overnight. It takes experience and effort, and it is largely tied to our "moral development"—that is, our view of the world and our place in it regarding how we should act, what kinds of duties we are obliged to carry out, and how we define ourselves in relation to others. We all go through a series of stages as we develop *morally* and grow into mature moral beings. This is a lifelong process. Psychologists and other theorists have proposed several different ways to understand this process of moral development. Many say we develop morally just as we develop physically—through phases, each of which requires completion of the preceding one. They also suggest that our moral development largely parallels our intellectual growth. Two important theorists in particular provide useful frameworks with which to understand how we develop morally: Lawrence Kohlberg and Carol Gilligan.

Kohlberg: An Ethic of Justice

Kohlberg (1981), a Harvard psychologist, constructed six stages of moral development that were based on his research. He said we all develop through these stages, though not at the same pace, and very few people reach the final, sixth stage. His framework is largely based on how our understanding of the idea of *justice* evolves as we mature. We begin as self-centered children only concerned with our own gratification, and as we grow, our sphere of concern—and our application of certain principles—gradually expands to include more people. For example, the ideas of sharing and turn-taking require considerable time for children to learn, but the notion of reciprocity is a prominent feature in morally developed adults. A child's rudimentary notion of what is right is that which is allowed, but among morally developed adults, avoiding punishment is no longer an acceptable reason for doing or not doing something.

Kohlberg calls the first two stages "preconventional" since they are associated with childlike behavior that reflects a primitive grasp of morality. In Stage 1, we act solely to avoid punishment and to obey power figures. For example, a company spokeswoman who knowingly misleads an audience about the value of a product because corporate executives ordered her to do so might exemplify a Stage 1 approach. In Stage 2, we act largely on the desire to be rewarded, and we perceive actions as "right" if they serve our interests and desires. A photojournalist intent on capturing the most sensational shot and who is driven largely by the possibility of winning awards might reflect Stage 2 thinking.

Stages 3 and 4 are what Kohlberg calls the "conventional" stages since he said they reflect society's expectations, and the majority of adults reach and remain at these stages. In Stage 3, we are driven by the need for social acceptance. Being perceived as a good team player and adherence to the Golden Rule becomes primary. Based on thinking at this stage, a reporter unsure about how to handle a particular question might seek to conform with the conventions of the newsroom and act as her peers might do in the same situation. In Stage 4, Kohlberg said, we recognize that we have duties as members of society, which include upholding the law and maintaining social order. A journalist at this stage will strive to uphold the law or follow company policy without questioning its legitimacy.

The final two stages are what Kohlberg calls "postconventional"—that is, right and wrong are no longer dictated by authority or social norms, but are based on one's own efforts to use reason and rise above self-interest or institutional rules. In Stage 5, we are driven by our sense of *social utility,* or our belief that decisions ought to benefit society and be made impartially. In this stage, we begin insisting that society's rules be based on the broad moral principles of fairness and justice, not political power. A public relations executive at this stage who discovers that a client's product poses a danger to consumers might disclose this information as a matter of public service, even though such disclosure might adversely affect the client. And finally, in Stage 6, we recognize the *universality* of moral principles— that we have moral obligations to the human community regardless of any particular law or culture. At this stage, we embrace the Kantian maxim that humans are ends in themselves. A journalist might be reflecting Stage 6 thinking if she argues that certain information should be left out of a story in response to valid concerns of the story subject.

Gilligan: An Ethic of Care

Carol Gilligan (1982) was a student of Kohlberg's and became increasingly dissatisfied with his explanations of how individuals develop morally. She argued that Kohlberg's system was based on several questionable assumptions. First, she said, his stages assumed that people were isolated individuals whose moral development was not contingent on relationships or interacting with others. It presumed that we live exclusively in a world dominated by the existence of individual "rights" rather than a world of social connections, duties, and obligations. Kohlberg, Gilligan said, described a moral system in the "language of rights that protects separation" (p. 210). Second, Gilligan said, Kohlberg based his moral development system almost entirely on research with adolescent boys and then assumed that his findings were true for girls and women as well. This, she concluded, was inherently simplistic and sexist. Gilligan studied groups of young women and found that, in contrast to Kohlberg's work, they approached dilemmas and grappled with decisions very differently than Kohlberg's model suggested. They were driven more by their perceptions of how people were connected with each other and by their interests in *maintaining* those connections. Gilligan's resulting book, *In a Different Voice,* validated women's ways of thinking, according to Seyla Benhabib (1992). "The contextuality, narrativity and specificity of women's moral judgment is not a sign of weakness or deficiency, but a manifestation of a vision of moral maturity that views the self as a being immersed in a network of relationships with others," Benhabib wrote (p. 149). Instead of a morality of justice or one based on individual rights and separation, Gilligan proposed a "language of responsibilities that sustains connection" (Gilligan, 1982, p. 210). Instead of six stages, Gilligan proposed three levels of moral development:

Level I: Orientation to individual survival. The individual is concerned solely with herself, and she perceives herself as powerless. In the "first transition" from this stage, the individual begins to empathize with others and feel that it is selfish and immature to be concerned with one's own desires. However, she still fails to take responsibility for her actions.

Level II: Self-sacrifice. The individual begins to define being "good" as sacrificing herself for the good of others. This comes to mean being a good caretaker and holding herself responsible for the actions of others while simultaneously holding others responsible for the choices she makes. In the "second transition," the individual begins to consider how taking her interests into account in decision making is not necessarily selfish but honest. She sees the importance of caring for oneself and is no longer dependent on others' perceptions of her worth as a caretaker as a measure of her value.

Level III: Nonviolence. The individual is no longer troubled by a perceived conflict between caring for oneself and caring for others. Once the obligation to care for all persons is understood, it automatically includes the self. She embraces nonviolence as the ultimate principle: acting morally means minimizing pain and harm for everyone (Elliott, 1991, p. 22).

While Gilligan did not claim that girls and boys have different, gender-based patterns of moral development, she proposed a "morality of care" intended to complement the picture of what a morally mature individual looks like. Her morality of care and Kohlberg's "morality of justice," in other words, are two important ways to consider the complexity that comes about with moral maturity. So for example, within a morality of justice, individuals are defined as separate in relation to others, whereas in a morality of care, individuals are defined as connected in relation to others; within a morality of justice, conflicting claims are resolved by invoking impartial rules, whereas in a morality of care, moral problems are considered as issues of relationships and of proper response. In a morality of justice, an act is moral if all parties are treated equitably; in a morality of care, an act is moral if it enables relationships to be maintained or restored (Lyons, 1993). Ethicist Deni Elliott (1991) offered a valuable way to consider the approaches of Kohlberg and Gilligan as equally important:

Metaphorically, we might say that Kohlberg provides a highway map through the territory of morality. Gilligan provides a map of secondary roads. One can reach moral maturity by either route, but the trip will be different depending on the road chosen. Looking at a map that contains both sets of roads gives a more complete understanding of the territory. (p. 23)

Notice how, in both systems, as we move through the stages or levels, the *scope of concern* widens, though in different ways. In each system, we move from a somewhat *relativistic* orientation, where what's considered ethical is strictly up to the individual, to a recognition of *universal* principles that transcend individual codes. Indeed, one of Kohlberg's aims in building his theory of moral development was to defeat ethical relativism on psychological grounds (Lapsley & Narvaez, 2004, p. 190).

In the 1970s, a test was developed to measure how people's moral reasoning skills reflected Kohlberg's various stages. Since its development, the Defining Issues Test (DIT) has been used with hundreds of thousands of Americans and dozens of different professional populations. Media researchers Lee Wilkins and Renita Coleman (Wilkins & Coleman, 2005; Coleman & Wilkins, 2009) applied the DIT to hundreds of journalists and public relations professionals. How the scores of people in the different professionals stack up is worth noting (Table 11.1). The DIT assigns individuals a "P" score that reflects the person's "stage" of moral reasoning.

Recall in Chapter 1 the discussion of our "ethical ideologies," which are largely shaped by two things: the level of our *idealism* and our degree of *relativistic* thinking. Donelson Forsyth (1980), who devised the Ethics Position Questionnaire to measure people's ethical ideologies, said that there is no one "correct" ideology, or one "right" level of idealism or relativism to have. However, moral development theories do suggest a directional growth away from selfishness toward a recognition that being a moral agent means acting out of

Table 11.1 Mean P (Moral Reasoning) Scores of Various Subject Groups

Seminarians/philosophers	65.1	Veterinary students	42.2
Medical students	50.2	Navy enlisted personnel	41.6
Practicing physicians	49.2	Orthopedic surgeons	41
Journalists	48.7	U.S. adults in general	40
Dental students	47.6	Business professionals	38.12
Nurses	46.3	Accounting undergraduates	34.8
Public relations practitioners	46.2	Accounting auditors	32.5
Lawyers	46	Advertising managers	31.6
Graduate students	44.9	Business undergraduates	31.35
Undergraduates students	43.2	High school students	31
Pharmacy students	42.8	Prison inmates	23.7

From Wilkins & Coleman (2005), p. 39; Coleman & Wilkins (2009), p. 333.

a concern for others based on principles that are *universal* in nature and not *relative* to our personal, often self-interested, definitions of goodness. An extensive study looking at the factors that influence ethically questionable business decisions concluded that relativistic thinking served as reliable predictors of perceived ethical and unethical conduct. Individuals with an internal, accessible belief prohibiting harming others were found less likely to make unethical choices (Kish-Gephart, Harrison, & Treviño, 2010). Another study assessed the moral reasoning skills and degrees of idealistic and relativistic thinking among two dozen "exemplar" journalists and public relations professionals known for their ethical leadership. The study found that the media exemplars uniformly rejected relativism and generally had high levels of idealism. The study also showed that while all the media exemplars insisted that avoiding harm was a primary concern in everything they did, they tended to be pragmatic in their application of moral absolutes, depending on what specific situations required (Plaisance, 2013).

Yet all this is not meant to imply that the opposite of relativistic thought is a sort of rigid absolutism that claims moral perfection based on an external "truth." As we mature morally, we are more willing to entertain a *pluralistic* view of the world: to acknowledge the existence of multiple human truths and the conflict of a range of legitimate human values and goals. This is exactly what is suggested by the relationship between idealism and moral reasoning in the recent study of media exemplars: As they are at high levels of moral development, they show a greater ability to adapt their principles to best fit the often complex range of contingencies in which they find themselves having to work. Too wise to believe they can insist on a rigid application of moral rules that can fit all circumstances, the exemplars' correlations appear to represent the American pragmatist strain of philosophy that strives to balance a principled life with a sense of accountability regarding necessary outcomes. A critical distinction between the strength of one's moral beliefs and how successful one is at manifesting those beliefs in daily life is useful here. In their landmark study of moral exemplars of various walks of life, Anne Colby and William Damon concluded that their exemplars did not stand out because their moral beliefs were stronger than those of average people or that they were more morally resolute:

> [E]xemplars' moral commitments are extensions in scope but not in kind from most people's typical moral engagements. Such extensions are made possible by a progressive uniting of self and moral goals during the course of development. This progressive uniting does not rest upon greater capacities for moral reflection, . . . [but] reflects an increasingly functional integration between one's sense of self, one's moral beliefs, and one's habits of social conduct. (1992, pp. 307–308).

People who exhibit high levels of idealism tend to judge unethical behavior more harshly, but they also exhibit a stronger ethic of "caring" for others (Forsyth, Nye, & Kelley, 1988). In contrast, people who display high degrees of relativism tend to be more Machiavellian—in other words, they tend to be more comfortable using any means necessary to achieve success (Leary, Knight, & Barnes, 1986; McHoskey & Hicks, 1999). Using Forsyth's Ethics Position Questionnaire, other researchers found that potential corporate whistleblowers described as nonrelativistic were more likely to report peer wrongdoing

(Barnett, Bass, & Brown, 1996). Other researchers (Keyton & Rhodes, 1997) found that ethical ideology has an effect on employees' ability to identify verbal sexually harassing behaviors. Those who displayed high degrees of relativism, they found, appeared less able to identify verbal harassing behavior than most others.

This and other research suggests that growing out of our tendency to be relativistic is a worthwhile goal as we mature morally. Our ability to embrace a more pluralistic approach to the world helps us put our interests and beliefs in the context of our moral duties and to see our lives in global terms. "Our truths are not only plural; they are fallible," media ethicist Stephen J. A. Ward (2006, p. 268) said in his book on the nature of objectivity. "There is no guarantee that our most fundamental and seemingly secure beliefs will not need revision" (2006, p. 268). Isaiah Berlin (1969), a noted philosopher of history, suggested that our ability to embrace a "pluralistic" view of the world, acknowledging the existence of multiple truths instead of a single "truth," is a measure of our moral maturity. He cautioned us on the danger of seeking black-and-white certainties and suggested that such a need might be human nature, but it was also self-delusional. "Principles are no less sacred because their duration cannot be guaranteed," he wrote in his landmark essay, "Two Concepts of Liberty." "Indeed, the very desire for guarantees that our values are eternal and secure in some objective heaven is perhaps only a craving of certainties of childhood or the absolute values of our primitive past." But to be guided by this impulse, or craving, in our postmodern world is, he said, "a symptom of an equally deep, and more dangerous, moral and political immaturity" (Berlin, 1969, p. 172).

IMPLICATIONS OF A UNIVERSAL MORAL THEORY

Morally developed communication professionals are not seduced by competitive pressures, technological marvels, or the god of convenience. They are keenly aware that having an ability to use the power of public channels of communication entails a serious ethical responsibility. Acts of communication—whether they be news reports, a promotional package, a corporate announcement, or a marketing campaign—that do not foster trust, greater understanding, or a willingness to engage others often fail to reflect long-standing principles of ethical conduct. Communication professionals understand that autonomy means upholding our moral duties rather than merely doing whatever feels good or promotes our interests. They understand why the principles of justice and minimizing harm ought to be reflected in our decision making. They understand that ideas of privacy and community are really two sides of the same coin of social engagement.

An ethic of media practice based on these principles requires us to think not only pluralistically, but globally. The media system is now a *global* entity: What is posted on the Web—whether on a corporate page or on a newspaper Web site—reaches people around the world and has the potential to influence how groups and governments act and how people understand the world. With this potential for global impact comes a new sense of global responsibility. A global media ethics requires media professionals to think differently about their audiences. It requires them to be *cosmopolitan* in their view of the world—to regard all people as "citizens of the world" and not just members of a tribe, a region, or a country, as Martha Nussbaum and other theorists have argued. Nussbaum (1996) referred to the call by the Greek Stoics for everyone to aspire to become "world citizens" whose views are not limited by narrow local, or even national, interests:

> The Stoics stress that to be a citizen of the world one does not need to give up local identifications, which can be a source of great richness in life. They suggest that we think of ourselves not as devoid of local affiliations, but as surrounded by a series of concentric circles. The first one encircles the self, the next takes in the immediate family, then follows the extended family, then, in order, neighbors or local groups, fellow city-dwellers, and fellow countrymen—and we can easily add to this list groupings based on ethnic, linguistic, historical, professional, gender, or sexual identities. Outside all these circles is the largest one, humanity as a whole. Our task as citizens of the world will be to "draw the circles somehow toward the center" (Stoic philosopher Hierocles, 1st–2nd CE), making all human beings more like our fellow city-dwellers, and so on. We need not give up our special affections and identifications, whether ethnic or gender-based or religious. . . . But we should also work to make all human beings part of our community of dialogue and concern, base our political deliberations on that interlocking commonality, and give the circle that defines our humanity special attention and respect. (p. 9)

For journalists, this means framing issues with an internationalist perspective and serving a "global public sphere," as Stephen Ward (2006) suggested, and not just validating the interests or perspectives of one's country. "Serving the public means serving more than one's local readership or audience or even the public of one's country," Ward argued. "Journalism should work against a narrow ethnocentrism or patriotism" (p. 329). Doing so, of course, will not win journalists many popularity contests.

The fact that we must work in and respond morally to an increasingly pluralistic world often complicates the ethical dilemmas we face. We cannot be absolutists in any sense. More often than not, using a "deductive" ethical approach to problems—where we start by adopting a general moral theory and applying it in a given situation—is not going to help us much. Instead, we need to be "contextualist" in our thinking, according to contemporary philosophers. That is, we need to realize that the complexities of a dilemma will often dictate how we might apply certain principles, and that these principles are not one size that fits all (Winkler & Coombs, 1993). Dutch theorist Cees Hamelink describes this "bottom-up," or inductive, approach to moral decision making:

> In the course of the inductive moral argument, questions are asked about the institutional and cultural settings and their value orientations in which choice situations are located. In this light questions are also asked about the consequences of choice and the interests involved: "Where does the choice lead to?," and "Is this desirable?" "How are benefits versus damages of choice distributed?" And "Whose interests are served with a particular choice?" "Who gains and who loses?" (Hamelink, 2000, p. 5)

Notice that these questions mirror those included in the Multidimensional Ethical Reasoning and Inquiry Task Sheet (MERITS) model of ethical decision making presented in Chapter 3.

MEDIA ETHICS IN CYBERSPACE

And finally, a few words about ethics and digital technology. Clearly, technologies offer new opportunities and new problems regarding how we communicate, whether it be about e-mail use, crowdsourcing, viral marketing strategies, or copyright issues. But if we understand ethics as concerned with how we incorporate the principles explored in this book into daily practice, then we realize that technologies don't actually require "new" ethical thinking in the sense of replacing our priorities of justice, minimizing harm, autonomy, and so forth. Indeed, technology often does the opposite: It tempts us to relax our long-standing ethical standards or to exempt new technology from those standards. For example, the anonymity allowed by cyberspace makes deception exceptionally easy and allows nearly effortless copying of data, and yet both issues can be considered simply the latest manifestations of ethical questions of transparency and justice or fairness.

> Deceptive behavior in cyberspace is, however, not a new moral issue though it raises the problem of "moral distance" with extra urgency. . . . The speed of digital communication does not create new forms of immorality, but makes it possible to commit immoral acts so fast one hardly notices. (Hamelink, 2000, pp. 34–35)

Technology tempts us to disregard ethical standards because the prime values that drive technology use and development are efficiency and expediency, not ethics. This is not to say that our moral standards are eternal and unchanging—obviously they are not. Our beliefs about slavery, spiritualism, sex, and so on are quite different than they were 300 years ago. New technology can indeed bring about morally important changes that require new ideals to replace traditional norms (Ladd, 2000, p. 46). But as moral agents, it is important for us as media professionals to demand that our ethical standards drive our technology use, not the other way around. That's part of what makes us "professionals" and what always will require a degree of moral courage.

REFERENCES

Barnett, T., Bass, K., & Brown, G. (1996). Religiosity, ethical ideology and intentions to report a peer's wrongdoing. *Journal of Business Ethics, 15,* 1164–1174.

Benhabib, S. (1992). *Situating the self: Gender, community and postmodernism in contemporary ethics.* London, England: Routledge.

Berlin, I. (1969). *Four essays on liberty.* London, England: Oxford University Press.

Colby, A., & Damon, W. (1992). *Some do care: Contemporary lives of moral commitment.* New York, NY: Free Press.

Coleman, R., & Wilkins, L. (2009). The moral development of public relations practitioners: A comparison with other professions and influences on higher quality ethical reasoning. *Journal of Public Relations Research, 21*(3), 318–340.

Elliott, D. (1991, Autumn). Moral development theories and the teaching of ethics. *Journalism Educator,* 18–24.

Forsyth, D. R. (1980). A taxonomy of ethical ideologies. *Journal of Personality and Social Psychology, 39,* 175–184.

Forsyth, D. R., Nye, J. L., & Kelley, K. (1988). Idealism, relativism and the ethic of caring. *Journal of Psychology, 112,* 243–248.

Gilligan, C. (1982). *In a different voice: Psychological theory and women's development.* Cambridge, MA: Harvard University Press.

Hamelink, C. J. (2000). *The ethics of cyberspace.* London, England: Sage.

Keyton, J., & Rhodes, S. C. (1997). Sexual harassment: A matter of individual rights, legal definitions or organizational policy? *Journal of Business Ethics, 16,* 129–146.

Kish-Gephart, J. J., Harrison, D. A., & Treviño, L. K. (2010). Bad apples, bad cases and bad barrels: Meta-analytic evidence about sources of unethical decisions at work. *Journal of Applied Psychology, 95*(1), 1–31.

Kohlberg, L. (1981). *The philosophy of moral development.* San Francisco, CA: Harper & Row.

Ladd, J. (2000). Ethics and the computer world: A new challenge for philosophers. In R. M. Baird, R. Ramsower, & S. E. Rosenbaum (Eds.), *Cyberethics: Social and moral issues in the computer age* (pp. 44–55). Amherst, NY: Prometheus Books.

Lapsley, D. K., & Narvaez, D. (2004). A social-cognitive approach to the moral personality. In D. K. Lapsley & D. Narvaez (Eds.), *Moral development, self and identity* (pp. 189–212). Mahwah, NJ: Lawrence Erlbaum.

Leary, M. R., Knight, P. D., & Barnes, B. D. (1986). Ethical ideologies of the Machiavellian. *Personality and Social Psychology Bulletin, 12,* 75–80.

Lyons, N. (1993). Two perspectives: On self, relationships and morality. *Harvard Educational Review, 53*(2), 125–145.

McHoskey, J. W., & Hicks, B. (1999). Machiavellianism, adjustment and ethics. *Psychological Reports, 85,* 138–142.

Nussbaum, M. C. (1996). Patriotism and cosmopolitanism. In M. C. Nussbaum (Ed.), *For love of country: Debating the limits of patriotism* (pp. 3–20). Boston, MA: Beacon Press.

Plaisance, P. L. (2013, May). Virtue in media: The moral psychology of U.S. exemplars in journalism and PR. Paper presentation at the annual conference of the International Communication Association, London.

Ward, S. J. A. (2006). *The invention of journalism ethics: The path to objectivity and beyond.* Montreal, Quebec, Canada: McGill–Queen's University Press.

Wilkins, L., & Coleman, R. (2005). *The moral media: How journalists reason about ethics.* Mahwah, NJ: Lawrence Erlbaum Associates.

Winkler, E. R., & Coombs, J. R. (Eds.). (1993). *Applied ethics.* Oxford, UK: Basil Blackwell.

Index

compelling/equally legitimate
justifications and, 8
conflicting values, compromise and, 11, 14
culturally grounded moral values and, 7, 11
deliberative process, quality of, 10, 11
ethics standards/ethical engagement and, 2–3
expediency, pressures of, 2
front-end work of, 2, 4
goals of, 9–10
gut-level responses and, xiii, 8, 10–11
idealism and, 17, 18
individualism, Western bias toward, 9–10
moral values/moral behavior, link between, 18
normative/epistemic completeness and, 9
prioritized values and, 11, 14
rational justifications and, 10–11, 25
relativism and, 17–18
values, focus on, 7, 11, 14, 23
See also Ethics theory; Media ethics; Moral
development theories; Philosophical
frameworks
Ethics Position Questionnaire (EPQ), 18–19
(table), 235, 236–237
Ethics theory, 1, 7
culturally grounded values and, 7, 11
deliberative process, quality of, 10, 11
Enlightenment assumptions and,
xv, 12–13, 16
ethical dilemmas and, 7–8, 10, 39–40, 44–45
ethics, definitions of, 9–11
ethics principles, media behavior and, xiv, xv
ethics vs. morality and, 7, 8–9, 10
goodness, nature of, 7, 9
intent vs. consequence theorizing and, 19–20
key thinkers/writers, evolving ethics thought
and, 11–17
male-dominated ethics theory, 16, 17, 82, 98,
112, 113, 155, 215, 219
means vs. ends theorizing and, 20–21
morality, definitions of, 8–9, 10
moral system elements, conflict among, 9
rational justifications and, 10–11
rightness of action and, 9, 10
theory-practice linkages and, xiv–xv
See also Consequentialist ethics; Duty ethics;
Ethics deliberation; Media ethics;
Philosophical frameworks; Virtue ethics
Ethnocentrism, 238
Etzioni, A., 213

Eudaimonia, 25, 26, 27
Evan, T. J., 135
Evil, 2, 28–29, 31, 124
Exemplar practitioners, 155, 236–237
External goods, 26

Facebook, 59, 62, 65, 66, 67, 194, 218, 226
Fackler, M., 207, 212, 216, 221
Fairness, 15, 27, 99, 101, 103, 104–105,
109, 110, 112, 115
Fallows, J., 217
Famine. *See* World hunger/starvation
response case
Federal Trade Commission (FTC), 38, 60,
90, 92, 117, 119
Feinberg, J., 128, 129, 137, 152
Feminist theory, 16, 17, 82
community, priority of, 214–215
freedom, privileging public vs. domestic
domains and, 155
interactional fairness, myth of, 112
male-dominated ethics and, 16, 17, 82, 98,
112, 113, 155, 215, 219
women's moral judgment, moral maturity
and, 234
Ferré, J. P., 207, 212, 216, 221
Fey, T., 87
Fidelity duty, 14, 31
Fifth Amendment rights, 178
Finnis, J., 158
First Amendment rights, 82–83, 141,
161–162, 163, 178, 180
Fischer, N., 211
Fisher, M., 138
Fiss, O., 163
Fitzpatrick, K., 89
Flannery, D. C., 43
Flight, 87
Flourishing. *See* Human flourishing;
Self-actualization
Folkerflik, D., 214
Food and Drug Administration (FDA), 135
Food Lion sales practices case, 79
Foot, P., 9, 15–16, 27, 68
goodness, conventional wisdom about, 15
goodness, objective features of, 15–16, 27–28
human flourishing, moral behaviors and,
16, 27–28
natural world, model of goodness and, 15, 16

pleasure and, 13, 25, 32
properties of, 9
subjective definition of, 15
teleological approach and, 13–14, 77
utilitarianism and, 13, 33–35
See also Ethics theory; Moral agency;
    Philosophical frameworks; Rightness of
    action; Virtue ethics
Good News: Social Ethics and the Press, 214
Google, 59, 193, 194, 195
Google flu trends modeling case, 105
Google Glass, 195
Google Street View, 194
Gorovitz, S., 107, 108, 110
Graham, M., 75
Gratitude duty, 14, 31, 124
Greater good ideal, 14, 17, 26, 32, 33, 77–78,
    105–106, 107, 155, 205, 212–213
    See also Common good; Community;
        Highest good
Greenwashing practice, 117
Grogan, J., 133
Groundwork of the Metaphysics of Morals,
    76, 83, 84, 86, 150, 158
Grsiwold v. Connecticut (1965), 178
Grunig, J. E., 116, 167, 223
Grunig, L. A., 167
Gun violence:
    Amish school shooting case and, 132–133
    gun-owner mapping case and, 159
    photojournalism standards and, 189
    Sandy Hook Elementary school shooting, 159
    Virginia Tech shooting case, 195
    Washington, D.C. sniper shootings, 39
Gut-level responses, xiii, 8, 10–11

Habermas, J., 155, 218, 219
Hackett, R., 217
Hallahan, K., 192, 196, 197, 221, 227
Hallett, M., 153
Hamelink, C. J., 56, 238, 239
Hampden-Turner, C., 207
Hansen, M., 105
Harbour, P. J., 38
Harm, 123
    advertising industry and, 130, 131–132,
        135–136, 139
    Amish school shooting case and, 132–133
    blameworthiness, judgment about, 126,
        133–134

codes of ethics and, 129–130
consent and, 126
constituents of, 126–129
content value/integrity, assessment of, 145
culturally-bounded concept of, 129,
    131–132
cyberspace contexts and, 142–143
datamining practices and, 142
definitions/understanding of, 124–126, 128,
    131, 137–139, 140
duties/harm concerns, conflict
    between, 143–145
economic/transactional harm, 128, 134, 135
gender stereotyping and, 135–136,
    138, 139, 141
greater good ideal and, 17
human dignity, respect for, 123
human flourishing, moral behaviors and, 16
journalistic practice and, 123, 126–130,
    136–137, 138
justice, Western conceptualization
    of, 98–99
legal perspectives on, 128–129, 143
marketing communication and, 130
media contexts and, 126–128, 132–139
Mill's harm principle and, 123–124,
    138, 139–142
moral harm and, 126, 138
moral uncertainty, embrace of, 32
nonmaleficence principle and, 14, 28, 31, 124
offensive material and, 134–135, 138
Pan Am flight 103 bombing case and, 132
pedophile sting operations
    case and, 126–128
prima facie obligations, 14, 28, 31–32, 124
psychological harm and, 135
public relations industry and, 123, 130,
    135, 136–137
risk of harm and, 29, 32, 127–128
setting back others' interests and,
    128, 129, 139, 140
sexual suggestiveness in advertising and,
    131–132, 139, 141
suicide cases, coverage of, 133–134
theorizing about, 126, 137–139,
    140–141, 144–145
truth telling, tolerable harm and,
    10–11, 32, 39–40, 44–45, 47, 48
utilitarianism, harm principle and, 123–124
values, harm and, 124–125, 131–132

About the Author

Patrick Lee Plaisance is an associate professor in the Department of Journalism and Technical Communication at Colorado State University, where he teaches media ethics, reporting, and mass communication theory on the undergraduate and graduate levels. His primary research areas include media ethics, moral psychology, newsroom socialization, and the philosophy of communication. His work has focused on analyzing how ethics theory can be more effectively brought to bear on media practice as well as on conducting qualitative and quantitative social science research in media-related settings. He worked for nearly 15 years as a journalist at newspapers around the country, including papers in Los Angeles, south Florida, New Jersey, and Virginia. He received a PhD in mass communications from Syracuse University. He also is the author of *Virtue in Media: The Moral Psychology of Excellence in News & PR*. He has contributed chapters and case studies to numerous journalism and media ethics books and has published more than a dozen peer-reviewed articles in journals, including *Communication Research, Journalism & Mass Communication Quarterly, Journal of Mass Media Ethics, Communication Theory, Journalism & Mass Communication Educator,* and *The International Journal of Applied Philosophy.*

$SAGE researchmethods

The essential online tool for researchers from the world's leading methods publisher

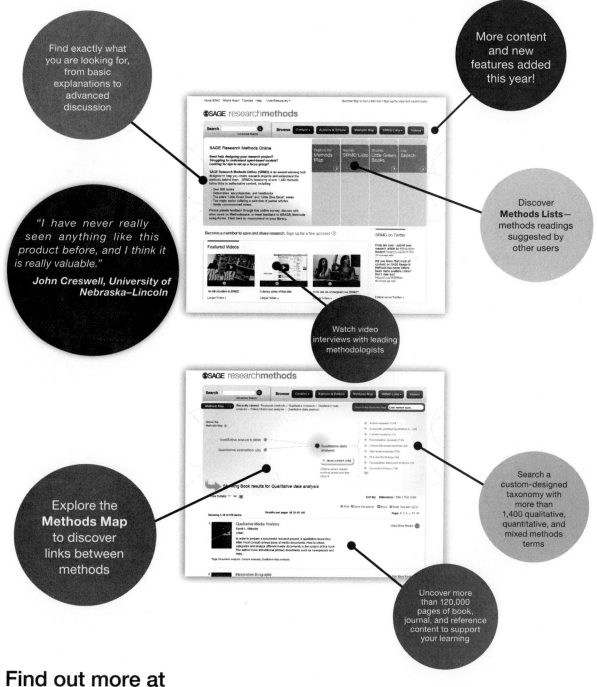

Find exactly what you are looking for, from basic explanations to advanced discussion

More content and new features added this year!

"I have never really seen anything like this product before, and I think it is really valuable."

John Creswell, University of Nebraska–Lincoln

Discover **Methods Lists**— methods readings suggested by other users

Watch video interviews with leading methodologists

Explore the **Methods Map** to discover links between methods

Search a custom-designed taxonomy with more than 1,400 qualitative, quantitative, and mixed methods terms

Uncover more than 120,000 pages of book, journal, and reference content to support your learning

Find out more at
www.sageresearchmethods.com